DUAL NATIONALITY, SOCIAL RIGHTS AND FEDERAL CITIZENSHIP IN THE U.S. AND EUROPE

DUAL NATIONALITY, SOCIAL RIGHTS AND FEDERAL CITIZENSHIP IN THE U.S. AND EUROPE

The Reinvention of Citizenship

———————

Randall Hansen and Patrick Weil

Berghahn Books
New York • Oxford

First published in 2002 by **Berghahn Books**

www.BerghahnBooks.com

© 2002 Randall Hansen and Patrick Weil

Library of Congress Cataloging-in-Publication Data

Hansen, Randall.
  Dual nationality, social rights and federal citizenship in the US and Europe : the
reinvention of citizenship / Randall Hansen and Patrick Weil.
      p. cm.
  Includes index.
  ISBN 1-57181-804-9 (alk. paper) -- ISBN 1-57181-805-7 (pbk. : alk. paper)
    1. Dual nationality--United States. 2. Dual nationality--Europe. 3. Conflict of
laws--Citizenship. I. Weil, Patrick, 1956- II. Title.

K7128.D8 H36 2002
342.73'083—dc21   2001052621

British Library Cataloguing in Publication Data

A catalogue record for this book is available
from the British Library.

Printed in the United States on acid-free paper

ISBN 1-57181-804-9 (hardback)
ISBN 1-57181-805-7 (paperback)

CONTENTS

ACKNOWLEDGEMENTS

We are grateful to the German Marshall Fund of the United States and the French Ministry of Social Affairs for the support of a June 1998 Paris conference on nationality law, immigration and integration in Europe and the U.S. Thanks also goes to all the participants at the conference, and to Daniel Cohen, Stéphane Dufoix and Paul Dixon for their assistance before and after the meeting. We also owe a debt to Sean Kingston and Marion Berghahn of Berghahn Books for their support of this volume and their efforts to ensure its efficient production. Finally, our gratitude goes to the scholars and policymakers – too numerous to name – whom we have met on both sides of the Atlantic, and whose conversations have greatly influenced our thoughts on dual citizenship, social rights and European citizenship.

LIST OF CONTRIBUTORS

OLIVIER BEAUD is Professor of Public Law at the University of Lille II

PETER BULTMANN is a Wissenschaftlicher Mitarbeiter at the Institut für Anwaltsrecht, Humbolt University, Berlin.
Email: Piet.Bultmann@rz.hu-berlin.de

JOSEPH CARENS is Professor of Political Science at the University of Toronto
Email: jcarens@chass.utoronto.ca

CARLOS CLOSA is Senior Lecturer in Politics at the University of Zaragoza
Email: cclosa@posta.unizar.es

PETER FRIEDRICH BULTMANN is completing his *Habilitation* at the Humboldt University, Berlin.
Email: peter=bultmann@rewi.hu-berlin.de

KAY HAILBRONNER is a Professor of Law at the University of Constanz
Email: Kay.Hailbronner@uni-konstanz.de

RANDALL HANSEN is a Fellow and Tutor in Politics at Merton College, University of Oxford
Email: randall.hansen@merton.ox.ac.uk

RIVA KASTORYANO is a Research Fellow at CNRS/CERI, Paris.
Email: kastoryano@ceri-sciences-po.org

PEGGY LEVITT is an Assistant Professor at Wellesley College and an Associate at the Weatherhead Centre for International Affairs, Harvard University.
Email: plevitt@wellesley.edu

MICHAEL JONES CORREA is Professor of Government at Cornell University
Email: mj64@cornell.edu

DAVID MARTIN is the Henry L. & Grace Doherty Charitable Foundation Professor of Law, University of Virginia.
Email: dmartin@law5.law.virginia.edu

SUSAN MARTIN is Director of the Institute for the Study of International Migration, Gerogetown University.
Email: martinsf@gunet.gerogetown.edu

GÉRAUD DE LA PRADELLE is Professor of Law at the University of Paris X, Nanterre

PETER SCHUCK is Professor of Law at Yale University
Email: SCHUCKP@juris.law.nyu.edu

PETER SPIRO is an Associate Professor at Hofstra University Law School.
Email: lawpjs@hofstra.edu

PATRICK WEIL is Director of Research at CNRS, La Sorbonne, Paris.
Email: Patrick.Weil@univ-paris1.fr

INTRODUCTION

DUAL CITIZENSHIP IN A CHANGED WORLD: IMMIGRATION, GENDER AND SOCIAL RIGHTS

Randall Hansen and Patrick Weil

This volume is devoted to the study of dual citizenship. As such, it is the first volume in over thirty years to make dual nationality[1] its major concern (Bar-Yaacov: 1961). For the first three decades of the postwar period, questions of citizenship received little academic attention within mainstream (English language) sociology and political science. Beyond one essay by T. H. Marshall, the study of citizenship was at best marginal. Since the 1980s, citizenship has become a major focus – almost an obsession – of scholars and graduate students. A cursory glance at the major journals, single-authored manuscripts and edited volumes produces a plethora of studies devoted to it. Although intellectual curiosity and a professional need for publication tend to exhaust all aspects of whatever topic fires academic imagination, the massive interest in citizenship has not spilled over into a concern for dual nationality.[2] This is despite the fact that in several countries it is the most important political issue linked with citizenship; it is increasing and impossible to prevent, and both the rules governing it at an international level and scholarly opinion on its strengths and weaknesses are in their infancy. The first purpose of this volume is to address this lacuna. Equally importantly, however, the volume also gives substantial attention to issues, related to dual nationality, that helped place it on the political and academic agenda: social rights, integration, the institution of citizenship itself, European citizenship and the conditions under which the rights of membership can be legitimately claimed. Given the novelty of debate over dual citizenship, much of this volume – including this introductory chapter – concerns both empirical/historical and normative issues. It examines the experience of dual citizenship in certain key countries, how and why nationality laws are changing and what they should look like.

Dual nationality: divergent responses to an increasing phenomenon

Since the French Revolution, the fundamental basis of individual belonging is citizenship of a nation-state. In its original formation, and in state practice, the dominant approach to dual citizenship was one of hostility. Yet, two phenomena have both led to its increase and rendered its prevention impossible: migration and the equalisation of rights between men and women.

The interaction of migration and different rules for attributing citizenship led, and leads, directly to increases in dual nationality (Weil, 2000). Nationality law depends on four distinct legal tools, two of which are invariably present:

1. citizenship at birth, or *jus soli*: [C]itizenship flows from the fact of being born in a territory over which the state maintains, has maintained, or wishes to extend its sovereignty.
2. Citizenship through descent, more crudely 'blood,' or *jus sanguinis*: citizenship flows from the parent(s)' or more distant relative(s)' nationality.

Two further factors are often neglected:

3. Marital status, as marriage to a citizen of another country can lead to the acquisition of the spouse's citizenship.
4. Past or current residence in the country's past, future or intended borders, including colonial borders.

The 'mix' of these features determines both the conditions under which nationality is granted in any country in the world and the methods through which citizenship is acquired. Together, they form the basis of legislation in any one country. As nationality is the exclusive purview of the nation state, emigration and immigration result in an intermingling of laws, leading to the expansion of dual citizenship (or, less often, to statelessness, the disappearance of an individual's legal link to a state). A child born of foreign parents coming from country X where nationality is defined by *jus sanguinis* in a country determining citizenship through simple *jus soli* (Canada, the U.S., Ireland) will have, at birth, two citizenships: that of its country of birth along with (under *jus sanguinis*) that of his parents. Thus, even if all nations were to oppose dual citizenship, it would tend to increase directly with population movements.

These trends towards dual and triple nationality have been magnified by recent developments in nationality laws governing marriage. Whereas women in the prewar period lost their citizenship when marrying a non-citizen, generally acquiring his citizenship, a trend toward equalisation has touched all liberal democracies. Today, men and women have the same right to maintain their nationality in marriage and to pass it on to their children. The change is a recent one in some European countries (Hansen and Weil: 2001), and it contributed substantially to increases in dual citizenship. Thus, in situations where a citizen from country X meets and marries a citizen from country Y, their child will inevitably be a dual national, even if X and Y oppose dual nationality. To make it even more complex, a German marrying a Turk and giving birth in the U.S. will give birth to a Turk and German by descent, and an American by birth.

The permanence of dual citizenship in the context of migration, and its further augmentation following the equalisation of the rights of men and women in nationality, have not consistently been matters of political controversy. The development of such controversy has been dependent upon contingent political factors of the sort that have arisen in two of the countries examined by this volume: Germany and the U.S.

In Germany, dual citizenship has become the major issue linked with questions of immigration, integration and citizenship. Dual citizenship's highly divisive nature is a somewhat recent feature of German politics: The *Reichs-und Staatsangehörigkeitsgesetz* of 1913, formally in operation until 1 January 2000, tolerated dual citizenship (at least for Germans abroad) as a means to furthering Germany's interests as a state of emigration and empire. As an American observer noted at the time,

> the most important features of this law are the abandonment of the provision of the old law of nationality that residence abroad of ten years results in the loss of German nationality, and the introduction of a quite novel provision, according to which Germans residing in foreign countries may retain their German nationality, under certain conditions, after obtaining naturalisation as citizens of such countries. This seems to carry the principle of dual nationality further than it has ever been carried before. (Flournoy: 1914)

Dual citizenship in Germany

Following Germany's transformation into a country of immigration, its hostility to dual citizenship for non-Germans developed into hostility *tout court*. Derided in a famous constitutional court (*Bundesverfassungsgericht*) decision as an 'evil' (*Übel*), the failure of Germany's integration policy (or absence of it) brought dual citizenship to the centre of political debate in the 1990s. Germany today faces a permanently resident foreign population of some 7.3 million individuals (8.9 percent of its population), the numerically largest in Europe. Despite significant reforms of naturalisation policy in 1990 and 1993, Germany's naturalisation rate remains (excluding ethnic Germans) low, while births to foreigners are disproportionately high – 13.3 percent in 1996 – and projected to grow (Green: 2001). Acting on the widely accepted belief that Germany's prohibition of dual citizenship was an essential block on naturalisation, the SPD/Green government announced a fundamental overhaul of its nationality law following its 1998 election victory. Expressing its commitment to the goal of integrating Germany's 7.3 million resident aliens, the coalition announced an expansive reform of its citizenship law, one tolerating dual nationality as a matter of course. It was not to be. The opposition Christian Democratic/Christian Socialist Union (CDU/CSU) made dual citizenship the focus of its opposition to the proposal. Denouncing dual citizenship as a security threat, an impediment to integration and a threat to the national constitution, the Union launched a national petition against it. Although legally meaningless, the petition was politically effective: it garnered over five million votes, and the SPD lost *Landtag* elections – and the government's Bundesrat majority – in Hessen. Sensing that public opinion was not on its side, the Schröder government retreated. It subsequently announced and secured the adoption of a less ambitious reform that retains a liberal *jus soli* policy, but requires those benefiting from it to decide between German nationality and any other by the age of twenty-three (Hailbronner: this volume). The FDP (Liberal) party, whose position was endorsed, was delighted; the CSU and large parts of the CDU remained unconvinced; migrant organisations, the Green party and many SPD members and academic activists were bitterly disappointed.

Although the government was keen to secure a consensus around its second proposal, the issue of dual citizenship will not go away in Germany. For many permanent residents, repudiation of former citizenship remains an obstacle to their naturalisation. In addition, there will almost inevitably be a challenge to the law by dual nationals when the first of them have to decide between their nationalities (thirteen years from the law's enactment). Although the respected lawyer and legal academic, Kay Hailbronner, defended the new law before the constitutional court, it remains to be seen whether a German court can bring itself to strip German citizens of their citizenship against their will. The ghosts of the 1930s will watch over whatever they decide.

Dual nationality in the US

In the U.S., dual nationality has emerged on the academic, and, to a lesser extent political, agenda as a side effect of a 1996 reform to social entitlements, and in response to changes in sending countries' policies. American social programmes are notoriously inferior to those in Europe,[3] and recent policy has aimed at excluding legal and illegal migrants from those that remain. At the same time, immigration polices are, in a comparative perspective, expansive and generous, and the U.S. treated – as part of what Lyndon Johnson referred to as a 'covenant conceived in justice, written in liberty' – legal immigrants as citizens in waiting, entitled to the same social and economic rights (S. Martin: this volume). In the 1990s, this covenant, and immigration more generally, became politicised.

The American political debate over social policy towards migrants, and the academic debate over the relationship between social rights, immigration and naturalisation, reached a *Wende* in 1996. In that year, the U.S. Congress, fired by a mix of fiscal conservatism and anti-immigrant sentiment, deprived both legal and illegal immigrants of many of their entitlements to social rights. The legislation contributed to a rush towards naturalisation among legal immigrants: in 1996 alone, a million individuals acquired American citizenship, and in 1997 applications for naturalisation exceeded 1.6 million (S. Martin: this volume). This rise in U.S. citizenship acquisition has not been accompanied by an expansion in political participation among immigrants-turned-citizens. Among Hispanics, voter registration rates have only just kept up with the increase, occasioned in part by naturalisation, in the voting age population. In other words, a large increase in Hispanic naturalisations – reflecting in part reactions to anti-Hispanic sentiment, Proposition 187 (which attempted to deny illegal immigrants in California social services) and the 1996 Congressional legislation – have not been followed by an increase in Hispanic voting, the most basic form of political participation (Jones Correa: this volume).[4] Likewise, Peggy Levitt concludes, on the basis of her study of Dominican and Brazilian migrants in Boston, that 'naturalisation no longer signals a shift in allegiance and an end to sending country involvements (this volume)'. In attempting (in part) to revalue a citizenship believed to be debased by immigration and easy access to it, the 1996 law succeeded only in devaluing that citizenship, by encouraging its instrumental acquisition, and by opening up a larger gap between naturalisation and participation.

Since 1996, some social rights have been restored (following intensive domestic lobbying and a healthier budget) for aliens in the country before the legislation took effect, but the decision made a mockery of claims – circulated contemporaneously – that the (previously) relatively secure position of legal migrants in democracies had ushered in a postnational age in which the benign influence of 'universal personhood' rendered national citizenship redundant (Soysal: 1994) or in which large-scale migration, laid against the globalisation of capital, commodity and service markets, has undermined the logic of national citizenship by breaking the link between it and the nation state (Feldblum: 1998; Sassen: 1998; Soysal: 1994). The decision made crystal clear the lingering vulnerability of immigrants without citizenship (Jones Correa: this volume). Declared dead or dying more often than New York City, the nation-state again demonstrated its capacity to exercise its sovereignty over populations present on its territory (On this, see Freeman: 1998; Joppke: 1999).

Partly in reaction to the 1996 reform, and to anti-immigration sentiment in mid-1990s U.S. more generally, the sending countries of Brazil, the Dominican Republic and Mexico loosened their rules against dual citizenship. Their moves reflected a global trend. One of the most recent developments in dual citizenship is its acceptance and use by sending countries. Following the path opened at the beginning of the century by Germany, and recently carried further by Greece, Portugal and Italy (Hansen and Weil: 2001), Latin American nations have come to view dual citizenship as a means to maintaining ties with the national community abroad. Dual citizenship provides them with greater security in the receiving countries (by acquiring local citizenship) and can even secure influence over politics in these states. This is the case for Turkey, Algeria and Morocco. In Latin America, Brazil explicitly reversed its opposition to dual citizenship in 1993 to allow its citizens abroad (especially in the U.S.) to gain access to social services, while the Dominican Republic followed suit several years later in response to pressure from political parties and migrant associations (Levitt: this volume). When Mexico followed suit in 1998, dual citizenship came onto the academic, though not, to a large extent, the political, agenda in the U.S.

American policy towards dual citizenship was, like that of many other countries, contradictory. The country traditionally combined, more or less successfully, an official opposition to dual nationality with a variable acceptance of it in practice, and with the (arguably successful) integration of large numbers of immigrants. During the early years of the Cold War, American hostility to dual nationality was at its peak. Naturalisation in a foreign state, oaths of allegiance in foreign countries, service in the armed forces where an individual had nationality, or holding government offices restricted to nationals were all grounds for expatriation (Spiro: 1997, 1443). The legislative hostility had the backing of the Supreme Court, which ruled that efforts to limit dual nationality were constitutional. Since the 1970s, hostility to dual nationality has eased; voting in a foreign election, for example, no longer leads to expatriation. Yet, the Immigration and Naturalisation Service (INS) remains officially opposed to dual nationality, and individuals acquiring American citizenship through naturalisation make a (non-enforceable) pledge to abandon their previous citizenship. In practice, though, the INS knows that there is nothing that the U.S. can do about dual citizenship.

Elsewhere in Europe, dual nationality provokes only minor opposition, if any at all. Indeed, one of the intriguing aspects of dual citizenship is that it provokes such highly divergent responses among nations sharing broadly similar liberal democratic values. The United Kingdom is perfectly indifferent towards dual nationality, and has been for decades. France is located somewhere between the German (pre-2000) and the British approaches. French legal tradition, as articulated by legal scholars, is instinctively suspicious of dual citizenship (de la Pradelle: this volume). The republican state however, partly reflecting a Great Power's confidence, was tolerant of it in practice. As a 1915 Ministry of Justice note put it, '[French] law cannot capitulate (*s'incliner*) to foreign legislation and no longer consider French, simply because it pleases foreign law, those upon whom France considers it within its interest to confer its nationality, retaining them within its allegiance'.[5] Today, French citizens can naturalise abroad without losing their French nationality, and migrants can acquire French citizenship without renouncing other nationalities, unless their country of citizenship is a signatory to the 1963 European Council convention on the prevention of dual nationality. As further evidence of a liberalising trend, French jurisprudence has recently incorporated, though in limited form, recognition of dual citizenship (de la Pradelle: this volume).

The case against dual citizenship

The contributions on dual citizenship all consider the factors in favour and against dual citizenship. There are broadly five factors cited against dual citizenship.[6] First, loyalty is indivisible; as one cannot serve two masters, one cannot serve two countries. Second, dual nationality creates a security threat, as dual citizens may use the nationality of country A to obtain sensitive information that is passed on to country B. This threat becomes intensified when dual citizens hold high office. Third, dual citizenship impedes integration, as it encourages an attachment to a foreign culture and language. Fourth, it increases international instability, by creating conflicts over tax, inheritance, marriage and, especially, military service. Finally, it violates principles of equality, as it provides dual nationals with a wider range of rights and opportunities relative to their fellow (single) nationals.

Responding to these arguments, the first is essentially contestable; although loyalty may be defined as exclusive, in the same way as allegiance was once defined as perpetual, it may also be defined as dual or multiple. Besides which, it is evident that no EU member state takes the strict definition seriously. The very project of European integration is based on the implicit recognition of multiple loyalties – to the state of one's citizenship, to the institutions of the EU, and to citizens of other member states. Following the introduction of European citizenship in 1992, all member-state citizens are dual nationals (Closa: this volume). As Olivier Beaud argues (this volume), federations once recognised in law – and today imply in theory – a duality of commitment: to the federation itself and to its constituent units: the state, province or *Land*. The institutional arrangements in neither the EU nor the U.S. give much credence to the exclusive loyalty thesis.

The putative threat to security posed by dual nationality is a myth. There is little evidence that dual nationals have been disproportionately represented among the treasonous in the countries under study (Shuck:

this volume; Spiro: this volume). More importantly, the threat to security exists independently of dual citizenship. Any citizen, whether they are such through birth, descent, or naturalisation, can use a privileged position in one state to pass sensitive information on to another country, with or without the latter's citizenship. Indeed, those with treacherous intent have an interest in avoiding dual citizenship, as it might draw attention to them.

Arguments about international stability do raise a substantive problem, but one that is lessening, as states abandon military service (France) and change inheritance rules (Turkey). They can arguably resolve those that remain through bilateral negotiations; in 1983, France and Algeria resolved the previously vexed issue of dual nationals' military service by allowing dual nationals to serve it once in the state of their choice (Weil: 1995). Such negotiations depend, however, on a will in both states to accept some measure of dual citizenship and to reach a mutually satisfactory compromise in this context. Unsurprisingly, such will is not always present: Germany's efforts to convince Iran of the merits of renegotiating the German–Persian treaty of 17 February 1929 (which grants each state a veto over any citizen of either state seeking naturalisation in the other) have met little success (Green: 2001; interview with German Ministry of Interior officials, Bonn, February 1999).

Of all the arguments against dual citizenship, the equality argument is particularly compelling. Citizenship is premised on equality among citizens, and, if dual citizenship violates this equality, this is a serious mark against it. Peter Spiro provides one riposte against this concern: as life is full of multiple, and often overlapping, inequalities (in wealth, skill, parentage and so on), it is arbitrary and perhaps hypocritical to select inequality generated by 'conationality' for particular opprobrium (Spiro: this volume). Another contributor suggests that this response is inadequate. On this view, citizenship requires equality among citizens *irrespective* of the equalities that exist or develop over the course of citizens' lives. Indeed, the fact of pervasive inequality – far more marked in the U.S. than Europe – makes equality of citizenship more pressing, not less. Equality in citizenship should be nurtured precisely because it is one of the few institutions through which it might be achieved (D. Martin: this volume).

One might, however, raise a normative counter to the equality concern. Following Michael Walzer, dual citizenship might be said to violate simple but not complex equality (Walzer: 1983). According to Walzer, complex equality is not universal, but limited to particular spheres; thus, whereas inequality is acceptable *between* spheres, it is unacceptable – as a violation of complex equality – within them. As Walzer argues,

> Simple equality is a simple distributive condition, so that if I have fourteen hats and you have fourteen hats, we are equal . . . Complex equality means

that no one citizen's standing in one sphere or with regard to one social good can be undercut by his standing in some other sphere, with regard to some other good. Thus, citizen X may be chosen over citizen Y for political office, and the two of them will be unequal in the sphere of politics. But they will not be unequal generally so long as X's office gives him no advantages over Y in any other sphere – superior medical care, access to better schools for his children, entrepreneurial skills, and so on (Walzer: 1983, 18–19).

Applied to citizenship, simple equality would require that all citizens have the same entitlements regardless of which national citizenship generated them; they would have to be equal *within* and *across* polities. By contrast, complex equality only requires that each citizen possess the same range of entitlements as all others holding the same citizenship. Thus, a situation in which a German citizen secures greater rights, *on the basis of her German citizenship*, than another German citizen would be inadmissible, but a German citizen claiming greater rights outside Germany than another German citizen, *on the basis of his Turkish citizenship*, would not be. Thus, a dual national in either of the spheres – countries in this case – could claim no more rights than another citizen. German/Turkish nations have the same rights and obligations as German nationals in Germany, and Turkish/German nationals have the same rights and obligations as Turkish nationals when in Turkey. There is functional equality of citizenship. The shift is more than an intellectual sleight of hand: it has intuitive appeal. If those concerned about simple equality were to take their opposition to dual citizenship seriously, they should also oppose citizens of country A enjoying social and economic rights (on the basis of permanent residence status, for instance) in country B, as this surely gives them more rights than other country A citizens. No one, however, finds this objectionable.

A caveat should be added here: such a citizen could not also claim greater rights within Germany on the basis of his Turkish citizenship. In practice, doing so is impossible: international and national law prevents dual nationals from invoking their foreign nationality *vis-à-vis* the second state of which they are nationals.

The case in favour of dual citizenship

The case against dual citizenship is thus highly debatable, empirically and normatively. But what of the case, from the state's point of view, in its favour?[7] There are essentially three arguments. First, dual citizenship is inevitable, and even states opposed to it might as well grit their teeth and bear it. As one state cannot dictate the nationality requirements of another, and as there is no international arena for seeking agreement on common nationality definitions, dual nationality will, even holding all else constant, drift upwards along with increased mobility.

Peter Spiro has developed a second argument in favour of dual citizenship: it can be a value generator. That is, far from the U.S. (and, by implication, other liberal democracies) fearing dual nationals' active participation in other polities whose citizenship they hold, they should see this as an opportunity to export Western liberal democratic values abroad (Spiro: this volume). When dual nationals hold citizenship(s) of non- or less-than-fully democratic countries, this might be of great value to the U.S., the West and the world itself.

Thirdly, far from impeding integration, dual citizenship furthers it. This thesis essentially turns on the relationship between dual nationality and naturalisation. In Germany, there is an academic consensus that a prohibition on dual citizenship is behind the country's low naturalisation rate (Brubaker: 1992, 78, Neuman 1998), and other countries – such as Holland – have witnessed a direct link between toleration of dual citizenship and naturalisation (Groenendijk and Heijs: 2001). The disincentive effect is both mechanical and psychological (Hansen: 1998). In the former, citizens are hesitant to give up the instrumental benefits of a second passport: the right to work in another country, pension and inheritance rights, the ability to pass the nationality and its attendant advantages on to their children and so forth. Psychologically, they may continue to identify themselves as citizens of another country and do not wish to truncate this aspect of their identity. In such cases, the host country's opposition to dual citizenship may be taken as a (further) indicator of its refusal to accept newcomers. In Germany, for instance, those opposed to immigration, in favour of strict naturalisation requirements and opposed to dual citizenship are rarely in opposing camps. At the very least, dual citizenship cannot be said to have impeded immigrants' integration in France and Britain (which generally tolerate dual citizenship); indeed, the U.K. views dual citizenship as a central, if secondary, element in its integration policies (Hansen: this volume; Kastoryano: 1998, Weil: 1995).

The relative weakness of the case against dual citizenship, set against one measurable positive benefit flowing from it – a higher naturalisation rate among migrants – and one hypothesised benefit (the spread of democratic ideas), suggests that the argument carries in its favour. This argument is reinforced when it is historicised. The experience of immigration countries demonstrates that when states adopt a position of legal neutrality towards the effects of dual citizenship – that is, when they ignore it – dual citizens tend to 'practice' only the citizenship of the country of residence. If this is not entirely the case with the first generation, it becomes more so at the second and beyond. Dual nationality should not be an obstacle to access to the nationality of the country of residence. If it is, the prohibition not only blocks the integration of migrants, but encourages political mobilisation in favour of dual citizenship, notably among those who valorise a world in which all citizens have two, three or more nationalities. Such developments risk the provocation of a counter-reaction – of the sort seen in Germany in 1999 – among the vast majority of citizens who are and will remain single nationals. As long as the world is divided into nations serving as the basis of individual identity, ignoring dual nationality will probably be the path of least resistance for those wishing to facilitate the integration of the millions of immigrants residing in Western countries.

As this suggests, support for dual nationality should not be unbridled. Taken to their logical extreme, the arguments of enthusiasts in favour of dual citizenship lead to the conclusion that there should be no distinction between citizens and non-citizens. If the exercise of political rights in multiple polities is so unproblematic, then why not distribute passports indiscriminately and let everyone vote everywhere? Citizenship remains the fundamental link between individuals and the state, guaranteeing the full range of rights and distinguishing them from those whose connection to the state is incomplete or non-existent. There clearly must be some limitations imposed on dual nationality. David Martin's contribution explicitly addresses this issue, and it is also touched on by Peter Shuck and Peter Spiro. However, it is worth drawing out an essential limitation. Dual citizenship should be constrained by the same criterion engendering a claim among non-citizens to nationality: residence. In the same way that length of (legal) residence correlates positively with a normative claim to citizenship (a thesis defended by Carens: this volume), it should also correlate with our tolerance for dual citizenship. Those individuals who have been resident in a country the longest have the strongest claim to acquire a member state's nationality while retaining another. The logic is simple: such individuals will have contributed most to the society, have built-up a web of social relations, will be best equipped to make informed voting decisions and – importantly – will have to live with the consequences of them (Carens: this volume; D. Martin: this volume). If implemented, this policy would reverse common practice, especially in Europe. Turks and other residents in Germany and Austria would have an entitlement to dual citizenship, while Austrians and German descendants in North America and elsewhere would have none.

Outline of the book

The volume opens with Peter Spiro's provocatively titled – 'Embracing Dual Nationality'. Spiro argues that dual citizenship should not only be accepted – as states can do little to prevent it – but wholeheartedly embraced. Suggesting the less pejorative term 'conationality' as an alternative, Spiro argues that it will both encourage further naturalisation (and thus integration) at home and serve to spread democratic values abroad. David Martin offers a more circumspect view of dual citizenship. Although he agrees with Spiro that dual citizenship does not generally create security or loyalty problems, Martin rejects the claim that it is a prerequisite to naturalisation, and he argues that an expansion of dual nationality should be accompanied by (ideally global) rules governing it. In particular, dual nationality should reflect genuine and lasting ties to a national community; it should be denied to individuals holding high office; and the exercise of political citizenship should be limited to one state – that of residence. Peter Shuck finds himself in agreement with Martin and Spiro on some of the factors encouraging dual citizenship. Shuck also agrees that the oath of allegiance – taken upon acquiring American citizenship – is anachronistic, but he argues – against Spiro – that the oath should be modified, not abandoned, to require that new citizens swear primary loyalty to the U.S. This is what can be reasonably expected of individuals acquiring citizenship, and it is consistent with a broad tolerance of dual citizenship. Joseph Carens, in the final contribution to this section, broadens the discussion by examining the normative foundations of distinctions between citizens and aliens. Carens argues that, when aliens have resided permanently in a country for a number of years, these distinctions are untenable. Liberal democratic societies are bound to grant entitlements expansively on the basis of continued and lengthy residence.

Kay Hailbronner's chapter is the first of three examining citizenship, dual nationality and naturalisation in Germany. Hailbronner considers the issue of dual nationality through an analysis of the influence on Germany and German nationality law exercised by immigration, including two 1999 proposals (one of which was successful) designed to amend at last the country's 1913 law on citizenship. He argues that while some concerns over dual nationality are legitimate, they do not outweigh the positive benefits if it serves to encourage naturalisation among Germany's large and growing resident alien population. In a similar vein to David Martin, he argues that dual citizenship must be accompanied by rules delimiting its growth – notably, its loss after prolonged periods of residence abroad – and that it cannot be viewed as the sole instrument of integration policy. Only full participation, and a willingness among residents themselves to participate actively in German political life, will ensure their integration. Peter Bultmann examines dual nationality and naturalisation from a neglected and central angle: that of the *Länder* (states). Although the German federation draws up rules and laws on naturalisation, these are implemented by the *Länder*. Examining *Länder* implementation from the point of view of local justice, Bultmann explores – and verifies – the hypothesis that variation among *Länder* naturalisation rates reflects their (relatively restrictive, or relatively generous) view of the naturalisation rules, and that these in turn reflect contrasting views on how naturalisation serves the interests of migrants, and Germany itself. Riva Kastoryano examines the Turks resident in Germany through the lens of citizenship and dual nationality. Highlighting the extent to which they enjoy economic and social citizenship, she argues – against postnationalism – that full integration presupposes political citizenship. In the third section, Randall Hansen and Géraud de la Pradelle broaden the analysis of Europe by examining, respectively, Britain's and France's approaches to dual citizenship. For Britain, dual citizenship has long been a matter of indifference. France, although historically more suspicious, today also treats it leniently.

The fourth section of the book examines social rights, naturalisation and integration in the U.S. Susan Martin analyses the 1996 legislation withdrawing social rights from both legal and illegal immigrants. Martin argues that the legislation drew support from a number of sources – including, curiously, those who supported immigration but feared that welfare 'abuse' would undermine it – but that the measure resulted in a devaluation of U.S. citizenship. She offers a series of recommendations for democracies interested in encouraging a robust citizenship. Michael Jones Correa also considers the 1996 law, using it as a basis for a reflection on postnationalism and political participation. Jones Correa argues that the law underlined the inadequacies of postnationalism for two reasons: first, it demonstrated the precarious nature of the socio-economic privileges of permanent residents; and, second, its aftermath highlighted the gap in the U.S. between naturalisation and political participation. Postnationalism, with its emphasis on entitlements received passively from the state, accords little attention to the latter. Peggy Levitt examines the transnational ties developed by Dominican migrants (from the village of Miraflores) and Brazilian migrants (from the city of Governador Valadares). She argues that the interlocking patterns of contact and exchange between these residents, the U.S. and their home countries demonstrate that neither citizenship nor dual citizenship is the sole basis on which migrants form their identity. Levitt also discusses divergent patterns of political participation between the groups, and examines a series of hypotheses explaining these differences.

The final section of the book considers citizenship and dual citizenship against a wider canvass. Carlos Closa examines European Union Citizenship, through a consideration of the 1996 Intergovernmental Conference (IGC). EU citizenship is central to debates about dual citizenship, as the manner of its institution (European citizens are those who hold member state passports) means that all member state nationals are dual citizens: French, British, German citizens, on the one hand, and European citizens, on the other. Olivier Beaud closes this section by historicising debates about dual citizenship. He examines the relationship between dual citizenship and federal citizenship, drawing on the Swiss, American and German federations in the nineteenth century. Beaud argues that the very idea of a federation implies dual citizenship: at the national and subnational (state/Land/Canton) levels. The implications for contemporary America, and especially Germany, are clear.

References

N. Bar-Yaacov, *Dual Nationality*, London, 1961.

R. Brubaker, *Citizenship and Nationhood in France and Germany*, Cambridge, MA, 1992.

W. Cornelius, P. L. Martin and J. Hollifield, *Controlling Immigration: a global perspective*, Stanford, 1994.M. Feldblum, 'Reconfiguring Citizenship in Western Europe', in *Challenge to the Nation-State: Immigration in Western Europe and the United States*, ed. C. Joppke, Oxford, 1998.

G. P. Freeman, 'The Decline of Sovereignty? Politics and Immigration Restriction in Liberal States', in *Challenge to the Nation-State: Immigration in Western Europe and the United States*, C. Joppke, ed. Oxford, 1998.

R. W. Flournoy, Jr, 'Observations on the new German Law of Nationality', *American Journal of International Law*, July 1914, 8, no. 3, p. 478.

S. Green, 'Citizenship Policy in Germany: The case of ethnicity over residence?' in *Towards a European Nationality: Citizenship, Immigration and Nationality Law in the EU*, eds. R. Hansen and P. Weil, Houndmills, 2001.

K. Groenendijk and E. Heijs, 'Immigration, Immigrants and Nationality Law in the Netherlands 1945–1998', in *Towards a European Nationality: Citizenship, Immigration and Nationality Law in the EU*, eds. R. Hansen and P. Weil, Houndmills, 2001.

R. Hansen, 'A European citizenship or a Europe of citizens? Third country nationals in the EU', *Journal of Ethnic and Migration Studies*', 24, no. 4 (1998).

R. Hansen, 'The Problems and Promises of Dual Nationality in Europe', *ECPR News*, 11, No. 2, 2000, 19–20.

R. Hansen and P. Weil, eds, *Towards a European Nationality: Citizenship, Immigration and Nationality Law in the EU*, Houndmills, 2001.

C. Joppke, ed. *Challenge to the Nation-State: Immigration in Western Europe and the United States*, Oxford, 1998.

C. Joppke, ed. *Immigration and the Nation State: The United States, Germany, and Great Britain*, Oxford, 1999.

T. R. Marmore et. al., *American's Misunderstood Welfare State*, New York, 1992.

G. Neuman, 'Nationality law in the United States and the Federal Republic of Germany: structure and current problems', in *Paths to Inclusion: The Integration of Migrants in the United States and Germany*, eds. P. Schuck and R. Münz, Providence RI, 1998.

F. Pastore, 'Nationality law and International Migration: the Italian case', in *Towards a European Nationality: Citizenship, Immigration and Nationality Law in the EU*, eds R. Hansen and P. Weil, Houndmills, 2001.

C. L. Rozakis, 'Nationality Law in Greece', in *Towards a European Nationality: Citizenship, Immigration and Nationality Law in the EU*, eds R. Hansen and P. Weil, Houndmills, 2001.

S. Sassen, 'The de facto Transnationalizing of Immigration Policy,' in *Challenge to the Nation-State: Immigration in Western Europe and the United States*, ed. C. Joppke, Oxford, 1998.

Y. N. Soysal, *Limits of Citizenship: Migrants and Postnational Membership in Europe* Chicago, 1994.

P.J. Spiro, 'Dual Nationality and the Meaning of Citizenship', *Emory Law Journal* 46, no. 4 (1997): 1411–85.

M. Walzer, *Spheres of Justice*, New York, 1983.

P. Weil, *La France et ses étrangers*, Paris, 1995.

P. Weil, 'Access to citizenship: A comparison of twenty five nationality laws', in *Comparing citizenship: Contexts and Perspectives*, eds Alex Aleinikoff and Doug Klusmeyer, Washington D.C., 2000.

Notes

1. In this volume, we adopt the legal definition of 'dual nationality' and 'dual citizenship,' which treats them as synonymous.
2. Or even, in the main, for nationality law as such.
3. Though, for a spirited defence of it, see Marmore (1992).
4. Even in the 8 November 1994 California election, viewed as a critical election in which Hispanics mobilised to vent anger at Proposition 187, almost as many registered Hispanic voters stayed home as voted; whereas eighty percent of registered non-Hispanic whites voted, only fifty-five percent of eligible Hispanics did. See Jones Correa (this volume). As Jones Correa argues, what Proposition 187 did succeed in doing was mobilising existing registered voters, though it did not greatly encourage the registration of new voters.
5. *Note du bureau du Sceau*, 1915, Archives du ministère de la Justice, (France).
6. This section includes arguments made, in briefer form, in Hansen (2000).
7. There are, to be sure, many advantages to dual citizenship from the individual's point of view. On these, see Schuck (this volume).

I

THE PROBLEMS AND POSSIBILITIES OF DUAL CITIZENSHIP

CHAPTER 1

EMBRACING DUAL NATIONALITY

*Peter J. Spiro**

Few societal aversions have seemed as automatic as those directed against dual nationality. It is a condition whose disadvantages have long been assumed and accepted without further explication. Indeed, the status seems antithetical to the traditional conception of the state and its relationship to individuals, a conception dominated by notions of loyalty and allegiance that have left little room for multiple attachments. In the common understanding, dual nationality has been associated with shadowy fifth columns and reviled as an intolerable sort of political polygamy, and this status was once the source of major diplomatic controversies. Even as the dictates of national security and the threat of subversion have diminished in the post Cold War world, dual nationality has, until recently, remained the object of lingering but prevalent distaste.

That distaste may finally be dissipating. Today, the prospect of serious international frictions or security risks arising from dual nationality has been reduced to almost nil. To imagine even hypothetical situations in which dual nationality poses a threat to the national interest is now increasingly difficult. Reflecting this reality, dual nationality is now completely tolerated under U.S. law and practice. Even recent changes in Mexican law, which laid the groundwork for a concentrated population of several million dual Mexican/American nationals, were hardly remarked upon by U.S. policymakers. Complete toleration should now move towards encouraging the status. Full, express acceptance of dual nationality may reap actual benefits for the American national interest. Such acceptance would facilitate the political and cultural assimilation of immigrants unwilling, either for economic or sentimental reasons, to forsake their countries of origin. It could also advance the global cause of democracy, as those who become steeped in the constitutional values of their adopted American homeland are able to apply them in other polities.

Embracing dual nationality in the United States may also pave the way for more complete acceptance of the status by other nations. Although nationality policy is to some extent context dependent, global forces are pushing some countries towards some recognition of the status. Even as some – Germany, most notably – remain resistant, the long-term trend suggests a universal toleration of dual nationality, perhaps even to the point that its acceptance becomes mandatory as a matter of international law. As a matter of discourse, perhaps the time has come as well for a new designation to reflect the shedding of old baggage, so that those who have more than one status are characterised not as 'dual' but rather as binationals.

Sources of dual nationality

There are four significant sources of Americans that hold dual nationality. First, historically the largest number of dual nationals has resulted from the interplay of different birthright nationality laws under which citizenship at birth can be ascribed both by location (the rule of *jus soli*) and by parentage (*jus sanguinis*), so that the child born in one nation to a parent holding citizenship in another nation will hold both nationalities at birth. The United States applies a strict rule of *jus soli*, under which all children born in the territorial United States (save those of diplomats) are extended citizenship at birth. Most countries, however, have adopted descent by the rule of *jus sanguinis*. Thus, for example, a child born of Canadian citizens in the United States will be a dual Canadian-American citizen at birth.

Second, dual nationality has more recently resulted from the marriage of persons with different nationalities. Whereas in the past a woman marrying a foreigner would, as a general rule, automatically lose her original citizenship and assume that of her husband (true under U.S. law until 1932), now both husbands and wives are entitled to retain their original citizenship and, in many cases, to acquire that of their spouse. The children of these unions will often be entitled, through *jus sanguinis* rules, to the nationalities of both parents. In cases where two parents of different nationality have a child in another country applying *jus soli*, that child can be born with three nationalities.

Third, a native-born American citizen will become a dual national if he or she naturalises in another country. Traditionally, naturalisation elsewhere resulted in forfeiture of U.S. citizenship – indeed, those born with dual nationality could lose their citizenship for the mere act of voting in their state of alternate nationality. Beginning with its 1967 decision in *Afroyim v. Rusk*, however, the Supreme Court has increasingly limited the circumstances in which native-born citizens can be deprived of their nationality. Today, an individual will almost never lose his or her American citizenship without specifically intending that result. A citizen who naturalises elsewhere is presumed to retain American citizenship, not to abandon it.

Finally, dual nationality in the U.S. arises where a foreign national naturalises there but retains his or her original nationality. This fourth category was long a source of dual nationals, not where a naturalising American sought to retain his or her original nationality, but rather where his or her country of origin refused to recognise the transfer of allegiances, under the so-called 'perpetual allegiance' approach to nationality ('Once a subject, always a subject.') To take the most notable example, Great Britain did not recognise the capacity of its subjects to shed British nationality upon naturalisation in the United States until 1870. Today, the right of expatriation is almost universally recognised, but many who naturalise in the United States seek to maintain their original nationality as a matter of choice. Naturalising citizens are required to renounce their original nationality, but this requirement has never been enforced.

No national or international statistical surveys of the incidence of dual nationality have been conducted to date, but the trend across these four categories has clearly been upward. As national borders become increasingly porous, the number of individuals who are either born with or become eligible for more than one nationality will steadily increase. The progeny of recent immigrants will be born with American citizenship and will also be eligible for that of their parents (and, indeed, of their grandparents, as is true, for instance, under Greek, Irish and Italian law). The incidence of marriage between nationals of different countries continues to rise, and so grows as a source of dual nationality. Many of the estimated four to five million Americans who now permanently reside outside of the United States hold, or will acquire, citizenship in their country of residence while remaining American citizens.

The last of these four categories – aliens who naturalise as Americans while retaining citizenship in their country of origin – will likely generate the most significant population of dual nationals, as a consequence of high immigration levels complemented by record levels of subsequent naturalisation. (More individuals naturalised in 1997 alone than in the entire decade of the 1970s.) At the same time, this source of dual nationals is also being magnified by changes in the laws of other countries. With the abandonment of perpetual allegiance in the late nineteenth-century, most nations automatically cancelled the citizenship of persons naturalising abroad. The renunciation oath then became self-enforcing, and the number of dual nationals from this category was limited to those from the few countries that tolerated their acquisition of U.S. citizenship.

In recent years, however, several countries have amended their nationality laws to allow individuals to retain their citizenship even when they naturalise in another country. Thus, applicants from such major 'sending' states as the Dominican Republic, El Salvador, Ireland and Italy will not necessarily lose their original citizenship upon naturalisation in the United States. Given the minimal costs of maintaining both nationalities (those who would be required to undertake military service in their country of origin presenting the only significant exception) and the nonenforcement of the renunciation oath, many are presumably holding on to first citizenships as a matter of default. On the numbers, the consequences of a change in Mexican law allowing for the retention or re-acquisition of Mexican nationality will be most significant. In the past, Mexicans who naturalised in the United States lost their Mexican nationality. Since March 1998, they have been able to retain Mexican nationality, and those who lost it through prior naturalisation will be able to regain it. This change presents the prospect of a population of dual nationals both large (as many as five million will be eligible) and geographically concentrated (largely in the Southwest, especially southern California and Texas).

Despite an increasing incidence of dual nationality, the issue has not received significant attention from U.S. policy-makers in recent decades. Indeed, dual nationality has quietly come to secure almost complete toleration under U.S. law. On the one hand, the *Afroyim* line of United States Supreme Court cases has protected the citizenship of Americans who naturalised in other countries, and on the other, no move has emerged to enforce the renunciation oath, though many naturalisation applicants elect to retain their original nationality.

Contrary to some predictions among academics and policy analysts (myself included) the changes in Mexican law have not, as yet, generated significant controversy in the U.S., and there are few signs that dual nationality is on the policymaking horizon. Nevertheless, the evident rise in the number of dual nationals does nonetheless warrant an examination of the roots of its traditional disfavour as well as the reasons for its more recent toleration. It is on this historical foundation that a modern approach is best formulated.

An old-world threat to international stability

One might expect a historical examination of dual nationality to reveal sensational tales of disloyalty and deceit, divided allegiances and torn psyches. In fact, the roots of its disfavour are far more prosaic. Dual nationality has seldom presented a direct threat to national security in the sense that its incidence has not, for instance, increased America's vulnerability to spying and sabotage. It has, however, posed an indirect threat of almost the same proportion. By blurring otherwise distinct lines between national populations, dual nationals invited the human equivalent of turf contests among countries in an era in which they could treat their own nationals as they pleased but were constrained in their treatment of others by international law. A hostile world in which the smallest spark might ignite conflict could not tolerate the instability posed by dual nationals.

At certain times during the nineteenth century, the problem of dual nationality came to dominate some bilateral relationships. The War of

1812 was triggered by the impressment of former British nationals whose naturalisation as Americans Great Britain refused to recognise. This refusal made these naturalised Americans subject to the dual claims of conflicting sovereignties. Even after Britain discontinued this practice, the problem persisted when naturalised Americans returned on visits to home countries throughout Europe, especially when an individual had not satisfied military service requirements in his country of origin; a naturalised U.S. citizen from Europe might find himself conscripted upon return to his homeland. Pursuing its obligation to exercise the diplomatic protection of its citizens, the U.S. government would intercede with the other state of nationality, asserting that naturalisation in the United States should absolve the individual of his obligations to his country of birth. In response, the other state would assert its right to define the terms of nationality (and the loss thereof) as well as the duties extracted from its own nationals. The refusal of other countries to recognise U.S. naturalisation proved a serious irritant to U.S. relations with every major European state at various points throughout the nineteenth century. At times the issue even inflamed the public imagination, as when Britain put several naturalised Irish-Americans on trial for treason as British citizens.

In some cases, foreign states had justifiable cause to resist U.S. entreaties. These cases generally involved naturalised Americans who had permanently returned to their land of birth but who nonetheless continued to assert U.S. nationality against the claims of their countries of origin. Such cases could also pose a genuine threat to U.S. interests when the government was obliged to expend diplomatic capital on behalf of an individual who might not count in any effective way as an American. In his 1874 annual message to Congress, President Ulysses S. Grant decried the phenomenon of

> persons claiming the benefit of citizenship, while living in a foreign country, contributing in no manner to the performance of the duties of a citizen of the United States, and without intention at any time to return and undertake those duties, to use the claims to citizenship of the United States simply as a shield from the performance of the obligations of a citizen elsewhere. (Quoted in Spiro: 1997, 1432–33)

Similar laments relating to tenuous claims of diplomatic protection were expressed by senior U.S. policy-makers for decades thereafter.

Some of these difficulties were resolved by domestic expatriation laws. A 1907 act provided for the loss of U.S. citizenship upon three years' residence in the country of origin. In other instances, bilateral agreements resolved competing claims to military service requirements and the transfer of nationality (most notably the Bancroft treaties of the 1860s and 1870s, with German and Scandinavian states). But success in addressing the problem on a universal basis proved more elusive; most countries were unwilling to cede their sovereign capacity to make rules respecting nationality. As a result, the United States faced continuing frictions over this subject in its relations with nations such as Italy and France well into the twentieth century.

Although statements of disapproval have historically been framed in terms of loyalty and allegiance (as when someone owing no real loyalty to the United States sought its protection), they have rarely focused on the direct threats that dual nationals potentially posed to national security. Since at least 1940, dual nationals faced with the problem of warring sovereignties have been afforded a choice between them. The choice may often be a difficult one, but its availability makes an inescapable commission of treason against one or the other sovereign nation unlikely. Those with both Japanese and American citizenship, for example, automatically forfeited their U.S. citizenship upon enlistment in the Japanese forces, and thus faced no criminal charges under U.S. law for that service. Nor did such dual citizens raise a particular threat to the American war effort by virtue of their (former) U.S. citizenship, any more so than did Japanese resident aliens who were allowed to return home. Finally, there appear no notable cases of dual nationals who worked as spies. Indeed, it is the spies and other saboteurs that one would most expect to avoid the status, with its obvious and open implication of possibly divided allegiance in war or warlike situations.

Dual nationals thus presented a serious threat to the national interest only in an indirect way – increasing the risks of bilateral tensions – rather than as a direct source of subversion. But however indirect the concrete drawbacks, dual nationality was still draped in a heavy mantle of moral condemnation. As George Bancroft observed in 1849, states should 'as soon tolerate a man with two wives as a man with two countries; as soon bear with polygamy as that state of double allegiance which common sense so repudiates that it has not even coined a word to express it'. Writing in 1915, Theodore Roosevelt labelled the 'theory' of dual nationality 'a self-evident absurdity'; others criticised it as 'unphilosophical' (quoted in Spiro: 1997, 1430–31).

Indeed, although dual nationality was at the heart of many international controversies for more than a century (from roughly the middle of the nineteenth century through to the middle of the twentieth), not a single commentator appears to have spoken in support of its acceptance or even its toleration. This view has persisted into more recent decades. The last major scholarly study of dual nationality concluded that the status 'is undesirable and should be abolished' (Bar-Yaacov, 1961: 266); a 1974 decision of the German constitutional court characterised it as 'an evil that should be avoided or eliminated in the interest of states as well as the interests of affected citizens' (quoted in Neuman, 1997: 277).

Interrogating entrenched conceptions

Today many continue to refuse to accept the status of dual nationality as a legitimate one. The issue seems chronically tied to the marriage metaphor; columnist Georgie Anne Geyer, for example, has asserted that dual citizenship dilutes patriotic commitments and 'mak[es] citizenship akin to bigamy' (Geyer: 1996, 68). Analyst John Fonte recently testified before Congress that dual nationality is 'philosophically inconsistent with our liberal democracy', and the prospect of a large Mexican/American dual national population has prompted a number of unfavourable editorial responses in the South and Southwest.

Nonetheless, dual nationality has come, as a practical matter, to be almost completely tolerated under U.S. law. Those born with dual nationality are not required to elect one or the other. Native-born Americans do not lose their U.S. citizenship upon the acquisition of additional nationality. Although required to take the renunciation oath, naturalising citizens face no sanction for the retention of their original nationalities.

This tolerance can be explained piecemeal. Birthright dual nationals have never been forced to choose between nationalities (at least when the individual has not been politically active in the other polity) perhaps on the presumption that many birthright dual nationals will hold the status as a technical matter only, as the children of immigrants. (Indeed, many may not even be aware that they have another nationality.) The U.S. Supreme Court has severely restricted the federal government's power to deprive individuals of their citizenship on the basis of ties to other nations. The renunciation oath has never been enforced, in part because for much of the modern era other countries have refused to recognise expatriation, and so enforced renunciation would have greatly diminished the numbers eligible to naturalise.

Toleration of dual nationality can also be both explained and justified in functional terms. If dual nationality once presented a threat to international stability, it no longer does today. The protection of persons is no longer so dependent on the particular state of the affected national, as such protection is found under the umbrella of international human rights, under which the international community shields individuals irrespective of nationality. The intersection of diplomatic protection and dual nationality was far more uncomfortable in a world where states could treat their own nationals as they pleased.

Now that nation states owe certain obligations *ergo omnes* respecting the treatment of individuals – that is, they have an obligation to all other states to respect the human rights of all persons, regardless of their nationality – dual nationality no longer adds much risk of international conflict. If, for instance, Germany mistreats a German citizen, that mistreatment will be sufficient cause for diplomatic protest by other states. Resulting international difficulties may be more pronounced if that person is a dual national, at least *vis-à-vis* the country of alternate nationality, but that will be more a matter of politics than of law. Diplomatic protection is itself now hardly the stuff of State of the Union addresses. Whatever diplomatic complications do arise are unlikely to push countries to the brink, assuming such a brink continues to exist at all.

As the prospect of armed conflict diminishes (especially among democratic states), so too does any indirect risk presented by dual nationals. This change in the international context should also answer any objections that evoke the spectre of security risks. To the extent that dual nationals ever posed such a direct risk – examples of which are not prominent in the historical record – it is surely slight today. Even where real conflict is involved, it is not clear that dual nationals should present a significant concern. Who is to say, for instance, that those with both Iraqi and American nationality would have sided, or did side, with Saddam Hussein during the Persian Gulf War and since?

Nor can dual nationals be indicted as presenting the lower-order loyalty problem of potentially playing the Trojan horse on the American political scene in the service of their other state of nationality. The extent to which U.S. citizens are motivated to act in the interests of their country of origin need not depend on a continuing formal attachment to that state. Americans have long voted their ethnic affiliation, even where they have not maintained their original nationality. As Peter Schuck argues, such motivations are not antithetical to national interests; on the contrary, they actually define the national interest, which is, after all, nothing more than an 'aggregation of interests.'

In this respect, maintaining an attachment to one's country of origin seems increasingly less distinguishable from the sorts of institutional attachments maintained by most citizens. A dual national of Mexico and the United States who advocates policies that benefit Mexico is little different from a Catholic who advocates policies endorsed by the Church or a member of Amnesty International who writes to his congressman at that organisation's behest. Why memberships in other polities are so fundamentally different in today's international dynamic as to render them a continuing concern is no longer clear.

This observation should also rebut the claim (most often made in the German context) that dual nationality should be restricted because it leads to inequality, to the extent that dual nationals have rights beyond those holding only one nationality. This argument seems suspect against a backdrop in which inequality results from the full range of institutional associations. An employee of Siemens or a member of the Catholic Church enjoys rights and resources that others may not, for example, and yet that is a fact of life. One might ask whether sole nationality ethnic Germans would trade situations with German-Turkish dual nationals by way of securing the advantage that is alleged to come with the status. Arguments vaunting equality may, in this context, mask less appealing exclusionary agendas.

Beyond toleration

The traditional bases for combating dual nationality have thus dissipated. The lingering distaste for the status is one that no longer enjoys substantial justification. Toleration of the status should not be reversed, as either a matter of law or one of practice. Indeed, strong arguments may be advanced to move beyond mere toleration toward full acceptance, even encouragement, of dual nationality. These arguments break down into two categories: recognition of the continuing societal harms of the existing approach, even if tolerant in historical perspective, and the possibility that embracing dual nationality may actually advance the national interest.

The harm of the existing approach comes in the form of deterred naturalisations. Some individuals refuse to secure U.S. citizenship because of dual nationality rules, even though they are otherwise eligible for it. Some are deterred because their home country will automatically expatriate them upon naturalisation, with possible concrete economic as well as sentimental consequences. Under old rules, for instance, a Mexican who acquired U.S. citizenship lost his or her Mexican citizenship, along with the right to own certain types of property. Historically low Mexican naturalisation rates can, in part at least, be ascribed to this legal consequence. Although the United States can do little to reform the laws of other countries on this score, many, including Mexico, are amending nationality laws to allow for the retention of citizenship elsewhere.

Available anecdotal evidence suggests that the renunciation oath itself deters some eligible aliens from naturalising. As Peter Schuck notes, the oath is hardly clear in what it requires of applicants; taken at face value, however, it appears to demand the severing of all ties to one's country of origin. (Schuck, 1998: 244) In flagrantly archaic phrasing, an applicant must 'absolutely and entirely renounce and abjure all allegiance and fidelity to any foreign prince, potentate, state, or sovereignty of whom the applicant has heretofore been a subject or citizen.' Not all eligible aliens understand that the oath is not enforced, and the U.S. government does nothing to publicise that absence of enforcement. Misconceptions apparently abound as to the manner in which the oath is administered. One study of the issue by Michael Jones Correa recounts the belief of some Colombians in New York City that naturalising aliens were required to spit and stomp on the Colombian flag as part of the naturalisation ceremony. (Jones Correa: 1998, 195) Others may refuse to take such an oath on principle (some people still take oaths seriously, after all), even equipped with the knowledge of its lack of practical effect.

Deterred naturalisations harm society in at least two respects. First, they deprive individuals of the rights that come with citizenship - a more substantial quantum in the United States since 1996, when welfare laws were amended to disadvantage individuals on the basis of citizenship status. Obviously, society sometimes deprives individuals of certain rights (one could not justify the naturalisation of war criminals, for instance), but liberalism requires that rights only be deprived where justified by some other good. Insofar as dual nationality by itself no longer poses a threat to the national interest, the deprivation here seems unfounded.

Deterred naturalisations also pose a harm from the self-interested perspective of the community. Aliens who reside permanently in our midst are far less likely to fully assimilate as long as they remain aliens. This situation is true almost by definition with respect to political assimilation, because aliens (with a few exceptions, notable as such) lack the franchise. This barrier to full participation in the political process is no small matter, because political identity is fundamental to the American identity (indeed, for some political theorists the American identity goes no further). The political exclusion of aliens inevitably retards their assimilation as a general matter. To the extent that even moderate numbers of aliens refuse to naturalise on account of the renunciation oath, the rest of us suffer a culturally separated and politically disempowered concentration of fellow residents within the community. Fully accepting dual nationality would thus help facilitate the cultural and political incorporation of new immigrants who would otherwise fail to naturalise.

These arguments suggest why dual nationality should be fully tolerated, if not actively encouraged, in the national interest. With the political incorporation of those who retain their original citizenship, dual nationality may present affirmative benefits as a function of dual nationality itself. The dual national who becomes politically assimilated in the United States will presumably come to internalise its constitutional values. If that person remains politically active in his or her country of origin, he or she will also presumably apply those values there. As this occurs, dual nationality may become a vehicle for advancing the cause of global democracy.

This kind of democratic influence already seems to have contributed to the democratic evolution of the Dominican Republic. In recent elections there, the Dominican community in New York played a significant role in electing a democratic progressive candidate as President (himself a product of a childhood on Manhattan's Upper West Side). That role may now be institutionalised, not only by the acceptance of dual nationality under Dominican law but also by the proposed allocation of two seats in the Dominican parliament for Dominican New Yorkers. Similar possibilities would be presented with respect to any of the transitional democracies, and there are now many with a significant number of emigrants in the United States. Indeed, virtually every country in the realm of second-tier states of Central America, the Caribbean, Eastern Europe, and South and East Asia can count a substantial population of its nationals (or former nationals) in the United States.

This potential to advance the spread of democratic values is a direct product of the dual national's distinctive status. When the naturalising American cuts ties to the home country, he or she loses the potential (at least in the average case) to influence its political development. Given the choice between a naturalisation applicant who intends to sever those ties and one who will retain them, the United States may now have cause to prefer the latter. The observation should apply to member states of the European Union as well. If, for instance, Germany were to accept the dual nationality of immigrant populations, one might confidently expect the step to promote democracy in Turkey. Dual nationality becomes not just a neutral status, but a beneficial one.

Policy possibilities

In light of the cost of existing rules that discourage dual nationality (resulting in suppressed levels of naturalisation) and the possible gains that may be won from embracing it (advancing the spread of democratic values), the challenge to those who would curtail its rising incidence must be to articulate even hypothetical situations in which dual nationality would pose an actual threat to the national interest. In the overwhelming majority of cases, that challenge has not, and cannot, be met.

Even with respect to the prospect of several million people with Mexican and American citizenship concentrated in the American Southwest – much less the more geographically diffuse examples involving other nationalities – any looming dangers are difficult to detect. Restrictionist Dan Stein ventures to ask, 'If Mexico sought in the future to re-occupy parts of the southern U.S., whose side would these dual nationals be on?' Yet he has to follow his own query with a tepid, 'maybe this danger is not realistic, but it should be considered.' Once one acknowledges that dual nationality cannot be opposed on grounds of political influence (as explained above, the assertion of ethnic political interests has nothing to do with the formal attachment of citizenship), no compelling reasons remain to justify stigmatising the status.

Thus dual nationality should be facilitated rather than discouraged. As a policy matter, that conclusion demands the elimination of the renunciation oath. The oath adds little, from society's perspective, to the value of a would-be citizen. To the extent that it deters some from naturalising, the oath retards the assimilation of new immigrants. To the extent that it encourages others to abandon their original citizenship, we lose the possible gains of having individuals export democratic values and practices. Others, including T. Alexander Aleinikoff and Peter Schuck, have suggested replacing the renunciation oath with one of 'primary' or 'core' loyalty to the United States, which would allow for the retention of prior nationality at the same time that a priority of loyalty is established. (Aleinikoff: 1998, 38–39, Schuck: 1998, 245) In my view, no real substantive need exists for a loyalty oath of any kind relative to other states, because such notions of loyalty are now themselves largely outdated. Moreover, to the extent that other nations have followed suit (the same proposal has already been made in Canada), a new oath of primary loyalty would soon assume the falsely symbolic status that has long infected the renunciation oath.

Once dual nationality is accepted as a legitimate status, it should not remain subject to special regulatory measures, with the relatively insignificant exception (in terms of number of persons affected) of service in foreign-policy posts in the federal government. Aleinikoff has suggested that such issues as voting rights might be the subject of bilateral accords on dual nationality. (Aleinikoff: 1998, 36) When necessary, such accords are not objectionable. But today, in contrast with the past when issues such as the military service obligations of dual nationals prompted numerous bilateral undertakings, the new phenomenon of binationality does not appear to have generated problems requiring diplomatic resolution. If the Dominican Republic wants to allow (or deny) Dominican dual nationals in the United States the right to vote in Dominican elections, that is for the Dominican Republic alone to decide. The United States would surely chafe at the intervention of other nations with respect to whether American citizens resident in those countries could vote in U.S. elections. The possibility of foreign nationals lining up in large numbers at foreign consulates in the United States to vote in foreign elections would present an odd spectacle, but a benign one.

Peter Schuck has proposed that dual nationals not be permitted to hold high public office in another nation, presumably at risk of expatriation. (Schuck: 1998, 245–46) But what better way to export constitutional values than at the top? Permitting foreign office-holding would be acceptable even from a traditional national-interests perspective, insofar as U.S. influence over another country's policies would likely be enhanced by the presence of U.S. citizens among the latter's policy-making ranks. The retention of U.S. citizenship does not even pose concrete dangers in the extreme situation in which a U.S. citizen leads another nation in war against America, for he or she gains no advantage by virtue of retained citizenship itself. Indeed, such a person would be merely a fool, because only an American citizen can be found guilty of treason.

One might more persuasively object to dual nationals assuming high office in the United States government. Here the possibility of divided loyalties could pose serious difficulties, even in an era in which national interests are less easily demarcated. It would not, for instance, likely serve U.S. interests to include a holder of Mexican and U.S. citizenship on the U.S. delegation in trade negotiations with Mexico; some international dealings may still include a substantial win-lose element, in which one country's gain is the other's loss. Indeed, the Mexican government's revision of its own nationality laws, while permitting dual nationality as a general matter, bars dual nationals from assuming certain elective, judicial, and military offices.

In the U.S. context, the imposition of such blanket ineligibilities on dual nationals would seem unnecessary. The service of dual nationals in the vast majority of public sector positions would not present even abstract risks to the polity. Rather, the problem of divided loyalties would be better addressed within a standard conflict-of-interest framework. When a public official is faced with an issue that directly implicates his own finances, that official is typically required to recuse himself from the matter. Broad or significant financial interests might disqualify one from some jobs altogether. One would not, for instance, find a large stockholder of a meatpacking company at the head of the Department of Agriculture (at least so one would hope).

Similarly, one could require dual nationals in appointive public office to recuse themselves from matters directly implicating the interests of their country of alternate citizenship. They would be disqualified altogether from positions in which the breadth and frequency of such recusals would prevent the discharge of full responsibility. Under this approach, a holder of both Mexican and American citizenship could not serve as Assistant Secretary of State for Latin American Affairs but could hold most other federal offices, including elsewhere in the Department of State. (Current Defence Department regulations denying security clearances to those who exercise dual citizenship, recently deployed to refuse an Irish and American congressional staffer access to classified campaign-finance related documents, should be shelved.) This practice would hardly be unprecedented. The use of non-nationals as diplomatic personnel has a long pedigree; the diplomatic corps of imperial Russia, for instance, was composed mostly of Germans. That the additional citizenship would compromise the dual national's suitability, even at high levels, in such departments as Health and Human Services or Education, much less as teachers or police officers in state or local employment, seems far-fetched.

The political discretion of the electorate would likely limit the number of dual nationals with a prospect of securing federal elective office, but dual nationals should not be excluded from federal office as a categorical matter, at least not under federal law. If the voters of New York's Washington Heights believe that someone with both Dominican and American citizenship would best represent them in Congress (as well they might), then it is not clear why that preference should be denied. Of course, the leadership would be unlikely to appoint the dual citizen to the Select Committee on Intelligence; but the status would not seem in any way to compromise most duties of the federal legislator. In the United States, the president must be native-born, which makes the prospect of a dual national in the highest office even more implausible than political realities would already dictate.

These policy approaches are sketched in broad outline, but any gaps can be more closely addressed as the growing incidence of dual nationality demands. From our standpoint today one thing seems clear: calls for stricter enforcement of the renunciation oath should be rejected. In any event, it would be difficult today to enforce effective restrictions on dual nationality. Enforcement of the renunciation oath could be readily circumvented in two ways. First, in what might be called the new perpetual allegiance, home countries might refuse to abandon citizens who naturalise in the United States; that is, they would not allow expatriation. Unlike the old perpetual allegiance, the new perpetual allegiance would be to the benefit of the citizen, not the sovereign state, but it would force the United States either to refuse to naturalise any individual from that country (an unlikely possibility) or to accept the fact of dual nationality.

Second, a naturalisation applicant could cancel his or her original nationality for purposes of naturalisation, but then reacquire it thereafter. Under the *Afroyim* line of cases, depriving an individual of U.S. citizenship in such circumstances would likely be found unconstitutional. The rule of *Afroyim*, of course, has set the precedent for the full acceptance of dual nationality when the second, non-U.S. citizenship is acquired through naturalisation. It remains unclear why as a policy matter dual nationality in those instances should be less threatening than when the U.S. citizenship is by naturalisation. Indeed, one might argue that those who move to another country and participate in its polity might pose more of a threat, to the extent that they are more likely to lose touch with their American roots and values.

The strongest practical argument against eliminating the renunciation oath is a political one. Merely broaching the possibility might provoke a firestorm of opposition that would ultimately work to the detriment of dual nationals in particular and of aliens in general. Politics looms over all immigration issues, as shown by the 1996 experience with immigration reform legislation. One may still wonder, however, if such a firestorm would develop on the dual nationality issue, despite a large Mexican-American dual national population. The issue would presumably mobilise many of the more powerful ethnic groups (the Irish and Jewish American communities most prominent among them) to defend the status and to promote a popular understanding of it as no special threat.

Perhaps that understanding can also be facilitated by adopting 'binational' as a label for those who hold more than one citizenship. Where one confronts entrenched negative conceptions, changing labels may present an important step toward securing acceptance. Dual nationality suffers from long-standing disfavour, dictated once, but no longer, by the realities of the old international system. Binationality, by contrast, may become a defining feature of a new global dynamic.

References

T. A. Aleinikoff, *Between Principles and Politics: The Direction of U.S. Citizenship Policy*, Washington D.C., 1998.

N. Bar-Yaacov, *Dual Nationality*, London, 1961.

G.A. Geyer, *Americans No More*, Atlantic Monthly Press, 1996.

G. L. Neuman, 'Nationality Law in the United States and the Federal Republic of Germany: Structure and Current Problems,' in *Paths to Inclusion: The Integration of Migrants in the United States and Germany*, eds. P.H. Schuck and R. Münz, Oxford, 1997, 247–97.

P.H. Schuck, *Citizens, Strangers, and In-Betweens: Essays on Immigration and Citizenship*, Boulder, Co., 1998.

P.J. Spiro, 'Dual Nationality and the Meaning of Citizenship,' *Emory Law Journal* 46, no. 4, 1997, 1411–85.

M. Jones-Correa, 'Comments on Peter Schuck's 'Dual Nationality in an Era of Migration,' in *Immigration & Citizenship in the 21st Century*, ed. N.M.J. Pickus, Lanham, Md., 1998, 193–98.

Note

* This contribution is revised from its original publication as an occasional paper of the International Migration Policy Program of the Carnegie Endowment for International Peace. © 1998 Carnegie Endowment for International Peace.

CHAPTER 2

NEW RULES FOR DUAL NATIONALITY

David A. Martin*

Dual citizenship has reemerged as a contentious issue.[1] For the United States, Mexico's adoption in March 1998 of constitutional amendments governing nationality precipitated the latest round of controversy. Departing markedly from Mexico's historic hostility to dual citizenship, the legislators explicitly meant to foster ongoing nationality links with Mexican emigrants who naturalise in the United States and perhaps thereby to encourage more to obtain U.S. citizenship (Vargas: 1996; Gutierrez: 1997; Verhovek: 1998, A12). Coming on the heels of similar legal changes by other countries (such as the Dominican Republic and El Salvador) that have traditionally sent large numbers of migrants to the United States, and at a time when U.S. naturalisation demand is at an all-time high, the change has evoked alarm in some quarters and praise in others. The new Mexican law is generally careful and nuanced in its approach to dual nationality, especially in distinguishing the Mexican nationality now being offered from full Mexican citizenship. Its newly recognised dual nationals resident north of the border will be exempt from certain restrictions on property holding and inheritance that formerly applied to them as foreigners, but, as Mexican nationals rather than citizens, they may not vote or hold high public office. Mexico's care in assigning rights and privileges, however, usually has not been matched by equal precision among U.S. commentators, who tend to manifest polar reactions.

Some – I will call them oppositionists (Geyer: 1996, 68, 312; Geyer: 1997, 1, 19) – who are suspicious of the other countries' law reform motives and worried about divided loyalties on the part of new U.S. citizens, call for a return to the traditional opposition to dual nationality that has marked U.S. policy, and indeed that of most of the world, throughout the first half or more of this century (Borchard: 1922, 733). Others – I will call them endorsers – welcome the new developments, believing them consistent with the realities of *fin de siècle* America in a shrinking globe, and advise that it is high time that we overcame our allergy to multiple citizenship (Spiro: this volume; Schuck: 1998; Shuck and Spiro: 1998, A22; Spiro: 1997; Franck: 1996; Legomsky: 1994; McGarvey-Rosendahl: 1986).

Nor is this by any means solely an American debate. Developments in Europe, both lingering controversies over how to treat large immigrant populations and head-scratching over the expanding reach of the European Union (EU) into political and social spheres, have prompted renewed attention to dual nationality, and Europe has its own line-up of endorsers and oppositionists. Germany has witnessed the most intense debate. The Social Democrat-Green alliance that won control of the German government in 1998 proposed a new law that would reduce from 15 to 8 years the residence period required before a foreigner could naturalise, and, most controversially, would have permitted such persons to retain their original nationality. The bill triggered such heated opposition that it was generally blamed for the Social Democrats' defeat in a state election in Hessen in February 1999. Having thereby lost control of the Bundesrat, the alliance withdrew its first proposal and replaced it with a more modest bill that countenances dual nationality only in limited circumstances (Hailbronner: this volume).[2]

Especially for the endorsers, embracing dual nationality seems an appropriate worldwide prescription. Meanwhile, oppositionists generally focus most closely on their own nation's policies. Nevertheless, sometimes harking back to their antecedents in the world leaders who drafted the 1930 Hague Convention,[3] most would probably be happy if the rest of the world accepted their resistance to the practice.

In this paper I want to pay close attention to both contending camps, but mainly as a way of getting beyond them. With the end of the Cold War, and a host of other developments that promote a more tightly linked, more peaceful, and more democratic globe, it is indeed time to reconsider the classic aversion to dual nationality, and to eliminate some of the rules and practices that have constricted it. Thus, I begin tentatively finding sympathy with the endorsers. But they often overread the existing evidence. It is hardly time to embrace dual nationality without qualification, or to treat choice of citizenships as an absolute human right, left only to the will of the individual. My endeavour here is to pick out the key features of the new world order that should have a bearing on establishing a new global citizenship regime, and then to sketch out precisely what those features may mean for more detailed rules governing the gain, loss, and exercise of multiple citizenship. The effort is to identify those new globalising developments that make dual citizenship more likely and more acceptable, but also to apply greater rigor to their analysis, and to discover thereby certain limiting principles implicit in the trends the endorsers find so compelling. My time horizon begins with the 1990s, the end of the Cold War, and the paper attempts to speculate about the next four or five decades, not farther. In this time frame, I am convinced, we will not observe the funeral of the nation-state. Instead, that entity will remain the most important political unit on the world stage, albeit in a more complex environment stemming from the growth in number and ambition of supranational institutions, more complex arrangements for internal autonomy, and perhaps an expanding global role for nonstate actors.

My inquiry here takes the form of an endeavour to sketch a set of global rules or guidelines, intended for wide and uniform implementation by modern states. A uniform global code governing nationality has long been wished for, yet never achieved; I do not pretend that this set is any more likely to be adopted. For now, political realism is not the objective. Instead, I offer this sketch in the form of a global framework as a somewhat artificial device, useful, I believe, for promoting more disciplined thought and debate about the new world realities that cause, in different circles, such hopes and fears about dual nationality. Thinking about these issues in the form of widely used rules, rather than simply spinning suggestions for a particular nation's law reform, keeps the debate at a more global level, and helps keep one focused on principle rather than national particularities. This is the kind of discussion we need now, as citizenship studies enter a new period of heightened activity – a discussion about the 'ought' in view of the new world order that is, in major part, the very reason for the new buzz of interest in citizenship.

The building blocks for the endorsers' case

The endorsers' case rests primarily on certain claims about how world conditions have changed since the current regime of nationality rules crystallised – crystallised in a form generally resistant to multiple nationality. This section picks up those claims, analyses them, and explores for inherent limitations, tensions, or contradictions. The next section moves beyond the endorsers' arguments to examine other relevant features of today's global system that should be taken into account as we fashion a new set of approaches toward dual nationality. The third section of the paper then draws on these building blocks as it tenders for discussion a proposed new set of dual nationality rules.

Globalisation

Endorsers of dual nationality plausibly wrap themselves in the mantle of social and economic realism. Our globe has shrunk, and the occasions for cross-national commerce, travel, and communication, as well as residence beyond the borders of one's native state, have multiplied. Business, tourism and the needs of academic inquiry all feed the momentum of global migration, as do poverty, war and human rights abuses. Short of environmental catastrophe or nuclear war, this development will not disappear or even weaken. Indeed, it will almost surely expand.

These trends obviously result in increasing numbers of persons living for lengthy periods outside their state of nationality. Greater cross-national contact results in an increasing incidence of cross-national marriage, which not only gives incentive for one spouse to take the other's nationality, but today also generally gives rise to eased rules of naturalisation in such a situation. Even without such marriages, increasing numbers of children are born while parents reside in a state other than their own. The world's current mix of *jus sanguinis* and *jus soli* rules quite often results in children having multiple nationality at birth.

Classic oppositionist doctrine had ways to accommodate such developments, while still adhering to the goal that all persons should have only a single nationality. The initial step was the mandate that married women take the nationality of the husband, or at least lose their former citizenship upon marrying outside the national family. Laws of this stripe certainly reduced dual nationality of children, but for those children nonetheless born dual nationals, owing to a confluence of *jus soli* and *jus sanguinis* rules, there remained two possible remedies. Some advocates proposed a uniform global code adopting one or the other rule exclusively, or some modest combination that would still result in only one nationality at birth (Flournoy: 1921, 545, 693, 705–06). These proposals made little practical headway, however, as states either proved stubborn in clinging to their own prerogatives in these matters, or remained convinced that their own regime of transmission rules made sense for their own national story, whatever may be the view elsewhere. Hence the second device: a required election. at or around the age of majority, usually meant to result in the dual national's assumption of the single nationality of the state of habitual residence (Ibid. 559–64, 693–70).

Neither of these approaches can be expected to work today. Forced loss of a wife's nationality was an early target of feminist political mobilisation and has now been widely rejected – although changes to this effect in some countries are surprisingly recent (Weis: 1979, 96–99; Bar-Yaacov: 1961, 177–192; Stratton: 1992, 202–05, 235–39). Some national codes still require election of a single nationality at majority, but the practice has been fitful. Even in the heyday of oppositionism, the Hague Conference rejected an article requiring election that was put forward by the prestigious Harvard Research Project.[4] Today, with the reasons for concern about dual nationality in decline (as the later sections of this part will discuss), it hardly seems likely that the will can be found for rigorous enforcement of such a choice upon persons born dual nationals. In the absence of a return to such measures, dual nationality will inevitably multiply.

Limiting principles

Globalisation, as a process, is a reality, and it will surely continue to expand the incidence of plural nationality. But it does not make nationality irrelevant. The nation-state has not disappeared, and it seems extremely unlikely to do so within the time frame we are addressing here. It remains the primary locus of governance, even as more and more webs of cooperation, treaty obligation, and international institution-building are spun. Even the experience of the region furthest along toward transnational governance reinforces this message, for the European Union's experimentation with EU citizenship has taken only baby steps. EU citizenship is a thin concept, and the treaty implicitly preserves the primacy of national citizenship (Martiniello: 2000). As long as this is true, nationality will count, and statelessness will still be regarded as an evil. The world still expects citizenship to serve, in Rogers Brubaker's phrase, as 'an international filing system, a mechanism for allocating persons to states' (Brubaker: 1992, 31). Even if the filing category is less likely than before to carry decisive weight for many purposes of international business and other endeavours, it still plays a significant role in resolving certain predictably arising, if residual, issues. For example, although neither state of nationality has the right to expel a dual national, third states still can. They will want to know who bears assured responsibility for accepting return, if the person's sojourn or even settlement in that third state is validly brought to an end. Nationality also remains important (even if in reduced measure) as a guarantee of mutual and reciprocal obligations between citizen and government.

One other concomitant deserves mention. Even as the world becomes more comfortable with dual nationality, it does not welcome endless discretion in taking up new nationalities. Under international law, for at least some purposes, a claimed nationality must reflect a genuine connection with the country involved (Nottebohm Case: 1955, 23), and for other purposes the 'dominant and effective nationality' will be given precedence (Case A-18: 1984; Highet et al.: 1993).

Peace

The end of the Cold War and the widening circle of countries sharing basic assumptions about democratic governance and market economies have also bolstered the endorsers' case for embrace of dual nationality. Dual nationality might provoke conflict or severely test a person's own sense of identity if the two nations found themselves on opposite sides of significant international disputes, to say nothing of war. But as nations' interests increasingly converge, so this argument goes, there is far less reason to expect such basic conflict (Spiro: 1997, 1461). Moreover, to the extent that national armies shrink and conscription either plays a reduced role or is abolished altogether, one of the ongoing flash points for conflict stemming from dual nationality declines in significance.

Limiting principles

The trend toward peace and convergence is of course most welcome, and this particular epoch seems firmly rooted in true mutuality of interest among a wide array of states, rather than in mere peaceful coexistence. To the extent that competitive energies can be channelled constructively into business and trade, the peace holds still greater promise of durability. This peace is not the rock the endorsers sometimes envision, however, and on which they would build a mighty edifice of new citizenship rules. Empirical studies on the 'democratic peace' show that it is durable and that it *almost* always holds, but they do not show that it is inevitable, even between democracies (Russett: 1993, 11; Chan: 1984, 639). An especially worrisome cloud on the horizon consists of the rise in ethnic tensions in many parts of the globe, along with the increasing incidence of identity politics that seems designed to increase the fissiparous tendencies of polyglot nations. This is not a counsel of doom; integrative tendencies and the demography of intermarriage provide strong countercurrents. Nevertheless, it is a counsel of prudence. Nationality rules need to take some account of the risk that states currently enjoying harmonious relations may someday come into serious conflict. Some constraints on dual nationality may be appropriate if only because conflict and tension have not been wholly banished – and their quiescence is by no means guaranteed in the future.

Complexity of loyalties, identities, and national interests

Oppositionists tend to assume that loyalty is one-dimensional; loyalty to a second dilutes or destroys loyalty to the first. Dual nationality then draws condemnation as akin to bigamy (Geyer: 1996, 68). But as Peter Spiro, Thomas Franck, Sanford Levinson, and others have pointed out, this is weak as psychology (Spiro: 1997, 1473; Franck: 1996, 376–383; Levinson: 1986, 1463–1470). Allegiance is a far more complex phenomenon than the oppositionists' metaphors suggest. All of us have multiple loyalties, to family, community, church, college, club or sports team, and they are not usually seen as incompatible with allegiance to the nation. Sometimes such non-national loyalties may stand in tension with the latter (acutely felt, for example, by newlywed conscripts), but some such conflict simply comes with living in a rich and complex civil society. It can usually be managed, bridged, accommodated.

Societies that lack or suppress those other affiliations, allowing only allegiance to the nation-state, are rightly condemned as totalitarian. National allegiance does not have to crowd out all other commitments. If this point is conceded, then there is no reason why national allegiance must *ipso facto* crowd out loyalty to another nation. Of course there may be instances where two nations may be so at odds, either ideologically or militarily, or both, that equal allegiance to both seems possible only through self-deception. Those instances would seem to be rare, however – rarer today in a post-Cold War world, where national policies tend to differ at the margin rather than the core.

Moreover, the one-dimensional view of loyalty fails to capture the complexities of emotion and commitment felt even by those naturalising citizens who take a renunciatory oath and take it seriously. They may be proud new American or Canadian or French citizens and fully committed to serving their new country and building a new life for themselves and their children there. But pangs of regret or wonder, emotional ties to the old country, and especially continuing relations with family still residing there, make it impossible to accomplish a full and complete break. This human reality lies behind some of the recent campaign in Germany to ease that country's ban on dual nationality. Proponents argued that resident aliens resist naturalising in Germany because they cannot bring themselves to make so decisive a break with their former nationality. Greater acceptance of dual nationality would more fully honour these complexities of emotion and identity, while encouraging an important step toward identification with Germany (Seibel: 1997, 927–28, 935; Rittstieg: 1994).

The oppositionist objection that grows from suspicions about dual nationals' loyalties sometimes takes a stronger form, at least when sparked by legal changes undertaken to encourage emigré citizens to naturalise in a wealthy or more powerful nearby country. The charge is that the new citizens will become a lobby voting for the preferences of the foreign state, rather than voting based on their own assessment of wise policy for their country of residence (Geyer: 1995, 19; Rodriguez: 1997, B5). To my knowledge, however, there is no empirical support for such a claim, and indeed it would seem virtually impossible to construct a valid empirical test. Even if a foreign state tried to instruct its dual nationals to vote for certain candidates or policies, and even if one could isolate the votes of dual nationals from those cast by other voters, how could the evaluator distinguish an instructed vote from the voter's independent judgment that reaches the same conclusion? Voting as urged by the foreign government might truly be in the best interest of both states.

In any case, even if there were some genuinely identifiable problem here, barring dual nationality would hardly solve it. A naturalised citizen who has severed all nationality ties with her previous country may still seek out candidates whose policies would be favourable to the former homeland. Indeed, native-born mono-nationals can equally well develop sympathy for a foreign country or a foreign cause, and let that sympathy guide their votes. This is inescapably their prerogative. Democracy means that citizens themselves are ultimately in charge of deciding what is in the national interest. That their judgment may coincide with the position of another polity on certain issues hardly demonstrates disloyalty. This is not to say that the 'national interest' is an empty concept, but in modern democratic polities, it is certainly not monolithic. Its calculation is too complex to sustain this oppositionist objection, at least in any situation short of war (Spiro: 1997, 1469–1472; Legomsky: 1994, 295; Neuman: 1992, 329).

Limiting principles

The picture painted here of complex loyalties supports reducing barriers against dual nationality. Yet complexity is not necessarily to be multiplied. Proponents of Germany's acceptance of dual nationality posit that Germany's renunciation requirement is a major psychological obstacle to naturalisation by its long-resident alien population (including many aliens born in Germany who have not known life elsewhere). The U.S. experience should spark some scepticism toward accepting this as a plausible overall explanation for low naturalisation in Germany. America's strong formal ban on dual nationality for naturalised citizens, enshrined in the renunciatory oath required by statute, did not deter a sixfold increase in naturalisation applications between 1991 and 1996.

The salient point is that some aliens may *want* a fresh start, may want to use the occasion of naturalisation to break official affiliation with another polity, and hence cut off duties and obligations (as well as rights) that flow from those earlier ties. Any new rules tolerating dual nationality by naturalising citizens should respect this form of complexity as well. They should facilitate an informed choice by applicants for naturalisation, aware of all the options a new dual nationality code might permit. If the citizen's choice is for cutting the old ties, both old and new country should help effectuate the choice, through eased procedures and, if necessary, diplomatic protection by the new country of nationality against the old.

A second conclusion may follow. Respecting the complexity of loyalty and identity requires no greater acceptance of plural nationalities than such notions of loyalty and identity can sustain. The immigrant generation can certainly be expected to feel those contradictory pulls, and so may its children, raised around a hearth where accounts of the old country are frequently shared, perhaps in that country's tongue. But as generational distance increases, multiple formal nationalities will usually lose any claim to reflect real identification. Any new global rules should act on this reality and avoid the perpetuation of nationality after genuine links have been broken.

A more effective international human rights regime

As noted by Peter Spiro (Spiro: this volume), some of the notorious controversies that prompted states to discourage dual nationality grew from difficulties in exercising diplomatic protection. The stakes were significant, because under classic international law the would-be protecting state either had full standing to take action against mistreatment of an individual – in cases where the individual was its national and did not also have the citizenship of the offending state – or it had no role at all. In this classic view, treatment by a state of its own citizens or subjects was entirely a matter for domestic jurisdiction.

Today that view of exclusive domestic jurisdiction is discredited. International action to protect human rights, even against abuses committed by a state solely against its own citizens, is almost always treated as legitimate, although it is far from reliably effective. A citizenship link between protector and abused is not required to justify action. This, argues Spiro, provides another argument against hostility to dual nationality. And if this was ever a significant part of the oppositionist case, he is surely correct.

Some scholars have gone further. Because of the growth of human rights protection at the international level, they contend that we have entered an era of post-national or transnational citizenship. In the more extreme versions of this theory, the new condition seems to render classic nation-state citizenship virtually irrelevant (Jacobson: 1996; Soysal: 1994).

Limiting principles

Arguments based on the increasing acceptance of international human rights norms and institutions must still acknowledge significant practical limitations on the efficacy of international human rights initiatives. Though the globe has come a long way from the hands-off doctrine (regarding a state's treatment of its own nationals) that held sway before World War II, international human rights machinery is still weak and episodic in its application. In any case, nation-states remain the key players on international human rights matters. For example, the Haitian generals left power in 1994 not because they feared an unfavourable report by the UN Human Rights Commission, but because a nearby and powerful national government was willing to use military force to assure the return of President Aristide. In less visible human rights initiatives – the day-to-day give and take over particular prisoners of conscience, government reaction to demonstrations, or restrictions on the electoral process – diplomatic interchange initiated by foreign ministries still plays a central role.

Beyond this, and of principal importance here, national governments are, and will remain, the principal stewards of the primary apparatus needed to honour human rights as a matter of routine within their own borders. If true observance of human rights is to be achieved in Haiti, it must rest on far more than occasional interventions by foreign militaries or denunciations by international bodies. It must be built patiently through the nurture of domestic institutions that will routinely respect such rights or help correct their violation – institutions such as well-trained police forces with effective internal disciplinary mechanisms, courts that function in a timely and decisive fashion according to a real rule of law, criminal punishments that fall on both private violators and corrupt or abusive government officials, and elections that hold leaders accountable. International initiatives are important, but they cannot supplant such domestic activity. The nation-state's governmental apparatus inescapably provides the principal arena for such work, laborious, chronic, and disappointing as it can sometimes be. And citizens of that country – full participants in its politics – will play a far more important ongoing role than international institutions or NGOs.

Citizenship rules should recognise this principal role and help to foster it. Premature declarations about the arrival of transnational or post-national citizenship obscure the true contribution of national institutions, and may even be counterproductive. More concretely, any new citizenship regime must attend to the need for citizen engagement in the polity – a matter addressed more thoroughly in the next section.

Expanding democratisation

The 1990s have witnessed a remarkable expansion of democratic regimes, along with a fairly decisive conceptual victory for electoral democracy as the principal foundation for a regime's legitimacy. International conferences now speak with conviction of a human right to democratic governance (Franck: 1992). When economic woes or popular uprising lead to the ouster of an old leader, the new caretakers almost always seek to bolster their own legitimacy by pledging early elections. Suharto's fall from power in Indonesia in 1998 exemplified this pattern, but similar pledges can be found in recent history from Southeast Asia to Central America to West Africa to Eastern Europe.

Limiting principles

In many respects, this development obviously bolsters the endorsers' case. It reflects a growing convergence of thinking about political institutions and human rights, which may be seen as a hallmark of globalisation. But in ways that endorsers usually fail to acknowledge, the expanding consensus on democracy should also be seen to entail constraints on the way in which dual nationals exercise their options.

Democracy is built on citizen participation, and its ideal is meaningful participation – of an engaged and informed citizenry. This presupposes a certain level of devotion to the community enterprise, to approaching public issues as a unified community, even while leaving much to individual choice in deciding on the aims the polity should pursue or on specific policies to address specific public issues. Such devotion is most closely associated with civic republicanism, whose advocates tend to call it 'civic virtue' (Neuman: 1994; Martin: 1994). It need not be thought of as solely a civic republican conception, however; any concept of healthy democracy requires a significant level of voter engagement.

Democracy, in short, requires commitment to the majoritarian process. This entails, within broad outer limits, an agreement to live by the consequences of majoritarian choice, even if one's own party or candidate or policy preference did not prevail – at least not at this particular election. It means accepting being a loser on the issues, and still coming back to contend another day, in another election. It means, in short, looking overwhelmingly to voice, in Albert Hirschman's formulation, rather than exit, as the primary way of contending with disagreeable actions or policies (Hirschman: 1970, 15–17). Such devotion also entails certain obligations for electoral winners. They too should ordinarily be prepared to live by the consequences, to stick around to experience the effects and implications of the policies they successfully supported, and not simply to witness them from afar. All these considerations point toward voting rules for dual nationals that focus their political activity on the country of habitual residence.

Additional underlying observations

A few other central features related to citizenship should be taken into account in considering new rules for dual nationality. Because they are not necessarily part of the endorsers' case, they were not treated in the previous section.

Sentiments of attachment – loyalty, patriotism, solidarity

In speaking of citizenship, we sometimes refer only to its formal, legal dimension – a recognised relationship between citizen and state that carries with it certain reciprocal rights and obligations. At other times the term connotes a richer, deeper vein of sentiment, commitment, emotion – affective ties among citizens that derive from an important common bond. This section tries to unpack the latter meaning.

There are two stories to be told about the affective dimension of citizenship. In one, it appears dangerous, exclusionary, overblown. Appeals to loyalty in the name of citizenship ask the audience to suspend judgment about government actions, to follow blindly, to join the herd. Patriotism descends to chauvinism. To emphasise fellow-feeling toward other citizens, in this account, is simultaneously to emphasise the otherness of the alien, to hijack the language of solidarity and to use it to suppress those feelings of solidarity that should extend to all persons. In its worst forms, this use of the concept helps deny the very humanity of the noncitizen, as in the notorious *Dred Scott* decision of the U.S. Supreme Court, which declared blacks permanently ineligible to citizenship and helped provoke the Civil War (Scott v. Sanford: 1857).

The other story sees citizenship as a call to individuals to rise above self-absorption, a foothold for genuine efforts to transcend selfishness, a way station toward a larger conception of obligation or community. History's slow, painful evolution may have seen feelings of loyalty and devotion expanding from family to clan to tribe, and then to wider fields. Perhaps someday it will expand to embrace all humanity. But until one is sure that day has arrived, one would do well not to abandon the foothold citizenship represents against too-narrow loyalties, particularly in a decade when appeals to the smaller horizons of ethnic or sectarian attachment have brought violence and atrocity in their wake. In this second account of the affective dimension, citizenship evokes some of the warmest and most generous feelings of solidarity – even more so when the citizenship at issue represents membership in a democratic society that is relatively open and inclusive. As Michael Ignatieff has observed, 'The only reliable antidote to ethnic nationalism turns out to be civic nationalism, because the only guarantee that ethnic groups will live side by side in peace is shared loyalty to a state strong enough, fair enough, equitable enough to command their obedience' (Ignatieff: 1993, 243).

Both stories carry weight and deserve attention. The rules advocated here, however, rely primarily on the second account. They assume that there is something valuable in the institutions that can sustain loyalty and solidarity among a circle so wide, and potentially so diverse, as that encompassed by most modern nation-states. They acknowledge that the first story contains necessary cautions. But they reflect a concern that a thorough-going scepticism about national sentiments springs from either a premature cosmopolitanism or a cynicism that dismisses the possibility of genuine affection or loyalty in human relationships.

Equality

The choice of stories described in the previous section is bolstered by recognition of another central and powerful feature of citizenship, its linkage to equality. When members of the French third estate embarked on their quest for *liberté, egalité, fraternité*, they chose *citoyen* as the appellation best capturing this new way of looking at social and political relationships. To be a citizen rather than a subject is to claim this equal station with all others. T.H. Marshall described citizenship as 'the basic human equality associated with . . . full membership of a community'(Marshall: 1965, 76). Rainer Bauböck opens his important recent book with similar observations: Citizenship means in part 'that people are equals as members of an inclusive polity. There may be large inequalities and wide cleavages in society but each citizen is counted as one and as one only and all citizens are counted together' (Bauböck: 1994, vii).

The norm of equality supports broader claims as well, of course. For a variety of rights, membership in the human species, not citizenship in a particular country, provides the only qualification for a claim to equal treatment. This recognition forms a key building block in the endorsers' case, and even more so in the highly ambitious claims made by those who speak of postnational citizenship (Soysal: 1994; Jacobson: 1996). For the latter, human equality combined with durable residence in a particular territory suffices to mark out the most relevant form of 'citizenship' or belongingness. As rights of permanent resident aliens have expanded over recent decades, this implication of equality undeniably played an important role.

Nevertheless, these qualifications still do not displace or erase the importance of equality among citizens, or more precisely, the almost definitional feature of citizenship that signifies equality among those who hold that status. Hard work is required to achieve equal rights in practice, no matter what may be proclaimed in international instruments. Progress toward equality must take advantage of whatever footholds it can find. The traditional and powerful notion of equal citizenship should be nurtured for these purposes. New rules on dual nationality should be attentive to this fact and at the very least should not undermine the sense that citizens are, and of right ought to be, equal.

A right to expatriate, and its qualifications

In the mid-1860s a Britain that still clung to the perpetual allegiance theory sought to discipline as British subjects three natives of Ireland who had naturalised in the United States. The resulting U.S. outcry produced the Expatriation Act of 1868, which pronounces a right to shed old nationalities in the broadest possible terms. It labels expatriation 'a natural and inherent right of all people, indispensable to the enjoyment of the rights of life, liberty, and the pursuit of happiness', and it directs the executive branch to defend the right (Expatriation Act: 1868). Confronted with this response, Britain appointed a commission to study the issue, and within two years it acknowledged a right of expatriation in statute and bilateral treaty (Mikva and Neuman: 1982, 307–29). Within roughly 80 years, the rest of the world had essentially come along, to the point that, in 1948, the UN General Assembly adopted without dissent a resolution stating that 'No one shall be . . . denied the right to change his nationality.' This, of course, is Article 15(2) of the Universal Declaration of Human Rights (Universal Declaration: 1948).

National practice has not readily conformed, however. Some states make it hard to secure official recognition of loss of nationality – which is sometimes a formal prerequisite to naturalisation under the laws of the state whose polity the individual wants to join. This reluctance or resistance may reflect real disagreement with the asserted right, but it might also indicate only bureaucratic inertia. In some cases it may even bespeak a kind of quiet deal whereby the nationals at issue can wind up retaining both nationalities, because many European states waive their renunciation requirements when the country of origin will not readily acknowledge or permit a change of allegiance. In any case, a new global code of nationality rules should incorporate some obligation on the state of origin to honor this right more fully and with fewer obstacles, in those instances where an informed citizen chooses to relinquish the earlier affiliation and would not thereby be left stateless.[5]

This last discussion suggests one further limiting principle that deserves more recognition than the 1868 U.S. statute acknowledges, at least in its text. The right of expatriation is a right of the individual against the state of original nationality; it does not provide a right as against any other polity. That is to say, no matter how disillusioned an individual becomes with his native state, he plainly obtains thereby no right to claim the citizenship of another. Only when he has otherwise obtained the chance for citizenship elsewhere, or at least a mature right of permanent residence, does this right of expatriation become ready for meaningful exercise. This limitation is not manifest in the text of the 1868 Act, but it is certainly not inconsistent with the practical realities of the time. Of chief importance, immigration controls were not then highly developed, indeed were not developed at all in much of the world. An expatriate then, unlike the situation 130 years later, could find somewhere else to live, provided only that he could meet the expense and endure the physical hardships of getting there. Moreover, the event that precipitated the 1868 Act clearly involved persons who did have another national affiliation. The Act stands less as a statement of pure individual right and more as a statement of the mutual rights held in common by the naturalised citizen and his new country of citizenship. The situation is potentially quite different today when immigration is closely regulated even by the traditional countries of immigration.

To put the matter another way, the right to expatriate must be balanced against countervailing norms against statelessness (Universal Declaration: 1948, article 15(1)). The state of origin retains certain duties *vis-à-vis* other states, if not indeed *vis-à-vis* the individual, no matter how disaffected. It must continue honoring a certain set of obligations, mainly for permitted residence and acceptance of return if deported from another country (Weis: 1979, 45–59), until such time as another polity enters into the reciprocal relationship of citizenship so as to displace the first. The international filing system has a justifiable bias against lost files.

Oath and ceremony

In the United States, naturalisation ceremonies are among our most joyous and hospitable public events. Both the naturalising citizens and their families, along with all the assembled public officials, dignitaries, orators, and high school bands, come together to recognise that a deeply important milestone is being passed. The ceremony is, customarily, a time of emotion, pride, and welcome. Within this ceremony, the taking of a solemn oath by the new citizens, right hands raised in unison, provides the pivotal moment. New citizenship rules should not discard the mysterious powers of ceremony, if only for the sense of solidarity that it tends to instill both in the new citizens and in all other participants as well.

Oaths also deserve attention for another reason. The U.S. State Department (along with other government agencies) has moved with the *Zeitgeist* toward a position far more welcoming of dual citizenship, but it has done so in ways that carry real costs for the sanctity of solemn oaths. This consequence plays out in two settings: loss of U.S. citizenship upon taking an oath of naturalisation elsewhere, and the consequences for other citizenships of the oath persons take when naturalising in the United States. I consider each in turn.

Because of constitutional rulings by the Supreme Court, one cannot lose U.S. citizenship upon taking up the citizenship of another country, or holding office or serving in the military there, unless one specifically intends thereby to surrender U.S. nationality. In only one circumstance is evidence of such specific intent readily available: when the other country's naturalisation rules (or induction formalities for officeholders or military personnel) require express renunciation of all other allegiances. If they do so, the requirement usually takes the form of an oath of renunciation. Since 1990, however, the State Department apparently treats such oaths, even with express language renouncing other citizenships, as 'routine' and hence not expatriating – unless of course the individual independently insists that she wanted that act to mark the loss of U.S. citizenship (Kelly: 1991, 446).

In the second setting, the treatment of persons who naturalise in the United States, U.S. law is formally hostile to dual nationality. The required oath expressly renounces all other allegiances. Nevertheless, State Department officials now routinely advise prospective citizens that even this act will not result in the loss of their earlier citizenship. The standard explanation rests on an assertion that most other states will not recognise the loss of citizenship; hence the person would remain a dual national in the eyes of that other state. Whether this is technically accurate is bound to vary depending on the detailed laws of the other jurisdiction. But the real question would seem to be the viability of dual nationality in such circumstances in the eyes of U.S. law, whatever the stance taken under foreign law. To give assurances that dual nationality may continue, in the teeth of an express oath, is virtually to invite false swearing and to place the individual at some (minor) risk of a perjury prosecution and even denaturalisation. At a minimum it must breed confusion or cynicism over the solemnity of the naturalisation oath. New rules for dual nationality obviously need to do better.

New rules for dual nationality: a first sketch

This section presents a proposed set of new rules for dual nationality for the first half of the twenty-first century that are consistent with the principles, observations, and factual assumptions described in the first two sections of this paper. I do not claim that all of them are compelled by the earlier sections. I offer them instead as a first sketch, hoping to stimulate broader discussion of the middle ground between oppositionist and endorser positions.

1. *States should accept dual nationality where it represents a genuine link with the two states concerned.*
    It should by now be obvious that the endorsers' case for general acceptance of dual nationality makes sense in the conditions of the early twenty-first century. The factors of globalisation, peace, human rights, and complex loyalties all point in this direction. Consequently it should be accepted that states will continue to choose their own rules for acquisition of nationality at birth, employing, within broad limits, whatever mix of *jus soli* and *jus sanguinis* they find appropriate for their own national history and character, even if the attribution of nationality results in dual citizenship. Further, at the time when a person naturalises, states should neither require renunciation of other national affiliations nor treat naturalisation elsewhere as an event that automatically triggers loss of the original nationality. Mere change in *de facto* administrative practice is not sufficient. Actual revision of any required oath should be secured.
    This rule would also continue the now well-established principle that a state may not impose nationality after birth without the consent of the individual concerned (or the consent of the parent in the case of a minor). This principle is probably best understood as a particular application of the broad outer limit on nationality attribution: that it should rest on a genuine link with the state involved. Clearly such a link exists in the normal application of *jus soli* and *jus sanguinis*, and also when a person naturalises in a new country of residence upon voluntary application. The genuine link test is meant only to screen out highly tenuous misuses of the citizenship system, not to become a demanding filter. Moreover, it does not give a country the power to strip citizenship whenever it determines that the citizen's actions have weakened the link.

2. *States should ease voluntary expatriation for those who choose this path, at the time of naturalisation or otherwise, provided the person will not be rendered stateless.*
    Even while becoming more tolerant of the individual choices that lead to dual citizenship, states need not promote or encourage the proliferation of nationalities. The complex psychology of loyalty and identity means that some will wish to change their nationalities decisively. On limited occasions, such as outbreak of war between their two nations, they may perhaps even be put to an obligatory or near-obligatory choice. Moreover,

encouraging full engagement in a single polity is a valid goal, consistent with healthy democracy (and especially so within a civic republican conception of democracy). Provided that the person concerned has obtained nationality elsewhere (or, at a minimum, durable residence rights) and that the change is not part of a scheme to escape criminal prosecution or other liability, he or she should be permitted to shed national allegiance. The person also need not have the new nationality in advance. Renunciation of prior allegiances can be a part of a naturalisation procedure, for those who choose this step knowing that it is a matter of personal choice. The state of initial nationality should facilitate whatever administrative processes are needed to secure full recognition of the surrender.

Because expatriation signifies a change of major significance, states should require formalities that promote mature deliberation and take other steps to help assure that the person truly has nationality (or at least secure residence rights) elsewhere. At its most elemental, this may mean that states require formal renunciation to be performed outside the national territory. States also should generally provide full information about the consequences entailed, perhaps on an informed consent form to be signed by the renouncer; impose waiting periods to assure time for ample deliberation; allow renunciation only after a full interview with a consular or other administrative officer who can plumb the person's intention and understanding and also, in most circumstances, help assure that the person will not thereby be rendered stateless; and finally require that the step be memorialised through the taking of an oath or other formality of equal gravity.

3. *States of initial nationality should reduce the material disadvantages that follow from acquiring a new nationality or from expatriating.*

This rule addresses the situation where persons are discouraged from naturalising because they will lose property rights, rights of inheritance, pension coverage, or similar entitlements in the state of initial nationality. If rule 1 is fully honoured, of course, this problem will greatly diminish, because most such consequences follow from loss of nationality, not simply the acquisition of a new one. To the extent that states do seek to discourage acquisition of a dual status through such material exactions, however, the present rule asks them to cease, so as to help assure full realisation of the rights and interests that underlie rule 1.

Whether the same strong protection should obtain in the case of fullscale voluntary expatriation (rather than the addition of a second nationality) is more problematic, especially if observance of the earlier rules has achieved a situation where expatriation reflects the uncoerced will of an individual who could have retained both nationalities. The transfer of allegiances is then clearly a choice of the individual, not a condition exacted as part of the second state's naturalisation process. Free-will choices properly carry consequences.

It is basic, almost definitional, that voluntary expatriation from country

A entails the loss of any assured residence rights in A. This is a focused and proportional reciprocal effect of the person's choice to shed ongoing obligations to A. But most of the material losses that states impose go beyond this, and they then carry the flavour of a gratuitous infliction. Owned property or earned pensions reflect claims that are more in the nature of vested rights, based on prior work or exchange. Inheritance rights, in contrast, cannot be seen as vested; the testator can generally change the allocation nearly until the moment of death. For the state to step in and block the bestowal of such bounty based on the break of national ties, however, seems more an unnecessary or retaliatory intrusion into family choices than a legitimate government measure – particularly as the world becomes more tightly linked in a global market system. On the other hand, broader social insurance schemes not closely founded on the individual's own contributions appear in a different light. Here the right to claim might properly be ended, for the expatriate should henceforth look to his new country for that sort of protection. Obviously this dichotomy is not a clean one, and difficult line-drawing problems regarding social security systems will arise.

Where this analysis leads to preserving material entitlements, there may still be overriding exceptions based on national security or other strong state interests. For example, a state might properly deny the expatriate the right to own land in sensitive border locations or to retain controlling interests in highly sensitive industries, such as fighter aircraft manufacture. The basic message of the rule remains, however: eliminate the material exactions unless they are solidly supported by valid policies other than deterrence or punishment of changes in citizenship status.

4. *The primary obligations of a dual national run to the state of residence, and that state should serve as the primary protector of the individual.*

While in the territory of a state, even aliens owe the measure of allegiance reflected in obligatory observance of the laws enacted by its government. Even more so does this apply to a dual national residing there. With regard to military service obligations of dual nationals, international treaties on the subject have generally given primacy to the obligations owed to the state of residence and generally provide that the fulfillment of mandatory service there discharges the obligation to serve in the other state's military (Protocol Relating to Military Obligations in Certain Cases of Double Nationality: 1930; Convention on Reduction of Cases of Multiple Nationality: 1968; Council of Europe: European Convention on Nationality: 1997). These treaties have not gained wide acceptance, but the principles they embody set a sensible pattern for a new century when dual nationality will be more common. Taxes present a more complex picture, because states have often asserted the power to tax nonresident nationals. Nevertheless, most of the time treaties or national laws allow offsets against that tax bill for taxes paid to the state of residence. This is hardly the place to consider all the complexities of international tax policy, but the basic framework just described would seem generally compatible with a rule of thumb giving primacy to obligations owed to the state of residence.With regard to one of the central potential benefits of citizenship, the dual national would have, *prima facie*, a claim to diplomatic protection by either state of nationality. Nonetheless, one would expect the state of residence to take the lead in pursuing such protection. An emerging rule of international law holds that the state of dominant and effective nationality (ordinarily the state of habitual residence) may exercise diplomatic protection and pursue international claims on behalf of its national even against that person's other state of nationality.

5. *A dual national should vote only in the state of residence, and rapid changes of residence should not be recognised for purposes of qualifying to exercise the franchise.*

Exercise of the right to vote by dual nationals has perhaps provoked the greatest controversy (Editorial: 1998, A30). The classic treatment of naturalisation elsewhere, coupled with the renunciation requirement often imposed by the receiving state, in principle eliminated most double voting. It thereby served the aims discussed in Sections I and II above, promoting democratic engagement (for the person thereafter had direct access to the political life of only one polity) and encouraging the kind of participation from which a healthy sense of attachment can grow.

As dual nationality nevertheless proliferated, national laws made a variety of arrangements either encouraging or forbidding voting by such persons while resident elsewhere. Some states have allowed voting only by resident citizens and have not permitted absentee voting from abroad. Overseas dual nationals therefore would be able to vote (if at all) only in the other country, and nonresident mono-nationals would be disenfranchised until they return to the home country. As a middle position, other states accept absentee voting by persons temporarily residing overseas, but they must have a demonstrated residence, usually at their last place of abode, within the national territory. They thus elect candidates to seats pertaining to that geographic district in the core national territory, a district with which they presumably retain some familiarity. At the opposite pole, some states make special arrangements for representation of overseas residents, who may or may not be dual nationals. France, for example, reserves thirteen seats in its Senate for residents of overseas departments and territories, and another twelve to represent French nationals residing outside France and its territories. Significantly, however, no comparable arrangements exist for representation in the more powerful branch of Parliament, the National Assembly. The limited empirical research available suggests that even when the state of origin makes a significant effort to encourage absentee voting by its overseas residents, participation is low (Jones-Correa: 1998, 125). Nonetheless, such voting does occur, and doubtless it sometimes includes votes cast by dual nationals.

In the face of such wide diversity, caution is appropriate before prescribing an overarching electoral rule for global application. But it may be that the matter has been left to national peculiarities by default. For the last century, at least, the dominant black-letter international doctrine has strongly discouraged dual nationality. Such a baseline scarcely invites hard thinking about rules on a worldwide basis for voting by dual nationals. Hence, states have made their own national arrangements for what has traditionally been seen as a small class of aberrant cases. As we have seen, however, the growth of that class shows every sign of continuing. Because dual nationality is no longer an insignificant aberration, a harmonious global approach is worth thinking about.

In the new system coming into being for the new century, I suggest that the rule should be: if you are a dual national, vote only where you are resident. In a democratizing world, this rule focuses political activity in a way that corresponds closely with the locus of primary obligations pursuant to rule 4. It also helps promote mature deliberation and seriousness about the vote, because the voter will have to live with the consequences in the most direct way. Focusing political activity in the place where you live encourages a deeper engagement in the political process – perhaps even civic virtue – and also helps develop affective citizenship and a sense of solidarity.

This rule also builds on an analogy to national systems. Modern societies certainly tolerate persons owning multiple homes, but I submit that we would regard it as objectionable, even fraudulent, for a person to vote twice within the same electoral cycle in two different locations, even if she did spend a portion of the year in each location. At least this is true of voting for higher level general-purpose legislative and executive branch positions. (Voting at the municipal level, where revenue may be based primarily on property ownership and authority may be divided among a variety of bodies with specialised powers, presents different considerations (Briffault: 1993, 340–41).) This rule would also seem to hold even within the U.S. federal system, deemed for some purposes to be characterised by dual sovereignties. 'One person, one vote' is normally taken to mean that one does not vote in two places.

It must be conceded that the claims made in the two preceding paragraphs, if pushed to their own limits, would argue strongly against dual nationality in the first place. If focusing primary political activity in this fashion carries such benefits for solidarity, democratic engagement, and civic virtue, how much more could these goods be expected to flow from channelling *exclusive* political activity? The point is even stronger if the person, by surrendering, or being required to renounce, all other national ties, has thereby foresworn use of the exit option when policies do not turn out as she favours. I concede all this. Indeed, these may be the strongest theoretical arguments to be mustered in the oppositionists' case against dual nationality. In the end, however, one arrives at the oppositionists' conclusion only by ignoring the other unmistakable features of the current world scene described in the first section of this chapter. These factors must be weighed in the balance against a dogmatic conclusion that all persons should be mono-nationals: globalisation with increasing cross-national contacts, cross-national marriages and births outside the parents' home state; increasing convergence of interest among an expanding circle of democratic states; and an honest recognition of the realities of complex loyalties and identities. Moreover, this part of the oppositionists' argument has not really considered the alternative set of rules proposed here, which can capture most of the benefits they seek in the realm of politics and solidarity. That is, much of the debate has proceeded as if there were only two possible systems – either a multiple nationality system that leaves it entirely up to the individual where and how often he will exercise his political rights, or a system that roots out dual nationality wherever possible.

The proposal here tries to escape such polarities. The dual national may vote in either polity, but only in one at a time (McGarvey-Rosendahl: 1986, 325). His voting exercise must generally correspond to the country where he chooses to take up residence; to vote in the other polity then requires transferring his domicile. To avoid opportunities for persons to game the system by taking advantage of different electoral cycles in the different polities, it makes sense to recognise a change of residence for these purposes only after a significant waiting period and perhaps other proof of a *bona fide* change in domicile. My starting intuition would be a one- or two-year period, but the exact contours are, of course, open for argument.

Meeting objections

When I have discussed preliminary versions of this proposal at scholarly gatherings, they triggered a variety of reactions, usually strongly felt. A minority share my own sense that there is something objectionable about multiple voting, but most, who would generally admit to endorser-camp leanings, protest that there really is no problem. Or if there is, they argue, then it is a problem solely for the polity that permits absentee voting, and that nation's officials have the legal capacity to end the practice when they judge that it brings concrete disadvantages.

Why is multiple voting so often seen as a nonproblem? One response I have met is that of course double voting within a single polity is bad, but the issue here involves separate polities – and not just separate units within one system, but two different sovereignties. The implication is that sovereign states are sufficiently separate that a vote in each of the units really does not count as double voting.

Endorsers who offer this response have not taken an adequate measure of their own case for easing acceptance of dual nationality to begin with. Their case rests on globalism and democratic convergence, hence on the diminishing importance of national boundaries. There is then a deep and unrecognised irony to find persons of a globalist bent invoking the hoary concept of sovereignty, whose importance they are otherwise seeking to deflate. I do of course agree with one part of the objector's case, *viz.*, that it is too early to count the nation-state out of the picture. Ironically, however, I want to make less of this observation than do these objectors from the endorser camp. Sovereignty, thankfully, is not quite what it used to be.

As the globe shrinks and international cooperation increases, political decisions made by other nations have an increasing effect outside their own borders. The beginnings of a functioning global political system are upon us, and some regional supranational institutions (especially the EU) run far ahead in blazing the trail. Human beings are generally represented in these settings by elected national political leaders, or by their delegates. A person who has a say in selecting two or more sets of those leaders, while their fellow citizens can participate in selecting only one, secures an advantage.

What is most fundamentally at stake is the equality that has been a key element in the basic understanding of what it means to be a citizen. Advocates of a new and more open era of citizenship rules should not at the same time display unconcern about this central feature, even if it is mainly symbolic. Equality must be considered across a wider canvas – precisely because of the globalisation on which endorsers rest so much of their case.

Similar points can be marshalled against the argument that double voting is really only a concern for one of the states, the state of nonresidence. This argument apparently rests on an understanding that the objections against double voting are solely instrumental – i.e., that double voting may lead to undesirable outcomes because nonresidents will be less informed and also may take extreme positions since they do not have to live with the full consequences. Those two instrumental objections, which carry some weight, do indeed have their direct impact on the state of nonresidence. But there is no reason why the rest of the world, in a more global era, should stand indifferent to such political distortions elsewhere. In any event, leaving the remedy to the actions of that single state does nothing to address the departure from equality.

6. Upon assuming policy-level positions in a national government, dual nationals should relinquish their other nationalities.

As we have seen, some oppositionists oppose dual nationality because they charge that dual nationals will make for disloyal voters, a kind of fifth column undermining the national interests of their new state of residence and distorting its policies to the advantage of their state of birth. Section I discussed how these objections are overblown with regard to simple voting. When it comes to the assumption of policy-level positions in a national government, however, the concerns come closer to the mark. This is emphatically not to say that dual nationals in office will ordinarily be spies or traitors. On most decisions or actions for which such an officer would be responsible, one can expect that the two states' interests would be harmonious. The differing pulls of two nationalities would not even arise as an issue. If there is some modest separation of interest, the odds are heavy that the officer's instincts and inclinations would run overwhelmingly with the state of residence, the state in whose government he serves.

The case for divestment of a second nationality in these circumstances still holds, nevertheless. In part this rule serves a prophylactic function. Even if cases of real conflict between the interests of the officer's two nations are rare, such conflicts are quite likely to arise unexpectedly, without warning, and to trigger heated controversy when they do arise. Even if the officer were at that point to surrender the other nationality, or perhaps only to recuse herself from further involvement in the controversy at issue, questions would surely be raised about her decisions earlier in the process. It is simply too late to wait until the point of recognised conflict to deploy such cures.

The case for relinquishment of nationality in these circumstances is more fundamental. In a democratic polity, a government officer is an agent of the people, and the people are entitled to assurances of undivided loyalty. Even more is this true of policy-level positions giving the officer discretionary authority in designing and executing national decisions. Broader authority of this sort places the person in the position of a fiduciary, and domestic law frequently imposes higher obligations on fiduciaries.

Some recent national practice supports the case for drawing the line at policy-level positions. Mexico, for example, in its new law allowing dual nationality, has provided that dual nationals may not hold certain high public offices. Israel, throughout its history a state deeply hospitable to dual nationality, provided in 1988 that members of the Knesset would have to be nationals only of Israel (Seib: 1992, A6). Just before Valdas Adamkus became President of Lithuania, after living for fifty years in the United States where he was a federal government official, he surrendered U.S. citizenship, even though the laws of neither country required it (Paddock: 1998, A4). His example deserves emulation.

7. A particular nationality should not be continued indefinitely into future generations if the family has lost a genuine link with that state.

Plural nationality deserves carefully measured but straightforward acceptance in the modern world, primarily because of the way it reflects the genuine and complex commitments held by individuals who have links with two or more societies. Plural nationality is not a virtue in itself, however, and should not be proliferated beyond the point where it serves this fundamental purpose. The issue arises primarily when nationality is attributed to distant generations long after the family has lost real connection with the home society. Most states, in any event, do not allow such endless transmission. Acquisition of nationality *jure sanguinis* is typically allowed only to children born of parents who themselves had a specified period of residence in the home state, and its continuation is often conditioned on the child's taking up a stated period of such residence before a prescribed age. Such rules are not universal, however, and some states permit the continued descent of citizenship without generational limitation, subject perhaps to some obligations of registration.

What could tolerably be left to isolated national decisionmaking in an era when fewer people migrated and married across international boundaries is no longer acceptably left exclusively to the national forum. Continued attribution of citizenship, even when the family has lost all realistic links, amounts to a self-aggrandising state effort to expand its own rights, claims and jurisdiction beyond justification. To say this is not to imply that the world needs complete uniformity of rules on this subject, but only to advocate some outer limits on transmission to future generations. I do not attempt here to paint exactly what those outer boundaries should be, but some required period of parental or personal residence (and not mere paper registration) would seem to provide the key measures – as noted, measures already used by most states anyway. If some states wish to establish special rules easing the requirements for descendants of its nationals who want to gain that country's citizenship, this should not be prohibited, again within certain outer limits. To make sure that this practice does not represent mere citizenships of convenience, however, it too should ordinarily be based on a residence requirement, rather than mere registration and proof that a distant ancestor once enjoyed that nation's citizenship.

One other corollary follows. If the children of emigrant families living abroad for two generations are to lose their rights *jure sanguinis* to the citizenship of the former state, they need ready access to the citizenship of the family's state of residence and of de facto allegiance. At this point, in order to avoid statelessness, a small required dose of *jus soli* may be required. We already see some developments in this direction on the part of states whose attribution rules were once strictly limited to *jus sanguinis* (such as the so-called 'double *jus soli*,' recognising citizenship of children born in the territory to alien parents who themselves were born there).

Conclusion

Both the hopes and fears surrounding the greater incidence of dual nationality in the modern world are exaggerated. Opposition to dual nationality paints scenarios of disloyalty and failure of allegiance that are not realistic in the more peaceful, democratic, and connected globe we now inhabit. But oppositionists are on to something. Not only are peace and democracy perishable; citizenship still represents an important arena for exercising the virtues of democratic participation and engagement, for developing a sense of civic solidarity that can overcome ethnic divisions, for reaffirming a fundamental equality that transcends barriers of race, class, religion, or ethnic group. Those who ask for an unqualified embrace of dual nationality often overlook these advantages. They risk treating citizenship as something unserious, something akin to joining a social club.

This paper has tried to sketch out a middle position between endorsers and oppositionists, drawing as much as possible on the strongest of the insights tendered by each camp. But it is only a sketch, a tentative first step, offered in the hope that it might enrich the debate.

References

N. Bar-Yaacov, *Dual Nationality*, New York, 1961.

R. Bauböck, *Transnational Citizenship*, Brookfield, Vt., 1994.

E. M. Borchard, *The Diplomatic Protection of Citizens Abroad or the Law of International Claims*, New York: The Banks Law Publishing Company, 1922.R. Briffault, 'Who Rules at Home?: One Person/One Vote and Local Governments', *University of Chicago Law Review* 60, 1993, 339.

R. Brubaker, *Citizenship and Nationhood in France and Germany*, Cambridge, Mass., 1992.

Case A-18, *Iran-United States Claim Tribunal Report*, 1984, 251.

S. Chan, 'Mirror Mirror on the Wall ... Are the Freer Countries More Pacific?', *Journal of Conflict Resolution* 28, 1984, 617.

Council of Europe: European Convention on Nationality, art. 7, done Nov. 6, 1997, 37 *ILM* 44.

Convention on Reduction of Cases of Multiple Nationality, art. 5, entered into force March 28, 1968, 634 U.N.T.S. 221.

Editorial, 'What Makes a Citizen?', *Washington Post*, 5 June 1998.

Expatriation Act of July 28, 1868, ch. 249, 15 Stat. 223, R.S. § 1999.

R. W. Flournoy, Jr., 'Dual Nationality and Election', *Yale Law Journal* 30 (1921), 545.

T. M. Franck, 'The Emerging Right to Democratic Governance', *American Journal of International Law* 86, 1992, 46.

T. M. Franck, 'Clan and Superclan: Loyalty, Identity and Community in Law and Practice', *American Journal of International Law* 90, 1996, 359.

G. A. Geyer, 'Mexico's Cynical Push for Adoption of Dual Nationality', *Chicago Tribune*, 2 June 1995.

G. A. Geyer, *Americans No More*, New York: Atlantic Monthly Press, 1996.

G. A. Geyer, 'Dual Nationality Not in America's Best Interests', *Chicago Tribune*, 10 January 1997.

P. Gutierrez, 'Mexico's Dual Nationality Amendments: They Do Not Undermine Citizens' Allegiance and Loyalty or U.S. Political Sovereignty', *Loyola Los Angeles International & Comparative Law Journal* 19, 1997, 999.

Hague Convention of 1930, Convention Concerning Certain Questions Relating to the Conflict of Nationality Laws, opened for signature 12 April 1930, 179 L.N.Treaty Series 89.

Harvard Research Project, 'Code on the Law of Nationality', *American Journal of International Law* 23, 1929, 14.

K. Highet, G. Kahale III and D. J. Bederman, 'Iran-U.S. Claims Tribunal – Dominant and Effective Nationality Test – Beneficial Ownership of Claims', *American Journal of International Law* 87, 1993, 447.

A. O. Hirschman, *Exit, Voice and Loyalty: Responses to Decline in Firms, Organizations, and States*, Cambridge, Mass., 1970.

M. Ignatieff, *Blood and Belonging: Journeys into the New Nationalism*, London, 1993.

D. Jacobson, *Rights Across Borders: Immigration and the Decline of Citizenship*, Baltimore, 1996.

M. Jones-Correa, *Between Two Nations: The Political Predicament of Latinos in New York City*, Ithaca, 1998.

H. A. Kelly, 'Dual Nationality, the Myth of Election, and a Kinder, Gentler State Department', *Inter-American Law Review* 23, 1991, 421.

S. H. Legomsky, 'Why Citizenship?' *Virginia Journal of International Law* 35, 1994, 279.

S. Levinson, 'Constituting Communities Through Words That Bind: Reflections on Loyalty Oaths', *Michigan Law Review* 84, 1986, 1440.

T.H. Marshall, *Class, Citizenship and Social Development*, Westport, Conn., 1965.

D. A. Martin, 'The Civic Republican Ideal for Citizenship, and for Our Common Life', *Virginia Journal of International Law* 35, 1994, 301.

M. Martiniello, 'Citizenship of the European Union' in *From Migrants to Citizens: Membership in a Changing World*, ed. T. Alexander Aleinikoff and Douglas Klusmeyer, Washington, D.C., 2000.

P. McGarvey-Rosendahl, 'A New Approach to Dual Nationality', *Houston Journal of International Law* 8, 1986, 305.

A. R. Mikva and G. L. Neuman, 'The Hostage Crisis and the "Hostage Act"', *University of Chicago Law Review* 49, 1982, 292.

G. S. Neuman, '"We are the People": Alien Suffrage in German and American Perspective', *Michigan Journal of International Law* 13, 1992, 259.

G. S. Neuman, 'Justifying U.S. Naturalization Policies', *Virginia Journal of International Law* 35, 1994, 237.

Nottebohm Case (Liechtenstein v. Guatemala), 1955 I.C.J. 4, 6 April 1955.

R. C. Paddock, 'Lithuania's President-Elect Gives Up U.S. Citizenship', *Los Angeles Times*, 26 February 1998.

Protocol relating to Military Obligations in Certain Cases of Double Nationality, art. 1, opened for signature 12 April 1930, entered into force 25 May 1937, 178 L.N.T.S. 227.

Helmut Rittstieg, 'Dual Citizenship: Legal and Political Aspects in the German Context', in *From Aliens to Citizens: Redefining the Status of Immigrants in Europe*, ed. Rainer Bauböck, Brookfield, Vt., 1994.

Roberto Rodriguez, 'Dual Citizenship from U.S., Mexico Spurs Hope, Hate', *Fresno Bee*, 24 February 1997.

B. Russett, *Grasping the Democratic Peace: Principles for a Post-Cold War World*, Princeton, N.J., 1993.

Peter H. Schuck, 'Plural Citizenships', in *Immigration and Citizenship in the Twenty-First Century*, ed. Noah M. J. Pickus, Lanham, Md., 1998.

P. H. Schuck and P. J. Spiro, 'Dual Citizens, Good Americans', *Wall Street Journal*, 18 March 1998.

Scott v. Sandford, 60 U.S. (19 Howard) 393 (1857).

G. F. Seib, 'Many Americans Choose East Europe but Few Renounce the Citizenship', *Wall Street Journal*, 24 August 1992.

A. M. Seibel, 'Deutschland ist doch ein Einwanderungsland geworden: Proposals to Address Germany's Status as a "Land of Immigration"', *Vanderbilt Journal of Transnational Law* 30, 1997, 905.

L. Stratton, 'The Right to Have Rights: Gender Discrimination in Nationality Laws', *Minnesota Law Review* 77, 1992, 195.

Y. N. Soysal, *Limits of Citizenship: Migrants and Postnational Membership in Europe*, Chicago, 1994.

P. J. Spiro, 'Dual Nationality and the Meaning of Citizenship', 46 *Emory Law Journal* 46, 1997, 1411.

Universal Declaration of Human Rights, G.A. Res. 217A(III), U.N. GAOR, UN Doc. A/RES/217A(III), A/810 (1948).

J. A. Vargas, 'Dual Nationality for Mexicans? A Comparative Legal Analysis of the Dual Nationality Proposal and Its Eventual Political and Socio-Economic Implications', *Chicano-Latino Law Review* 18, 1996, 1.

S. H. Verhovek, 'Torn Between Two Nations, Mexican-Americans Can Have Both', *New York Times*, 14 April 1998.

P. Weis, *Nationality and Statelessness in International Law*, Germantown, Md., 1979.

Notes

* A revised and expanded version of this essay was published in the Georgetown Immigration Law Journal (volume 14, 1, 1999).

1. For convenience I use virtually interchangeably the terms 'dual citizenship' and 'dual nationality' to describe the phenomenon I address, as the technical distinction between a citizen and a national is rarely important for my purposes. My main focus is on rules to be applied by states and the international community to persons who have or desire recognised, formal affiliations with more than one nation-state, whether that affiliation amounts to citizenship, as will ordinarily be the case, or mere nationality.

2. As enacted, the revised bill grants citizenship at birth to children born in Germany to parents legally resident for at least eight years. Ordinarily such children would then have dual nationality, but by age twenty-three the bill requires that they would have to renounce the other nationality or lose their German citizenship. The reduced residence requirement imposed on applicants for naturalisation (eight years) was retained in the enacted law.

3. The preamble to that convention states: 'It is in the general interest of the international community to secure that all its members should recognise that every person should have a nationality and should have one nationality only' (Hague Convention of 1930).

4. See Article 12 of the Project's proposed Code on the Law of Nationality:

A person who has at birth the nationality of two or more states shall, upon the attaining of the age of twenty-three years, retain the nationality of that one of those states in the territory of which he then has his habitual residence; if at that time his habitual residence is in the territory of a state in which he is not a national, such a person shall retain the nationality only of that one of those states of which he is a national within the territory of which he last had his habitual residence (Harvard Research Project: 1929).

5. Restrictions on this right may be justified in limited circumstances, for a person should not be able to use expatriation to escape punishment for a crime or for desertion from properly exacted military or other national service. Blocking expatriation, however, would not be justified as a way of extracting debt payments or forcing repayment of the costs of education. In general, human capital belongs to the individual, not to the state.

CHAPTER 3

PLURAL CITIZENSHIPS

Peter H. Schuck

To reflect deeply on citizenship is to enter a bewildering gyre of reasoning. It is commonly held that citizenship entails a kind of membership, but there the consensus ceases and the contention begins. Membership in what? Why, in the polity of course. And what is a polity? It is a community of citizens. Oh. And does the polity include those who are not citizens? Well, it includes them in some senses but not in others. If it is the citizens who decide on the nature and conditions of non-citizens' inclusion, by what right did they acquire that power and under what limitations do they exercise it? Hmmm.

One cannot really answer these questions without first formulating some theory that can either justify or criticise existing practice. Failing that, a metaphor can sometimes serve as a placeholder or surrogate for theory; it is a kind of theory manqué whose power to persuade lies in its compressed, immediate, deeply felt associations and imagery. For this reason, citizenship talk usually unleashes a high-stakes rhetorical battle of metaphors. One picture portrays citizens as members of a family of origin, individuals who are linked to one another irrevocably by blood or by some equally binding historical integument. Another conceives of citizenship as a normative fellowship of belief, a dense community of shared value, what Robert Cover called a *nomos*. A third depicts citizens as members of a club who join and disaffiliate for their own purposes as and when they wish – so long as they meet eligibility standards and their dues are fully paid up. A fourth image of the civic relationship is that of a marriage formalised through solemn vows, designed to be permanent, and dissolved only with the consent of the state and upon certain proofs (Cover: 1983; Walzer: 1983: Levinson: 1986, 1440).

Each of these metaphors captures certain features of constitutive relationships like that between citizen and state. The idealised family imagery evokes our desire for security, permanence, and unquestioning devotion; a web of mutual commitments beyond choice or calculation. Yet it also presupposes a common experience and affinity of descent that are infrequent in a society as radically heterogeneous and open as that of the United States. The *nomos* metaphor, like that of marriage, draws much of its rhetorical power from our yearnings for commitments that are so intense and unique that they occupy our spiritual domain. The consensuality of marriage, however, preserves room for considerable self-definition and autonomy, whereas the totalising tendency of religion and the ascriptive tie of family tend to constrict such a space. The club is the most instrumental of these communal forms. Like marriage, club membership is contractual in nature and may generate affective ties but arises out of more calculated, reversible choices. Like markets, clubs require only a partial, episodic commitment from a member; they lay claim to a relatively narrow range of a member's identity.

When the debate turns to dual citizenship or nationality[1] and the question of divided loyalty arises, these metaphors continue both to clash and to converge. For those who invoke the family or *nomos* as the dominant image, dual citizenship[2] is an impossibility, a condition utterly at war with the logical, spiritual, emotional, and psychological presuppositions of such communities. For those who liken the polity to a marital relationship, dual citizenship amounts to polygamy, a diffusion of allegiance and affection that threatens the integrity of both relationships. In contrast, those who prefer the club metaphor are quite comfortable with multiple memberships, each for limited purposes defined by the member. Alternatively, one might abandon these relational metaphors altogether and view acquired citizenship as a 'new political birth,[3] or, focusing on citizenship's traditionally territorial dimension, regard it as a more or less permanent home.

This debate, of course, does not end here. One remains free to question the appropriateness of each of these metaphors as applied to a political community. One can also challenge the metaphors' normative integrity by pointing to certain inconsistent social practices that seem to compromise their coherence: America's separation of the religious and political domains; the multiplicity of family groupings to which Americans belong; the blending of families and the generation of new ones through marriage and remarriage and the cessation of relationships through divorce.[4] Such challenges invite the suspicion that although each of these images captures some significant aspect of citizenship, none provides an adequate account of it.

In this chapter, I hope to move beyond these metaphors by focusing instead on how we might think about dual citizenship without being distracted by such familiar, freighted and powerful images. This discussion will underscore the profoundly value-laden character of the increasingly incendiary dual citizenship debate, which threatens to polarise Americans in positions that will be difficult to compromise.

The first section of this chapter begins by explaining why dual citizenship is becoming both more common and more controversial. This requires some discussion of the legal and social contexts in which dual citizenship has been liberalised[5] and citizenship itself is being reassessed. Others have ably (and recently) covered this ground, so my summary can be brief.[6] The following section develops some distinctions that can add texture to our understanding of dual citizenship and help us to identify some leverage points for possible policy change. The next section – the heart of the chapter – analyses the arguments for and against permitting dual citizenship; it explores both the normative claims and the oft-suppressed empirical issues that underlie the normative debate.

Finally, on this analysis, the chapter considers how dual citizenship law might be reformed. I generally applaud the recent trend in U.S. law to accept dual citizenship and believe that this emerging regime should be refined rather than either rejected or extended. I focus on two problems with existing dual citizenship law that deserve reformers' attention. First, the statutory requirement that a naturalising citizen 'renounce and abjure absolutely and entirely all allegiance and fidelity to any' other state, language that dates back to 1795, is broader than necessary to secure the loyalty that the U.S. needs and has a right to expect of its citizens. This broad, indiscriminate formulation obscures what the oath should clarify: the kinds of ties to other states that are inconsistent with American citizenship and must therefore be renounced. It may suggest to new citizens that they are being asked to renounce more than a liberal polity should demand. Second, the renunciation requirement applies only to naturalising citizens, not to those dual citizens who acquired their U.S. citizenship by birth or descent. This difference creates an inequality among citizens that is difficult to justify and that appears to contradict fundamental constitutional principles. This inequality warrants public scrutiny and debate. By refining and clarifying the renunciation requirement and by calling on Congress to make the rights and obligations of citizens – old and new alike – as equal as possible, I hope to remedy both problems.

I readily acknowledge that if my approach to the first problem were adopted – if the oath were modified to require new citizens to renounce only the core political allegiance that they bear to another state – the U.S. dual citizenship policy and practice might change little. Americans (whether single or dual citizens) might continue to view their political rights and duties much as they do now, naturalisation officials and the courts might interpret the standards as before, and aliens' incentives and propensity to seek naturalisation might remain largely unaffected. Even if my proposal would change little in practice, however, this is hardly ground for objection. Since I do not regard the current permissive dual citizenship policy as being fundamentally 'broke', I see no strong reason to 'fix' it except for refining the renunciation language in the oath. On the other hand, my approach to the second problem – reducing the inequality among citizens with respect to their right to acquire dual citizenship – would affect the right of existing U.S. citizens to acquire additional nationalities in the future and to act accordingly.

Some commentators on citizenship issues, including me, have expressed doubts about the dominant conceptions of citizenship, the distribution of rights and responsibilities among those who reside in the polity, and the justifications advanced to support this distribution.[7] Although these criticisms raise interesting and important issues concerning citizenship, none of them doubts the fact that strong normative arguments can be made for retaining some distinctive citizenship status, although disagreement exists about which arguments are most persuasive. In what follows, I shall assume the essential validity of the status of citizenship,[8] even as I question certain conventional ways of thinking about and regulating it.

The contemporary debate and context

It is only a matter of time before Congress takes up the dual citizenship issue. A number of structural changes are stoking Americans' anxieties about the course of the nation's political development and about the coherence of its national identity. These changes include the globalisation of the economy; easier travel; instantaneous and inexpensive communications; increased immigration, especially by the undocumented; diminished American autonomy in the world; the expansion of multinational corporations and the emergence of influential transnational nongovernmental organisations; growing multicultural pressures prompting concerns about immigrant assimilation and English language acquisition; the loss of a unifying ideology; dizzying technological changes; the expansion and consolidation of the welfare state and what many perceive to be a devaluation of American citizenship.

In analysing these developments, I have suggested that together they are already precipitating a re-evaluation of the meaning of citizenship and of the legal and political practices that give shape and texture to that meaning (Schuck: 1997). This re-evaluation of citizenship is broader, more robust, and more radical than perhaps any consideration of the subject since the 19th Amendment was adopted in 1920. It is even more remarkable because much of the law governing citizenship is both old and relatively stable. With several extremely important exceptions – the 1798–1801 period when the Alien and Sedition Acts were in effect, the elimination of racial and gender barriers to eligibility in 1870, 1920, and 1952, and the more durable ideological exclusion and English language requirement added in 1906 (Neuman: 1995), the legal requirements for naturalisation have changed little since the First Congress. The principle of birthright citizenship (*jus soli*) was established even earlier, indeed, its English roots have been traced back to 1290 (Schuck and Smith: 1985; Spiro: 1997). Despite (or perhaps because of) their antiquity, both naturalisation and birthright citizenship principles are now under active reconsideration. In the wake of the political and legal imbroglio arising out of the naturalisation of thousands of ineligible aliens shortly before the 1996 elections,[9] as well as prosecutions of private naturalisation testing organisations for large-scale fraud,[10] Congress is investigating the administration of the naturalisation program and reviewing the naturalisation standards themselves. Legislation to limit birthright citizenship for the native-born children of illegal aliens is also under active consideration (U.S. Congress: 1997).

Because dual citizenship is a product, among other things, of naturalisation and birthright citizenship rules, controversy over those rules necessarily implicates dual citizenship as well, but dual citizenship raises a host of other controversial questions that extend well beyond the issues raised by naturalisation and birthright citizenship. The context in which dual citizenship operates, moreover, is being transformed. It is not surprising, then, that prominent academics and policy-oriented foundations are now taking a lively interest in the subject and are publishing important critiques of existing practices (Neuman: 1995; Spiro: 1997; Aleinikoff: 1998). The Immigration and Naturalisation Service itself has commissioned an outside consultant to study the possibility of 're-engineering' the naturalisation process.

No reliable data exist on the number of Americans holding dual citizenship, but there can be little doubt that the total is growing rapidly. With current legal and illegal immigration approaching record levels, naturalisation petitions quintupling in the last five years to almost 2 million a year and legal changes in some of the largest source countries that encourage (and are often designed to encourage) naturalisation in the U.S., dual citizenship is bound to proliferate. This fact alone would justify Congress's reconsideration of U.S. dual citizenship policy.

This reassessment reflects more than simply the growth of dual citizenship. Modern transportation and communication technology makes residence and effective participation in two polities easier than ever, converting many merely 'technical' dual nationals into functional ones.[11] Many Americans believe that immigrants today are naturalising for 'selfish' reasons – for example, to obtain social benefits for which only citizens are eligible – and that the rules should be changed to require, or at least encourage, purer motives for naturalisation. A decade ago, many commentators expressed consternation over Rupert Murdoch's naturalisation, which appeared to have been prompted primarily by Murdoch's desire to qualify under Federal Communications Commission rules limiting ownership of multiple media properties to U.S. citizens.[12] More recently, controversy over the judicial decision to free convicted rapist Alex Kelly on bail led critics to allege that he and his parents had acquired Irish citizenship for the sole purpose of facilitating his flight from the U.S. should he decide to become a fugitive rather than face prison. The government does not maintain a registry documenting the incidence of dual citizenship (much less one indicating how and why it is acquired) so it is far from clear that the 'opportunistic' use of the practice has increased.[13] However, there is a more fundamental reason why we cannot answer this question. Even if it were possible to discern and disentangle the complex mix of feelings that surround a decision to naturalise, no social or political consensus exists on the normative question of which motives are and are not legitimate, indeed, this issue has scarcely been discussed.

Whatever the motives for naturalising may be, the road to dual citizenship seems easier to travel today than it was in the past. Both of the social behaviours that create new opportunities for dual citizenship – marriage between individuals with different nationalities and international migration by individuals – have become more common, and the legal rules that govern dual citizenship are also changing in ways that permit migrants to exploit these opportunities. The interaction between these behaviours and rules, then, has increased the dual citizen population.[14] Many of the principal countries of origin have amended their nationality laws to enable their nationals in the U.S. to acquire American citizenship more easily. Mexico, the Philippines, the Dominican Republic, Canada, and India, for example now confer their nationality on the children born to their nationals in the U.S.; these infants simultaneously acquire birthright citizenship in America (Aleinikoff: 1998). The Council of Europe is also moving in this direction; its draft convention would permit those who become dual nationals in member states by birth to retain both nationalities (Spiro: this volume). States like Germany, traditionally hostile to dual citizenship, are under increasing pressure to accept it in order to facilitate the assimilation of their large population of permanent residents (Hailbronner: this volume; Kastoryano: this volume).[15]

More important for present purposes, major source countries are also making it easier for their nationals to retain that nationality when they naturalise in the U.S. – and easier to reacquire it thereafter if it is subsequently lost, as through mandatory renunciation in the course of naturalising in the U.S. Some of these countries have repealed provisions that required those wishing to renaturalise in their country of origin to renounce their other nationalities, while others decline to give effect to their own nationals' renunciations if those renunciations are required by the second state as a condition for naturalising (as in the U.S.) (Goldstein and Piazza: 1996, 517). Moreover, many countries of origin that might be prepared to effectuate their nationals' renunciation of citizenship may nevertheless fail as a practical matter to learn of the renunciations and thus will continue to treat them as their nationals.

An important instance of this liberalising trend – at least in terms of the number of individuals who may be affected-is a new Mexican law that took effect in March 1998. It reverses longstanding constitutional limitations on

Mexican dual nationality and enables Mexicans who naturalise in the U.S. – estimated to exceed 100,000 in 1996 alone – to retain (or reacquire) their Mexican nationality, which confers many economic rights in Mexico but not the franchise (Mexico would continue to require, as the U.S. does, that those who naturalise there must renounce their other citizenships). A second change limits its *jus sanguinis* transmission of citizenship/nationality to the first generation: children born in the U.S. to Mexican citizens will be Mexican nationals but their children will not (unless, of course, they naturalised there).[16] Although estimates of the number of Mexicans eligible to do so range from 2.3 to 5 million,[17] the new balance of incentives created by this law, coupled with legal and policy developments in the U.S. that are prompting record levels of aliens to petition for naturalisation, strongly implies that the number of Mexicans seeking to naturalise will be much larger than would be predicted from the group's traditionally low rate of naturalisation in the U.S.[18] In India, another major source country, one of the main political parties supports similar liberalisation of its dual citizenship law (Sengupta: 1996).

These changes clearly demonstrate the most significant change of all: other states increasingly *want* their own nationals to acquire U.S. citizenship – a striking departure from the historical pattern. Approximately sixty percent of Swiss nationals now live abroad as dual citizens, a fact evidently desired by Switzerland (Koslowski: 1997). Sending states in Central America attach enormous importance to the remittances by their nationals of funds earned in the U.S., which are likely to increase if those migrants can acquire dual citizenship (Lewis: 1997). The 'transnational communities' created through their nationals' dual citizenship in the U.S. – communities often reinforced by multinational enterprises and international nongovernmental organisations – increase the flow to these states not only of remittances but of technology, skills, and tourism (Levitt: this volume; Portes: 1998). These states also welcome the growing prospect that their nationals, once naturalised and able to vote in the U.S., may succeed in influencing American politics in ways that will serve the interests of the states of origin.[19]

The growth of the U.S. dual citizen population, however, reflects changes in domestic law as well as developments in foreign law. The U.S. has acquiesced in these external changes by not attempting to counter them, but it has also magnified their effects simply by its growing toleration of dual citizenship. For example, the Immigration and Naturalisation Service has steadily increased the resources and visibility that it devotes to the promotion of naturalisation. Yet the U.S. has also refrained from taking any meaningful steps to ensure that its new citizens' renunciation oaths are legally effective in their countries of origin.

Since the 1960s the U.S. courts have limited the government's authority either to denationalise its citizens or to denaturalise those who have acquired citizenship through misrepresentation (Aleinikoff: 1986, 1471; See also *Kungys v. United States*, 485 U.S. 759, 1988). Congress might have responded to these limits by framing narrower standards capable of sur-viving judicial scrutiny but it has not done so. Indeed, it has enlarged dual citizenship over time by narrowing the severe gender bias in prior law that made it easier for females to lose their U.S. nationality by marrying for-eigners and made it harder for females to transmit *jus sanguinis* citizenship to their children born abroad.[20] By substantially raising the level of legal immigration, the U.S. has multiplied the number of aliens who will eventually naturalise and who will, despite the renunciation requirement, retain or reacquire their prior nationalities. The U.S. State Department, bowing to such realities, has gradually shifted its official policy from one of opposition to dual citizenship to one of grudging acceptance.[21]

These liberalisations in law and policy advance important humani-tarian goals. They reflect both the efforts by countries of origin to facilitate their nationals' naturalisation in the U.S. (and elsewhere) by not auto-matically denationalising them when they do so, and the efforts by the U.S. to reduce the tension between the unwanted growth of dual citizen-ship and a commendable desire to avoid the potentially harsh effects of denationalisation and denaturalisation on individuals who often possess strong ties to the United States.

Noteworthy as these liberalisations have been, they do not necessarily mark an inexorable trend. Because they also entail some risks to the polity's interests (discussed in section III), they can generate a political reaction and reversal. Canada has recently had some second thoughts about its liberalised law (Aleinikoff: 1998), and the U.S. is likely to recon-sider its own changes in light of new developments, especially the new Mexican nationality law, which heighten the doubts and anxieties about dual citizenship that many Americans harbour.

Some policy-relevant distinctions

Before turning to the putative advantages and disadvantages of dual citizenship, it is worth briefly considering five distinctions that may help to clarify the debate over the effects, merits, and possible reform of dual citizenship policy. These distinctions concern (1) who is affected by dual citizenship; (2) the role of consent in citizenship law; (3) how Congress may regulate political and non-political rights; (4) the different treatments of original and newly acquired citizenship and (5) the effectiveness of renunciation of prior citizenships.

Entities Affected

Different entities may be affected by dual citizenship policy and will there-fore seek to shape the rules governing it (an appraisal of these effects is deferred until section III). Dual citizenship most obviously affects the *individuals* who may acquire, or be denied, that status. Many procedural and substantive rights turn on whether one is a citizen of the polity in which one lives or does business. Moreover, polities define the specific content of those rights differently, although international law seeks to reduce those differences. For example, one's ability or willingness to migrate and to work or receive public benefits in the destination country will vary with the state (or states) in which one can claim and exercise those rights.

Dual citizenship affects the interests of *states* quite apart from its impact on individuals. Because dual citizenship rules affect the incentive and opportunity to migrate to and remain in the destination state, they help to shape the political identities of states and their inhabitants, as well as the contours of public programs and budgets. Historically, at least, dual citizenship policies have also had far-reaching impacts on the military, diplomatic, political, and commercial relationships among states, which has occasioned bilateral and multilateral conventions seeking to regulate dual citizenship.[22] For these reasons, dual citizenship also affects the interests of the states' existing citizens. They will have strong feelings, of course, about who belongs to their community and under what terms. Like stockholders facing a possible dilution of their shares, they do not wish to see their own membership devalued by extending membership to others 'too cheaply.' As taxpayers, they want to ensure that their fiscal burdens are not increased unduly. Finally, the international community possesses a discrete interest in dual citizenship rules insofar as it hopes to minimise the risk that individuals will be rendered stateless, a goal that it has long sought to achieve through international agreements. States' general, *ex ante* interest in a system that minimises statelessness, of course, is not inconsistent with the *ex post* reality that particular states, when confronted with a potentially stateless individual's claim for citizenship in their polity, may decide to oppose that individual's claim. Although this interest might seem superfluous – dual citizenship, after all, presupposes an existing nationality in some other state – it is not. In a world of mass migration, poor record keeping, uncertain citizenship rules, and state incentives to deny nationality to some individuals who may claim it or to withdraw it from some who already possess it, the international community may view dual nationality as a kind of safety net for those who might otherwise fall between the cracks of the state system.[23]

Consent

Broadly speaking, one may acquire or lose citizenship consensually or nonconsensually. Naturalisation, of course, is the paradigmatically consensual mode of acquisition, at least for adults. (Parents' naturalisation can confer nationality on children without the latter's consent.)

The more nonconsensual modes of acquisition include citizenship conferred at birth and descent through the operation of *jus soli* and *jus sanguinis*. Marriage is a hybrid mode of acquiring citizenship. One might view it as either consensual or nonconsensual, depending on whether one focuses on the individual's awareness of the nationality consequences when marrying or on the automaticity of citizenship upon marriage (where that is the rule). Citizenship may be lost consensually through expatriation where one has renounced citizenship or performed some other act that has that legal effect (under U.S. law, one must also *intend* that it have that effect). It may be lost nonconsensually through a state's denationalisation or denaturalisation of a citizen without that alien's knowledge or assent, where the state's rule permits this.

The perceived consensuality of one's acquisition or loss of dual citizenship may affect the way in which it is evaluated by others and hence the consequences that they may wish to attach to that acquisition or loss. This is not to say that consent is the only criterion of legitimacy, only that it is, in some form, the most widely accepted and important (Schuck and Smith: 1985; Neuman: 1996).

In one view of the matter, a citizenship that one actively seeks through naturalisation – especially if accompanied by an express renunciation of another allegiance – is likely to be viewed as more genuine, deliberate, and morally deserving of recognition than one that is acquired adventitiously and without some measure of personal commitment or at least continuing connection to the polity. The perceived fairness and legitimacy of a citizenship acquired passively and automatically through one's parents may vary depending on whether the nationality-conferring event is defined as birth in a state to which the parents are significantly linked (what might be termed 'qualified' *jus soli*), birth in a state where the parents simply happen to find themselves at nativity (absolute *jus soli*), or birth to these parents *wherever* they may be located (*jus sanguinis*). By the same token, a loss of citizenship caused by a voluntary, knowing act of expatriation will probably be perceived as fairer and more legitimate than an involuntary, state-imposed denationalisation. This is not to deny that one's political or national identity may be powerfully shaped by a citizenship that is acquired nonconsensually, it is merely to call attention to the normative appeal of consent as a standard legitimating many important social practices (Schuck and Smith: 1985; Schuck: 1994, 889).

If the consensuality of an acquisition or loss of citizenship is viewed as an important indicator of its legitimacy, then the methods that a state uses to regulate acquisition and loss are likely to be designed to test its knowing, voluntary character. Requiring the individual to take a naturalisation oath is one such technique; mandating that the individual elect one nationality, as through renunciation of other allegiances or designation of one nationality as 'primary,'[24] is another. Some states are more lenient in permitting their nationals to retain a second citizenship if it was acquired involuntarily (as through *jus soli*) rather than through naturalisation. This same purpose of measuring and ensuring consent explains the requirement that a parent (or, under now-repealed law, the individual in question) establish some period of residence in the U.S. in order to acquire *jus sanguinis* citizenship, a requirement that the Supreme Court has held to be constitutional *(Rogers v. Bellei)*.[25] It also explains the constitutional (and now statutory) requirement that expatriation occur only through an unambiguous act and formal procedures, giving some assurance that the relinquishment of citizenship will be both knowledgeable and voluntary *(Afroyim v. Rusk*, 387 U.S. 253:1967).

Regulating political and non-political rights

Political membership in the polity is the hallmark of citizenship, and political rights are usually limited to citizens.[26] The most important of these, of course, is the right to vote, but other political rights such as eligibility to hold high public office and to contribute money to political campaigns may also be restricted to citizens. Congress defines political and nonpolitical rights and decides how they are to be distributed among citizens, noncitizen nationals and aliens; in this way it establishes the functional significance of these statuses.

This power is subject to constitutional constraints. The two most important ones are the mandate that naturalisation rules be 'uniform' and the equal protection principle, which the Supreme Court has interpreted to preclude distinctions between naturalised and other citizens, at least in the expatriation context *(Schneider v, Rusk*, 377 U.S. 163:1964). On the other hand, these principles might not prevent Congress from providing that U.S. citizens who subsequently naturalise in other countries may not exercise political rights there, so long as Congress did not discriminate unfairly between groups of U.S. citizens. Indeed, Congress might possess the constitutional power to prohibit U.S. citizens from naturalising elsewhere at all, even though *Afroyim* might preclude it from enforcing this prohibition through the harsh and thus constitutionally limited sanction of expatriation *(Afroyim v. Rusk*, 387 U.S. 253:1967).

Original versus new nationality

The coexistence of these congressional powers and constitutional constraints renders even more doubtful the continuing differences as to dual nationality between those who already possess U.S. citizenship and those who wish to acquire it through naturalisation. After all, the latter are required as a condition of naturalisation to renounce their earlier allegiances and thus be limited to a single citizenship, whereas the former are free to acquire new ones as they wish. How can this be justified in light of the *Schneider* principle of legal equality between all citizens? The truth is that little or no attention has been devoted to the question.

In the debate about dual citizenship, the assumption seems to be that one's original nationality is more binding and deeply felt and thus less problematic than one's subsequently acquired nationality. Americans seem to worry much more about the divided loyalties of those who are nationals of other states and wish to naturalise in the U.S. than they do about the loyalty of American citizens who choose to naturalise in other countries while retaining their American citizenship (as other states increasingly permit them to do). This interesting bias seems to drive the renunciation requirement, which is at the heart of American dual citizenship law. Why else would the law require naturalising citizens to renounce other national allegiances while permitting U.S. citizens to acquire other nationalities without constraint?

Yet the basis for this bias is far from clear. Recall that one can only naturalise in the U.S. by actively and solemnly renouncing one's original nationality – an act that provides some affirmative evidence of loyalty and commitment to the U.S. In contrast, American citizens who naturalise elsewhere may have never been obliged to acknowledge or even confront seriously their sentiments about the U.S. Americans simply infer allegiance from their continued residence and minimal law abidingness – surely weaker indicia of loyalty and commitment. As Sanford Levinson puts it, 'American law tolerates political bigamy so long as the second political marriage follows, rather than precedes, the acquiring of United States citizenship (Levinson: 1986, 1465).'

The explanations for this practice may be more chauvinistic than rational.[27] Perhaps Americans imagine that fellow citizens who naturalise elsewhere (or who take up residence in their country of origin) without renouncing their U.S. citizenship must be taking this step not out of dissatisfaction with American society but in order to serve some instrumental purpose (say, retirement or business) or to affirm a religious or ethnic tie (as with Ireland or Israel) and that doing so is not inconsistent with retaining their political loyalty to the U.S. Only if they use their new citizenship to shirk obligations to American society, such as avoiding taxes or military service, do their fellow Americans begin to question their suitability for continued citizenship.[28]

A more psychological explanation would be that the first allegiance (like first love?), because it grows out of an earlier acculturation in another society, is the dominant, deeper, and more durable one unless it is renounced (and perhaps even then). A newer allegiance thus seems more opportunistic and shallow: less legitimate. The opposite assumption, of course, also seems plausible. That is, an allegiance explicitly acknowledged during maturity and after some study of American institutions is likely to be more genuine than one for which no acknowledgement has been required and that may have never been put to a serious test.

Even if this is true on average (how would we know?), there will be many causes in which it is false. After all, many of those who naturalise do so after having resided in the U.S. for quite a long period of time during which they may have become fully assimilated, whereas birthright or (*jus sanguinis*) citizens may have spent little or no time in the U.S. (The requirements of physical presence and residence in the United States, which sometimes condition the transmission of *jus sanguinis* citizenship, now apply to the parents, not to the child who thereby gains citizenship.)

The Supreme Court has also played its part in creating and legitimating this asymmetry by refusing in *Afroyim* to recognize the effectiveness of congressionally defined expatriating acts unless they are voluntarily performed with the specific intention of relinquishing U.S. citizenship, a ruling that Congress accepted and codified in 1986. Although the Court primarily invoked textual and rights-based justifications for the position, it may well have been influenced by the assumptions that a first citizenship is less vulnerable to dilution than a subsequently acquired one and that Congress can always ensure the integrity of the latter by prescribing standards for naturalisation if it wishes.

Formal versus effective renunciation

U.S. law requires those who wish to naturalise to renounce their other political allegiances as a formal matter. Unlike Germany, however, the United States does not require that these prospective citizens make such renunciation legally effective by successfully expatriating themselves under the other state's law, much less that they provide proof of such expatriation to the naturalisation court. As Gerald Neuman has shown, even the German practice provides for exceptions (such as when expatriation is not possible or is unreasonable), and in any event this requirement is far from foolproof (Neuman: 1998). Evasion (by the naturalising citizen, the country of origin, or both) and nonenforcement are likely to be common in any such system. The arguments for and against requiring a truly effective renunciation are, of course, the arguments for and against dual citizenship, a subject to which I now turn.

An assessment of dual citizenship

Dual citizenship, like other complex social/legal phenomena, is difficult to evaluate. It is not simply that the normative criteria to be applied to it are deeply contested – although they are. It is also that the empirical consequences of the current regime of dual citizenship, and of the various reforms that might be adopted, are highly uncertain. We know what the rules of dual citizenship are (they are admirably clear, except for the standards for denaturalisation),[29] but we lack any reliable information concerning how those rules actually affect the sensibilities and behaviour of would-be and existing citizens and how those effects might change if the rules were altered in one way or another.

To render the evaluative enterprise manageable, one is tempted to elaborate models designed to capture the disparate values that might be brought to bear on it. In an earlier effort to appraise naturalisation policy, for example, Gerald Neuman did just that, sketching four 'simple normative models' or perspectives that he called unilateral liberal, bilateral liberal, republican, and communitarian. Although Neuman's article contained some very useful insights, his models did little analytical work for him. What was interesting in his analysis did not derive from the models, in part because they were characterised at so high a level of generality that many naturalisation practices could be justified under several or all of the models.

I doubt that an effort to develop more rigorously specified normative models of dual citizenship would be worth the trouble. Instead, I shall employ the less systematic, but perhaps more effective, approach of canvassing the advantages and the disadvantages for the American polity of dual citizenship (in various possible forms), drawing on a variety of normative perspectives including those that are suggested by Neuman's models. In each case, I shall try to highlight the most important but unanswered empirical questions on which the integrity of such evaluations may ultimately depend. The answers to such empirical questions will obviously determine – from a given normative perspective – the magnitude of benefits and costs that the evaluator will assign to some aspect of dual citizenship. Obviously, the variety of possible normative perspectives merely compounds these uncertainties by raising a further, more fundamental question of whether one should characterise dual citizenship as a benefit or as a cost in the first place.

In light of the indeterminacy of any overall assessment under these (quite common) conditions, it should not be surprising that I do not reach any crisp, rigorously derived evaluative conclusions. Nevertheless, at the end of the day I am inclined to think that the growth of dual citizenship is on balance a good thing. Moreover, I am able in the final section to recommend a nontrivial (or so it seems to me) policy change that seems broadly consistent with all of the leading normative perspectives.

Benefits of dual citizenship

As noted earlier, dual citizenship's benefits flow to a number of different entities. For individuals who hold dual citizenship, the status is advantageous because it provides them with additional options – an alternative country in which to live, work and invest, an additional locus and source of rights, obligations and communal ties. Despite the growing and enthusiastic literature on transnational communities, it is a fair question whether the quality of dual citizens' relationships to their polities and civil societies is diluted by the possible diffusion of attention, affection, and commitment that dual citizenship may entail. On one hand, people who commute between two communities, for example, often report that they feel a bit alienated from both and fully attached to neither. On the other hand, many people who are members of two nuclear families (perhaps through divorce and remarriage) seem to feel intense ties to both. Even if the quality (somehow defined) of each relationship were diminished, it might well be that the total satisfaction derived from the two families taken together is greater than before.

It is hard to know how to answer such questions, just as it is hard to know which of these (or other) analogies to dual citizenship is most appropriate in thinking about it. What is clear, however, is that the individual's choice is always a necessary, albeit not sufficient, condition of dual citizenship. Because it is usually acquired voluntarily and can be renounced when it is not (or no longer) desired, no individual is compelled to be a dual citizen against his will for very long (although the law may prevent some who wish to be dual citizens from becoming or remaining one). The individual who thinks that being a dual citizen is a benefit will become (or remain) one if he can (i.e., if the law permits it); otherwise not. From a liberal perspective – and perhaps under some versions of republicanism and communitarianism as well – this is justification enough for dual citizenship.

U.S. based business firms also benefit from dual citizenship. Employees, by acquiring dual citizenship, become more valuable to a firm because they can travel and work abroad more easily, are more likely to be bilingual, and can more readily build transnational market networks that will advantage the firm. By the same token, other states and their citizens benefit from the liberal availability of dual citizenship in the U.S. I have already noted that the steady flow of remittances from the U.S. is essential to the social and economic viability of many other societies, but the dynamic is a more general one. Just as genuinely free trade among nations tends to benefit all participants, so too does the international flow of human, financial, and technological capital that dual citizenship facilitates. For the same reason – and because (as noted earlier) dual citizenship reduces the risk of statelessness, which all countries have a strong interest in minimising – the international community of states benefits.

Finally, dual citizenship confers significant benefits on American society as a whole. In addition to the economic advantages (including tax) generated by a population with many dual nationals, there are exceedingly important social and political advantages. Citizenship probably facilitates (as well as reflects) the assimilation of newcomers by imparting a sense of welcome and belonging, reinforcing their attachment to American values and improving their English language skills.[30] Citizenship also helps to legitimate the exercise over them (and others) of governmental power; it reduces the risk that they will be subject to discriminatory treatment. To the extent that a liberal dual nationality policy encourages long-term immigrants to naturalise – a causal relationship assumed by most commentators[31] – it advances the essential democratic value of full political and social participation by all individuals who are subject to the polity's coercive authority.

Even a liberal state which, more than republican and communitarian polities, values individuals' rights to decide for themselves whether and how to participate, may nevertheless have a strong interest in actively encouraging resident aliens to naturalise. The reason, I have noted elsewhere, is that 'at some point . . . the ratio of aliens to citizens might become so high that aliens lack of direct or indirect political participation and representation would present a serious problem for democratic governance, (Schuck: 1995: 329). Sanford Levinson put the point this way: 'One must ask if a country consisting primarily of resident aliens can sustain itself as a community with ideals worth professing'(Levinson: 1986). Such a scenario, I suggest, is by no means far-fetched: if current trends continue, almost one-third of Germany's population by 2030 will consist of foreign nationals, and in large cities the figure could reach forty-five percent (Schuck and Münz: 1998).

Peter Spiro sees an additional attraction of dual citizenship. Citing as an example the 1996 elections in the Dominican Republic in which many U.S. dual citizens voted, he suggests that they may both absorb American constitutional values through participation and encourage the diffusion of these in their country of origin, thus expanding global democracy (Spiro: this volume).

Costs of dual citizenship

Were these benefits the only consequences of dual citizenship, it would hardly be the contentious public issue that it is and will increasingly become. A liberal dual citizenship policy entails costs, however, and they must be taken into consideration in evaluating its merits.

Some of these costs are rather mundane and unlikely to have much weight in any overall evaluation of the merits of dual citizenship policy. For example, dual citizenship can magnify legal uncertainties and hence the transaction costs associated with resolving them. Under conventional conflict of laws principles, an individual's citizenship can be a factor in determining the jurisdiction whose law applies to that person's conduct, transactions or status. This determination becomes correspondingly more difficult where the person possesses two nationalities.

A more significant cost of dual citizenship, which arises from the 1996 welfare reform statute, is fiscal in nature. Under this statute, which departs radically from prior law, most aliens – including those who have lived in the U.S. for many years – are no longer eligible for some valuable public benefits and services to which citizens may be entitled. Providing these benefits and services to resident aliens imposed a substantial fiscal burden on the federal government, which was a major reason why aliens were targeted as part of the deficit reduction effort in the first place[32] (the assumption of these fiscal burdens by the state and local governments, which have moved with surprising speed to narrow the gap created by the federal statute (Fix and Zimmerman: 1998), has merely shifted the costs rather than eliminating them). To the extent that a liberal dual citizenship policy confers public benefit entitlements on individuals who, if they remained aliens, would not otherwise receive them, those budgetary costs would again be borne by government.[33] To the extent that those marginal costs are occasioned by individuals who did not contribute commensurate taxes to the U.S., this fiscal effect will be even more objectionable to many existing citizens.[34]

Less quantifiable is the effect of dual citizenship on the state's obligation to provide diplomatic protection to its citizens. Peter Spiro recently analysed this consideration, noting that the traditionally unfettered right of a state to treat its own citizens pretty much as it likes sometimes clashes with the second state's right and obligation to protect its citizens (single or dual) when they are abroad, including when they are in their other country of nationality where the second state's protection responsibility was traditionally not applicable.[35] He maintains, however, that the establishment of a regime of general international human rights, in which one state may protest another states' mistreatment of individuals regardless of whether or not they are nationals of the protesting state, effectively reduces the protesting state's diplomatic protection burden. Spiro acknowledges that dual citizenship may intensify such interstate conflicts but asserts that this 'will be more a matter of politics than of law, and in any event the factor is unlikely to push anyone over the brink'. He also argues that one state is unlikely to hold another state responsible for the actions of its (their) citizen because 'states so clearly have lost the capacity to control the international activities of their citizens' (Spiro: 1997; Spiro: this volume).

Spiro's assertions concerning tendencies and probabilities may well be correct as a general matter. It seems plausible that when compared with other factors that influence state actions in the international sphere, the motivational significance of dual citizenship may have declined. At the margin, however, it also seems plausible that a state will intervene more readily and energetically on behalf of its own nationals than on behalf of strangers to whom it owes no special duty of protection, and that where the state's arguments for intervening are closely balanced, the existence of such a duty might furnish a real or pretextual reason that might affect, or even tip, the balance.[36] Ultimately, the magnitude of the protection burden posed by dual citizenship is one of those empirical questions to which we simply have no reliable answers, especially because it is likely to depend on many factors, and thus vary from situation to situation. In the debate over liberalising dual citizenship, the most divisive and worrisome concerns are of a fundamentally political nature. The fact that these concerns are perhaps the most speculative and least quantifiable of the consequences of dual citizenship does not mean that they are insubstantial and thus easily dismissed. Indeed, it is precisely the elusiveness of these political concerns that makes them such powerful rhetorical weapons in the hands of partisans.

Consider first the electoral implications of dual citizenship. Assume that a dual citizen is eligible to vote in the elections of both countries.[37] Should this be troubling to Americans? To the extent that the interests of the U.S. and those of the other country do not conflict, it is hard to see any good reason for objecting to a situation in which the individual asserts one set of interests in the American election and another, not inconsistent set of interests, in the other election. Here, Spiro's speculation seems plausible.

Sometimes, however, those interests will conflict in the sense that the other state's election may shape that state's policies – on trade or foreign policy, for example – in ways that either benefit or adversely affect the U.S. It is true – indeed, *increasingly* true given the growing diversity of the U.S. population in terms of national origin – that American citizens/voters often have policy preferences that accord some weight to the interests of other countries. This has always been the case – and always a source of concern to other members of the polity who think themselves exempt from such conflicts. Such preferences in fact exist whether or not the citizen voters are also citizens of those other countries, and whether or not the interests of those other countries might, under some views of America's national interests, be of an adverse nature.

Somewhat more controversially, I believe that we should conceive of the national interest of the U.S. as including those preferences. After all, if the national interest is in some fundamental democratic sense an (indeterminate) aggregation of the interests perceived by citizens/voters,[38] then this aggregation cannot exclude preferences that accord some weight to the interests of other countries. As Spiro puts it: 'A dual Mexican-American who advocates policies that benefit Mexico is little different from a Catholic who advocates policies endorsed by the church or a member of Amnesty International who writes to his congressman at the organisation's behest (Spiro: this volume).' There are no questions here of disloyalty, only of interests and identities and of different modes of social contribution. This seems correct, at least within very broad limits – that is, so long as Mexico, like the church and Amnesty International, is not an enemy of the U.S. capable of doing her great harm.[39]

Spiro also posits the harder case in which the Mexican government endorses candidates in American elections and seeks to influence the votes of its dual nationals in the U.S. Spiro dismisses this concern, arguing that states of origin have little leverage over their nationals in the U.S. and even less inclination to use it, and that retention of Mexican nationality would add little to the dual national's existing propensity, shared with other dual-nationality Americans, to give weight to ethnic affiliations. Again, this seems persuasive, at least given the current U.S.-Mexico alliance, the long-standing attitudinal differences among groups of people in the U.S. with Mexican ancestry (Skerry: 1993), and the propensity of voters, including dual-nationality Americans, to focus on local issues.

Voting, of course, is not the only way in which dual citizens participate in U.S. elections. Like single citizens and legal resident aliens, they may contribute to political campaigns and make independent expenditures seeking to influence the public debate. Although recent congressional hearings concerning apparently illegal campaign contributions by foreign companies and individuals fronting for them may eventually lead to additional restrictions on these practices (proposals to limit or ban legal aliens' campaign contributions are pending in Congress), extending such restrictions to dual citizens would be unwise and almost certainly unconstitutional. Their full participation benefits American politics for the same reasons that the participation of other citizens (and legal aliens) does.[40]

The reverse situation, in which U.S. citizens participate in elections in countries where they hold dual citizenship – conduct that once triggered denationalisation under U.S. law but due to the Supreme Court's ruling in *Afroyim* no longer does – also seems unproblematic from the American point of view, at least so long as this participation does not embroil the U.S. in unwanted disputes with the other country or involve situations in which the voter subordinates the interests of the U.S. to those of the other country, distinguished from merely taking the latter into account in determining the former. Indeed, Spiro's point, noted earlier, bears repetition here: this participation could help to disseminate abroad the liberal democratic values that the American polity seeks to inculcate in its citizens.

This analysis suggests that the electoral conflicts engendered by dual citizenship are, in principle, quite consistent with the aggregation of preferences that we call the national interest. It is true, of course, that the government will ordinarily find it impossible as a practical matter to discern, much less prove in a denaturalisation or expatriation proceeding, that the voter has in fact preferred another country's interests to those of the U.S. (properly defined). Accordingly, we must assess the risk of disloyalty in this sense on the basis of probabilities and magnitudes-the probability that a U.S. voter will subordinate American interests, and the number of Americans who are likely to go to the trouble of voting in foreign elections both seem exceedingly low. All of this, of course, still begs the most basic question raised by dual citizenship: who should be permitted to become U.S.

citizens and thus to vote and have their preferences counted in that aggregation process? In order to address this question, we must look beyond possible electoral conflicts to more transcendent concerns having to do with political unity, identity, community and loyalty.

If citizenship is anything, it is membership in a political community with a more or less distinct political identity – a set of public values about governance and law that are widely shared by those within it. As already noted, the United States does not require birthright and *jus sanguinis* citizens to affirm a commitment to those values and that identity, yet it permits U.S. citizens to acquire other citizenships without limit and without affirming their solidarity with and loyalty to American society. How, then, might dual citizenship threaten this American political identity (Schuck and Smith: 1985; Levinson: 1996)?

One answer is that although all citizens who are also members of other polities may threaten this identity, the government is in a position to minimise that danger by exerting a leverage (the oath requirement) over the individual who wishes to naturalise that it lacks over its existing citizens. This answer, however, ignores several possibilities. Congress could require existing U.S. citizens to take a loyalty oath too,[41] as they now do when they apply for passports and certain jobs. It might also limit their freedom to naturalise abroad or, if they are allowed to naturalise, might limit their freedom to take certain actions, such as voting in elections in other countries. As discussed earlier, such legislation should not raise constitutional difficulties so long as Congress neither discriminates among citizens in this regard nor seeks to enforce its restrictions by expatriating them.

One can also argue that dual citizenship threatens America's political unity and identity regardless of whether one thinks that it is inconsistent to require only naturalising citizens to swear an oath. In this view, dual citizenship dilutes America's political identity by adding members who are committed to other polities with other values. Put another way, in terms elaborated by Albert Hirschman, dual citizenship weakens loyalty by making exit easier (Hirschman: 1970). To be sure, a citizen in a federal system may owe simultaneous allegiance to two polities, but if both share essentially the same values, as in the American case, the danger of disunity would be less than in cases where the citizen is a member of two polities with quite different political cultures.

At least two responses to this claim are possible. One is to deny that this identity is unique; the polities from which most immigrants come today are committed to the same principles of governance to which the U.S. subscribes. This claim, however, is not convincing, at least in practice. Of the ten leading source countries in 1996, only Mexico, the Philippines, India, the Dominican Republic and Jamaica might be argued to be even qualified.[42] Another response, conceding that American values are indeed unique, might nevertheless despair of our ability to reduce them to a verbal formulation that can serve as a more discriminating naturalisation criterion than the existing standards, tests and oaths. In this view, there is little choice but to continue administering them in essentially their current form. This assumes, however, that Americans know what they are asking the individual to affirm and renounce. I challenge this assumption below.

Two variations on these disunity and dilution themes should be noted. The first was made by a Canadian parliamentary committee, which expressed a fear that dual citizens might 'import and perpetuate their strident ethnic or nationalistic self-interests here in their new country'; they might 'bring foreign quarrels to Canada'.[43] Insofar as this is not simply another way of voicing the electoral concerns discussed earlier, it seems to envision a more general threat to political civility and accommodation posed by certain types of conflicts that dual citizens are thought more likely to inflame.

The second variation is that many dual citizens naturalise for the 'wrong' (i.e., selfish or opportunistic) reasons.[44] This characterisation is already being made of the flood of naturalisation petitions following the 1996 welfare reform law that will likely be used to disparage naturalisations by Mexicans once the new Mexican law becomes effective. There is evidence that many aliens are indeed naturalising to preserve or obtain welfare benefits,[45] and this perception has had powerful political ramifications. In addition, Alex Aleinikoff cites a study of a 1994 change in the Dominican Republic's citizenship law similar to that being adopted in Mexico, which shows that the desire to facilitate the naturalisation of Dominicans in the U.S., without reducing their ties to the home country, was an important argument for the change (Aleinikoff: 1997).

Nevertheless, it is not clear what we should make of this 'wrong reasons' argument. It implies that we know and can define what the 'right' reasons for naturalising are, that right and wrong reasons either do not coexist or can be disentangled, that we can render transparent through evidence the motivational mix that particular individuals possess, and that existing citizens do not value their *own* citizenship, at least in part, for instrumental reasons. None of these propositions, however, has been demonstrated or appears likely. It is true – as public opinion surveys and the political support for the 1996 welfare reform law suggest – that most Americans are repelled by the notion that some aliens are naturalising in order to gain access to the welfare system. However, as Aleinikoff points out, other instrumental reasons, such as a desire to integrate and actively participate in American society and politics, are not only viewed as praiseworthy but reflect values that 'we look for in native-born citizens' (Aleinikoff: 1997). Lines that are both morally satisfying and administrable are exceedingly difficult to draw here.

This leads to a final complaint about the relation between dual citizenship and political community and identity concerns about the ability of immigrants to assimilate socially.[46] Dual citizenship, the argument goes, retards assimilation by encouraging newcomers to cling to old ties and refrain from unequivocally casting their lot with the U.S.[47] Dan Stein, a leading opponent of dual citizenship, states that immigrants 'ought to get on board or get out' (Sengupta: 1996). Naturalisation and assimilation are surely correlated, if only because one must have already achieved some level of English proficiency and knowledge about American society in order to qualify in the first place. Naturalisation does not merely reflect assimilation however; it probably also accelerates it, as discussed earlier. For this reason, one can argue that the government has an interest in promoting naturalisation more energetically than it does, rather than essentially relying on the initiative of individual aliens (Schuck: 1995).

For present purposes, however, the relevant question is not how naturalisation affects assimilation but how *dual* citizenship, as distinguished from single citizenship, affects it at the margin. It may be, as Spiro asserts, that dual citizenship will not retard the integration process, but he cites no evidence to support his assertion (Spiro: 1997; Spiro: this volume). There are reasons, however, to question his claim. If it is true that dual citizenship helps to build and reinforce 'transnational communities', that any individual possesses only limited affective and attentional resources, and, that allocating those resources between two communities necessarily reduces the level of commitment to either one, then it seems to follow that this lower level of commitment to the American community will slow the rate of assimilation into it. To return to the family metaphor, it is doubtful (although possible) that parents with two sets of children from different marriages manage to devote the same amount of time to each child as they would if they had only one set of children to raise.

Even if this is true, countervailing considerations may nonetheless support a more liberal dual citizenship policy. Spiro immediately adds, for example, that 'denying the possibility of naturalisation (or of raising its price too high, by requiring renunciation) *will* retard that process and weaken the bonds of community, at least as delimited in territorial terms' (original emphasis) (Spiro: 1997; also Spiro: this volume). Again, he cites no support for this important and plausible empirical claim about how the price of naturalisation (including renunciation) affects the speed and quality of assimilation. The opposite claim – that immigrants whom the law requires to make a firm, undiluted commitment to American society may assimilate sooner and better than those who can naturalise without having to affirm that commitment – is also plausible. In the end, we are left with no evidence, but an important research issue. In my view, the question of the marginal effects of dual citizenship on assimilation is indeed pivotal, but regretfully it is also unanswerable at present except on the basis of supposition.

Beyond the concern about assimilation, the debate on dual citizenship revolves around the issue of the loyalty of dual nationals to the U.S. The anxiety, of course, is that their allegiance to America is wanting – at best divided and at worst subordinate to their earlier allegiance. This is partly a concern about national security. In this view, people whose loyalties are either divided or lie elsewhere may be tempted to subvert the nation's safety and well-being in service to another state, even to the point of treason.

Traitors[48] do indeed dot American history, but it is doubtful that dual citizens – or even aliens, who have not sworn allegiance to the U.S. are disproportionately represented among them. Spiro believes that the national security risk posed by dual citizenship is minimal, as the spread of democracy has reduced the likelihood of war (Spiro: this volume). Moreover, the undemocratic regimes with which the U.S. might now go to war are 'less likely to instil the real loyalties of dual nationals even where they command their formal ones (Spiro: this volume).

As with diplomatic protection, one can acknowledge the general tendencies that Spiro identifies while still doubting that they will apply in every case and reduce the risks to zero. Our world is one in which hostilities may take the aspect not only of formal military campaigns[49] but also of clandestine acts of terrorism or theft of valuable technologies undertaken on behalf of undemocratic regimes that can nevertheless claim the fervent political aud religious loyalty of their people.[50] Although legal or illegal aliens can also engage in such conduct, citizens probably have somewhat greater opportunities at the margin to do so. In such a world, Spiro's assurances may be too optimistic. The fact that few dual nationals pose any greater danger of disloyalty than those with only one nationality does not preclude the risk that the dual citizenship of those few may place them in a better position to wreak immense damage. This risk is a cost (to be discounted, of course, by its presumably low probability) that must be assessed against a policy of more liberal dual citizenship. Again, any effort to quantify it raises empirical questions for which there are no obvious answers.

To view public concerns about the loyalty of dual citizens as being limited to the fear of treason is to risk trivializing those concerns. Even if divided loyalty does not culminate in active betrayal, it may create practical and moral conflicts as when both countries demand military service of their citizens. Beyond such concerns, such divided loyalties surely offend common-sense conceptions of the desired citizen-state relationship. I have already alluded to the variety of competing metaphors that may plausibly frame those popular views. As I also noted, these metaphors should not impoverish a reflective deliberation about dual citizenship; metaphors, after all should serve us rather than rule us. At the same time, however, such a deliberation should take seriously the public values that are embedded in the metaphors which American society invokes.

My guess – and it is of course only a guess – is that most thoughtful Americans, if asked to characterise the relationship between citizen and state that naturalisation and the oath ought to affirm and reify, would view marriage and the marriage vow as the most closely analogous. Americans simply do not think of their polity as a mere club – a transitory affiliation affording easy entry and exit for purely instrumental reasons with few strings attached (Hirschman: 1970) – and they do not think of naturalising citizens as entering an ideologically or spiritually defined *nomos* or a blood relationship.

If we think that naturalising citizens are entering into a kind of marital relationship with the polity, it might seem natural and morally compelling to insist that they make a firm choice of one polity or another. The law, after all, sometimes obliges us to make a firm choice between competing claims on our allegiance and identity. We must choose one U.S. state of residence,[51] one political party,[52] one name,[53] and one marriage at a time. Why not require us to choose one national citizenship? In marriage, we expect a certain exclusivity or (where not exclusive) at least a clear priority of commitment. One who marries, of course, does not thereby renounce all nonmarital affections, obligations, and trusts; the vow surely contemplates the maintenance of other deep attachments and other duties of emotional or financial support. However, virtually all marrying couples, not to mention the larger society, certainly expect that some of the most essential marital commitments, such as procreation and sexual intercourse, will indeed be exclusive, whereas others, such as friendship and Wednesday evening outings, may be more widely diffused. Yet even here, we expect the spouse to enjoy unequivocal pride of place in the event of conflict. Is the analogy of citizenship to marriage accurate? It is of course far from perfect. In particular, the intense intimacy that marriage entails is not always replicated in the relation of citizen to policy and vice-versa, as many unsuccessful marriages attest. Moreover, American political culture apparently does not regard dual citizenship as bigamous, for it now permits U.S. citizens to acquire other nationalities without constraint, which suggests that such conduct is not regarded as analogous to bigamy. It is also true that the 'transformed consciousness' of which Levinson speaks in connection with marriage (drawing on Hegel and David Hartman) is not quite the same as the 'new political birth' to which naturalisation is sometimes likened. Likewise, it is hard to imagine the civic counterpart of procreation, unless it be a citizen's inculcation of American values in their children.

Despite these differences, however, I nevertheless believe that marriage probably comes closer than any other common relationship to capturing the quality of enduring loyalty and priority of affection and concern that most Americans expect from those who apply to become their fellow citizens. If this is true, certain implications follow. First, the exclusive loyalty demanded of a citizen, like that demanded of a spouse, would be a circumscribed loyalty, one limited to the domain of political loyalty appropriate to the relationship between citizen and state in a liberal democratic polity. Even within that domain, loyalty is perfectly consistent with the most severe public criticism of the polity and its officials, and outside that domain loyalty is simply not a question, as the citizen's only essential duty is to observe the law (which may of course impose other duties on citizens), not to love the country.

Second, just as marital duties apply to all married persons equally and categorically, the political loyalty required of naturalised citizens should be the same no more, no less as that required of all other citizens, regardless of how they acquired their citizenship. This principle, affirmed in *Schneider v. Rusk*, lies at the heart of any polity committed to equal protection of the laws. Such a polity especially one whose civil society and public philosophy countenance large inequalities in private goods cannot flourish unless its members regard and treat each other as political and legal equals. In this sense, second-class citizenship is a pernicious oxymoron. Deviations from the equality-among-citizens principle should be tolerated only for the most compelling reasons.

As already noted, naturalisation imposes some requirements on would-be citizens that birthright and *jus sanguinis* citizens need not satisfy. Neuman calls these 'asymmetries.' Some are procedural and to that extent are inescapable in the case of naturalisation, but others such as good moral character and the renunciation of prior allegiances are deeply substantive. If the principle of equality among citizens means anything, it must mean that these substantive asymmetries demand justification. Neuman shows that some of the requirements themselves can be criticised from certain normative perspectives, but he does not view the asymmetries as problematic because the former do not yet possess their U.S. citizenship, and 'a power to revoke is more dangerous than a power to withhold in the first place'.[54]

Rather than justifying the asymmetries, however, Neuman's assertion begs the most significant questions about them.[55] First, the power to revoke is not always more dangerous than the power to withhold; for example, one who already has something may be in a better position to defend it (e.g., through political mobilisation) than one who still lacks it. Second, the persuasiveness of the revoke/withhold distinction depends on the nature of the asymmetry at issue. For example, the (good moral character) asymmetry probably strikes most people as less objectionable than, say, the ideological asymmetry, which excludes otherwise desirable citizens simply because they subscribe to unpopular views that existing citizens are perfectly entitled to advocate.[56]

Third, different asymmetries may have different rationales and no single justification is likely to work for all of them. The asymmetric requirements concerning knowledge of the English language and American government for example, might be defended on the basis of a strong presumption – not, true in every case, of course – that by adulthood birthright citizens have lived and been schooled in the U.S. long enough to acquire this knowledge, and that *jus sanguinis* citizens acquire it through their families. The (good moral character) asymmetry might be justified by the assumption that living in American society nurtures such character (this would be quite a stretch) or by the intuition that anyone applying for membership in a community should be expected to satisfy so minimal a requirement.[57]

Finally, none of these rationales can serve to justify either the ideological or renunciation asymmetries. Many existing citizens hold ideological views that might preclude their naturalisation, and many others have acquired plural nationalities along with the risk of divided loyalties, which the naturalising citizen must renounce. A defence of these asymmetries, then, must be based on something like the leverage argument that I noted earlier, which of course is less a justification than a raw assertion of power.

This analysis narrows, but does not resolve, the question of which forms of disloyalty other than treason should be counted as costs of dual citizenship. If (as I believe and Spiro does not) even a polity committed to a liberal dual citizenship policy can properly demand that new citizens affirm their exclusive political loyalty to the U.S., we must still decide what we mean by 'exclusive political loyalty to the U.S.' and which kinds of continuing commitments to other polities are deemed consistent with that loyalty. The answers, I believe, should be consistent with the content of the oath itself.

Possible reforms

Particular anxieties about dual citizenship imply particular questions that must be addressed and particular remedies that might then be proposed. Some concerns go to the standards and processes by which one may acquire and lose citizenship, others go to the rights and duties that attach to the status. Some concerns go to the criteria for naturalisation whereas others go to the criteria for dual citizenship. Overlap obviously abounds. As we have seen, the debate over dual citizenship today is largely a debate about what the appropriate standards for naturalisation should be. Reforms directed at particular concerns, then, risk being overly broad and should be carefully targeted at the specific problem that is perceived.

One set of possible solutions is based on the feeling that dual citizenship is now acquired too easily and/or for the wrong reasons. I have already expressed doubts about this opinion, but if that is the diagnosis, then certain remedial options would follow. For example, Congress could fashion eligibility standards for dual citizenship that are more stringent than they are now or than they are for single citizenship naturalisations. Instead (or in addition), it could reduce the benefits flowing from dual citizenship. In either case, it could distinguish these standards and rights from those that apply to people who naturalise for single citizenship. Again, however, any effort to create distinct classes of citizens – particularly with respect to their legal rights[58] – would raise constitutional difficulties.

I shall not discuss these possibilities further here, as I believe that the reformers have not met the burden of proof, which I think properly rests on them, that a significant problem in fact exists with regard to either the standards or the motivations for acquiring dual citizenship. I shall instead focus my attention on the naturalisation oath itself and on how it might be modified to address the threats to political identity and loyalty that I discussed above. I do so for several reasons. First, many Americans already take these threats seriously.[59] Second, these anxieties are likely to intensify in the future as the national origins of the immigration stream continues to diversify. Third, there is much merit, quite apart from whether these anxieties are justified, in attempting to be clearer about what it is that America imagines it is asking new citizens to affirm in their oaths. The delightfully archaic formulation of the oath, as well as its ambiguities, together make for considerable uncertainty as to its meaning and practical effects (Aleinikoff: 1997). If consent (as I believe) is the master concept underlying America's political arrangements, that consent should be knowing, discriminating, and authentic (Schuck and Smith: 1985). I argue below that the current oath, particularly the renunciation provision, fails these tests.

Before turning to my proposal,[64] let me make certain premises explicit. First, it should go without saying that I take the naturalisation oath requirement, and hence the content of the oath itself, seriously, as do most oathtakers.[60] Drawing on analogies to nuptial and religious vows, Levinson has reviewed the arguments for and against loyalty oaths, including the inconsistency of their professions with certain social realities and their possible ineffectiveness, hypocrisy, and even cynical uses. He correctly notes, however, that oaths – at least when solemnly performed in an appropriately focused and dignified setting – have the capacity not only to bind one in a psychological sense but also to generate 'a transformed (and socialised) consciousness' (Levinson: 1986, 1459). Having observed naturalisation ceremonies and discussed them with presiding judges and new citizens, I find that this claim rings true.[61]

Second, I believe that an effort by some immigration proponents to eliminate the renunciation requirement in the oath would constitute a colossal, even tragic political blunder. Such an effort, which Spiro urges, would arouse intense, widespread political opposition and animus, which would be directed against immigrants in general and naturalising immigrants especially Mexican-Americans and other Spanish-speaking groups in particular. The renunciation requirement would swiftly be transformed into a sacred shibboleth, a symbol of the integrity and security of the American polity with a prominence out of all proportion to its genuine significance.

I believe, however, that a suitably modified renunciation requirement should be embraced, even by those who now doubt its efficacy, as a useful instrument of immigrant assimilation, regardless of how that controversial idea is defined. The reason is that after all is said and done, after one acknowledges both the unpersuasiveness of some rationales for renunciation and the inconsistency between even the most persuasive rationales and some actual practices, few would seriously contest the notion that the U.S. may legitimately insist that those who naturalise in the United States owe it a core political loyalty. They will surely disagree about which sorts of commitments constitute that core, which of these are exclusive and which merely primary, and which commitments lie outside the core and thus may be made to other polities without violating a properly refined renunciation oath. My own view, which follows, is that the core is properly quite small, limited to those obligations that are essential to the flourishing of a polity as liberal as America. That there is *some* core that the U.S. may demand in exchange for the rights and blessings of citizenship seems indubitable.

A third consideration is that the current oath, which requires one to renounce 'absolutely and entirely all allegiance and fidelity to' another polity, utterly fails to define any such core. As already noted, its terms are simply too archaic, broad, and unqualified to communicate which duties Americans would truly place within this core were they to deliberate about the question. Because of this vague generality, the current renunciation oath cannot elicit the knowing, discriminating, and authentic consent of those that take the oath, which is necessary both to confer their full membership in the polity and to legitimate its exercise of power over them. People taking a solemn oath of renunciation should know precisely what they are accepting and forswearing. Accordingly, the requirement should be reformulated to provide a clearer, more refined definition of those loyalties that must and those that need not be renounced.

Finally, certain aspects of loyalty that the U.S. can legitimately demand of its new dual citizens are already encompassed in other parts of the naturalisation oath. Hence they need not be among those aspects of loyalty to which a redefined renunciation requirement should apply. Specifically, these aspects of loyalty include the duty 'to support and defend the Constitution and the laws of the United States . . . ,' the duty 'to bear true faith and allegiance to the same'[62] and the duty to bear arms or to perform equivalent public service. These duties obviously encompass an obligation to obey U.S. law.

Which aspects of loyalty, then, do dual citizens owe exclusively or primarily to the U.S. such that there is something that they must renounce? I am inclined to place only two duties of loyalty into that core. First, the naturalising citizen should be obliged to prefer the interests of the U.S. over those of any other polity. This duty to accept the primacy or superiority[63] of America's claim on a dual citizen will seldom come into question except in cases of war and other serious conflicts between the U.S. and the dual citizen's other country of nationality. In such situations, dual citizens may be obliged to make decisions (perhaps in voting or about military service) knowing that the interests of the two countries inescapably clash and that they must therefore choose between them, as distinguished from simply taking the interests of the other state into account in forming their views about where the national interests of the U.S. lie. Ordinarily, moreover, the oath taker's true state of mind and affection cannot be challenged as a practical matter. Since the government may not (and even if it could, should not) seek to control or punish oath takers' thoughts or feelings, their bad faith (if it exists) cannot be effectively sanctioned unless it relates to objective facts that they have misstated and that might be the subject of denaturalisation proceedings. Still, these realities do not render the duty meaningless. The fact that it will generally be unenforceable does not distinguish it from many other significant duties that we owe to others but whose observance must ultimately rest on our conscientious moral commitments.

Even this relatively constrained duty of primary loyalty, however, can be challenged as going too far. Stephen Legomsky, for example, argues that naturalising citizens should be required at most to accord *equal,* not greater, weight to U.S. interests in the event of a conflict, and he wonders how I think the U.S. should respond if other countries required primary loyalty from their dual nationals who are U.S. citizens and if such individuals took such an oath in the other country (Legomsky Letters: 1997). My answer, which presupposes that citizenship should be more demanding and hence exclusive than mere membership in a voluntary club, is that a nation has a legitimate claim to its citizens' primary loyalty (as I have narrowly defined it), and that one who cannot muster that minimal degree of loyalty should not be granted citizenship. Whether the government should be able to expatriate an American citizen who voluntarily, knowingly and solemnly pledges primary loyalty to another state in derogation of primary loyalty to the U.S. (again, as narrowly defined) is a separate question turning on several considerations, but in principle, and under current law as legitimated by the Supreme Court and confirmed by Congress in 1986, the answer is yes.

The second core duty is that the new citizen must not hold a high public office in another polity.[64] Although this proscription is likely to be overbroad in the sense that many official decisions that such an individual makes would not actually impinge on U.S. interests, a relatively clear prophylactic rule nevertheless seems warranted. Some of the official's decisions may create conflicts with that official's first duty to prefer the interests of the U.S.; the importance to the U.S. of these decisions may be disproportionately great, and drawing distinctions in general or on a case-by-case basis would be very difficult. Even so, some line-drawing would be necessary. For example, the offices that are 'high' enough to trigger this duty should probably depend on the breadth of their policymaking responsibilities, a familiar form of legal classification. Ordinary military service in another nation not at war with the U.S. would not necessarily implicate this duty but perhaps a military leadership position should.

Plausible objections to this duty can be anticipated as well. One is that the government could not constitutionally (or now, even statutorily) expatriate or denaturalise a U.S. citizen for holding office in another nation unless that person specifically intended thereby to renounce American citizenship. The Supreme Court, however, has never so held; *Afroyim* involved only voting in a foreign election, which, as I have just noted, poses a smaller risk of conflicting loyalties. However, even if the Constitution does bar the government from depriving a foreign officeholder of U.S. citizenship, it would probably not bar Congress from imposing other sanctions on that person. The question may be more one of appropriate remedy than of the power to implement a policy against foreign office-holding.

Stephen Legomsky makes another objection. Noting my belief that American citizens may properly take the interests of other groups and even countries into account in deciding where U.S. national interest lies, he wonders why I should be troubled by a U.S. citizen holding high office in another nation any more than if that person were holding high office in a corporation or other interest group and favouring that group's interests at the expense of the U.S. national interest (Legomsky Letters, 1997). My answer is that the risk of conflict in the government-government situation is likely to be far greater, the stakes for the U.S. in how such conflicts are resolved far higher, and the number of individuals who would be burdened by this duty far fewer than in the government-private entity situation that Legomsky posits.[65] Like my first response, this one will not satisfy those who find no justification for citizenship as a distinctive status carrying certain rights and responsibilities denied to non-citizens. As I noted in the Introduction, however, I am not such a person.

By solemnly affirming their primary loyalty to the United States and renouncing any inconsistent political allegiances in their naturalisation oaths, new dual citizens would minimise any risks to the American polity that their divided loyalties might seem to pose. They should not be required to renounce any ties to their other country that do not pose these risks for example, the intention to vote in foreign elections, serve in non-policymaking offices abroad, or seek to advance another country's interests. The naturalisation oath can be easily and succinctly revised to express these principles. The revised oath can take the form of either a renunciation or an affirmation. What is essential is that it define the core aspects of loyalty that the new citizen must accept.

This change, however, would not remedy the anomaly in current citizenship law, noted earlier, that naturalised citizens are obliged to accept these duties and renounce inconsistent allegiances, whereas citizens who are Americans through *jus sanguinis* are not, and may indeed acquire new allegiances (short of treason) without taking, much less violating, any oath.

Congress could address this anomaly (if anomaly it is)[66] by seeking to eliminate the differential treatment. It could do so by making these duties applicable to all citizens in two ways. First, it could oblige existing citizens to take the same loyalty oath. Precisely because many (like the author) would find such a requirement obnoxious, it would focus their minds on the troubling implications of demanding more of their new countrymen than they do of themselves. Congress could also (or instead) limit existing citizens' freedom to acquire new citizenships or to act upon them in particular ways (for example, voting) that naturalising citizens are obliged to renounce or forego. If new citizens can be forced to affirm their loyalty publicly, then why not existing ones? If existing citizens are unwilling to do this, then they may conclude that they should not force new ones to do so either. This conclusion would demonstrate once again the value-clarifying, unfairness-constraining function that the principle of legal equality among all citizens can play in democratic discourse and politics.

References

T.A. Aleinikoff, *Citizen and Membership: A Policy Perspective,* Carnegie Endowment for International Peace, Washington D.C., 1997.,

T.J. Chiappari, 'Expatriation Tax: Income Tax Liability of Expatriates and Departing Lawful Permanent Residents', in *1997–98 Immigration and Nationality Law Handbook, Vol. II,* American Immigration Lawyers Association, 1997.

N.C. Cott, 'Marriage and Women's Citizenship: in the U.S., 1830–1934, *American Historical Review,* 103, 1998, 1440.

R.M. Cover, 'The Supreme Court, 1982 Term: Foreword: Nonos and Narrative', Harvard Law Review 97, 1983.

M. Fix and W. Zimmerman, 'The Legacy of Welfare Reform' (working draft, The Urban Institute, February 1998), Washington, DC

E. Goldstein, and V. Piazza, 'Naturalisation, Dual Citizenship and Retention of Foreign Citizenship: A Survey', *Interpreter Releases* 73, 22 April 1996.

A.O. Hirschman, *Exit, Voice, and Loyalty: Responses to Decline in Firms, Organisations, and States,* Cambridge, Mass., 1970.

R. Koslowski, comments at roundtable discussion on plural citizenship, Carnegie Endowment for International Peace,Washington, D.C., 25 April 1997.

S.H. Legornsky, 'Why Citizenship?' *Virginia Journal of international Law* 35, 1995.

S.H. Legomsky, letters to the author dated August 21, 1997, and September 2, 1997

D.A. Martin, 'The Civil Republican Ideal for Citizenship, and for Our Common Life', *Virginia Journal of International Law* 35, 1995, 301.

N. Lewis, 'Reno Acts to Suspend Deportations', *New York Times, July* 11, 1997, A13,

S. Levinson, 'Constituting Communities Through Words That Bind: Reflections on Loyalty Oaths', Michigan Law Review 84, 1986, 1440

G.L. Neuman, Justifying U.S. Naturalisation Policies', *Virginia Journal of International Law* 35, 1995, 237–278.

G.L. Neuman, *Strangers to the Constitution: Immigrants, Borders, and Fundamental Law,* Princeton, N.J., 1996.

G.L. Neuman, 'Nationality Law in the United States and Germany: Structure and Current Problems,' in *Paths to Inclusion: The Integration of Immigrants in the United States and Germany,* eds Peter H. Schuck and Rainer Münz, Oxford, 1998.

N. Pickus, ed., *Immigration and Citizenship in the 21st Century*, Lanham, Md., 1998.

A. Portes, 'Divergent Destinies: Immigration, the Second Generation, and the Rise of Transnational Communities', in Schuck and Münz (1998).

J. Raskin, 'Legal Aliens, Local Citizens: The Historical, Constitutional and Theoretical Meanings of Alien Suffrage', *University of Pennsylvania Law Review* 141, 1993, 1391.

P.H. Schuck, 'Rethinking Informed Consent', *Yale Law Journal* 103, 1994, 899.

P.H. Schuck, and R.M. Smith, *Citizenship Without Consent. Illegal Aliens in the American Polity*, New Haven, Ct., 1985.

P.H. Schuck, Expert Testimony in *Lavoie v. The Queen*, Federal Court of Canada, Trial Division, October 1994.

P.H. Schuck, 'Whose Membership Is It, Anyway? Comments on Gerald Neuman', *Virginia Journal of International Law* 35, 1995, 321.

P.H. Schuck, 'Alien Rumination', *Yale Law Journal* 105, 1996, 1987–95.

P.H. Schuck, 'The Re-Evaluation of American Citizenship', *Georgetown Immigration Law Journal* 12 (1997a): Also in *Challenge to the Nation-State: Immigration in Western Europe and the United States*, ed. C. Joppke, New York, 1998.

P. Schuck and R. Münz, eds. *Paths to Inclusion: The Integration of Immigrants in the United States and Germany*, Oxford, 1998.

P.H. Schuck, 'Refugee Burden-Sharing: A Modest Proposal', *Yale Journal of International Law* 22, 1997b, 243.

S. Sengupta, 'Immigrants in New York Pressing Drive for Dual Nationality', *York Times*, December 30, 1996, B1.

P. Skerry, *Mexican-Americans: The Ambivalent Minority*, New York, 1993.

R.M. Smith, *Civic Ideals: Conflicting Visions of Citizenship in U.S. History*, New Haven, 1997.

P.J. Spiro, 'Dual Nationality and the Meaning of Citizenship', *Emory Law Journal* 46, no. 4, 1997, 1411–85.

U.S. Congress, 'Societal and Legal Issues Surrounding Children Born in the United States to Illegal Alien Parents', Joint Hearing before Subcommittee on Immigration and Claims and the Subcommittee on the Constitution, House judiciary Committee, 104th Congress, 1st Session, 13 December 1995, Serial No. 50 (Washington, DC: Government Printing Office, 1996); U.S. Congress, Hearing before Subcommittee on Immigration and Claims, House Judiciary Committee, 105th Congress, 1st Session, 25 June 1997 (unpublished).

J.A. Vargas, 'Dual Nationality for Mexicans? A Comparative Legal Analysis of the Dual Nationality Proposal and Its Eventual Political and Socio-Economic Implications', *Chicano-Latino Law Review* 18, 1996, 1–58.

M. Walzer, Spheres of Justice: A Defense of Pluralism and Equality, New York, 1983.

Notes

1. Following convention, I use the terms *citizenship* and *nationality* interchangeably for most purposes in this discussion, although the legal distinction between the two concepts does become important below when I discuss how the law should treat the franchise; paradigmatically, citizens possess it but

nationals do not. A recent essay urging that the two statuses be decoupled in order that their functional and normative aspects can be separated also observes that citizenship 'attempts to encompass in one word a legal status, a state of mind, a civic obligation, an immigration benefit, an international legal marking, and a personal virtue' (Harvard Law Review).

2. I shall continue to refer to 'dual' citizenship although, as noted below, triple and even more plural citizenships are becoming increasingly available to individuals as a result of the conjunction of modes for acquiring citizenship – and liberalising ones at that – deriving from, parentage, marriage, naturalisation, and reacquisition of former nationalities.

3. Spiro (1997): 1435, (citing President James Buchanan's secretary of state, Lewis Cass).

4. In addition to the widespread adoption of no-fault laws for dissolving marriages, at least one state, Louisiana, has created a consensual, dual-track regime for regulating the conditions for divorce. See Kevin Sack, 'Louisiana Approves Measure to Tighten Marriage Bonds', *New York Times*, 24 June 1997, 1.

5. Liberalisation can occur in the country of first nationality (when that country does not denationalise its citizens for naturalising elsewhere), in the country of second nationality (when it does not require naturalising citizens to renounce their earlier nationality), or in both.

6. See T. Aleinikoff (1997); Neuman (1995); and Spiro (1997).

7. See, for example, Smith (1997); Schuck and Smith (1985); Legomsky (1995); Aleinikoff (1990); and Neuman (1995).

8. In my view, citizenship can be justified, among other reasons, as creating an additional incentive to assimilate by acquiring a minimal competence in the dominant language, gaining minimal understanding of (and hopefully a love for) the nation's institutions, and affirming a minimal allegiance to the polity. Such assimilation is of inestimable value both to American society and to aliens in the United States. See Peter H. Schuck, Expert Testimony in *Lavoie v. The Queen*, Federal Court of Canada, Trial Division, October 1994.

9. U.S. General Accounting Office, 'Naturalisation of Aliens: INS Internal Controls', Testimony before Subcommittee on Immigration, Senate Judiciary Committee, 1 May 1997, GAO/T-GGD-97–98.

10. Katharine Q. Seelye, '20 Charged with Helping 13,000 Cheat on Test for Citizenship', *New York Times*, 28 January 1998, A12.

11. Neuman (1998). Neuman points out that 'before the 1860s the U.S. was full of dual nationals who thought of themselves as Americans'.

12. William Safire, 'Citizen of the World', *New York Times*, 16 May 1983, A31. The flip side of this selfishness-Americans who acquire foreign nationalities and renounce their U.S. citizenship in order to avoid paying U.S. taxes aroused such public resentment that Congress enacted a statute in 1996 to address the practice. See Chiappari (1997).

13. Alex Aleinikoff estimates that half a million children acquire dual citizenship in the U.S. *at birth* each year. See Aleinikoff (1998).

14. Aleinikoff (1998) identifies six discrete combinations of rules that can lead to dual citizenship. See Aleinikoff, *Citizen and Membership*. Peter Spiro (1997; this volume) notes that dual citizenship was expanded by the historical circumstances that states in the 19th century increasingly rejected other states' claims of perpetual allegiance, and that Europe's adoption of *jus sanguinis* in the 19th

century coincided with the application by the U.S. of an almost absolute rule of *jus soli*.

15. See Schuck and Münz (1998), 'Introduction'. Germany is sharply divided on this question; see Hailbronner (this volume).

16. Aleinikoff (1998); Vargas (1996). Aleinikoff believes that the net effect of these two changes, which trade off more dual nationals in the first generation against fewer in the second and subsequent ones, will be to produce fewer dual nationals eventually than under the old rules. Whether or not he is correct about this, the changes will surely encourage more Mexicans to naturalise in the U.S.

17. Spiro (1997); Sam Dillon, 'Mexico Woos U.S. Mexicans, Proposing Nationality', *New York Times*, 10 December 1995, 16.

18. Some observers doubt that the new Mexican law will significantly affect naturalisation rates in the U.S., arguing that discrimination against non-citizens in America is a more important factor driving naturalisations. See 'Dual Citizenship, Domestic Politics and the Naturalisation Rates of Latino Immigrants in the U.S.', Policy Brief, Tomas Rivera Cente; June 1996.

19. Indeed, Spiro notes that many states are now so eager for their nationals both to naturalise in economically advanced countries and to retain their ties to the state of origin that their nationality laws make it difficult or even impossible for their nationals to make an effective renunciation in the second state. In an arresting phrase, he calls this a 'new perpetual allegiance', different from the old in that the states now *encourage* their nationals to acquire additional citizenships. He suggests that this development poses a dilemma for the second state if it wishes to minimise dual citizenship among its new members by requiring (as the U.S. now does *not* require) an effective renunciation. If the second state refuses to naturalise migrants from states that will not effectuate such a renunciation, then in effect no migrants from the states will be able to naturalise. This refusal would create political and diplomatic difficulties, between the states and, by preventing naturalisation, would impede the assimilation of these migrants. See Spiro (1997).

20. Cott (1996); Spiro (1998); The Supreme Court is now considering a further challenge to this gender bias in connection with the transmission of citizenship to illegitimate children. See *Miller v. Albright*, 96 F.3d 1467 (DC Cir.), cert. granted 117 S. Ct. 1551 (1997). The case was argued on 11 November 1997.

21. 'Advice about Possible Loss of U.S. Citizenship and Dual Nationality', U.S. Department of State, reprinted in *Interpreter Releases* 67 (1990): 1093. Indeed, as David Martin has argued, the State Department not only tolerates dual citizenship through naturalisation elsewhere by U.S. citizens but actually makes it more difficult for citizens to renounce their American citizenship by not effectuating renunciatory language in the other state's naturalisation oath. Martin (1995).

22. Spiro (1997). Aleinikoff (1998) notes that some of the problems associated with dual citizenship today could be ameliorated through bilateral agreements between states.

23. For another example of an *ex ante* interest that even an insular state may have in an international safety net regime (for refugees), See Schuck (1997b).

24. A commission reviewing Canada's dual citizenship law recommended in 1994 that both new 'involuntary' dual citizens and naturalising citizens 'accord

primacy' to their Canadian nationality. Canada House of Commons, 'Canadian Citizenship: A Sense of Belonging,' Report of the Standing Committee on Citizenship and Immigration (June 1994), 15.

25. *Rogers v. Bellei*, 401 U.S. 815 (1971). Some have expressed concern that a liberal dual citizenship policy might encourage the proliferation of second- and third-generation dual citizenship in the U.S. by permitting those who naturalise in America to transmit their U.S. citizenship through *jus sanguinis* to children and grandchildren who live elsewhere and have no other ties to the U.S. Congress could respond to this risk, if it exists, by enacting the kinds of residency requirements for *jus sanguinis* citizens that *Bellei* upheld.

26. Usually, but not always. Well into the 20th century, aliens were permitted to vote in some states, and some municipalities permit them to vote in local elections a practice that is common in Europe. Indeed, even undocumented aliens are entitled to vote in local school board elections in New York City. See Raskin (1993).

27. One possible explanation that immigrants wishing to naturalise in the U.S. are aliens whose petitions give the government leverage over them that it lacks over Americans who are already citizens and wish to naturalise elsewhere simply begs the central policy and perhaps constitutional questions of which conditions the polity can, and, as a moral matter, should impose on the acquisition of citizenship through birth or consent, and why the status difference between the two groups should matter insofar as the supposed dangers of dual citizenship are concerned.

28. The U.S. has become increasingly aggressive in pursuing those who expatriate thus ending their dual citizenship status (if they had it) in order to minimise their U.S. tax obligation. Tax law changes enacted in 1996 are designed to defeat this stratagem. See Chiappari (1997).

29. The confusion about standards results from the Supreme Court's severely fractured decision in *Kungys v. United States*, which attempted to define them. These standards may become clearer as a result of denaturalisation cases that are being initiated in the wake of revelations that the Immigration Naturalisation Service has erroneously naturalised many ineligible aliens. See Seelye, '20 Charged with Helping 13,000 Cheat'.

30. Recent empirical research suggests that naturalisation affects English proficiency more strongly than any other indicator of durable attachment to the U.S. This effect, moreover, goes beyond the fact that one who naturalises must already have acquired some English proficiency: 'although there is a modest English prerequisite for U.S. citizenship, it is hard to imagine that this effect outweighs the substantial propensity for naturalised citizens to want to make long-term investments in many forms of U.S.-specific capital, including learning English'. Thomas J. Espenshade and Haishan Fu, 'An Analysis of English-Language Proficiency Among U.S. Immigrants', *American Sociological Review* 62 (1997): 300.

31. See, for example, Spiro (1997): 101–2. That the ease of acquiring dual nationality increases immigrants' propensity to naturalise in the second state seems self-evident and has been reported by some observers in some countries: see Sengupta, 'Immigrants in New York.' Participants in the Carnegie Endowment workshop reported that the average period taken by Italians resident in Canada to naturalise there declined from 17 to 6 years after Italy permitted

dual citizenship, and that the naturalisation rate of Irish immigrants in Australia increased when Canberra eliminated from its naturalisation oath an affirmation of loyalty to the British Crown. Mary Woods, comments at roundtable discussion on plural citizenship, Carnegie Endowment for international Peace, April 25, 1997. But see Tomas Rivera, Centre, 'Dual Citizenship'.

32. The 1997 budget agreement restored approximately half of these 1996 benefit cuts. See Robert Pear, 'Legal Immigrants to Benefit Under New Budget Accord', *New York Times*, 30 July 1997, A17. President Clinton proposed in his January 1998 State of the Union Message to fill much of the remaining gap. See Fix and Zimmerman (1998).

33. Strictly speaking, of course, it is not dual citizenship *per se* that imposes these fiscal burdens, but rather the naturalisation incentive created by a policy to deny benefits to aliens. Still the effect is the same: a liberal dual citizenship policy will cost the government more in benefits. These costs, of course, should be offset by any corresponding social benefits, such as food stamps and Supplemental Security Income, that are generated by making these individuals eligible for these transfer programs.

34. The Canadian parliamentary committee cited this concern, among others. Canada House of Commons, 'Canadian Citizenship', 15.

35. Recent examples are Sweden's effort to prosecute Argentine military officers for the death of a teenager who was a Swedish Argentine dual citizen, and Spain's effort to prosecute Argentine military officers for the murder of Spanish Argentine dual citizens.

36. Depending on how one views these complex imbroglios, China's increasingly bellicose protests against Taiwan, which governs millions of people whom China views as Chinese citizens, and Russia's threats against the Baltic republics for their alleged discrimination against resident Russians, might be considered examples. As Neuman (1998) points out, these are often cases not of dual nationality but of single nationality individuals who reside outside their country but have ethnic ties to it.

37. Under U.S. law, a dual citizen can certainly vote in American elections. Whether this citizen can also vote in the other state's elections depends on the law of that state. As noted earlier, the pending Mexican law will not permit Mexicans naturalising in the U.S. to vote in Mexican elections, although Mexico could amend its election law to allow them to do so, in effect rendering them citizens, not merely nationals, of Mexico. Mexico has already changed its election law to permit Mexican citizens who reside abroad to vote by absentee ballot.

38. The existence of Arrovian voting paradoxes does not substantially affect this argument.

39. Although the possibility that the church might harm U.S. interests seems farfetched, the risks of other nongovernmental organisations doing so may be worth considering at a time when NGOs can wield enormous influence, even qualifying them for the Nobel peace prize. As Spiro points out, NGOs enjoy the freedom of action to undertake certain conduct that states are unlikely to engage in because of the legal, political or diplomatic constraints under which they operate.

40. See Peter H. Schuck and Bruce Brown, 'Lessons froin Lippo', *Wall Street Journal*, 27 February 1997, A16.

41. I do not favour this approach, which is discussed in the final paragraph of this essay.
42. Obviously, there is room for interpretation here; if the criterion of an independent judiciary were used, for example, it is not clear that any of these countries (except perhaps India) would qualify. The others, in order of the number of immigrants sent, are Vietnam, China, Dominican Republic, Cuba, Ukraine, and Russia.
43. Canada House of Commons, 'Canadian Citizenship'.
44. The suspicion that many who naturalise do so for opportunistic reasons seems to animate a recent proposal to decouple functional citizenship (concerned with rights and duties) and nationality (concerned with affirming one's affective ties to the polity), *Harvard Law Review.*
45. Some other reasons for increased naturalisations include intensified Immigration Naturalisation Service efforts to encourage them: aliens' need to pay a fee for renewing their green cards that is only slightly lower than the naturalisation fee, and the large cohort of those legalised under the amnesty provisions of the Immigration Reform and Control Act of 1986 who have only recently satisfied the time limits required for naturalisation.
46. I shall not attempt here to define assimilation or to defend its importance as a preeminent value against which to assess immigration policy generally and dual citizenship policy in particular. I have discussed these matters elsewhere (Schuck: 1996), and there is a voluminous literature on the subject.
47. Alex Aleinikoff (1997) finds it 'interesting that this concern has never been stated for the six to eight thousand Canadians who naturalise in the United States each year, and have since 1977 been permitted to retain Canadian citizenship'. His innuendo – that racial animus distinguishes the two cases – may be correct, but the much larger number and perhaps residential concentration of naturalising Mexicans, and their lesser command of English, might also contribute to and justify the different reactions.
48. 'Traitor' is used here in its colloquial sense as someone who betrays the nation rather than its technical sense, which requires, among other things, that the traitor be a citizen of that nation. See *Kawakita v. United States*, 343 U.S. 717 (1952). For a nuanced discussion of treason and loyalty, including some cases in which citizenship was an issue, see George P Fletcher, *Loyalty: An Essay on the Morality of Relationships* (New York: Oxford University Press, 1993), especially chapter 3.
49. In such campaigns, of course, dual citizens are as entitled to serve in the armed forces as other citizens. Indeed, resident aliens may serve.
50. Indeed, Americans may also engage in such conduct on behalf of *democratic* regimes even close allies of the U.S., as is demonstrated by the fascinating case of Jonathan Pollard, who illegally transferred U.S. military secrets to Israel apparently in the belief that there was no conflict of interest.
51. My colleague Akhil Amar points out that a U.S. citizen may not simultaneously be a citizen of more than one American state because this would give her two votes for Congress and the Presidency rather than the one that her fellow citizens enjoy.
52. However, open primary states permit members of one political party to vote in the primary of another.
53. Many people, of course, use names that are different from their legal ones.

54. Other asymmetries may not be far off. The Commission on Immigration Reform, for example, considered whether to limit future immigrant admissions by restricting the right of newly naturalised citizens to petition for the admission of their relatives beyond the limits that apply to other citizens.

55. As Levinson puts it, native-born citizens 'are free to regard the Constitution as all abomination and even support its violent replacement by a more agreeable substitute; naturalised citizens, however, are formally bound to swear that their new self-definition of being 'American' will include at least the propositions laid out in their oath' Levinson, 'Constituting Communities', 1463. Neuman does seem to view this asymmetry as problematic. 'Justifying U.S. Naturalisation Policies,' 253–63.

56. This assumes, of course, that good moral character is defined in a minimalist fashion. This has not always been the case.

57. As a glance at the naturalisation statute reveals, the United States has long done so with respect to eligibility standards. Rights have not been exempt from discrimination. The most important example is voting rights, which were withheld from citizen women until the 19th Amendment, and are still withheld from citizen felons and citizen children under the age of eighteen.

58. Neuman suggests that their concerns may be pretextual and 'often a tactic for preventing naturalisation of Mexicans'. Gerald L. Neuman, letter to author dated 18 August 1997. As noted earlier, Aleinikoff harbors the same suspicion. In any event, nothing in my analysis turns on whether or not they are correct.

59. After circulating several drafts of this essay containing my proposal, I learned that Lawrence Fuchs in recent congressional testimony had made a similar one and that the Commission on Immigration Reform had recommended an oath like the one favored by Fuchs. We all emphasise the requirement of a primary loyalty to the U.S. I go beyond them, however, in seeking to specify (not necessarily in the oath itself) the duties that should define that primary loyalty.

60. Some evidence of oathtakers' seriousness, were it needed, appears in the report that Irish naturalisation rates in Australia rose when applicants were no longer required to swear allegiance to the British Crown.

61. For what it is worth, Congress seems to agree; only recently and reluctantly did it permit the Immigration Naturalisation Service, and not just judges, to conduct the ceremony and oathtaking.

62. This clause seems superfluous unless it means to affirm a state of emotion or veneration that might strengthen the inclination, already required, to support and defend the Constitution and laws.

63. The notion of a hierarchy of claims appears in the very same provision of the Immigration and Nationality Act that prescribes the naturalisation oath. Section 337 of the statute, in defining 'religious training and belief' for purposes of an exception to the duty to bear arms, provides that the phrase means a 'belief in a relation to a Supreme Being involving duties that are superior to those arising from any human relation'. The Canadian parliamentary committee, which as noted earlier, would require that certain new dual citizens accord 'primacy' to their Canadian nationality, does not define what such primacy means or would entail.

64. There are at least two recent examples: an American who was briefly the president of Yugoslavia, and another who is now president of Latvia (but has relinquished his U.S. citizenship). While this duty is important, however, it is likely

to be implicated so rarely that it need not be mentioned explicitly in the renunciation oath, which should retain its solemn dignity and lofty generality insofar as possible.

65. To be sure, one can imagine a scenario in which a government-private entity conflict would be more troubling than a government-government conflict for example, if the other state were an insignificant one that could not harm U.S. interests but the private entity were a multinational corporation with global interests that could harm the U.S., but such a possibility does not invalidate the prophylactic rule that I am proposing to govern the vast majority of situations.

66. Lawrence Fuchs writes, 'I do not worry about the asymmetries required between naturalised citizens and native born Americans. Not every inconsistency can be fixed'. Letter to the author dated 12 September 1997.

CHAPTER 4

CITIZENSHIP AND CIVIL SOCIETY: WHAT RIGHTS FOR RESIDENTS?

Joseph H. Carens

Do we want people to be virtuous? Then let us start by making them love their homeland. But how are they to love it if the homeland is nothing more for them than for foreigners and accords them only what it cannot refuse to anyone.

Rousseau, Political Economy

Contemporary liberal democratic states have not heeded Rousseau's advice. In Europe and North America legal distinctions between citizens and resident non-citizens have diminished significantly over time, especially during the period after World War II. Should we celebrate this development as a triumph for equality or deplore it as a devaluation of citizenship? What about recent actions contrary to this general trend, like the law passed in the United States that restricts the access of legal immigrants to various social welfare benefits? Is this sort of policy an appropriate redressing of the balance, an impermissible form of discrimination, or perhaps something in between? Rousseau speaks of one's 'homeland,' assuming implicitly that citizens acquire their status by birth – but some do not. What can reasonably be required of people as a condition of naturalisation? For example, are restrictions on dual citizenship a morally illegitimate restriction on individual rights or a morally desirable means of promoting loyalty (or perhaps something in between)? Finally, how generalisable are our answers to such questions? To what extent are they contextually specific, applicable only to a particular state and to what extent do they apply more broadly?

The questions I am asking are normative not empirical. I am concerned in the first instance not with what the law is but with what it ought to be, not with why states have adopted this or that policy but with what policies they ought to adopt. I say a bit more about the normative approach I employ in the paper in an appendix.

In addressing these questions, I will adopt four simplifying presuppositions that I want to make explicit. First, I am focusing only on questions about legal differences between citizens and non-citizens. This is obviously a very limited set of concerns from the perspective of a comprehensive theory of justice. It would be a mistake to assume that because a state acts justly with respect to these issues that it is a just state. Conversely, a state that has morally problematic policies in its treatment of immigrants may, nevertheless, be more just overall than one whose policies towards immigrants are less objectionable.

Second, I assume that questions about formal legal status matter. One might reasonably object that administrative interpretations and practices may differ from and be more important than formal rules and also that social and economic arrangements are more central in immigrants' lives than legal rules of any sort. Both objections have merit. I am not claiming that the issues I am addressing here are the most important ones, only that they do matter and are worth considering.

Third, in this paper I will set to one side questions that might be asked about the legitimacy of restrictions on initial admissions. My focus is on those who have been legally admitted, and, *for this purpose*, I will adopt the conventional assumption that states normally have considerable moral discretion in deciding whom to admit.[1]

Fourth, I will limit my analysis in this paper to non-citizens who have been lawfully admitted and who have a legal right to ongoing (rather than temporary) residence.

An overview of the argument

Given these preliminaries, what can we say about what justice requires and permits with regard to people who live in a state but are not citizens? In what ways (if any) may the legal rights and obligations of permanent residents legitimately differ from those of citizens?

In broad outline my answer is this. Liberal democratic justice, properly understood, greatly constrains the distinctions that can be made between citizens and non-citizen residents. The longer people stay in a society, the stronger their moral claims become, and, after a while they pass a threshold that entitles them to virtually the same legal status as citizens. Once people have been settled for an extended period, say, five years or so, they are morally entitled to the same legal rights (and ought to be subject to the same legal obligations) as citizens, except for the right to vote and the right to hold high public office. During the early stages of settlement it is permissible (though not required) to limit some other rights (e.g., to redistributive benefits or protection against deportation). With regard to naturalisation, the same principles apply. The longer the stay the stronger the claim to citizenship. At some point (ten years at most, probably five), citizenship should be made available upon demand, without any restrictions or requirements.

I will focus on four issues that I regard as particularly likely to be contested: deportation, social rights, political rights, and naturalisation.

Deportation

In most liberal democratic states non-citizens who have been admitted for an indefinite period enjoy considerable security of residence. Nevertheless, they are normally subject to deportation if convicted of a serious criminal offence or a series of offences. It is important to note that citizens may not be deported, not even if there is a place willing to take them. At one time exile was used as a punishment for citizens, but now it is considered morally unacceptable, a violation of human rights, to force even heinous criminals to live outside their own societies. Indeed the deportation of non-citizens convicted of crimes is usually presented not as a punishment but simply as a routine exercise of a state's power to exclude unwanted immigrants. Of course, from the perspective of the non-citizen, deportation is often a much harsher sanction than whatever penalty is imposed by the criminal justice system.

In most cases, the amount of time the non-citizen has been present is treated as legally irrelevant, or at most, as something that authorities have the discretion to take into account if they wish in deciding whether or not to seek deportation. It is not uncommon for people who have spent all but the first few years of their lives to be deported to a place where they know no one and sometimes whose local language they do not speak. I regard this practice as a scandal, the most blatant and severe injustice against non-citizens of any of the practices I shall criticise. Nevertheless, it is likely to be one of the most difficult to change, because convicted criminals are unpopular and courts tend to be highly deferential to political authorities on this issue.

I will offer three interrelated arguments for why the deportation of long-term residents convicted of serious criminal offences is morally wrong: membership; fairness to other societies; the rights of family members.

The first and most important argument – one that will be relevant to the other issues as well – is that long-term residents are members of society, and, for that reason, ought to be entitled to stay regardless of their conduct. Of course, by definition, the residents in question are not citizens, not formal members of the political community, but they are members of civil society. They participate in labour and housing markets, they pay taxes, they have families that connect them to others in the society in myriad ways, they send children to schools, they participate in neighbourhood and other associations, and they are involved in cultural and recreational activities. As a result, they form a wide range of human ties and social attachments that affect their lives in many ways so that they acquire a vital interest in being able to continue to live in the society where they have settled. The state, which has enabled them to acquire that vital interest by admitting them, has an obligation to protect their interest by granting them a legal right to remain. In sum, residents are members of society, and that membership matters morally. It radically constrains the state's right to deport them.

To elaborate this argument I will begin with the easiest case and then show why the principles for that sort of case should be extended to less obvious ones. So, consider first non-citizens who come to the society at a very young age, perhaps even are born there if the country has no *jus soli* rule. They grow up speaking the local language, using their parents' native tongue only at home if at all. Their schooling, their friendships, their cultural experiences (television, music, etc.), and their formal and informal socialisation are very similar to those of the children of the citizens in the land where they live and very different from those of the children in the land their parents came from. To suggest that such children are not integrated into society would be ludicrous. The society where they have been raised is their home. They are clearly members of that society. Because they are members, it would be wrong to expel them, no matter how they behave as adults.

On what grounds might someone say that such individuals are not morally entitled to remain in the society where they have always lived, whatever their conduct and behaviour? Two possible answers occur to me. First, one might claim that they are not entitled to stay because they possess citizenship in another country. Second, one might say that their failure to naturalise when they had the opportunity to do so implies a tacit consent to the conditions that distinguish permanent residents from citizens, including being subject to deportation for criminal behaviour. Neither is persuasive.

The right of such individuals to remain in the land where they live is not lessened if their parents' country of origin happens to grant them citizenship because that citizenship does not secure their place in the society to which they most clearly belong. If they are members of any society, they are members of the society where they have lived their entire lives, the society whose language they speak and whose culture they share. Surely they are much more members of that society than of the one from which their parents came, in a land where they have never lived and have no friends, whose culture and customs are unfamiliar at best. Perhaps they have some claim to membership in both societies, but to refuse them the right to stay in the land where they live, and thus formal legal recognition and protection of their status as members of society, is to treat them unjustly.

What about their failure to naturalise? Even for adults, consent counts as a justification only when it reflects a genuine choice or at least a free affirmation. In many cases, children do not become citizens because of their parents' choices (or inaction), and by the time they are old enough to choose for themselves, they have already become embroiled in the legal system in ways that preclude naturalisation. Even if these obstacles do not exist, it is unreasonable to infer from inaction the deliberate forfeiture of such a vital interest as the right to stay in one's homeland (even if it is not the place of one's birth). If people are to give up that sort of fundamental right, it must be done as a deliberate and conscious choice in circumstances that are not coercive. Finally, even those who do choose freely and consciously not to naturalise are entitled to protection against deportation, because the right to remain in a society of which one is a member, even if not a citizen, is a fundamental human interest that ought to be respected.

So far I have focused on people who have spent virtually their whole lives in the country. What about those who come at a later age? The general principle is that the longer the presence, the stronger the claims to membership. The shorter the presence the weaker the claims. A child who comes to a country as an infant is virtually indistinguishable, in moral terms, from one who was born there. People who spend all or most of their formative years as children in a country have powerful ties and a powerful moral claim to remain there. (Conversely, those who spend only a year or two in a country have little moral claim *per se*, even if they were born there and have an indisputable legal claim because a state happens to have a *jus soli* rule.) How long must children spend in a country before they have become members with a moral claim to remain? I can't answer that question precisely, but I would think that several years (especially years between the ages of six and eighteen) should be enough. If we turn now to the question of what claims people who come as adults have to remain, we find that the same sorts of principles apply. The longer one stays, the more one becomes a member. The shorter the stay the weaker the claim. If someone arrives as an immigrant and commits a serious crime within six months or a year, I do not think it would be wrong to deport him.[2] He will not have built up the kinds of social ties that make expulsion so inhuman. If he has been there for ten years, however, then the case is entirely different.

How long must adults spend before they have the kind of claim to membership that should bar deportation? Again, I won't try to answer this question precisely, but it is important to recognise that in assessing the claims that come from living in a society, there is a threshold after which the length of time does not matter because the claim should be regarded as absolute. Five years seems to me a reasonable length of time for such a threshold, though I don't pretend that the question can be precisely settled on the basis of a theoretical principle. After a while, the terms of admission become irrelevant. Regardless of the original conditions of entry, once people have established themselves firmly as members of society, they have a moral claim to stay.

'But these are criminals,' someone will object. 'They cause social problems. They are destructive to the rest of society. Isn't it in our interest to send them away?' Let us assume that this is true.[3] Why is it fair to dump such people on another society, a place where they have a legal membership but no real social connection? Are they any less likely to engage in criminal behaviour there? Every society has people who are involved in criminal activity and who create social problems. It seems only fair that a society should deal with its own problems, not try to foist them off on someplace else. The argument is especially powerful with regard to people who have grown up in the society that seeks to expel them. It is that society, not the one of their nominal citizenship, that is responsible for their social formation, for successes and failures in the inculcation of social norms and values and for the creation of opportunities and obstacles in social life. In short, one important response to the imagined objection is to say, 'These people may be problems, but they are *our* problems, not someone else's, and we should be the ones to cope with them as we do with criminals who are citizens.'

The final argument against deportation of non-citizens concerns the effect of such deportations upon family members who may themselves be citizens or who, in any event, have done no wrong themselves. I regard this argument as somewhat weaker than the preceding two, because the same objection can be posed against any sanction (i.e., that it affects not only the person against whom it is directed but also those to whom he or she is connected). Nevertheless, it appropriately draws attention to the particular nature of deportation as a harm, and a harm additional to what citizen criminals have to suffer. Ironically, it is this sort of argument, constructed on the basis of guarantees to family life, that has proved most effective in European courts in providing a barrier to deportation.

Social rights

Let me begin this section by recalling Marshall's famous distinction between civil, political, and social rights. As Soysal has pointed out, the pattern in Europe has been to extend first civil and then social rights to immigrants, with political rights the last and least extensively provided, thus altering the Marshallian sequence in which political rights preceded, and were instrumental in securing, social rights. (Soysal: 1994, 131) The same pattern has prevailed in North America.[4] (Schuck: 1984)

Some people describe the current arrangements as ones within which citizenship rights have been replaced by human rights or rights of the person. I think that can be quite misleading. There are indeed some rights –

mainly civil rights – that people enjoy simply because they are human beings, physically present within the territory of a given state. Among the rights that we would regard as fundamental in any liberal democratic regime are security of the person and of property, freedom of conscience and of religious practice, and the right to a fair trial if accused of a crime. Different liberal democratic states interpret and implement these rights in somewhat different ways, but in doing so they do not distinguish between citizens and others. For example, the police are supposed to protect *people*, not just citizens or even residents, from assault and theft, from religious persecution, and so on. Even people present without authorisation are, in principle, entitled to these protections. (In practice, of course, their desire to avoid contact with the authorities renders them more vulnerable.) Let's call rights of this kind 'general human rights' because they are enjoyed by everyone. Within the context of liberal democracy, no one, not even the most fervent chauvinist, argues that it would be proper to deny such rights to non-citizens.

On the other hand, there are many civil and social rights that are not enjoyed by everyone within a given territory but only by those who live there. Rights to get a job, to join a local union, and to receive unemployment insurance or health care are the sorts of rights normally enjoyed only by citizens and legal residents. Now these too, or at least some of them, can reasonably be described as human rights in the sense that they appeal to standards of justice that we think ought to constrain all regimes. For example, we may say that it is a violation of human rights when a regime makes it impossible for a member of society to find employment. However, to call the right to work a human right is to use the term in a somewhat different sense from the way it was used in the previous paragraph. These sorts of rights are derived not from one's general humanity but from one's social location, i.e., from the kinds of ties one has to the society. It is not a violation of human rights to deny a tourist the right to work. Rights of this second sort mark off both citizens and residents on the one hand from those who are present only on a temporary basis or without authorisation on the other.[5] If we call these rights human rights, we should call them something like 'membership-specific human rights.' Perhaps it would be simpler just to call them rights of membership.

In contrast to the virtual unanimity about general human rights, there are some people who think that liberal democratic states have gone too far in extending rights of membership to non-citizen residents. Recent initiatives in the United States have reduced the social benefits available to immigrants, and there are comparable proposals, if not yet comparable policies, in some European states.

To put the contemporary debates in proper perspective, however, it is essential first to note that most of the social rights enjoyed by non-citizen residents are also not seriously contested. Consider, for example, the right of access to the general labour market. It would hardly be reasonable to admit people to live in a society and then deny them the opportunity to earn a living. Moreover, to restrict them, at least for any extended period, to a single narrow area of the market is obviously to place them in a vulnerable and exploitative position. So far as I know, no one has actually advocated this. By the same token, to deny them the kinds of labour rights (e.g., health and safety legislation, unions, etc.) that other workers enjoy would be to place them at an unfair disadvantage. Again, I know of no one advocating such a course.

If we consider social insurance programs financed by compulsory deductions from workers' pay (old age pensions, unemployment compensation, compensation for workplace accidents), it would hardly be reasonable to require people to pay into these programs and then to deny them access to the benefits they provide. (Some programs of this sort have minimum periods of employment that must be fulfilled before one can collect, and, of course, it is appropriate to impose the same limits on noncitizens – but not longer ones.) Again, I don't think this principle is seriously contested even if it is sometimes breached in practice.

Finally, consider access to general social programs, such as publicly funded education and health care, that are provided to the general population. Of course, different states provide different levels of benefits, but one rarely hears arguments for treating legal permanent residents differently from citizens with regard to these programs.

The real debates, and the policy changes, have focused on one small sector of social programs: means-tested health and welfare benefits. In other words, what is at issue is whether immigrants should have access to redistributive programs that provide income and other benefits that are contingent upon one's income falling below a certain level.

Now let me distinguish between what justice requires and what would be a wise or even morally desirable policy. Justice sets a minimum standard (even if it is one we often fail to reach). It does not exhaust the moral universe. In my view, *as a matter of justice*, immigrants who have been settled in a society for a number of years are entitled to enjoy all of the social rights that citizens enjoy. The argument for regarding this as a matter of justice is the same one advanced above in my discussion of deportation. The longer one stays in a society, the stronger one's moral claims and after a certain point one is entitled to be treated simply as a full member. (Again, I recognize that it is impossible to say on theoretical grounds precisely how many years, but I think five is about the right number.) So, in my view, it is unjust to exclude permanent residents from any social programs, means-tested or not, for a much more extended period such as ten years (or even permanently as some have proposed in the U.S.).

Is it unjust, however, to insist that immigrants not be immediately eligible for such programs? On that issue, I am much less certain. I think that such a policy is unwise and mean-spirited, and that it scapegoats immigrants for fiscal problems they have not caused. As a citizen I would want my political community to welcome the immigrants who have been admitted and make them immediately eligible for the same programs as everyone else. But that is not the same as saying that such a course is morally required as a matter of justice. My general argument – the longer one stays, the stronger one's moral claims – implies that the claims of immigrants when they first arrive are not as strong as when they have been there for some time. I suggested above that that was true with regard to security of residence, and it seems to me that it is true also with regard to redistributive social programs whose goal is to compensate for economic disparities among members.

Political rights

Those who were inspired by my opening quotation from Rousseau may give a sigh of relief, feeling that at last we have arrived at a topic where citizens can claim something more than residents. So we have, but not as much more as one may suppose. It is common (though not universal) for liberal democratic states to restrict voting in national elections and the holding of high public office to citizens. While there is nothing that makes such a pattern morally obligatory, it is certainly morally permissible, in my view, provided that residents have proper access to naturalisation (a topic I take up in the next section). This sort of political activity is intimately connected to the idea of democratic citizenship, and we have recently been reminded in various parts of the world what tremendous importance people attach to the act of voting when they have been without it.

Some countries have begun to experiment with non-citizen residents voting in local elections, and, of course, the EU now mandates this for EU members, so it is hard to see the justification for excluding non-EU residents.

While voting is an important – symbolically the most important – form of political participation, there are many other ways that people participate politically and most of these ways are open to non-citizen residents and should be. For example, the expression of political opinions, in personal conversations or in written forums or in public speeches, and participation in public rallies are important kinds of political activity that non-citizens should be able to engage in. Most states also permit resident non-citizens to join political parties and to contribute time and money to political activities, presumably because they see such activities as intimately connected to basic civil liberties.

In sum, political rights are an area where it is easier to justify some differences between citizens and non-citizens, but even these differences are quite limited.

Naturalisation

Let me turn now to the question of what it is appropriate to expect of people who want to become citizens.[6] I want to argue that the only morally defensible arrangements regarding naturalisation are ones in which the applicant has a right to become naturalised once certain requirements have been met, rather than ones in which state authorities exercise some discretionary judgement about the applicant's acceptability. I want to argue further, and even more controversially, that the only requirement for naturalisation should be length of residence.

I suggest we distinguish between requirements, norms, and aspirations in the naturalisation process. Requirements refer to legally enforceable standards that must be met as a condition of naturalisation (such as length of residence, demonstrating a certain level of language proficiency, passing a test on the country's history and institutions, etc.). Norms refer to social expectations regarding the behaviour and attitudes of immigrants. These social expectations are not enforced legally, but they do have sanctions attached. Failure to meet them may evoke disapproval, perhaps even public criticism from other members of society, but will have no impact on legal eligibility for naturalisation. Finally, aspirations refer to hopes the receiving society has for the ways in which immigrants will adapt and the kinds of adaptation the society tries to foster without thinking it appropriate or even acceptable to criticise those who do not adapt in these ways. In my view, many of the things that are currently treated as legal requirements really belong in the second category (norms) and some belong only in the third (aspirations).

With respect to requirements then, I think the standards should be set very low. Indeed, as I just noted, I think that length of residence is the only standard that is ultimately justifiable for permanent residents. (By now this will be a familiar refrain.) I recognise that the standard I am proposing is not adopted as a general rule by any liberal democratic state, not even ones like Canada, Australia, and the United States that see themselves as countries of immigration, and it is still further from the practice of most other states. Nevertheless, I want to argue that, as a matter of fundamental justice, anyone who has resided lawfully in a liberal democratic state for an extended period of time (e.g., five years or more) ought to be entitled to become a citizen if he or she wishes to do so.

Why should the legal requirements be limited to residence? Once again, this is an argument about the moral priority of civil society in relation to political society. Living in a society is what makes a person a member of civil society. In living in a society one inevitably becomes involved in a dense network of social associations and acquires interests and identities tied up with other members of the society. Legal citizenship offers one important means by which those interests and identities can be protected and expressed. For many people it will seem an essential means.

Some will object that citizenship should be more than a means to private ends. Such a limited, instrumental conception of citizenship does not do justice to the political community and its needs for an active, engaged, committed citizenry. I understand and agree with this concern in many ways, but this more demanding conception of citizenship is not fit material for legal requirements either of current citizens or of potential ones. These are the sorts of concerns that we can make the subject of our aspirations and perhaps, to a lesser extent, of our expectations, but not of our requirements. We should not sacrifice the moral rights of particular individuals for the sake of such aspirations.

At the heart of the liberal democratic conception of politics is the notion that the state exists for the sake of the members of society, and that the fundamental interests of some members should not be sacrificed even if a majority would find that to their advantage. What makes a person a member of society with these kinds of claims against the state cannot depend on the state's own categories and practices. It depends instead on the social facts.

In many cases, the facts of social membership for non-citizens seem beyond dispute. Let me cite an example that is now familiar in discussions of citizenship. In Germany the descendants of Turkish guest workers have been generally excluded from citizenship. These are people who have been born and brought up in the society, whose parents may have been born and brought up in the same society, who may speak no other language and know no other home, but are nonetheless denied access to citizenship. It may be useful for us to consider why such a policy is morally objectionable. The answer, I think, is that these people are so obviously members of German civil society that it is wrong to exclude them from full political membership. Indeed, the Germans have begun to reform their citizenship laws in partial recognition of such claims.

Of course, to set five years as the threshold for this sort of membership is obviously a considerable leap from three generations, but it seems to me that the burden should be upon those who think much more should be required to say why. Whatever the length of time, there must be some sort of threshold within the life of a single individual after which additional time is unnecessary. So, a double *jus soli* rule is not an adequate solution. It is important to remember that I am talking about people who have been admitted on a permanent basis, i.e., with the right to live there as long as they want. In such a context, to exclude people from citizenship for an extended period seems deeply problematic from a democratic perspective.[7]

Most states, even ones with relatively easy naturalisation processes, have exams to test applicants' abilities in the official language, their knowledge of the history and government of the state they are seeking to join, and so on. When states seek to encourage naturalisation, these are not severe barriers, and so their presence is not a serious injustice. Nevertheless, I think they are undesirable.

Consider first naturalisation exams ostensibly designed to make sure that prospective citizens have the competence to participate in an informed and intelligent way. This sort of test never works very well regardless of the particular questions it asks. The tests are usually set at a very low level and so screen out very few people anyway. That's good from my perspective because it means the tests do less harm than they would if they were highly selective, but it also suggests that the tests don't actually function very effectively as screens. What about the few who do fail? Are we actually confident that they are not competent? My guess is that most who fail do so because of nervousness as much as lack of knowledge. Even if they don't know the answers, however, does that mean they are not competent to participate as citizens? The knowledge required for wise political judgement is complex, multifaceted, and often intuitive. It is not something that can be captured on a test of this sort. Moreover, we know that formal tests of this kind always have built in biases that inappropriately favor some class and cultural backgrounds over others, even if that is not intended. In sum, I am deeply sceptical about the capacity of any naturalisation exam to measure the competencies required for citizenship. All tests have flaws, of course, but sometimes we need them because we are obliged to sort and rank people for various purposes. In this case we have another alternative. We don't have to sort and rank. We can treat everyone equally.

My claim that language competence should not be used as a requirement for naturalisation is apt to be equally or more controversial. In my view, a person who has functioned in a society for several years without knowing its official language should be presumed to be capable also of participating in the political process without knowing that language. She will have many forms of information available from friends and neighbours and media in her own language, and that should be enough. One may wish and hope that citizens will be better informed, but it would be unreasonable to insist on a knowledge of the official language for the sake of an idealised form of political information that the average native-speaking citizen does not possess. The political knowledge of most citizens is heavily filtered through friends and neighbours and other trusted local sources, regardless of the language they speak. Moreover, we should not assume that minority language communities are monolithic in their political views or that local communities of native speakers are typically open to unconventional ideas and vigorous debate.

Some people may find length of residence a bit thin as a criterion of membership in civil society and prefer to emphasise labour market participation, participation in neighbourhood associations or other forms of more active engagement in civil society. These sorts of examples can certainly serve to bring home some of the many ways in which people are connected to one another in civil society and thus reinforce the sense of why access to citizenship may be both instrumentally necessary and associationally appropriate. Nevertheless, I want to be cautious about unduly emphasising forms of involvement in civil society that may be gender biased. Of course, many women also participate in the labour market or in neighbourhood associations, but some women are primarily involved in child rearing and household maintenance. These are forms of work that have generally been undervalued and sometimes excluded altogether from accounts of civil society through the construction of the family as a separate, private sphere, distinct from both civil society and political community. In fact, more careful attention to the way child rearing and household maintenance actually work would undoubtedly show that these activities also normally engage people in a dense network of social associations outside of the immediate family, but it seems to me that it would be a normative mistake to make a person's membership in civil society, and hence entitlement to citizenship, depend in any fundamental way on an empirical assessment of the number or quality of one's social interactions. It is one thing to construct social policies with the goal of helping people to escape from unwanted forms of social isolation, quite another to use social isolation, wanted or unwanted, as a criterion justifying exclusion from citizenship.

To avoid any misunderstanding let me distinguish the position I am defending here from what is sometimes described as a cosmopolitan view. Nothing in my argument rests on the proposition that we have to treat all human beings alike, that we cannot distinguish between members and strangers. My argument does not depend in any way on a claim that we are obliged to admit any immigrants who want to come. On the contrary, it rests on the fact that we have chosen to admit certain immigrants as permanent residents, and having admitted them to live among us on an ongoing basis, we are obliged not to marginalise them, not to exclude them from participating in shaping the choices and directions of society or from enjoying the fuller security and rights that citizenship brings. In sum, long term membership in civil society creates a moral right to political membership.

So, I would set the requirements threshold very low. What about the expectations imposed on immigrants? What sorts of norms can we establish? It is in the realm of norms rather than requirements that some of the concerns about language and values can be pursued. It is perfectly reasonable, in my view, to expect immigrants to send their children to schools where – if all goes well and as it is supposed to – they will learn the dominant language and will be encouraged to adopt liberal democratic values like tolerance, mutual respect, and so on. Of course, what students learn about liberal democratic values from the behaviour and attitudes of their teachers and fellow students is far more important than what they are taught in lectures and textbooks, so we need to be cautious about assuming that everything is fine if the right courses are in place, but in principle it is possible to justify this sort of expectation. I think it is also reasonable to expect that adult immigrants will try to learn the local language, so long as reasonable opportunities are provided and allowances made for the many different circumstances that affect people's capacities to acquire a new language. Finally, it is reasonable to expect immigrants to accept liberal democratic values as the principles that govern public life. That is about all we can reasonably expect, either of immigrants or citizens, as a matter of socially enforced norms.

What about loyalty, patriotism, and identity? Can't we expect immigrants to become attached to their new country? As an empirical matter we can, of course, because most do. As a normative matter, however, we should not try to impose such an expectation, much less make it a legal requirement. This is the sort of thing we can try to encourage and foster, but it's not the sort of thing we should try to command. In any event, such commands are probably doomed to failure. The heart does not normally respond well to coercion. If dual loyalties are a problem – and I think they are rarely a real problem – prohibitions of dual citizenship will do little to resolve them. People's feelings and identities may well remain divided, whatever legal status they choose.We can also hope to foster a more active form of citizenship. Again aspiration rather than requirement or norm is the right way to approach this sort of concern which is important but in tension with liberal norms about people's rights to choose their own ways of life and set their own priorities. Because of those liberal norms, even our aspirations ought to be severely limited. It would not be right, for example, to hope that Muslim immigrants would convert to Christianity or that gay immigrants would become straight. The commitment to respect individual freedom that is such a central part of liberal democratic ideals sets severe limits to the sorts of things that are an appropriate subject for collective concern, even in the form of aspirations.

Conclusion

In this final section, I want to address some possible objections to the basic enterprise of the paper. The first objection is that questions about citizenship are political not moral issues, and it is therefore inappropriate to use moral language in discussing them. I have heard this sort of objection on a number of occasions, and I confess I remain somewhat puzzled by it. Surely, there are some citizenship laws or policies that are appropriately labeled unjust, indeed whose injustice no one seriously disputes today. Think of the U.S. Supreme Court ruling that held that slavery was legal and that 'Negroes' (even if free) had no rights that whites were obliged to respect or the later ruling (after citizenship had been formally secured) that state imposed racial segregation was compatible with equal citizenship, or the Nazi Nuremberg laws, or the South African laws that excluded blacks from citizenship under the apartheid regime. To call such laws and practices unjust is to make a moral judgement.

A related objection takes the form of an assertion about sovereignty. Control over citizenship is at the heart of national sovereignty, people say. It establishes the boundaries within which questions of democratic politics and hence questions of liberal democratic justice arise. I think this sort of view confuses the issue of who has the right to exercise power with the question of whether power has been exercised rightly. We can accept both the idea of state sovereignty (other states should not interfere with a state's internal policies) and the idea of popular sovereignty (legitimate authority derives ultimately from the will of the people) without abandoning our capacity to make moral judgements and to criticise public policies, even of political communities to which we do not belong.

Another similar objection stems from the tendency among some political theorists to talk about rights and citizenship as if the two terms were inextricably linked. For example, Hannah Arendt claims in a famous passage that citizenship is essentially the right to have rights. (Arendt: 1958, 296) On some readings of Arendt (though I do not think they fully reflect her views), this implies that it is meaningless, or at least futile, to discuss the rights of non-citizens because having the status of citizenship is a necessary precondition for the secure enjoyment of any other legal rights. This is simply wrong as an empirical matter once one examines the well-established practices of contemporary liberal democratic states in which non-citizens enjoy many rights just as securely as citizens. Of course, even the rights of citizens are not always secure, but that simply reinforces the point I am making here that we should not assume that there is necessarily a radical disjuncture between the status of citizens and the status of all other residents of a state. It is possible to imagine that states would return to their former practices of drawing much sharper legal distinctions between citizens and non-citizens, but this possibility, merely as a hypothetical possibility, does not provide an adequate reason for regarding non-citizen rights as inevitably radically more contingent than citizen rights.

A final general objection to the enterprise rests on an argument from consent. On some accounts, whatever restrictions are placed on immigrants' rights are morally permissible so long as these are publicly announced and immigrants can reasonably be expected to know about them before they come. In choosing to come, the argument goes, immigrants – at least those who are not refugees – have consented to these restrictions and so waived whatever moral rights they might have had to equal treatment. I do not wish to deny entirely the moral relevance of the fact that (voluntary) immigrants have chosen to move. This may indeed partially justify certain kinds of adaptive demands by the receiving society, but such arguments must be used with great caution. In the first place, all consent arguments are limited by the principle that the consent of the parents cannot be construed as the consent of the children. More fundamentally, however, every plausible moral view sets some limits to consent. For example, no liberal democratic state permits people to sell their organs or to sell themselves into slavery. It is no doubt true, given the conditions in the world today, that many immigrants would readily agree to severe restrictions on their rights, even including terms of indentured servitude. Consent alone cannot legitimate that sort of arrangement, however. There are standards of fairness and justice beyond actual consent for assessing the ways in which states treat their own citizens and others. So, the mere fact that immigrants were informed in advance about the rules and restrictions would not make the rules and restrictions morally legitimate, not even if the immigrants were to say explicitly that they understand and accept them. States do indeed have an obligation to let the immigrants know what they expect, even if the expectations are morally permissible. To that extent the idea that informed choice matters is correct. But we have to employ independent moral standards for evaluating the legitimacy of the expectations themselves. At a minimum, they must be compatible with liberal democratic principles and respect for human rights to be morally defensible. Identifying what that entails has been the primary goal of this paper.

Appendix

In this appendix I want to make more explicit four features of my mode of inquiry in this paper. First, my approach is interpretive and contextual rather than foundational. I do not attempt to construct a theory of justice and situate my discussion of the ethics of immigration within that. Instead I start from the norms and practices of liberal democratic states and the principles and judgements of people committed to liberal democratic ideals. A contextual and interpretive approach is not uncritical, of course. Sometimes I begin with some concrete judgement or principle that I assume to be shared by my readers and then use that to interrogate another conventional practice or theoretical principle. Thus I use some features of the liberal democratic moral universe (which I take to be settled for these purposes) to call into question and criticise others.

Second, I am concerned primarily with questions about justice. Now justice talk is not the only sort of normative discourse. To talk about justice (or rights or obligations) is to focus on minimum moral standards. With this sort of language we try to identify what is morally prohibited and what is morally required, and thereby to mark out the range of the morally permissible. But there are other sorts of moral language as well, other virtues besides justice. When we ask what is good for a particular political community or what goals a state should pursue, we are asking normative questions. In addressing such questions, we may use words like wisdom, prudence, generosity and pride or terms like the common good or the national interest. This is clearly moral language but of a different sort from the first. In this discourse, which is closer to the ordinary language of politics, arguments about ideals, interests and identities tend to be intertwined.

The second sort of normative discourse rests, at least implicitly, upon the first in the sense that in making a claim about what is good for the community, people normally presuppose that the course being advocated falls within the range of the morally permissible. In fact most public policy debates within contemporary liberal democracies presuppose that the alternatives under consideration meet minimum moral standards. Of course, that presupposition can always be challenged. One can object that a policy is not only unwise but also unjust (or unjust even if otherwise in our interests).[8] For the most part in this paper I engage in the first sort of moral discourse. My goal is more to mark out the range of the morally permissible with respect to the treatment of non-citizens than to advocate particular choices within that range, though I do not entirely neglect the latter.

Third, I try to attend to the ways degrees matter in our moral judgements. Some issues are more important than others. Some departures from justice are more extreme than others. Moreover, it is important to take account not only of one's final judgement on an issue but also of the strength of competing considerations (even when they are outweighed). Degrees of certainty matter as well. In moral deliberations, what matters is not only the ultimate conclusion we reach but also relative importance of the issue, the considerations we regard as relevant, and the degree of confidence we feel in our judgements. These things matter because they affect our view of the range of reasonable disagreement which in turn affects our view of the kinds of differences that deserve respect (Gutmann and Thompson, 1996).

Fourth, my approach in the paper is comparative. I draw upon and evaluate the experiences of many different liberal democratic states. I do this with some trepidation. To evaluate the policies of states in which one is not a member raises questions of both capacity and standing. I have lived for extended periods in both Canada and the United States and have an intimate knowledge of and deep attachment to both societies. But I cannot claim the same familiarity with or connection to any European state. Who am I, as a North American, to criticise Europeans? In some parts of my argument, I advocate principles and policies that are much closer to the ones found in North America than to those in many European states. Some may see these arguments as a form of cultural imperialism, illegitimately projecting norms that may be appropriate for the histories and circumstances of North American societies onto European societies whose situations are very different. I regard that as a risk but one that is worth taking for two major reasons. First, general theoretical formulations about justice can sometimes impose blinkers that screen out some problems while addressing others and that can embody in disguised form moral insights that grow out of, and are only applicable to, particular contexts. One important way to reveal this is to confront these theories with concrete practices that seem just intuitively but are incompatible with the theoretical formulations. At the same time, an appeal to local circumstances, values and traditions is the first line of defence for every injustice. That is why we need to move back and forth between theory and practice. We need to confront our theories with the actual practices of states and to confront the practices of states with our theories. Second, comparative normative inquiry is something that we already engage in both as theorists and as ordinary citizens. States are neither moral nor intellectual islands. As theorists we read and evaluate the work of authors from other societies. We accept some arguments and reject others. As citizens we read about the practices of other societies and often form judgements, implicitly or explicitly. Sometimes we may conclude that a policy which is morally required in our own state may not be required in another. Other times we may conclude that what would be wrong in our own state would also be wrong elsewhere. The theoretical challenge is to articulate why and how we make these different judgements. It is a commonplace to say that history, context, and circumstances have to be taken into account in moral judgements. The crucial question is how they are to be taken into account and how much they matter. One way to answer that question is to evaluate the policies and practices of different states.[9]

References

Hannah Arendt, *The Origins of Totalitarianism*, 2nd ed., Cleveland, 1958.

Joseph H Carens,. 'Aliens and Citizens: The Case for Open Borders,' *Review of Politics* Vol. 49, No. 2, 1987, 251–273.

Joseph H Carens,.'Migration and Morality: A Liberal Egalitarian Perspective' in *Free Movement*, eds Brian Barry and Robert Goodin, London, 1992, 25–47.

Joseph H Carens 'Why Naturalisation Should Be Easy: A Response to Noah Pickus,' in *Immigration and Citizenship in the 21st Century*, ed. Noah Pickus, Lanham, Md., 1998, 141–146.

Joseph H. Carens, *Culture, Citizenship, and Community*, Oxford, 2000.

Amy Gutmann and Dennis Thompson, *Democracy and Disagreement*, Cambridge, Mass., 1996.

Ruth Rubio-Marin, *Immigration as a Democratic Challenge*, Cambridge, 2000.

Peter Schuck, 'The Transformation of Immigration Law,' *Columbia Law Review* 34, 1984, 1–90.

Yasemin N. Soysal, Limits of Citizenship: Migrants and Postnational Membership in Europe, Chicago, 1994.

Notes

1. For other purposes, one might want to challenge this assumption. See Carens: 1987.
2. I use the masculine pronoun advisedly here because most criminals are male.
3. In fact, it is not always true. Some of those deported are not hardened criminals. Others may not be guilty at all. I want to assume here, as a way of taking up the harder challenge, that the convicted non-citizens are in fact guilty. But, at least in North America, it is not uncommon for people, especially racial minorities, accused of crimes to be held without bail for several months and then offered an official plea bargain in which they will be sentenced only to the time already served if they plead guilty and will face the risk of years of incarceration if they insist on their innocence but are subsequently convicted by a criminal justice system that has already indicated its doubts by keeping them in jail for an extended period. They receive legal counsel from greatly overworked lawyers who have their own incentives for settling quickly. The clients, and sometimes even the lawyers, do not always understand that a guilty plea will make them liable for deportation. Nevertheless, I set this sort of problem aside in the discussion above, because there is no doubt that many of those convicted are in fact guilty, and my aim is to show that even they do not deserve to be deported.
4. This generalisation should be qualified by recognition of the fact that non-citizens enjoyed local voting rights in the nineteenth century in some jurisdictions although these were gradually eliminated.
5. Indeed, even citizens who reside abroad may not be entitled to some of these rights (e.g., access to social programs) if they have returned only on a temporary basis and are not establishing residence.
6. Parts of this section are adapted from Carens: 1998.
7. For a sustained and careful elaboration of this position see Rubio-Marin: 2000.
8. At the time of the Vietnam War, for example, many American opponents of the war contended that the war was unjust, but others based their opposition on the claim that the war was not in the national interest of the U.S. or unwise in other ways.
9. For a further discussion of this approach to political theory, see Carens: 2000.

II

DUAL CITIZENSHIP IN GERMANY

CHAPTER 5

GERMANY'S CITIZENSHIP LAW UNDER IMMIGRATION PRESSURE

Kay Hailbronner

Germany as a *de facto* country of immigration: some facts

By the end of 1998 there were 7.32 million foreign nationals living in Germany, accounting for 9 percent of the German Population (*Beauftragte*: 1997, 7). The largest groups of foreigners living in Germany came from Turkey with 2.11 million (28.8 %), the Federal Republic of Yugoslavia with 719,474 (9.8 %), from Italy with 612,048 (8.4 %), from Greece with 363,514 (5 %), from Poland with 283,604 (3.9 %), from Croatia with 208,909 (2.9 %), from Bosnia with 190,119 (2.6 %) and from Austria with 185,159 (2.5 %). Only 25.1 percent of all foreigners living in Germany were nationals from EU Member States. A survey of the foreign population shows that most foreigners living in Germany have done so for a long time. By the end of 1997, approximately 30 percent of all foreigners had been in Germany for 20 years or more, 40 percent for at least 15 years and almost 50 percent for more than 10 years.[1] The pattern is even more marked when we look at the nationals of the former 'recruitment' states. Almost two thirds of all Turks and Greeks, 71 percent of Italians and 80 percent of Spaniards have lived in Germany for more than 10 years. Of all foreigners 8.59 million (21.7 %) were born in Germany; among those foreigners of less than eighteen years, 1.11 million (65.4 %) were born in Germany. All demographic surveys forecast a substantial increase in Germany's foreign population over the next thirty years (Münz and Ulrich: 1997). Assuming net migration of approximately 190,000 foreigners per year on this basis (the average level of net migration witnessed for the past thirty-five years), the number of foreigners living in Germany will increase to 12.6 million by 2030; this figure would constitute 16.9 percent, in contrast to 8.9 percent of this population (Münz and Ulrich: 1997, 57). In the event of a substantial increase of naturalisations from 60,000 per year to 120,000 per year, the share of foreigners would increase to 14.6 percent (in absolute numbers 10.9 million) (Münz and Ulrich: 1997, 557).

The figures show a basic dilemma of German immigration policy: an increasing number of children of migrant workers are born in Germany and grow up in Germany, take their schooling and professional formation in Germany, will eventually work in Germany and yet have children of 'foreign' nationality in Germany. The children will be 'foreign nationals', although their citizenship has frequently become only an emotional attachment to the home country of their parents, and is sometimes considered a mere reassurance, a sort of 'alternate' nationality. There is, in principle, no dispute about the need to integrate large parts of the foreign population into Germany by encouraging them to become German citizens. All German governments have declared that there is a public interest in the naturalisation of foreigners living permanently in Germany.[2] There is no consensus, however, on the means through and conditions under which German citizenship should be acquired. It is particularly the issue of acquisition of German citizenship through birth on German territory, which would introduce an element of *jus soli* into the German citizenship conception, that has given rise to a heated controversy between the major political parties in recent years, until recently blocking any reform of the German Citizenship Law. An attempt to solve the fundamental dilemma arising from the exclusion of a substantial part of the population from political rights by granting limited voting rights at the local level to foreigners in some of the *Länder* has failed due to the decision of the Federal Constitutional Court declaring such an attempt to be unconstitutional (*Decisions of the Federal Constitutional Court*, 51). The Court stated that the concept of democracy as laid down in the Basic Law, the German Constitution, does not permit a disassociation of political rights from the concept of nationality. Nationality therefore is the legal prerequisite for the acquisition of the political rights that legitimise the exercise of all power in the Federal Republic of Germany. The Court, however, also stated that the only possible approach to solving the gap between the permanent population and democratic participation lies in changing the nationality law, e.g., by facilitating the acquisition of German nationality by foreigners who are living permanently in Germany and who have thereby become subject to German sovereignty in a manner comparable to German nationals (*Decisions*, 51).

Basic principles of German law on nationality and citizenship

The core of the German Citizenship legislation is the *Reichs-und Staatsangehörigkeitsgesetz* of 1913. Although it has been amended repeatedly, particularly by laws in 1955 and 1956 aimed at introducing equal treatment of men and women and by laws in 1990 and 1993 designed to facilitate the naturalisation of immigrants, its basic principles remained in effect until 2000. Under the 1913 law, German citizenship is basically acquired by descent, by legitimisation, by adoption or by naturalisation. According to § 4, a child acquires German citizenship by descent from a German mother or a German father. In the absence of a marriage, descent by a German father requires a formal procedure to determine fatherhood. Acquisition by naturalisation for foreigners living in Germany requires certain minimum requirements, notably the absence of criminal prosecution, the possibility to make a living and adequate accommodation. If these minimum requirements are fulfilled, the authorities have a wide discretion over whether to grant naturalisation. Administrative discretion is determined by binding administrative guidelines, which are enacted by the Federal Ministry of the Interior in accordance with the interior ministers of the *Länder* (*Einbürgerungsrichtlinien vom* 1. 7. 77, see Hailbronner and Renner: 1998, p. 863 ff). According to the Administrative Guidelines, the applicant must present sufficient evidence of having been a legal resident in Germany for at least 10 years. In addition, an attachment to Germany is required as well as a certain knowledge of the German language. A candidate for naturalisation must also not be opposed to the ideas inherent in the Basic Law of the Federal Republic of Germany. The requirement to give up a former nationality is not a binding legal requirement but is laid down in the Administrative Guidelines as a reflection of the general requirement of proof of attachment to the German way of life and the country's legal and social order. Therefore, dual nationality has always been considered to be inconsistent with the concept of loyalty and attachment to Germany.

Based on the belief that naturalisation is an exception rather than a regular procedure terminating a process of immigration,[3] discretionary naturalisations based on article 8 of the Nationality Act of 1913 have remained a rather exceptional measure. This is the case for the substantial number of migrant workers who had been recruited in the beginning of the 1970s and who were originally thought of as temporary workers who would eventually return to their home countries. Only about twelve thousand to seventeen thousand persons were naturalised each year from 1974 until 1989, in spite of an increasing number of persons having their permanent residence in Germany.

Spouses of German citizens had always been in a privileged position under the law of 1913. Originally, foreign women marrying a German national acquired German citizenship automatically while foreign husbands had a possibility of being naturalised. With the equal treatment legislation of 1969, spouses of German nationals acquired a right of naturalisation provided that they renounced their previous nationality and they fulfilled certain requirements of integration into the German living conditions. In the context of a general debate about Germany's immigration policy and its factual change into an immigration country, pressure increased in the late 1980s for a reform of German citizenship legislation. There were numerous proposals ranging from simplifying the naturalisation process and increasing the acceptance of multiple nationality to introducing a *jus soli* 'principle' for third generation foreigners born in Germany.[4] The *Bundestag* decided in 1990 to substantially facilitate the acquisition of German citizenship for young foreigners of ages 16 to 23, provided that they renounced their previous citizenship, had lived permanently and lawfully in Germany for 8 years, had attended a school in Germany for at least 6 years and had not been prosecuted for a criminal offence. In addition, the acquisition of German citizenship for the first generation of recruited migrant workers was also facilitated substantially by giving a right to acquisition of German citizenship, provided that certain requirements are met:

1. renunciation of previous nationality
2. absence of criminal conviction
3. capability to earn a living.

By a further amendment in December 1993, these rules were changed through establishing an individual right entitling every foreigner fulfilling certain requirements to demand naturalisation (Hailbronner: 1999a, article T 5, 1 ff). Although these provisions of the Aliens Act granting an entitlement to German citizenship still provided for a renunciation of the previous nationality, a number of exceptions were made which led in practice to a steadily increasing number of naturalisations with dual nationality. Exceptions were granted 'for instance' if a foreigner could not renounce his previous nationality or could do so only under particularly difficult conditions, especially if the original home country required military service before giving up nationality.

The recent figures show a substantial increase of naturalisations based on these provisions (See tables 5.3 and 5.4). The general number of naturalisations in 1995 increased to 313,606 compared to 34,913 in 1985.[5] However, it must be recognised that this figure includes a substantial number of naturalisations of foreigners who can be considered 'Germans' who acquire German citizenship very easily on the basis of a special provision. This provision gives them a constitutional right to obtain German citizenship as a refugee or expellee of German ethnic origin or as their spouse or descendant, provided that they had been admitted to the territory of the German Reich within the frontiers of December 31, 1937. Nevertheless, in

1990 naturalisations based upon the provisions of the Aliens Act for the immigrant population increased at a rate of approximately thirty-five percent compared to the preceding year. In 1994 this increased to fifty-four percent, levelling out somewhat, so that in 1995 the rate was only twenty-three percent, and in 1996, twenty percent.[6] With 1.18 percent of the total foreign population, the rate of naturalisations in 1996 was still relatively small compared to other western European states, although it had quadrupled since 1986. The share of women was substantially higher with 1.37 percent than the share of men with 1.03 percent.

Of a total of 82,913 naturalisations based primarily upon the provisions of the Aliens Act (§§ 85, 86) included: 39,111 (47.2%) Turkish nationals; 4,010 (4.8 %) Moroccans; 3,119 (3.8 %) Vietnamese; 1,989 (2.4 %) nationals from the Federal Republic of Yugoslavia; 1,942 (2.3 %) Polish; 1,789 (2.2 %) Croatians; 1,677 (2.0 %) Tunisians; 1,547 (1.9 %) Romanians; 1,454 (1.9 %) Afghans; 1,382 (1.7 %) Eritreans; 1,362 (1.6 %) Sri Lankans; 1,176 (1.4 %) Palestinians; 1,134 (1.4 %) Lebanese, and 1,118 (1.3 %) Italians.

There are very different naturalisation rates for the different nationalities. The Tunisians with 6.60 percent, the Moroccans with 4.78 percent and the Vietnamese with 3.55 percent have a relatively high naturalisation rate. Afghans (2.19 %), Turks (1.86 %) and Hungarians (1.29 %) are in a middle group. Very low rates of naturalisation were registered with Croatians (0.87 %), Iranians (0.81 %), Yugoslavs (0.28%), Italians (0.18 %) and Greeks (0.10 %). One of the reasons for these differences is obviously that EU citizens do not have a substantial interest in acquiring German citizenship as a result of union citizenship. Another reason for lower rates may be that certain states do not easily release their citizens from their original nationality. This usually implies a very difficult process for acquisition of German nationality while maintaining a previous nationality.

Statistics also show that there is a substantial number of dual nationals living in Germany which has steadily increased as a result of manifold exceptions made under the new provisions of the Aliens Act.

Of a total of 79,442 naturalisations (excluding Hamburg) in 1997 based upon the provisions of the Aliens Act, 17,423 (21.3 %) have been granted with the acceptance of dual nationality. Dual nationality has been particularly tolerated in the case of Iranians (90.1 %), Greeks (87.2 %), Moroccans (89 %), Eritreans (88.5 %), Lebanese (83.3 %), Afghans (82.7 %), Tunisians (82.3 %), Syrians (76.0 %), Bosnians (74.8 %) and Yugoslavs (63 %). Frequently, dual nationality is accepted in cases in which a release of the original nationality is dependent upon conditions that are difficult to fulfil. In spite of a substantial softening of Turkish laws on property, military service and heritage, dual nationality has been granted in the case of Turks in 8.45 percent of all cases. These figures, however, only partly reflect the reality of dual nationality, for two reasons. First, official statistics on the acceptance of dual nationality also register those naturalisations in which dual nationality has only been accepted temporarily, which means that naturalisation has been granted under the condition that the person deposit a formal application for renunciation of a previous citizenship. On the other hand, the true number of dual nationals in the case of the Turkish population may be even higher, because in many cases, Turkish citizenship was only formally renounced and, with the cooperation of the Turkish authorities, readily reacquired after naturalisation. This was made possible by a provision in German nationality law providing for a loss of German citizenship as a result of the acquisition of a foreign nationality *only* if the German national had a permanent residence abroad. Thus, Turks living in Germany would not lose their German citizenship if they reacquired their Turkish nationality immediately after formally renouncing their Turkish nationality. It was an open secret that Turkish authorities encouraged the reacquisition of Turkish nationality, since the Turkish concept of nationality is based on the idea that persons of Turkish origin should remain attached to the Turkish state through Turkish citizenship. It seems that this practice has only recently been changed, under the pressure of the German authorities, to prevent an 'abuse' of German legislation. There are estimates that a high percentage of Turkish nationals who have been naturalised are in fact dual nationals. Therefore, the debate about dual nationality as the major obstacle for a reform of the German citizenship law may justifiably be considered obsolete and unrealistic.

Proposals for reform

A quasi-nationality for immigrant children

According to a coalition agreement between the Christian Democratic Party (CDP) and the Liberal Party (FDP) of 1994, a special nationality for third generation children (*Kinderstaatsangehörigkeit*[7]) born in Germany was proposed. In order to be eligible for this special nationality, which was intended to ensure equal treatment between German nationals (through a German identity card), at least one of the children's parents would have to be born in Germany and both would have to reside lawfully in Germany during the ten years preceding the child's birth. Additionally, both parents would have to be entitled to an unlimited residence permit. The 'quasi-nationality' for children would require an application by parents before the child's twelfth birthday. With the child's eighteenth birthday, it would acquire full German nationality unless its previous nationality was not given up. It is very doubtful whether the proposal is practicable and whether a 'quasi-nationality' would be acceptable in international relations. The effects of such a limited nationality on, for instance, the application of international treaties relating to visa and travel documents is also unclear (*efms*, p. 11 and 19; Lübbe-Wolff: 1996, 57; Ziemske: 1995a, 380, 381).

Acquisition of German nationality by jus soli

According to a proposal of the *Bundesrat*, the upper house of Parliament (*Bundestagsdrucksache* 13/8157), German nationality would be acquired automatically by children whose foreign parents were born in Germany and who possessed a residence permit at the time of the child's birth. Children whose parents dispose of an unlimited residence permit and have been living in Germany for five years were to be given a right to naturalisation. In both cases, the acquisition of German citizenship would be independent of the renunciation of a previous nationality. The proposals of the Social Democratic Party and the Green Party go in the same direction. The Social Democratic Party has suggested supplementing the principle whereby German nationality is acquired by descent with the principle of territoriality (*jus soli*). Children of foreign parents therefore ought to automatically acquire German citizenship as a result of birth on German territory, provided that at least one parent has been born in Germany and has secured his or her permanent residence in Germany. Dual nationality is not to be prevented in such cases. Additionally, for permanent residents, individual rights to the acquisition of German nationality are to be created independently of a renunciation of their previous nationality. The draft suggests a facilitation of naturalisation for the following groups of citizens:

1. Foreigners with a permanent residence permit after 8 years of residence.
2. Foreigners belonging to the so-called 'second generation' of aliens who have grown up in Germany.
3. Spouses of Germans after three years of lawful residence, provided that they have been married for at least two years.

Additionally, the proposal provides for a facilitation of discretionary naturalisation which should be triggered after a residence of five years and be dependent only upon a capacity to earn a living, an absence of a criminal conviction for a serious offence and an absence of a reason for expulsion for endangering public safety or violent behaviour (see *Bundestagsdrucksache* 13/259).

A 'compromise' has been worked out by the Liberal Party, providing for the acquisition of full nationality at birth on German territory if both parents apply and at least one of the parents does have a right of residence in Germany. The Liberal Party proposal suggests a loss of dual nationality by obliging the naturalised person to opt for one nationality once that person has reached the age of twenty-one. If the previous (dual) nationality is not renounced, German nationality will be forfeited.[8]

The Greens' proposal

The proposal of the Green Party (*Bundestagsdrucksache* 13/3657; *Bundestagsdrucksache* 13/7677), a modified form of which found its way into the law taking effect on 1 January 2000, goes even further in the direction of an automatic acquisition of German citizenship on the basis of *jus soli*. The Green Party suggested that children of foreign parents were to acquire German citizenship automatically by birth on German territory if one parent is living in Germany with a permanent residence permit. Neither the application of a parent, nor the renunciation of a previous citizenship would be required for the acquisition of German citizenship. None of these proposals has received the necessary majority in the German *Bundestag* (see *Bundestagsdrucksache* 13/130 of March 4, 1998). Although a number of deputies from the Christian Democratic Party and the Liberal Party were in favour of some of the proposals submitted by the draft law in the *Bundesrat*, no majority was achieved and the circumstances of submitting the draft law were primarily directed towards splitting the coalition between the Christian Democratic Party and the Liberal Party.

Pros and cons

Although there is a consensus about the need to integrate second and third generation foreigners by facilitating the acquisition of German citizenship, opinion is deeply divided on the issue of whether this should be achieved by introducing elements of *jus soli* and/or accepting dual nationality. Difficulties arise with regard to constitutional law as well as international treaties, such as the 1963 Council of Europe Convention on the reduction of dual nationality.

Objections on the grounds of constitutional law are voiced in particular against the proposal for temporary dual nationality that is to be terminated automatically at the age of 18. Article 16 (1) of the Basic Law provides that nobody may be deprived of their German citizenship. Loss of citizenship may only occur pursuant to the law, and only against the will of those affected if they do not thereby become stateless. This provision, which is basically a reaction against Nazi legislation depriving Jews of their German citizenship, may be an obstacle to the technique of granting German citizenship which will be withdrawn if the dual national renounces his previous nationality at the age of 18. Whether an automatic loss of German citizenship as a result of maintaining the nationality of another state amounts to a 'deprivation' in the sense of the Basic Law is very much disputed (Lübbe-Wolff: 1996, 57, 59; Ziemske: 1995b, 273; *Decision of the Federal Constitutional Court* of June 22, 1990, *Neue Juristische Wochenschrift*: 1990, 2193; Kokott; Pieroth). Be that as it may, a number of practical problems will have to be solved in implementing temporary dual nationality. It will be necessary to introduce exceptions to the obligation to give up another nationality based upon those exceptions that are already admissible under existing legislation. This means that in every individual case an examination will have to take place as to whether a second or third generation foreigner is entitled to maintain dual nationality. A number of protracted and difficult legal proceedings can be easily foreseen.

A major debate has been focused upon the issue of dual nationality. It has been argued that dual nationality is inconsistent with integration and a certain loyalty towards the state. In addition, problems relating to diplomatic protection and the application of international treaties may arise in cases of dual nationality. Finally, increased acceptance of dual nationality may result in unjustified privileges in comparison to individuals with only one nationality (on this, see Blumenwitz: 1993,151; Löwer: 1993, 156, 158; von Mangoldt: 1993, 965; Marx: 1997, 67, 73; Badura, von Mangoldt and Löwer in *Protokoll*: 1993, Protokoll No. 75, 256, 43 and 164; an overview is offered by the *Wissenschaftliche Dienste*: 1996, 14).

The principle of avoidance of dual nationality has repeatedly been confirmed by the Constitutional Court, which has argued that dual nationality may lead to loyalty conflicts and uncertainty concerning diplomatic protection. The Court is frequently quoted for a doctrine laid down in its jurisprudence:

'It is accurate to say that dual or multiple nationality is regarded, both domestically and internationally, as an evil that should be avoided or eliminated if possible in the interest of states as well as in the interest of the affected citizen: most international conventions in the field of nationality concern this subject or at least attempt to ameliorate the difficulties that arise out of the possession of several nationalities . . . States seek to achieve exclusivity of their respective nationalities in order to set clear boundaries for their sovereignty over persons . . . they want to be secure in the duty of loyalty of their citizens which extends if necessary as far as risking one's life and do not want to see it endangered by possible conflicts with a loyalty owed to a foreign state. Accordingly, the duty of military service provides the principal reason for avoiding dual nationality. Conflicts between the two countries of nationality can also arise from such inconsistent duties and from competitive assertions of diplomatic protection, agencies and courts of third states face the problem of deciding which of the two nationalities they should give priority. (BT-Drs. 12/2035: 1992)

It seems doubtful, however, whether the traditional arguments voiced against dual nationality outweigh the need to integrate second and third generation foreigners into the political system of the Federal Republic. As a more practical argument, one may point to the steadily increasing numbers of dual nationals who are in fact living in Germany and so far have not created substantial problems in the application of international treaties or in the exercise of diplomatic protection. There is in fact no precise account of the exact number of dual nationals. Originally, dual nationality had to be registered. This was given up some years ago, and, therefore nobody knows the exact number of dual nationals. One can assume, however, that following the heavily increasing numbers of mixed marriages the number of dual nationals has grown substantially, particularly since, as a rule, children obtain the nationality of those parents by law.

As for the argument about loyalty, the concept of the German State has undergone substantial changes through both the immigration of a large foreign population and the process of European integration. As a *de facto* immigration country, Germany cannot ignore the fact that part of its population consists of migrant workers and their children. The basis of German nationality can no longer be seen in the attachment to the idea of a nation with a homogenous cultural identity, primarily transferred by descent. One may note, however, that the common observation that German nationality law is based upon blood is an incorrect interpretation of existing legislation. That German nationality is not exclusively based on 'blood' can easily be shown by the naturalisation provisions mentioned earlier. However, a different concept of German nationhood does not necessarily mean that pure *jus soli* should be introduced or that requirements of integration into the German society should be abandoned. There is a legitimate concern that foreigners joining the 'Club' fulfil those requirements, which are necessary to ensure integration into the social, political and economic order. One may therefore reasonably be asked to prove German language knowledge and absence of criminal convictions in order to acquire German citizenship. Under these conditions, however, dual nationality does not appear as serious an obstacle to naturalisation.

Still, dual or multiple nationality may create the problem of transferring nationality to descendants who may have little or no tie to Germany. With the reform of German citizenship law, the issue of the loss of German citizenship through permanent residence abroad will have to be solved. There should be an automatic loss of German citizenship for dual nationals if permanent residence is established abroad. That will, however, create constitutional problems in relation to the provision of article 16 (1) on deprival of German citizenship.

The debate concerning the introduction of *jus soli* is even more controversial. Proponents of the introduction of *jus soli* argue that problems relating to unequal treatment and growing discrimination can only be solved through an automatic acquisition of German nationality for third generation foreigners born on German territory. On the other hand, it may be argued that acquisition of German citizenship on the basis of *jus soli* has always been alien to the German nation, which never considered itself as a country of immigration. The fact that Germany has become a *de facto* country of immigration does not necessarily argue in favour of changing its basic rules as to who should be admitted to German citizenship. From a practical point of view, the disadvantage of *jus soli* is that it excludes any examination of whether there is a sufficient prospect of integration. One may object that the requirement of being born in Germany in connection with residence rights of parents should be sufficient to indicate integration. Recent experience, however, shows that this assumption is not always correct. An increasing number of foreigners are deliberately rejecting any attempt to integrate into German society. It is likely that children under these circumstances will not be integrated easily.

Recent developments and the new law of 15 July 1999

A renewal of the discussion was provoked when the coalition agreement of the Social Democrats and *Bündnis 90/Die Grünen* of 20 October 1998 was presented to the public. According to the coalition's intentions, German citizenship was to be conferred at birth to children born on German territory if one foreign parent was already born on German territory or if that parent entered Germany before the age of fourteen. It further provided that, in both cases, he or she must have a residence permit (*Aufenthaltser-laubnis*). Other amendments intended by the coalition were a facilitation of the naturalisation process when applying on the grounds of an entitlement to German citizenship. It was proposed that naturalisation be allowed if the foreigner is able to sustain himself and his dependants, if there are no convictions for criminal offences and, finally, if no grounds for expulsion or deportation have arisen. In addition, the residence requirement was to be reduced from fifteen to eight years. Other proposed amendments related to a right to naturalisation for minors and a reduction of the residence requirement to three years for spouses of German nationals. Dual or multiple nationality was to be accepted in all those cases (on dual and multiple nationality, see Hailbronner: 1999b).

Those intentions, however, have not been fully realised, although the first draft presented by the Ministry of the Interior provided for a broad acceptance of dual and multiple nationality and the introduction of the *jus soli* principle (*Zeitschrift für Ausländerrecht*: 1999, 50, 95; Barwig et al: 1999). Due to changing majorities in Parliament, a new proposal was submitted by the Social Democrats, *Bündnis 90/Die Grünen* and the Liberal Party (FDP) comprising not only the introduction of the *jus soli* principle, but also the insertion of the 'optional model'. Both chambers went on to adopt this draft with minor changes (*Bundestagsdrucksache* 14/867) in May 1999.[9] The new law on the reform of the German citizenship law of 15 July 1999 became law on 1 January 2000 (*Bundesgesetzblatt* I, 1618; on the amendments Hailbronner: 1999 c; Huber and Butzke: 1999, 2769 ff). In addition, administrative guidelines for its application are to be adopted.

One of the major changes is the introduction of the *jus soli* principle in § 4 of the German Nationality Law, the *Staatsangehörigkeitsgesetz* (StAG), meaning that a child of foreign parents acquires German citizenship under the condition that one parent has legally had their habitual residence in Germany for eight years and that he or she is in the possession of a residence permit, an '*Aufenthaltsberechtigung*' or an unlimited '*Aufenthaltser-laubnis*' for three years; the model of the double *jus soli* in force in some other European states has not therefore been introduced. Foreign children legally residing in Germany are entitled to naturalisation upon completion of the eighth year if the above-mentioned conditions had been fulfilled at the time of birth (§ 40b StAG). Due to the fact that children usually acquire the nationality of their parents by descent, the introduction of the *jus soli* principle will entail at least dual, if not multiple, nationalities for foreign children born in Germany. Therefore, § 29 StAG introduces the highly disputed optional model and the duty to decide upon completion of the eighteenth year which nationality to keep and which to renounce. If the young adult declares that he intends to keep his foreign nationality or if he does not declare anything upon completion of the eighteenth year, he will suffer the loss of his German citizenship. If the person, on the other hand, declares an intention to keep his German citizenship, the young adult is obliged to prove the loss or renunciation of the foreign nationality (§ 29 (2) StAG) unless German authorities have formally approved the retention of his foreign nationality. According to § 29 (4) StAG, this permission to retain the former nationality (*Beibehaltungsgenehmigung*) is to be issued if renunciation of the foreign nationality is either impossible or unreasonable or if – in the case of naturalisation – multiple nationality would be accepted according to § 87 AuslG (Aliens Act).

As well as the introduction of the *jus soli* principle, the naturalisation process has been facilitated. The foreigner now is entitled to naturalisation after a residence of eight years, rather than fifteen, under the condition that he declares himself bound to the free and democratic order of the constitution (*'freiheitliche und demokratische Grundordnung'*), that he is in the possession of a residence permit (*'Aufenthaltserlaubnis'* or *'Aufenthalts-berechtigung'*), that he is capable of earning a living without any recourse to public assistance or unemployment benefits (except in those cases in which the dependence on those benefits is not attributable to the applicant's fault or negligence), that there is no criminal conviction and, finally, that loss or renunciation of the previous nationality take place. Dual nationality is accepted in more cases, e.g., if the applicants are elderly persons and dual nationality is the only obstacle to naturalisation, if the dismissal of the previous nationality is related to disproportionate difficulties, and if a denial of the application to naturalisation would constitute a particular hardship (§ 87 (1) no. 4 AuslG). Moreover, dual nationality is accepted in cases in which the renunciation of the previous nationality entails – in addition to the loss of civil rights – economic or financial disadvantages (No. 5), or in the case of EU-citizens, provided that reciprocity exists (§ 87 (2) AuslG). According to the new § 86 AuslG, naturalisation is not permissible if the foreigner does not demonstrate sufficient knowledge of the German language, or if there is actual evidence that the applicant pursues or supports activities contrary to the constitution.

Due to the fact that the acquisition of German citizenship has been facilitated, some amendments relate to the loss of German citizenship and the limitation of acquisition by descent. On the one hand, acquisition of German citizenship abroad is excluded if the German parent who has his habitual residence abroad was born abroad after 31 December 1999, except in those cases in which statelessness would be the consequence. Despite this provision, the acquisition of German citizenship remains possible if both parents are in the possession of German citizenship or if the one parent who has German citizenship notifies the competent diplomatic representation at the time of birth. According to the amended § 25 StAG, the loss of German citizenship, which did not occur automatically at naturalisation if the person continued to have a vital interest in Germany, now should also apply in those cases in which the applicant continues to live in Germany when acquiring another nationality.

After years of discussion, new provisions concerning the German citizenship law have finally been adopted. Nevertheless, some issues concerning legal aspects are still under discussion.[10] Other aspects relate to the implementation of the new provisions, especially the handling of the duty to opt for or against German nationality at the age of eighteen and the fact that, besides some practical problems, this might be the starting point for a broad acceptance of dual and multiple nationality in those cases.[11] Thus, in the future, further reforms, particularly relating to dual nationality, the acquisition of German citizenship when returning to the country of origin, and the assertion of minority rights, have to be discussed. It should be noted, however, that although changes in citizenship law might influence the integration of foreigners, they are not by themselves a sufficient means to integration. The main objective should be the active participation of Germany's resident aliens in political life.

References

G. Apel, 'Gedanken zu einem zuwanderungspolitischen Konzept,' *Zeitschrift für Ausländerrecht*, 1992, 99–111.

K. Barwig et al. (eds.), *Neue Regierung – neue Ausländerpolitik?*, Baden-Baden, 1999.

Beauftragte der Bundesregierung für Ausländerfragen, *Daten und Fakten zur Ausländersituation*, eighteenth ed., Bonn, June 1999, 7 (Government Commissioner for Issues Concerning Foreign Nationals in Germany).

D. Blumenwitz, 'Territorialitätsprinzip und Mehrstaatigkeit,' *Zeitschrift für Ausländerrecht*, 1993, 151–156.

Bundestagsdrucksache 13/3657 – *Mindestkriterien für eine Reform des StaatsangehörigkeitsrechtsBundestagsdrucksache* 13/7677 – *für eine sofortige Reform des Staatsangehörigkeitsrechts*.

BT-Drs. 12/2035, *Antwort der Bundesregierung auf eine Kleine Anfrage der Abgeordneten Ulla Jelpke und der Gruppe PDS/Linke Liste*, 1992.

Decisions of the Federal Constitutional Court, Vol. 83, 31 October 1990, 37–60.

efms (Europäisches Forum für Migrationsstudien), *Staatsangehörigkeit und Einbürgerung*, Bamberg, 1995.

H. Eylmann, 'Rechtspolitische Zielsetzungen der CDU/ CSU in der 13. Legislaturperiode,' *Zeitschrift für Rechtspolitik*, 1995, 161–165.

K. Hailbronner and G. Renner, *Staatsangehörigkeitsrecht*, second ed., Munich, 1998, third edition forthcoming.

K. Hailbronner, *Ausländerrecht, Kommentar*, Heidelberg, March 1999a.

K. Hailbronner, 'Doppelte Staatsangehörigkeit', *Zeitschrift für Ausländerrecht*, 1999b, 51–58.

K. Hailbronner 'Die Reform des deutschen Staatsangehörigkeitsrechts,' *Neue Zeitschrift für Verwaltungsrecht*, 1999c, 1273–1280.

S. Hobe, 'Das Staatsvolk nach dem Grundgesetz,' *Juristenzeitung*, 1994, 191–195.

P. M. Huber and K. Butzke, 'Das neue Staatsangehörigkeitsrecht und sein verfassungsrechtliches Fundament,' *Neue Juristische Wochenschrift*, 1999, 2769–2775.

H.U. Jessurun d'Oliveira, 'Tendenzen im Staatsangehörigkeitsrecht', *Zeitschrift für Ausländerrecht*, 1990, 114–119.

B. John, 'Vom Stammesangehörigen zum Clubmitglied-Plädoyer für weitere Einbürgerungserleichterungen', *Zeitschrift für Ausländerrecht*, 1991, 81–86.

J. Kokott, in Sachs (ed.), *Grundgesetz, Kommentar*, Article 16, No. 11, München, 1999.

S. Leutheusser-Schnarrenberger, 'Liberale Rechtspolitik in der 13. Legislaturperiode', *Zeitschrift für Rechtspolitik*, 1995, 81–85.

W. Löwer, 'Abstammungsprinzip und Mehrstaatigkeit', *Zeitschrift für Ausländerrecht*, 1993, 156–160.

G. Lübbe-Wolff, 'Entziehung und Verlust der deutschen Staatsangehörigkeit- Art. 16 I GG', *Juristische Ausbildung*, 1996, 57–64.

H. von Mangoldt, 'Ius sanguinis- und ius soli- Prinzip in der Entwicklung des deutschen Staatsangehörigkeitsrechts,' *Das Standesamt*, 1994, 33–42.

R. Marx, 'Reform des Staatsangehörigkeitsrechts: Mythische oder rechtlich begründete Hindernisse?', *Zeitschrift für Ausländerrecht*, 1997, 67–74.

R. Meireis, 'Aspekte einer Neuregelung des deutschen Staatsangehörigkeitsrechts, Oder ein Versuch, über die Betrachtung von Bäumen den Wald nicht aus den Augen zu verlieren', *Das Standesamt*, 1994, 241–249.

I. von Münch, 'Darf es ein bisschen mehr sein?, Gedanken zur Mehrstaatigkeit', *Neue Juristische Wochenschrift*, 1994, 1199–1201.

R. Münz and R. Ulrich, *Das zukünftige Wachstum der ausländischen Bevölkerung in Deutschland, demographische Prognosen bis 2030*, Berlin, November 1997.

Neue Juristische Wochenschrift, 1990, 2193.

Neue Juristische Wochenschrift 1995, XVII, XVIII.

B. Pieroth, in Jarrass H. and B. Pieroth, *Grundgesetz, Kommentar*, fifth ed., Article 16, No. 5, Munich, 2000.

H.-U. Predeick, 'Staatsangehörigkeitsrecht und Ausländerpolitik, Verfassungsrechtliche Probleme der Einführung des ius soli- Prinzips', *Deutsches Verwaltungsblatt*, 1991, 623–631.

Protokoll der Sachverständigenanhörung im Innenausschuß des Deutschen Bundestages, 27 Sept. 1993, 12th term.

G. Renner, 'Ausländerintegration, ius soli und Mehrstaatigkeit', *Zeitschrift für Familienrecht*, 1994, 865–872.

II.-J. Schrötter, and A. Möhlig, 'Staatsangehörigkeit in der Diskussion, Rechtliche Aspekte und politische Ansätze', *Zeitschrift für Rechtspolitik*, 1995, 374–380.

R. Scholz and A. Uhle, 'Staatsangehörigkeit und Grundgesetz', *Neue Juristische Wochenschrift*, 1999, 1510–1517.
Wissenschaftliche Dienste des Deutschen Bundestages, report of 11 June 1996, WF II/113/96.
Zeitschrift für Ausländerrecht, 1999, 50, 95.
B. Ziemske, 'Über den Versuch, sachliche Probleme durch neue Begrifflichkeit zu lösen', *Zeitschrift für Rechtspolitik*, 1995a, 380–381.
B. Ziemske, *Die deutsche Staatsangehörigkeit nach dem Grundgesetz*, Berlin, 1995b.

Notes

1. See *Daten und Fakten*, at footnote 1, page 9; For other statistics on Germany, see also *Bericht der Beauftragten der Bundesregierung für Ausländerfragen über die Lage der Ausländer in der Bundesrepublik Deutschland*, June 1999, p. 19 ff. *Migration und Integration in Zahlen, ein Handbuch*, November 1997
2. See for example the statement of the Federal Government in Official Records of the Bundestag, Bundestagsdrucksache 10/2071.
3. No. 2.3. of the Guidelines on Naturalisation: 'The Federal Republic of Germany is not an immigration country; it does not seek to increase the number of German citizens through naturalisation.'; correspondingly Federal Administrative Court, BVerwG, Buchholz 130 § 8 RuStAG No. 10, 14, 16.
4. On the topic of the reform debate see: Apel (1992), 99; Blumenwitz (1993), 151; Hobe (1994), 191; d'Oliveira (1990), 114; John (1991), 85; Löwer, (1993), 156; Lübbe-Wolff (1996), 57; Mangoldt, (1994), 33; Marx, (1997), 67; Meireis, (1994), 241; Münch (1994), 1199; Predeick (1991), 623; Renner (1994), 865; Schrötter/Möhlig (1995), 437.
5. In 1997, however, the number decreased to 278,662 naturalisations.
6. See *Daten und Fakten zur Ausländersituation*, June 1999, 11; in 1997, however, the number of naturalisations decreased by about 4 percent.
7. *Neue Juristische Wochenschrift*: 1995, XVII, XVIII; on the coalition agreement, see Eylmann (1995), 161, 163; Leutheusser-Schnarrenberger (1995), 81, 85. On the issue of the '*Kinderstaatszugehörigkeit*' also see Ziemske (1995), 380, and the parliament's Plenarprotocol 13/18, p. 1217
8. On the optional model see the report by the German Parliament's 'Wissenschaftliche Dienste' 11 June 1996, WF III-113/96.
9. Plenary protocol 14/40, p. 3415 ff.; *Bundesratsdrucksache* 296/99. On the consultation of the Committee on the Interior (*Innenausschuss*), see protocol no. 12 dated 13 March 1999.
10. On the concept of 'nationality' and its constitutional aspects, see Hailbronner 1999c, examining in particular the views of Scholz and Uhle, 1999, 1510, at 1511 and Ziemske (1995b), 221, at p. 230 ff. On the optional model and the prohibition of any deprivation of citizenship in Article 16 (1) of the Constitution as well as the principle of equal treatment in Article 3 (1) of the Constitution, also see Hailbronner 1999c.
11. Cf. to these political aspects Hailbronner 1999c.

CHAPTER 6

DUAL NATIONALITY AND NATURALISATION POLICIES IN THE GERMAN LÄNDER

Peter Friedrich Bultmann

Naturalisation is the allocation of citizenship to aliens. As naturalisation is always restricted by national laws, citizenship is a scarce in-kind good.[1] Every distribution of scarce goods – and, thus, the distribution of citizenship – is subject to questions of justice. The federal German naturalisation law, the administration of this law, and the naturalisation policies in the old West German states (*Länder*)[2] will be examined in terms of justice, and, as there are differences among the states, in terms of local justice. These issues will be explored through a focus on dual citizenship.[3]

Local justice

The empirical study of local justice concerns the distribution of scarce goods and necessary burdens by local institutions. It is a branch of the empirical study of justice. The term 'justice' is used as an analytical category based on the assumption that those in charge of the allocation of scarce goods have some conception of an appropriate solution. A specific procedure for an allocation, then, indicates a certain attitude towards justice. Local Justice encompasses such issues as immigration, college admission, organs for transplant, layoffs, military service and child custody.[4]

In describing the distribution of a certain good, one can distinguish between its criteria and the mechanisms for achieving it. Typical criteria are distribution according to equality, desert, equity, efficiency, merit, need, or some social or legal status. These criteria are 'pure,' i.e. they are never used exclusively but rather are mixed. They can be implemented by several mechanisms: for instance, queueing, lotteries, point systems, intuitive trade-offs. Distributive criteria and mechanisms can be combined in different ways subject to a distribution's conditions, circumstances and intentions. The regulations can be either relatively mechanical or relatively discretionary. In the latter, the local administrators have a considerable freedom of choice in their decisions. That makes it necessary for them to develop their own judgments and intuitions.

Distributive regulations are set and administered by actors on different levels and in different institutional locations. Basically, the first-order decision-makers determine the amount of the scarce good that is available for distribution. The second-order actors choose the particular distributive procedure. As there is a broad variety of possible combinations of several criteria and mechanisms, one can assume that different second-order allocators determine varying distributive patterns. In fact, the local-justice-studies show that this is the case. The schematic distinction between first- and second-order actors hardly explains the division of allocative decisions in contexts where laws play an important role, for example, for the distribution of German citizenship. Parliamentary laws typically lay down precise prerequisites for individual claims against the state. The crucial point for the possibility of local justice, then, is whether or not the laws leave some freedom of choice to the local decision-makers. The more precise the first-order regulations are, the more restricted the freedom of choice for the local decision-makers is and the less heterogeneity can be found between localities. Therefore, discretionary law gives local allocators the opportunity to implement local patterns of justice.

The German naturalisation law as a distributive procedure

In what follows, the German naturalisation law is discussed and evaluated as an allocative procedure.

1. The German naturalisation law is laid down in the *Reichs- und Staatsangehörigkeitsgesetz* (RuStAG) of 1913[5] and in the *Ausländergesetz* (AuslG) ('aliens-law') of 1990[6], and in some other laws.[7] These federal norms are administered by the *Länder*. As the naturalisation rules are quite abstract[8], they are put in more concrete terms by the '*Einbürgerungsrichtlinien*' (EinbRL) of 1977.[9] These are administrative agreements between the Federal Government and the *Länder* that are internally binding for the administration.

One can distinguish between naturalisations based on right from those that are discretionary. The former gives a legitimate claim to become naturalised. Beneficiaries are, for example, ethnic German emigrants[10] or young aliens of the second generation of immigrants[11]. Several special discretionary norms privilege certain groups of aliens, for example spouses of German citizens[12] or of aliens acquiring German citizenship[13]. Nevertheless, the basic norm in German naturalisation law is § 8 RuStAG which is a discretionary norm: as a rule, alien residents have no right to be naturalised. Every decision is discretionary. Aliens may only be naturalised if they meet certain prerequisites.

The character of the local understandings of naturalisation, the local attitudes towards a 'just' regulation of the distribution of citizenship, are particularly visible by observing the use of discretionary naturalisation rules. The emphasis of the study, therefore, lies on § 8 RuStAG.

The prerequisites of § 8 RuStAG in combination with the EinbRL are complex: permanent residence in Germany for ten years, no serious penalties, no dependence on the welfare system – i.e., an ability to support oneself and one's family – knowledge of the language and political system, and loyalty to democratic principles. These requirements guarantee that only those aliens can be naturalised who are completely assimilated and integrated within the German population. This includes the legal demand from the applicants to give up the legal ties to their nationality, thus, their former citizenship.[14] Another condition is that an alien should not be naturalised if this would cause different citizenships within one family, because this would cause uncertainty in international private law, Nr. 4.1 EinbRL. Many *Länder*, though, gave up this naturalisation condition. A special precondition for naturalisation that can be neglected here concerns aliens from the developing countries who came to Germany to study, cp. Nr. 5.2 EinbRL. Germany seeks to limit a potential brain drain from developing countries.

There are many exceptions to the general naturalisation prerequisites.[15] These privileges are made for three groups of applicants: a) those who are related to German citizens, cp. Nr. 6.1 EinbRL; b) those who have a special relationship to Germany, cp. Nr. 6.2 EinbRL; c) many exceptions are made for humanitarian reasons, e.g. stateless persons, refugees, those that are entitled to political asylum or those who had to suffer under the Nazi regime, cp. Nr. 6.3 and Nr. 6.4 EinbRL. A typical naturalisation privilege for these groups is a shorter duration of permanent residence in the Federal territory. In general, naturalisation conditions have to be fulfilled before someone may become a citizen.

Even if the legal prerequisites are fulfilled, the applicant has no right to be naturalised. To comply with the legal preconditions is a minimum and necessary but not a sufficient condition for naturalisation, Nr. 2.2 S. 1 and 2 EinbRL. Every naturalisation is subject to the general reservation of the public interest. The state's interest in a particular naturalisation is only given if the applicant is 'a valuable addition of the population'[16]. When a particular naturalisation does not seem to be in the state's interest, the naturalisation can be denied, Nr. 2.2 S. 3 EinbRL. Whether or not a naturalisation would be in the public interest has to be proved in every single case, Nr. 2.1 S. 3 EinbRL. This is due to the policy that the 'Federal Republic of Germany is not and cannot become a country of immigration,' Nr. 3.2 EinbRL. Naturalisation is an exception to the rule that the German citizenship can be gained only by descent from German citizens (*jus sanguinis*). This motive for the German model of naturalisation law illustrates at the same time the goal of naturalisation in Germany: The alien, to whom the

German citizenship is conferred, shall already approximate a German citizen. Naturalisation is meant to be the coronation of a completed process of integration.

2. The primary allocative principle in German naturalisation law is efficiency: The naturalisation law shall meet the intention to naturalise restrictively and only those aliens who are integrated within the German society. This basic principle is implemented by the secondary criteria of desert and character. Every applicant has to 'earn' German citizenship. The applicants have to learn the language, they have to find employment, they have to live a legal and settled life. All these prerequisites prescribe some required traits of a successful and social worthy citizen. Another criterion for desert is implemented by the demand to give up the former citizenship. Public interest does not allow the state, though, simply to follow efficiency. The exceptions to the normal procedure implement additional distributive criteria. These are kinship, ethnic status, and need. The exceptions for ethnic and family reasons, however, do not interfere with the particular goal of limiting naturalisation to assimilated aliens. The conditions for successful integration within the German society are better for these aliens than for those who have no relationship to Germany or German citizens.

German naturalisation law is 'open' in two ways. First, the prerequisites are abstract and not definitive. They leave discretionary powers to the administrators. Second, for every single naturalisation the applicant has to be deemed worthy of German citizenship. The combination of a reconsideration of the naturalisation decision and the reservation of the public interest enables the administrators to take equity concerns of single cases into account. The *Länder* may have special practices in applying the naturalisation law. They could, for example, perform a traditional policy in accordance to the German *'Volk'* as a *'Kulturnation'* or they could stick to a modern liberal attitude in order to integrate resident aliens via naturalisation within the political society, or they could perform some sort of communitarian approach, i.e. that the applicants would have to fit certain criteria that guarantee the preservation of a 'community of character'[17]. Different administrators could handle the exceptions to the general procedure in different ways, as well. Therefore, in concrete cases the range of possible decisions for the *Länder* is broad.

An empirical study of naturalisation regulations in the German states

Even though the *Länder* naturalise according to the same law, the statistics of discretionary naturalisation rates differ considerably among them. This is shown by the data given in the following tables. Tables 6.1 to 6.6 contain the naturalisation data of the *Länder* from 1991 until 1996. Table 6.7

contains the absolute number of aliens in the *Länder* for the years 1981 until 1990. Table 6.8 contains some computations: For each year of naturalisation the approximate number of eligible applicants is given by the absolute number of aliens in the *Länder* ten years before that year. This is due to the naturalisation prerequisite of ten years' residence in Germany. In order to level out fluctuations between different years, the average number of aliens in the *Länder* has been taken to estimate the eligible naturalisation candidates. These numbers are put in relation to the sum of discretionary naturalisations of the years 1991 until 1996. The computed naturalisation quotas can be compared.

The bar chart shows the differences between the *Länder*.[18] The difference is striking between Bayern and Berlin. Bayern, Baden-Württemberg, Nordrhein-Westfalen and Bremen form a group with the lowest rates. Hessen, Rheinland-Pfalz, Schleswig-Holstein, Niedersachsen and the Saarland form another group. Hamburg and Berlin form a group with the highest rates.

In order to explain the differing naturalisation rates, I test the hypothesis that these differences are caused by a divergent use of the federal naturalisation law in the Länder. A content analysis of minutes was made: although each state has the exclusive administrative power, the states cooperate on and discuss current problems of naturalisations in practice. Higher level bureaucrats of the Ministries and Senates for Internal Affairs of the *Länder* meet about two times a year. In accordance with suggestions

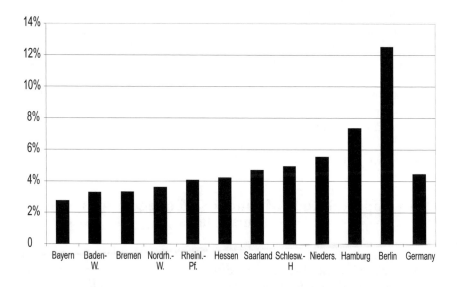

Figure 6.1 Bar chart: naturalisation quota of the Länder

Table 6.1 Naturalisation data of the *Länder* for 1991

State	total number of naturalisations	rights-based naturalisations	discretionary naturalisations	§ 86 (II) AuslG – naturalisations
1991				
Baden-Württemberg	33,641	29,696	3,945	- not available
Bayern	18,538	15,391	3,147	
Berlin	7,515	1,844	5,671	
Bremen	477	219	258	
Hamburg	5,277	3,786	1,491	
Hessen	9,016	6,511	2,505	
Niedersachsen	15,038	13,166	1,872	
Nordrhein-Westfalen	36,905	31,571	5,334	
Rheinland-Pfalz	10,206	9,295	911	
Saarland	1,196	678	51	
Schleswig-Holstein	2,214	1,520	694	
Germany	141,630	114,335	27,295	

Table 6.2 Naturalisation data of the *Länder* for 1992

State	Total number of naturalisations	rights-based naturalisations	discretionary naturalisations	§ 86 (II) AuslG – naturalisations
1992				
Baden-Württemberg	36,006	31,837	4,169	- not
Bayern	29,487	26,243	3,244	available
Berlin	9,743	976	8,767	
Bremen	392	83	309	
Hamburg	4,233	1,751	2,482	
Hessen	11,835	8,295	3,540	
Niedersachsen,	17,993	15,257	2,736	
Nordrhein-Westfalen	44,058	37,174	6,884	
Rheinland-Pfalz	17,671	16,303	1,368	
Saarland	1,868	1,466	402	
Schleswig-Holstein	2,234	1,379	855	
Germany	179,904	142,862	37,042	

Table 6.3 Naturalisation data of the Länder for 1993

State	total number of naturalisations	rights-based naturalisations	discretionary naturalisations	§ 86 (II) AuslG – naturalisations
1993				
Baden-Württemberg	39,981	33,862	6,119	- not
Bayern	30,692	26,633	4,059	available
Berlin	9,458	1,482	7,976	
Bremen	1,734	1,446	288	
Hamburg	5,234	2,122	3,112	
Hessen	14,485	9,719	4,766	
Niedersachsen	21,454	17,798	3,656	
Nordrhein-Westfalen	49,900	39,264	10,636	
Rheinland-Pfalz	14,422	13,127	1,295	
Saarland	1,954	1,524	430	
Schleswig-Holstein	3,127	2,298	829	
Germany	199,443	154,493	44,950	

Table 6.4 Naturalisation data of the *Länder* for 1994

State	total number of naturalisations	rights-based naturalisations	discretionary naturalisations	§ 86 (II) AuslG – naturalisations
1994				
Baden-Württemberg	47,534	43,691	3,843	1,258
Bayern	32,900	30,077	2,823	663
Berlin	9,903	7,029	2,874	1,131
Bremen	3,178	3,002	176	4
Hamburg	4,929	3,527	1,402	498
Hessen	21,453	18,943	2,510	978
Niedersachsen	31,204	29,070	2,134	38
Nordrhein-Westfalen	73,021	65,048	7,973	2,527
Rheinland-Pfalz	18,004	17,166	838	248
Saarland	2,372	2,093	279	51
Schleswig-Holstein	5,591	5,025	566	155
Germany	259,170	232,875	26,295	7,570

Table 6.5 Naturalisation data of the *Länder* for 1995

State	total number of naturalisations	rights-based naturalisations	discretionary naturalisations	§ 86 (II) AuslG – naturalisations
1995				
Baden-Württemberg	50,932	45,895	5,037	2,303
Bayern	40,200	37,202	2,998	992
Berlin	12,228	8,904	3,324	1,778
Bremen	3,544	3,173	371	28
Hamburg	7,730	6,017	1,713	798
Hessen	27,116	23,271	3,845	1,832
Niedersachsen	39,893	37,173	2,720	1,211
Nordrhein-Westfalen	86,136	77,116	9,020	3,602
Rheinland-Pfalz	19,605	18,533	1,072	362
Saarland	3,305	3,014	291	66
Schleswig-Holstein	7,248	6,554	694	291
Germany	313,606	281,718	31,888	13,290

Table 6.6 Naturalisation data of the *Länder* for 1996

State	total number of naturalisations	rights-based naturalisations	discretionary naturalisations	§ 86 (II) AuslG – naturalisations
1996				
Baden-Württemberg	45,760	39,119	6,641	3,373
Bayern	39,806	36,616	3,190	1,310
Berlin	10,268	7,308	2,960	1,787
Brandenburg	2,734	2,600	134	10
Bremen	3,208	2,913	295	179
Hamburg	8,726	6,552	2,174	1,168
Hessen	27,278	22,185	5,093	2,555
Mecklenburg-Vorpommern	1,298	1,170	128	5
Niedersachsen	38,423	35,352	3,071	1,413
Nordrhein-Westfalen	85,542	74,733	10,809	5,173
Rheinland-Pfalz	18,102	16,618	1,484	634
Saarland	2,772	2,460	312	94
Sachsen	6,621	6,324	297	16
Sachsen-Anhalt	3,311	3,198	113	–
Schleswig-Holstein	6,578	5,824	754	352
Thüringen	2,403	2,254	149	1
Germany	302,830	265,226	37,604	18,070

Table 6.7 Number of aliens in the States in the years 1981 to 1990

State	1981	1982	1983	1984	1985
Baden-Württemberg	933,100	919,800	874,800	845,200	840,000
Bayern	708,500	709,700	686,900	666,300	667,800
Berlin	225,900	234,700	236,200	240,300	254,300
Bremen	51,200	51,700	50,300	46,800	46,900
Hamburg	151,600	172,600	173,100	168,600	170,800
Hessen	516,900	522,800	516,100	506,300	512,300
Niedersachsen	299,100	300,600	290,700	273,700	274,900
Nordrhein-Westfalen	1,435,200	1,443,600	1,403,000	1,324,200	1,319,800
Rheinland-Pfalz	169,200	170,900	166,500	161,500	161,700
Saarland	45,600	46,000	45,000	44,500	45,400
Schleswig-Holstein	93,300	94,500	92,500	86,200	85,100
Germany	4,629,700	4,666,900	4,534,900	4,363,600	4,378,900

State	1986	1987	1988	1989	1990
Baden-Württemberg	863,500	867,700	912,100	968,600	1,010,500
Bayern	691,100	631,600	679,200	736,700	842,600
Berlin	257,800	228,900	246,500	276,400	317,600
Bremen	48,700	46,400	50,200	56,800	63,900
Hamburg	175,800	150,200	154,700	166,200	198,600
Hessen	528,400	481,800	509,200	552,400	615,500
Niedersachsen	286,700	268,400	283,800	310,800	338,800
Nordrhein-Westfalen	1,358,900	1,289,100	1,358,700	1,453,700	1,590,100
Rheinland-Pfalz	167,700	155,600	166,200	182,800	205,500
Saarland	47,100	44,200	46,700	50,800	57,600
Schleswig-Holstein	87,100	76,800	81,700	90,800	101,900
Germany	4,512,700	4,240,500	4,489,100	4,845,900	5,342,500

Table 6.8 Naturalisation quota of the *Länder* 1991 until 1996

State	Mean of aliens between 1981 and 1990	Sum of discretionary naturalisations 1991–1996	Quotient sum of naturalisations 91–96 and mean of aliens 81–90 (Q_91_96) in %
Bayern	702,040	19,461	2.77 %
Baden-Württemberg	903,530	29,754	3.29 %
Bremen.	51,290	1,697	3.31 %
Nordrhein-Westfalen	1,397,630	50,656	3.62 %
Rheinland-Pfalz	170,760	6,968	4.08 %
Hessen	526,170	22,259	4.23 %
Saarland	47,290	2,232	4.72 %
Schleswig-Holstein	88,990	4,392	4.94 %
Niedersachsen	292,750	16,189	5.53 %
Hamburg	168,220	12,374	7.36 %
Berlin	251,860	31,572	12.54 %
Germany	4,600,490	205,074	4.46 %

of the *Länder*, the Federal Ministry of Interior Affairs arranges the agenda and writes the minutes of the meeting discussions.

The minutes show which *Länder* make which statements and which arguments. It is not the aim of these meetings to find consent for concurring procedures and rules but to exchange experiences and express opinions in an informal setting.

The analysis includes 76 items of minutes from 1991 until 1996. The 504 counted statements of the *Länder* were classified to the categories 'extensive interpretation/decision' or 'restrictive interpretation.' The 404 counted arguments were classified in the categories 'legal argument' or 'non-legal argument.' As the analysis was done under the premise of confidentiality, the *Länder* had to be made anonymous. The *Länder* with the highest naturalisation rates, Berlin and Hamburg, form the group 'Few.'[19] The middle group 'Less' contains Hessen, Niedersachsen and Rheinland-Pfalz. The group with the lowest rates contains Baden-Württemberg, Bayern and Nordrhein-Westfalen and is named 'Least.'[20] The empirical work cannot be described here in any detail.[21] Also, the competing hypotheses have to be neglected. Only the results are discussed in full.

Results: four models of naturalisation decisions

It is clear from the content analysis that the *Länder* administer the Federal naturalisation law differently. There is a considerable correlation between a divergent use of the federal law and the differing naturalisation rates. The *Länder* with the lowest naturalisation rate interpret the law predominantly restrictively. They employ mainly legal arguments and references to what the laws say. The *Länder* with the highest naturalisation quota employ for the most part non-legal arguments with extensive interpretations following. The group Less represents a medium position which lies in between these two extreme positions. These formal characteristics of the naturalisation administration of the *Länder* can be described in detail for the different groups. These descriptions are, however, conceptual because the *Länder* within the groups differ in their naturalisation policy and because the general differences among the groups are emphasised. Every group represents a certain model of naturalisation policy. The Federal administrative body represents a fourth model.

The group Least naturalises only upon consideration of the reservation of the public interest. The legal prerequisites are strictly interpreted, only as minimum conditions for a naturalisation. Naturalisation is an exception. The group Least is mainly engaged to fulfil this basic principle of the German naturalisation law. Therefore, the character based and the desert criteria for the allotment of citizenship are taken seriously. The *Länder* of this group insist on the legal requirements for naturalisation. They scrutinise whether or not an applicant is a 'valuable' increase to the population. The basic idea is that only those aliens who are really integrated into German society are 'wanted.' Exceptions to rules on the ten-year residence in the Federal territory, the penal prerequisites, and the dismissal of the former citizenship are only hesitatingly made even if the law approves exceptions. They argue for the most part dogmatically. A freedom of choice is used to further the state's rather than the applicant's interests.

The group Less basically ignores Nr. 2.2. S. 1 EinbRL, which prescribes that the legal prerequisites are only minimum conditions for a naturalisation. Once the legal requirements are fulfilled, naturalisation logically follows. The *Länder* of this group take the legal demands for a naturalisation seriously but not formally. They deal with the special circumstances of the single case. They take the interests of the applicants into account. Their argumentation profile shows more non-legal arguments than the profile of the group Least. While the group Least is mainly efficiency oriented, the group Less is basically equity oriented. A general tendency towards the state's interest or the applicants' interests cannot be found. The conscientious check of the naturalisation prerequisites is disinterested.

3. *The group Few* is comparable to the group Less. The *Länder* of the group Few, however, show even more understanding of the applicants' needs and interests. Of all groups they make most use of the exceptions from the general naturalisation prerequisites. Within the framework of the law they seem to be more interested in naturalising alien residents than in refraining from doing so. Only if the applicants resist playing their part in the naturalisation procedure, i.e. bringing the necessary information or at least trying to dismiss their former citizenship, is the naturalisation denied. The argumentation profile of this group contains the most non-legal arguments, which is a sign of a political use of the naturalisation law. The desire of the aliens to become a full member of German society is respected.

4. The Federal administrative body plays a special role in the analysed minutes. However, the Federal administration has, apart from exceptional cases, no responsibility for naturalisation. It is the first-order actor in the allocative system of the naturalisation law. The Federal administration must agree on every single naturalisation.[22] In practice this is done through abstract, general approvals.

The naturalisation policy of the Federal administrative body is a mixture between the models Less and Few on the one hand and the model Least on the other hand. It is similar to the models Less and Few in its argumentation, but the consequences are different from these models as it interprets the law predominantly restrictively. The circumstances of the single case are seriously considered. Thus, the argumentation profile contains more non-legal than legal arguments and especially many equity considerations. The Federal administration takes the needs and interests of the applicants into account. It is open to exceptions to the normal procedure. Nevertheless, it does not lose sight of the restrictive character of the naturalisation law. It tries to find a balance between the legal and practical aspects of the cases, and between the state's and the applicant's interests.

The special role of the Federal administration gives rise to some specific features of its naturalisation policy. It acts globally, not locally. Therefore, it takes more (foreign-) policy arguments into account than the other groups. It seems to be the patron of the naturalisation law. It is interested in a homogenous Federal naturalisation policy, legal security, just decisions in the single case, and the preservation of the restrictive policy of the naturalisation law. The exceptions to the normal procedure shall remain exceptions and not become a rule.

The avoidance of dual nationality, Nr. 5.3 EinbRL: a particular aim

1. The principle of single nationality is only mentioned in § 9 (I) Nr. 1 RuStAG but it is, via Nr. 5.3. EinbRL, extended to § 8 RuStAG. It is also generally[23] required for privileged naturalisations according to the aliens law, §§ 85 (I) Nr. 1, 86 (I) Nr. 1 AuslG. Several exceptions to this rule are allowed in Nr. 5.3.3–6 EinbRL and § 87 AuslG: a) in exceptional cases, which would occur if the applicants had no chance to get rid of their former citizenship,[24] unless they were themselves responsible for that failure,[25] Nr. 5.3.3 EinbRL[26]; b) in cases involving stateless persons, asylum seekers, and refugees, Nr. 5.3.3.3 EinbRL; c) on grounds of a special public interest in the naturalisation, Nr. 5.3.4 EinbRL; d) in case of marriage to German citizens, Nr. 5.3.5 EinbRL, and e) for former German citizens, Nr. 5.3.6 EinbRL.

The political struggle over the reform of the nationality law in early 1999 suggested that opposition to dual citizenship was the naturalisation law's most controversial element.[27] It is, indeed, the core of the idea of citizenship and, thus, the crucial point of the German naturalisation law:[28] According to public opinion polls in January 1999, around 50% of the German population are against dual nationality.[29] According to the EMNID-poll only 65% of the population knew what dual nationality was. Nevertheless, it can be assumed, and it is explicitly mentioned in Nr. 5.3.1 EinbRL, that dual nationality is considered to be an obstacle to loyalty to the state.[30]

The withdrawal of the former citizenship is a desert criterion [i.e., it has to be fulfilled before one can claim an entitlement] for distribution as it requires an action and a decision by the applicants.[31] The other distributive criteria mentioned in the above described typology are also represented in this concern: Nr. 5.3.3.3 EinbRL regards those who have special needs. Further, exceptions are made on grounds of kinship and ethnic status. The basic principle of efficiency is in itself represented in the requirement to give up the former citizenship. It is tightly interwoven with the other distributive criteria as the system of exceptions is obviously the outcome of a careful trade-off.

2. In principle, the *Länder* consent to the legal requirement to withdraw the former citizenship and they all try to enforce this rule.[32] This, of course, includes as well the enforcement of the exceptions: in accordance with Nr. 5.3.3.1 EinbRL, for example, the *Länder* accept the fact that success in withdrawing the former citizenship is dependent not only upon the applicant's attempt but also upon the will of the home state. Thus, there is no profound discussion on the pros and cons of dual nationality. The minutes report only twelve topics on the question of dual nationality. These are single cases, where dual nationality could not be avoided because of legal or practical conditions in the home countries of the applicants. Twelve topics are an insufficient basis for generalisation. Nevertheless, it could be observed that some *Länder* follow the rule of single nationality less strictly than others.

The federal administrative body and most *Länder* usually ask for the renunciation of the former citizenship. They want a clear decision by the applicant. They usually waive this rule when the attempt to renounce a previous citizenship was rejected by the home state. Only one *Land* of group Least is very restrictive in this concern. It is supported by the other *Länder* of that group, which seems to be somewhat less rigid, but is also afraid of an abuse of exceptions from the rule of single nationality. This is congruent with the observation that they favour the desert and efficiency criteria for distribution. One *Land* of group Less follows their opinion. For the other *Länder* of that group a homogeneous pattern could not be observed. Some *Länder* are less strict. They allow applicants to keep their former citizenship on humanitarian grounds or if their attempts to withdraw their former nationality have failed. Other *Länder* are more reluctant in these cases. One *Land* of group Less and one *Land* of group Few express their will to privilege minors.[33] One *Land* of group Few clearly sticks to the need criterion. The other *Land* of that group shows no trend in favour or against dual nationality.

Overall, about 30 % of the naturalisations on discretionary grounds lead to dual nationality.[34] The real number is probably much higher: it is a well known practice of some applicants to renounce their citizenship, if they want to apply for German citizenship, and to re-naturalise after German citizenship had been granted to them. There is a gap in the German nationality law, as § 25 RuStAG does not automatically withdraw citizenship in these cases.[35]

The different attitudes on dual nationality are one reason for the differing naturalisation rates. They also have the effect that the relative contribution to the number of dual nationalities differs among the *Länder*. The influence of the different practices in the enforcement of the single nationality rule cannot be quantified. Due to the confidentiality of the examined material it may not even be possible to detect which *Länder* of which group were more strict than others. An independent survey revealed that dual nationality is mostly accepted on the grounds of Nr. 5.3.3.6 EinbRL, i. e. those who were mainly educated in German schools and who had to serve in the military in their home country first to be released from their citizenship. § 87 (II) AuslG states the same for naturalisations according to §§ 85 and 86 AuslG.

Conclusion: the meaning of citizenship, naturalisation, and dual nationality

The naturalisation policies of the *Länder* indicate different understandings of the meaning of citizenship, particularly in regard to dual nationality. The attitudes toward and understandings of citizenship diverge even within one country. The range may be small, but is significant, as the data and the analysis show. Dual nationality is thus central to the broader question of citizenship, making clear that there is no consensus on it in Germany.[36]

All conceptions of a European citizenship and complementary naturalisation laws must take account of local differences. The various conceptions of citizenship between states can only differ more than those different *Länder*/departments/regions.

The various naturalisation policies could be adjusted to each other by a nondiscretionary naturalisation law with formal distributive criteria that make a mechanical administration of the law possible. The local understandings of citizenship would have then no effect on the naturalisation of aliens. Broadly speaking, it can be said that a communitarian perspective would prefer a localized variant of the overall conception of citizenship. A liberal approach might favour a globalized, generous variant, instead.[37]

The different meanings of citizenship and, thus, reforms of the naturalisation procedures have to take special account of the matter of dual nationality. Even though the proportion of acceptance of dual nationality in the total number of naturalisations is high, changes in the law would still raise enormously the number of candidates that would be eligible for naturalisation.[38] Because of privileges for relatives of German citizens in the *Ausländergesetz*, the number of people who were entitled to immigration and permanent residence would rise. The problem of dual nationality, therefore, has to be considered carefully. A number of strong arguments have been brought up against dual nationality,[39] but its occurrence is a fact and the number of people with dual nationality is increasing constantly. It also seems to be a necessity when seeking equalisation of citizens and permanent residents, especially in regard to political rights.[40]

The controversy surrounding dual nationality, however, could, legally and politically, be considered as a proxy for the core issue of integration of immigrants: which rights should be granted to which group of immigrants. Particular questions concerning voting rights for aliens or the privilege of kinship in immigration law, for instance, give rise to similar controversies. The different answers to these questions derive from different attitudes towards another question: the extent to which a nation should strive for homogeneity and an exclusive binding of the individual to the state. This study makes it clear that prohibiting dual citizenship is detrimental to the goal of encouraging loyalty; a positive integration policy should favour dual citizenship.

References

W. R. Brubaker, 'Citizenship and Naturalisation: Policies and Politics,' in ed. Brubaker 1989, 99.

W. R. Brubaker, *Immigration and the Politics of Citizenship in Europe and North America*, Lanham, Md., New York, London, 1989.

P. Bultmann, *Lokale Gerechtigkeit im Einbürgerungsrecht*, Berlin, 1999.

J. Elster, *Local Justice in America*, New York, 1995.

J. Elster, *Local Justice: How Institutions Allocate Scarce Goods and Necessary Burdens*, New York, 1992.

F. Franz, 'Einbürgerungsanspruch für Nichtdeutsche mit Bleiberecht,' in *Zeitschrift für Ausländerrecht*, 1988, 148.

K.-M. Groth, *Einbürgerungsratgeber : Einführung in das Recht der Ermessenseinbürgerung für Ausländer*, Frankfurt, 1984.

K. Hailbronner, 'Citizenship and Nationhood in Germany,' in ed. W. R. Brubaker, 1989, 67.

K. Hailbronner/G. Renner/(C. Kreuzer), *Staatsangehörigkeitsrecht: Kommentar*, 2nd ed., Munich, 1998.

T. Hammar, *State, Nation, and Dual Citizenship*, in Brubaker, 1989, 81.

A. N. Makarov./H. v. Mangoldt, *Deutsches Staatsangehörigkeitsrecht: Kommentar*, 3rd ed., Neuwied, August 1993.

R. Marx, *Kommentar zum Staatsangehörigkeitsrecht*, Berlin, 1997.

R. Münz and R. Ulrich, *Migration und Bevölkerung*, Berlin, 1999.

R. Münz, W. Seifert and R. Ulrich, *Zuwanderung nach Deutschland: Strukturen, Wirkungen, Perspektiven*, Frankfurt, New York, 1997.

M. Walzer, *Spheres of Justice*, New York, 1983.

P. Q. Yang, 'Explaining Immigrant Naturalisation,' in *International Migration Review*, vol. 28, no. 107, Fall 1994, 449.

Notes

1. There is, of course, no natural limit for the distribution of citizenship, but because of the particular demands of the naturalisation laws one can speak of an artifical scarcity caused by the system itself.
2. There was not enough reliable data available for an analysis of the newly formed German states.
3. It should be noted that the chapter analyses the period before the adoption of a 1999 nationality law, which took effect on 1 January 2000.
4. For a brief introduction to the concept of local justice, see e.g. Jon Elster (1995) p. 1 ff. The basic local-justice-book is Jon Elster (1992).
5. BGBl. III 102–1, the present form is of 16. 12. 1997 (BGBl. I S. 2942).
6. BGBl. I S. 1354; the present form is of 16. 12. 1997 (BGBl. I S. 2970).
7. The illustration of the German naturalisation law is based on Marx (1997); Makarov (1993); Hailbronner and Renner (1998). The laws are reprinted in, for example, Bergmann, Korth, Ziemske (1995).
8. Illustrations in William Rogers Brubaker, ,Citizenship and Naturalisation: Policies and Politics,' in Brubaker (1989), 99, 108.
9. The present form is of 7. 3. 1989, reprinted in Bergmann, Korth and Ziemske (1995).
10. Cp. § 6 Abs. 1 1. *Staatsangehörigkeitsregelungsgesetz vom 22. 2. 1955* (BGBl. I S. 65), reprinted in Bergmann, Korth and Ziemske (1995). Cp. also Art. 116 Grundgesetz (Basic Law).
11. Cp. § 85 AuslG.
12. § 9 RuStAG.
13. § 86 Abs. 2 AuslG.
14. Germany is obligated under international law to limit dual citizenship, cp. Makarov/ v. Mangoldt (1993), § 8 RuStAG, Rn. 51 ff.; Hailbronner, Renner (1998), § 8 RuStAG, Rn. 44 ff.
15. This paragraph simplifies extremely. It is just intended to describe some more characteristics of the German naturalisation law.
16. Cp. e.g. Marx (1997), § 8 RuStAG, Rn. 48.
17. Concerning this term cf. e.g. Walzer (1983), 31.
18. The §§ 85 and 86 (1) AuslG were changed from discretionary to rights-based naturalisation norms. In order to find out whether or not theses changes influenced the relation between the naturalisation data of the *Länder*, the quotas were also computed for the years from 1990 until 1993 and from 1993 until 1996. The influences were negligible. The affect of §§ 85 and 86 Abs. 1 AuslG can, thus, also be neglected here.
19. This is due to the fact, that compared to naturalisation data in other countries, the naturalisation rates are low in Germany.
20. Some *Länder* are missing because there was not enough reliable data available.
21. For these, see Peter Bultmann (1999), 96.
22. According to § 3 S. 1 of the *Verordnung über die deutsche Staatsangehörigkeit of 05. 02. 1934* (BGBl. III 102–2), reprinted in Bergmann, Korth and Ziemske (1995).
23. Exceptions in § 87 AuslG.

24. Nr. 5.3.3.4 and Nr. 5.3.3.5 EinbRL privilege old people and minors in this concern: dual nationality is accepted not only if it is inevitable but also if it would be considerably difficult to avoid it. Nr. 5.3.3.6 EinbRL privileges those who were mainly educated in German schools: dual nationality is accepted if the withdrawal of the former citizenship was only possible after they had served in the military in their home country.

25. For example, because the applicants refuse to contribute to the procedure (e. g. to pay a fee or to fulfill their duty to military service).

26. Nr. 5.3.3.7 (aliens, who have not been in their home country for twenty years) and Nr. 5.3.5 EinbRL (persons, who are married to German citizens) state exceptions from the exception of Nr. 5.3.3 EinbRL, which is an exception of Nr. 5.3.1 EinbRL.

27. On these events cp. the report on http://www.demographie.de/aktuell website.

28. It is, in fact, very important for the 'living' aliens law: Relatives of German citizens are, for instance, privileged by the immigration rules.

29. EMNID-poll: 39% pro, 53% contra; ALLBUS-poll: 39% pro, 49% contra, cp. Münz and Ulrich (1999), 3, or http://www.demographie.de/aktuell website on March, 23th, 1999. For the scientific controversy to this question cp. e. g. Hailbronner and Renner (1998), § 8 RuStAG, Rn. 66; Marx (1997), § 8 RuStAG, Rn. 118; BVerwG, EZAR 271, Nr. 22 and, concerning EU-citizens, BVerwG, EZAR 271, Nr. 23.

30. Hammer (1989), pp. 81, gives a good discussion on the matter of dual nationality on a general level.

31. Yang (1994), 449 discusses the marginal utility of a change of citizenship for the U.S.-naturalisation law.

32. This is astonishing, if the discussion about a reform of the German nationality law in early 1999 is considered. Part of the reform is a broader acceptance of dual nationality. It has to be considered, however, that the proposed changes priviledge the naturalisation of minors only. Basically, this would be compatible with the traditional concept of citizenship as those minors in consideration would be educated in German schools and integrated in and influenced by the German society, and thereby 'made into Germans.' Proposals that go further by granting dual nationality to adults are controversial. It also has to be kept in mind that the empirical study deals with administrative bodies, not with opinions of politicians. It might also be assumed that the discussants do not express their opinions on dual nationality frankly because they might have anticipated a controversial and rather rigid attitude on the topic by other representatives and because it was the meaning of the discussions to remain within the legal framework.

33. There is general acceptance of dual nationality for minors that may not, under their home state laws, give up their citizenship before they are adults, under the premise that they will renounce their former citizenship, once they are legally allowed to do that.

34. 1990: 4,279 of 20,237; 1991: 6,700 of 27,295; 1992: 10,296 of 37,042; 1993: 16,880 of 44,950; 1994: 8,929 of 26,295; 1995: 11,086 of 31,888; 1996: 10,33 of 37,604 – Source: *Statistisches Bundesamt* – VII B – 175. Münz and Seifert (1997), 113, who estimate that in 1993 40 % of all naturalisations (30,000 of 74,058) lead to dual

nationality. Franz (1998), 148, 151 exaggerates somewhat when he says the exceptions to the rule of single nationality had become the rule.

35. Of course, the problem is as well that the information about such a re-naturalisation is not easily obtained for the naturalisation bodies.

36. This was obvious at the beginning of 1999: Lacking the legal possibility to launch a federal plebiscite, the Christian Democratic Party (CDU) collected signatures against the proposed draft for a reform of the nationality law, which allows dual nationality within a much broader framework as the former nationaliy law. The draft version can be found on http://www.demographie.de/aktuell website on 23 March 1999.

37. That topic and the question, whether or not local justice can be considered as being 'just' is addressed in Bultmann (1999), 231. Hints for the current reform discussion on the mentioned: http://www.demographie.de/aktuell website.

38. On the basis of the mentioned draft nationality law it has been estimated, that around four million aliens would be eligible for naturalisation and that around two million really would apply for German citizenship, cp. http://www.demographie.de/aktuell website.

39. See, for example, Hailbronner (1989), 67, 78.

40. On this argument cp. Hammar (1989), 81.

CHAPTER 7

TÜRKEN MIT DEUTSCHEM PASS: SOCIOLOGICAL AND POLITICAL ASPECTS OF DUAL NATIONALITY IN GERMANY

Riva Kastoryano

Introduction

Since the 1980s, questions linked with immigration and integration have become questions of citizenship.[2] Against the background of contrasting geographies and histories, France and Germany have debated the conditions under which third country nationals are to be integrated into the national community. In 1987, France transferred the debate over citizenship and nationality law to a commission of the 'Great and the Good' (*Commission des sages*).[3] Germany found itself confronted with a similar issue two years later, following the fall of the Berlin Wall and the collapse of the Soviet Union. Both led to a massive influx of *Aussiedler*, migrants from central Europe and Russia enjoying immediate citizenship on the basis of their German ancestry. Since then, the debate has developed around the question of dual nationality, rejected by the German constitution but demanded by Turks, as a prerequisite to their naturalisation and accession to equal citizenship.

This chapter examines the place of Turks in German society through the lens of citizenship. It has three goals. First, drawing on Marshall's classic tripartite distinction, it examines the Turkish position in terms of social, economic and political citizenship, noting that the exclusion of the Turks from the political community masks their full participation in the social and economic life in Germany. Second, it argues that the Turks' robust enjoyment of social and economic citizenship is insufficient; only political citizenship secures the right to full participation in the polity, a fundamental prerequisite to active citizenship. Third, it offers a modified critique of the debates surrounding dual citizenship. Although dual citizenship can serve as a provisional and practical aid to integration (suggesting that conservative claims that it is by definition a barrier to citizenship may be overstated), individuals can, by definition, only be full citizens of one state. As full citizenship presupposes active involvement in a political community, and as this can only be exercised in the country of residence, the state of citizenship and of residence provides full citizenship. Dual citizenship, along with recognition of cultural diversity, at least in the private sphere, can ease individuals' integration into national citizenship in their country of residence, but this remains the only guarantee of full inclusion. It is the task of citizenship *tout court* to redefine itself in a manner that maintains the link between the individual and the nation-state while accommodating pluralism and multiple attachments.

Citizenship and dual citizenship

The question of citizenship in Europe relates both to the rights of third country nationals in member states and, in a larger sense, to the construction of Europe. These two developments, seemingly independent, call into question the nation-state and its constitutive components: citizenship and nationality.

The same holds true for the question of dual nationality. Nationality and citizenship, concepts that are interdependent and 'interchangeable' in the framework of the nation-state (Leca: 1992), are based, above all, on an individual's belonging to a political community. Individuals' status as citizens is expressed through rights – social, political and cultural – and obligations that together embody the very idea of citizenship. The legal act institutionalising this principle, naturalisation, implies the inclusion of the 'foreigner', within the national community, and he or she is naturally expected to share its moral and political values.

Such are the requirements. They rely on the founding principles of the nation-state, its political traditions and in short, its national identity. They are legitimately expected of those naturalising.[4] This holds in France as much as it does in Germany. As a number of scholars have emphasised (Brubaker: 1992), the claim that the two republics, with contrasting histories, constitute opposing 'models' of citizenship and nationality. These differences structure political rhetoric, public debates and clearly shape *mentalités* and attitudes themselves. They also influence public policy and determine the legal principles governing access to citizenship: France privileges *jus soli*, while Germany maintained, until very recently, a legal regime based exclusively on the cult of ancestry, expressed in *jus sanguinis*.[5] But since January 2000, Germany has switched to *jus soli*, with the new citizenship law granting German citizenship to a child born on German soil to foreign parents.

In practice, however, sociological reality had already narrowed the differences between the two countries. Both countries face a large population of migrants and their descendants who arrived in the 1960s. In both countries, these 'migrants' have multiple attachments: to the country of origin, to a linguistic, ethnic or religious community, and even to a local community in the country of residence. These developments have led to doubts about the allegiance of immigrants in both states. Their doubts intensify with every debate over citizenship and immigration, and are reflected in an unmistakable elite fear that national citizenship will be 'desacralised' through the spread of instrumental citizenship (*citoyenneté pour les papiers*), that is, citizenship acquired only to avoid expulsion. Such fears are inspired by the attachment – real or imagined – of the 'immigrants' or 'foreigners' to their country of origin, expressed through identification with the migrant/religious community within the host country. Based on this logic, both France and Germany are, on the face of it, hostile to dual citizenship. In France, political rhetoric – often founded on ignorance – rejects political attachment to any community other than the national. In Germany, the constitution required the renunciation at naturalisation of all other citizenships as proof of the applicant's 'complete' attachment to the German nation.

The debate over the dual citizenship claimed by the Turks turns on questions of loyalty, belonging and assimilation. It concerns different conceptions of a political community's moral and political values, as well as the civic duties demanded of those residing within it (Pickus: 1998). Moreover, the increasing fluidity of the borders since the collapse of the Soviet Union has led immigrants to develop transnational networks linking the country of origin to the country of residence and to participate actively in both spaces; in such instances, the country of origin becomes a source of identity and the country of residence a source of right. In this perspective, dual citizenship stems from political participation in both political communities, which brings to light multiple membership and to some extent multiple loyalties. The result is a confusion between rights and identity, culture and politics, states and nations. At the very least, the question seems to be whether dual citizenship can be the institutional expression of multiple belonging.

Dual citizenship also raises empirical and normative questions. Empirically, it results from the interaction of states and immigrants. Dual citizenship flows from a duality that appears, *a priori*, contradictory but is in fact complementary: the construction of a minority status and the creation of a citizen's identity. Both emerge within the country of residence's institutions. Normatively, it is a question for a state of defining new modes and new mechanisms for integrating migrant populations (and their descendants) into the national political community. For individuals and groups within civil society, it is a question of combating all forms of exclusion, whether political, social or cultural, a process that is itself a precondition to migrants' and permanent residents' accession to full citizenship. Together, these tasks amount to a negotiation of interests that takes the form of a 'negotiation of identity' between the state and its migrant population

(Kastoryano: 1997). This ultimately involves striking a balance between citizenship within national institutions and citizenship within what can be called 'communitarian' institutions, as well as within civil society itself. This balance inevitably requires a redefinition of the classic link between political and cultural belonging; between rights and identity. The first step in such a redefinition concerns civic participation with equal rights, the second step implicates the source of one's identity. It is this link that underlines the relevance of dual citizenship.

States and immigrants

The dual citizenship claimed by Turks resident in Germany, is founded on a logic that has two consequences: it transforms nationality into an ethnicity, an identity rooted in the country of origin, and it makes citizenship an entitlement within the country of residence. On such a view, citizenship becomes simply a legal status, and nationality is defined along religious, ethnic or cultural lines.

Germany and its 'foreign citizens'

The Turks' claim for dual citizenship raises a series of searching questions concerning the relationship between the state and its 'immigrants'. Does the Germans' own foundation of national identity on descent drive non-Germans to define themselves through similar ethnic criteria derived from their previous nationality? Is it the case that law and politics in Germany lead migrants/permanent residents to view their (country of origin) citizenship as a constitutive element in the construction of a collective identity to be nurtured, and, through dual citizenship, institutionalised? Does Germany's immigration policy, referred to as a 'foreigners' policy' (*Ausländerpolitik*) and/or its national legislation on naturalisation (referred to as a law for foreigners, *Ausländergesetz*) serve to keep the Turkish foreign? Does the Turks' self-definition reflect the goal, expressed, and at times forcibly pursued, by successive German governments, of seeing them return one day to their own country, effectively making the Turkish state – rather then the German state – a refuge and a source of security and right?

Germany's policy towards migrants has rested, for a long time, upon an official discourse consistently emphasising that 'Germany is not a country of immigration'. Although the phrase contradicts sociological fact, there is no question that it translates into a willingness to separate the migrants – in effect, future citizens – from the German nation and German citizenship. For foreigners, naturalisation itself can only be the result of full assimilation, not a contributor to it. By contrast, *Aussiedler* from Eastern Europe or Russia, sharing with Germans a common ancestry but a foreign language and culture are attributed citizenship immediately upon their arrival. Their 'naturalisation' is nothing more than the extension of a citizenship founded on their belonging to the German people (*das deutsche Volk*), and it is further evidence of the organic character of the political community within the very definition of the nation.

Nationality founded on *jus sanguinis* already posed practical and conceptual problems in 1871, at the time of German unification, in that the new frontiers led to a blurring of the concepts of people and territory. 'Little Germany' excluded foreigners in neighbouring states and included, in principle, ethnic Germans living outside its borders. The result, as Rogers Brubaker noted, was two forms of citizenship: a political citizenship, corresponding to territory, and a spiritual and ethnic citizenship, founded on a common ancestry (Brubaker: 1992). The ethnic dimension of German citizenship was reinforced by a 1913 law 'on belonging to the State and Empire', which permitted Germans living outside the *Reich's* borders to keep German nationality while denying foreigners born within Germany citizenship. In 1949, the German Basic Law confirmed the principle of ethno-cultural citizenship. Article 116 defines as German anyone of German ancestry living within Germany's 1937 borders. *Deutschtum* (Germandom), or the quality of being German, includes in principle ethnic Germans living in other states. This justifies the *Aussiedler's* access to citizenship and the 'privilege' of being permitted to keep their previous nationality.

In a replay of events a century ago, citizenship today is a question of 'imported workers' (Bade: 1997); [6] in the four decades after the war, the presence of foreigners changed nothing in the laws on 'Germanness' or German citizenship. The latter, though criticised as a violation of democratic principles, appeared to conform to the definition of German nationhood – founded on common ancestry – that it embodied. In 1990, however, in reaction to a wave of migration from Eastern Europe, the government adopted a new law on foreigners (*Ausländergesetz*) with the goal of facilitating their integration. Such a policy was the inevitable result of Germany's 'moral obligation' to the guestworkers, who had been resident in the country for as many as three generations. This law introduced, for the first time, naturalisation criteria based on the socialisation of the guestworkers' children. According to the new legislation a young foreigner had the right to naturalise if he or she requested to between the ages of sixteen and twenty-three, had resided regularly in the Federal Republic since the age of eight and had been educated for six years (at least four of which at the secondary level) and was free of criminal convictions. The law also reduced the price of naturalisation – which had varied between three thousand and five thousand Deutsche Marks – to one hundred Marks for youth. Although the prohibition on dual nationality was maintained, a sharp increase in naturalisations followed: varying between twenty thousand and thirty thousand from 1973 to 1989, they reached 101,377 in 1990.

In 1994, the CDU/CSU-FDP coalition agreed to a further reform proposal aimed at third-generation Turks. The debate concerned a quasi-citizenship referred to by Turkish activists as 'children's citizenship' (*Kinderstaatszugehörigkeit*). The measure proposed granting German nationality to foreign children at birth if one of their parents had been born in the Federal Republic. It thus would have introduced an element of *double jus soli*, which had been instituted in French nationality law for over a century, although one that depended on parental proof of ten years' residence in Germany. The *Kinderstaatszugehörigskeit* would have been obtained by application before the age of twelve years, and it would become void if the child did not apply for full naturalisation and obtain release from his/her previous nationality within one year of the age of majority. Practically, the measure would have involved granting the child a 'guarantee of naturalisation' (*Einbürgerungszusicherung*), which would have been clearly indicated on their identity card (*la lettre*: 1998). It is worth recalling that the expression of willingness to naturalise found a place in German nationality law, as it did in the 1993 French reform (*l'expression de la volonté*), the option in favour of one nationality would have resulted from German constitutional provisions concerning the renunciation of other nationalities.

Since 1990, negotiations over nationality have been on the agenda of each government. Most recently, in the Autumn of 1998 the new SPD/Green coalition announced a reform that would have allowed dual citizenship as a means to encouraging alien residents – especially Turks – to naturalise. In other words, the measure would have involved amending the constitutional provision requiring renunciation. This project, which made dual citizenship and its links with national identity, as well as the respect for the constitution, the anchor of debates over citizenship, led the opposition to organise a national petition against it. At the same time, representatives of the Turkish community made clear that dual citizenship was a precondition to their acquisition of German citizenship.

Turkey and 'its' citizens

Turkey has intervened in the complex relationship between the German State and its immigrants, and there is little doubt that it constitutes a positive force in its nationals' campaign in favour of dual citizenship. Their efforts implicate the very definition of Turkey as a nation-state. For Turks, their (home country) national identity has become – through the experience of immigration – a source of 'ethnic pride', to borrow from Max Weber, articulated through the image of a people and an independent Turkish nation. It is this identity that is reflected in the discourse, the action and the political mobilisation of various voluntary organisations in favour of the recognition of the Turkish language as an affirmation of a collective ethnic/national identity. Religion plays a similarly important role; despite the ideological distance between language and religion, the Turkish State has found itself driven to make official appeals to Germany in favour of courses in both. Perhaps this is one of the consequences of the bilateral agreements signed between Turkey and Germany in 1961. These agreements, which facilitated Turkish immigration, originally concerned with culture (notably the teaching of Turkish) and religion, became for Turks in Germany 'identity ressources'. Today, most of the Turkish voluntary associations in Germany, which in principle developed independently of political movements in Turkey, appear to be an extension of agreements between the two countries, leading their leaders and members to define themselves with reference to both Germany and Turkey.

Regarding the Kurds (who make up approximately thirty percent of immigration from Turkey), they have cultivated an 'ethnic pride' in their ethnic identity that has persisted despite the assimilationist policy of the Turkish Republic. Nationalist movements in Europe highlight the role of demands articulated not only through the status of immigrant but through a 'double minority' status – as a minority in the country of origin as much as in France and Germany.

Recourse to the Turkish State also arises for the representatives responsible for the integration of Turks in Germany. At times, this task involves relations between diverse workers' associations and German charity associations, on the one hand, and official representatives of the Turkish State on the other. At others times, it entails official state to state relations over issues of concern to Turkish nationals in Germany. There are also instances in which official representatives, emerging from German civil society but maintaining their links with the country of origin, serve as intermediaries between Turkish families in Germany and public authorities in Turkey.

Clearly, such recourse to the Turkish state is an important variable factor in the debate over dual citizenship. It is also a resource for the construction of an ethnic minority defined by a common nationality. In effect, Turkish nationals' claim of dual citizenship originates in an ethnic identity expressed through Turkish nationality and claimed through the status of 'minority', the latter of which rests on both a Turkish national identity and a Muslim religious identity. The national minority defines itself by its foreign legal status, while the religious minority defines itself by the lack of an official institutional recognition of Islam, recognition of the sort granted to other religions by German public law. This logic pushed the members and leaders of associations close to the SPD to adopt the expression *türkische Minderheit*, Turkish minority. Its use is almost ironic. For Germans, the concept of 'minority' is usually reserved for themselves, as they were in a minority following their exile in the Second World War. They are naturally ill-disposed towards its application to the Turks.

This leads in turn to the question of the role of the Turkish and German states in the construction of such a minority. In contrast to official French integration policy, based upon the discouragement of all religious and/or (non-French) national communities seeking political representation, German officials have expressed their desire to see the Turks organised through a unified ethnic community and around interests that transcend ideological, religious, ethnic or linguistic cleavages. The declared objective of the Foreigner's Commission (*Ausländerberauftragte*) is to aid migrant populations, in forming organisations representing 'a community guided by consensus' rather than seeing a proliferation of formal and informal groups in conflict with one another. It is a means through which the public authorities resist the social, economic and political compartmentalisation or marginalisation of foreigners. It is also a way of organising them into unified and solidaristic communities modelled on German churches. The idea is to aid the migrants in helping themselves (*Selbsthilfe*) through associations to create their own institutions for combating delinquency, poverty and crime. It is an approach reminiscent of American liberalism, in which ethnic voluntary organisations are at the same time self-help institutions, sensitive to addressing the social problems disproportionately affecting their members. The logic of ethnic communities – structured, integrated and socially active – implicitly involves a parallel struggle for recognition. Above all, it becomes the only means to obtaining legitimacy and a 'recognition of their permanent presence in Germany'.

In such a perspective, members of the migrant organisations take on board the official discourse, following the official lead in organising or structuring such a community. They pool their resources in order to create umbrella organisations (*Dachorganisation*), that is, federal organisations in each *Land* through which Turkish nationals are themselves organised. This strategy is manifest in the organisational leadership's efforts to unify organisations of different – even opposing – political tendencies in *Land*-level federal associations, such as the *türkische Gemeinde zu Berlin*.[7] In the last analysis, an ethnic community defines itself through its programme of action, and it is in this context that its organisations and members express their identification.

The stakes in these developments are of equally important consequence for the Turkish population and Germany itself. For the former, it is a question of projecting an image of a community no longer segmented, divided and conflictual, but, on the contrary united by common interests and better equipped to combat inequality, discrimination and racism. For Germany, aiding the foreign population in uniting existing networks between different groups with the aim of ending their isolation and overcoming internal cleavages, is a matter of ensuring social peace. Even more than this, it is a matter of preserving democracy by ending the policies and practices that exclude the foreign population and of fully integrating them into civil society.

That which public officials refer to as the ethnic community resonates transformed in the Turkish community's leaders' and members' notion of an ethnic minority. They refer through this term to the structural presence of a culturally distinct population including almost two million individuals from all social categories – the unemployed, skilled and unskilled workers, students, managers, shopkeepers and industrialists – who express their attachment to different regional, linguistic or ethnic cultures in Turkey. They collectively constitute, as Faruk Sen puts it, 'Turkey in Germany'. According to him, the expression 'a Turk from Germany' or a 'German Turk' will become a terminology that will impose itself on public opinion. Emphasising the presence of a structured minority looking to consolidate itself, he continues: 'Our artists, our businessmen, our culture, our language, our religion, our television and our press are only one aspect of Turkey in Germany. We have also established a network of internal communication made up of several daily papers, a weekly and a monthly paper published in Germany'(Sen: 1990). It is this that leads him to propose the term *türkische Minderheit* in political debates within the SPD, of which he is a member.

In addition, the Turkish minority finds its common denominator in nationality. Inspired by the American example, and by affirmative action programmes aimed at 'minorities' on the other side of the Atlantic, Turkish interest group members demand political recognition. Nonetheless, two significant elements differentiate the German situation from the American: first, the contrasting histories – of both their particular relationship with the state and their own immigration – of 'minorities' in the U.S. and 'foreigners' in Germany, and, second, their legal status – the groups categorised as 'minorities' are American citizens, while the Turkish 'guests' in Germany remain, in the vast majority of cases, foreigners. This difference results in a contrasting definition of 'minority' in the two countries: an ethnic minority, whose status is based on race, national origin (or sex) in the U.S., and a largely national minority in Germany.

The leaders of Turkish organisations have also looked to the European level, notably the Council of Europe and its programme on the rights of minorities. In doing so, they recast their demands in terms of a minority culture, particularly when they demand recognition of the Turkish language and its teaching in public schools, seeking as well to align themselves with programmes legitimised by the Council.

When the German State seeks legitimate representatives in the logic of communitarian and ethnic politics, the Turks respond by using its efforts as a means to claim recognition as an ethnic minority. Turkey itself seeks – through the existence of such a minority – to nurture a lobby in Germany able to defend the interests and image of Turkey both in Germany and in European supranational institutions.

The identity of citizen

There is neither a normative nor an empirical tension between the Turkish minority pursuing its interests through its links with the German state – the sole legitimate framework defining the limits and terms of its recognition – and through German society, in which its organisations and political actions take shape. The relations that Turkish representatives develop with German civil society shape both their own self-identification and their actions. In practice, this involves relying on the intermediary bodies present in any strong civil society. Participation in them is justified by residence in Germany and respect for the principle of legal equality, which together constitute a form of citizenship. Such a definition of citizenship expresses itself in the Turks' willingness to integrate – through a minority and/or community – into the social structure of the Federal Republic, in a manner that accords primacy to these intermediary bodies as they do to the classical social and economic institutions which have always played a central role in civil society and in political decisions.[8]

Social participation and citizenship

Integration within civil society implies access to social citizenship. This integration, however, in no way implies full citizenship, that is, full integration into the political community. Only political citizenship grants them the ability to participate, and it remains largely unrealised. Under such conditions, dual nationality could be selectively conceived as a practical and provisional measure for achieving full citizenship.

In the United States, interest in dual citizenship is based not only on the dual citizen's meaningful ties to the country of origin, but also on a rational calculation of the social advantages provided by citizenship in both countries (Schuck: 1998). In the latter, social rights flow from, or logically follow, political rights; since 1996, one must be a citizen to take advantage of most social programmes. Such a conception of social citizenship is inspired by the famous lecture by T.H. Marshall who – in the aftermath of the Second World War – emphasised the expansion of citizenship from civil, to political, then finally to social rights, in areas such as health, education and social provision in general.[9]

In European countries, Marshall's evolutionary path is reversed. Legal foreign workers and their families acquire a social citizenship – in the form of social entitlements and constitutional protections of universal human rights equal to those of full citizens – upon arrival. They constitute what Habermas referred to as 'passive citizenship', a citizenship legitimised by the development of the welfare state. The passage from this social citizenship to a legal (or active) citizenship is achieved through naturalisation, which depends upon the length of residence, work and service, but also, it is worth adding, on an expected identification with the country of residence.

Citizenship expresses itself through participation – direct or indirect – by individuals and groups, by foreigners and citizens. It is the expression of individual involvement in the political community.[10] It occurs as much in the framework of officially recognised migrant associations, in the cultural or local activities, in short in civil society itself, as in the national political community. From the 1980s, citizenship has become a support for the 'politicisation of identities', which led 'foreigners' to act within a public space, a common space of socialisation where power is exercised, and to manifest their involvement and belonging, at least in practice, in a political community by situating themselves over and against the state.

Political involvement increases not only participation but also the exercise of citizenship. Even more, it contributes to the formation of an 'identity of citizen'. This identity is constituted by action, and it grants legitimacy both to struggles against exclusion and to demands for legal and practical equality. It also gives birth to a sentiment of pride, motivated by the foreigners' integration in established institutions – whether national or community-based – representing the interests of their members. In sum, it is the result of a process of 'political acculturation' – to borrow from Habermas – that is, the internalisation of the country of origin's national values and its rules of political conduct. It is a process that does not, however, result in complete socialisation (Habermas: 1992). Social citizenship, based on participation in intermediate institutions, especially migrant associations, falls short. Only legal citizenship integrates foreigners directly into the political community, translating into civic participation: the right to vote.

Naturally, the laws governing citizenship affect individuals' strategies and modes of participation. The absence of direct participation in the political community, reserved for those with legal citizenship, leads foreigners to develop compensatory strategies that make citizens not merely 'spectators who vote', as Rousseau put it, but actors who approximate the vote (*faire voter*) through their influence on public opinion and/or public policy. Such moves do not exclude participation; on the contrary, they seek indirect means to achieving it. The absence of electoral channels is compensated for at the local level by a form of citizenship deriving essentially from its exercise in society itself, a citizenship defined through the formation of migrant associations that press their claims before the federal state or the *Länder*.

Economic participation and citizenship

These channels are multiple. In addition to the association's influence on public opinion, it is a matter of reinforcing integration through economic success (Walzer: 1994). A report published in Brussels in 1991 estimates the direct or indirect benefit of the Turks at approximately 57,000,000DM per annum. The figure greatly exceeds the figure of some 16,000,000DM paid to Turks for all forms of social assistance (Migration News Sheet: 1991). The association of Turkish businessmen included, in 1992, thirty five thousand entrepreneurs, from restaurant owners to industrialists. They collectively employed at that time one hundred and fifty thousand Turks and seventy five thousand Germans, resulting in a turnover of around 25,000,000DM and, in 1991, taxes of 1,000,000DM.[11] These economic actors play an important role not only in relations between Turkey and Germany, but also in financing Germany's investment projects in the Turkish republics of the former Soviet Union. The statistics regularly demonstrate the extent of this investment, the media draws attention to the Turk's economic consumption and German companies express their civil solidarity with the Turks and seek to influence the politics that concern them.

The question that remains, however, is whether a security founded on an economic role can compensate for a political insecurity resulting from a lack of legal protection. In other words, can economic integration open the door to political rights? History provides a partial response to this question insofar as Germany's economic elite was able to integrate the country into international economic competition during the Great Depression of 1873–1896. It was on this basis that economic interests acquired importance and were able to make their influence felt in the country's political decisions. According to the same logic, economic interests, such as the organisation of Turkish doctors from 1990, then the Turkish business associations of the different *Länder*, were prepared to act as interest groups able to pursue collective interests, including the defence of social and cultural rights and the support of measures against xenophobia. In a manner reminiscent of the role played by economic factors in the redefinition of German identity after the war, they used their success in this area in order to transform themselves into a credible political force.

A further question is whether it is necessary to see this method as a means to appropriating the 'economic miracle' with the hope that prosperity and well-being will provide German identity with a new content, going beyond the old ethnic basis. Or does such an approach assume another, no less traditional, interpretation of 'citizenship,' linked with the medieval status of 'bourgeois' (*Bürger*), or economic citizen? In Germany, this second vision of citizenship refers more to belonging in a civil society than allegiance towards a political community; civil society is here understood as 'bourgeois society' (*die bürgerliche Gesellschaft*), which not only distinguishes a state from its institutions but positions them against one another. In this sense, all individuals who participate in a public life dominated by economic competition can be considered (economic) citizens. This suggests 'citizen' is a synonym for 'bourgeois', that the two are 'two sides of the same coin', as Ralf Dahrendorf writes (Dahrendorf: 1988). It is perhaps in this logic that the term 'foreign co-citizens' *ausländische Mit-bürger*, introduced into the debate by the Greens, must be interpreted. The formula amounts to an acceptance, in the absence of political citizenship, of Turkish nationals through economic citizenship. It raises the question of whether their gentrification (*'embourgeoisement'*) will be a step on the road towards naturalisation – as the German term *Einbürgerung* suggests, if the former is used in reference to the state (*Staatsbürger*) and not, as in the case of 'bourgeois', the town. This highly specific conception of citizenship puts politics in a derivative position relative to economics, in contrast with the French case, in which – at least in theory – politics takes precedence over economics. In Germany, it gives political power to Turks who are otherwise excluded by the cultural definition of citizenship (Gosewinkel: 1998).[12]

As in the case of social citizenship, if economic citizenship creates direct participation in civil society, it is at best indirect political citizenship. Only legal citizenship provides a *right* to participate fully in the political community. Nevertheless, the creation of a 'citizenship identity', expressed within community or ethnic organisations (such as voluntary associations), goes against classic republican understandings of citizenship as an amalgam of political involvement and national sentiment. On such understandings, citizenship is integrally linked with the framework of the nation-state, which merges its aspects of politics and identity. In reality, whether citizenship is political, judicial, social or economic, and whether its element of identity is cultural or legal, the combination is captured by a sentiment of multiple loyalty, directed simultaneously towards the group, the community, civil society and the state. It is through their interpenetration that actors' strategies reveal themselves. In doing so, they disrupt the overlapping relationship of the national and political community, the link between identity and rights, as well as between culture and politics.

In Germany, the language of politics uses a terminology separating citizenship from nationality and identity. Although both citizenship (*Staatsbürgerschaft*) and nationality (*Staatsangehörigkeit*) are defined with reference to the state, the first is defined as an instrument, the second as a belonging. The turn to dual citizenship (*die doppelte Staatsbürgerschaft*) is founded on this duality, a duality that, in reality, is complimentary. It combines the construction of an ethno-national minority in Germany with the development of an identity of citizenship reflecting political and institutional assimilation. This analysis stands against a pessimistic thesis holding that retaining the country of origin's citizenship could lead to a delayed assimilation.[13] In effect, dual citizenship – claimed by the Turks themselves – could be viewed as a right, permitting the negotiation of a ethno-national and moral identity (*personalité*) on a triple basis: that of German civil society (through residence and the exercise of the rights and civil obligations linked with it), that of Turkish nationality (for those whose identity is bound up with it), and that of an attachment to the German state itself. It is through this multiplicity that citizenship is negotiated (Kastoryano 1997).

In effect, the 'minority' in question expresses a willingness to integrate into the political community, through the request for citizenship, while still expressing its 'attachment' to the nationality of origin. In this perspective, dual citizenship, for the groups that express a specific identity, can be a means to escaping their political marginalisation. Consequently, it amounts to a struggle for emancipation. In this perspective, emancipation contrasts with the emancipation linked with the enlightenment, which separated religion from public life and the individual from his community with the goal of assuring a primary identification with the national community. Emancipation through dual citizenship is founded on a *willingness to participate*, with the equal rights granted to religious or community-based identities, within the nation-state.

These terminological and conceptual distinctions concerning the nation-state, a source of confusion, are echoed in the terms hesitantly used to describe foreigners with ties to Germany: 'non-Germans' for the conservative right, 'foreign compatriots' for the Greens and, finally, the 'Turks with a German passport' (*Türken mit Deutschem Pass*) for others. 'Non-Germans' are naturally defined with reference to German citizenship, and as a result with reference to their non-belonging, both to the German state and in the German nation. 'Foreign compatriots'(co-citizens) are defined, as seen above, by their integration and belonging in civil society. Finally, the 'German Turks' are defined in terms of their 'ethnic identity,' which the acquisition of a German passport cannot change. According to the statistics, there are over two hundred and fifty thousand of them.

The political parties already see in dual citizens an important electoral potential, and they compete with one another to define the place offered them in the political community. According to a 1994 study, had the Turks possessed German citizenship, forty-nine percent would have voted for the SPD (compared with sixty-seven percent in 1986), eleven percent for the Greens, ten percent for the FDP and six per cent for the CDU. Although the number of Germans of Turkish origin over the age of eighteen does not exceed thirty five thousand, political parties publish propaganda in community journals as if they wished to realise a sort of electoral investment. The FDP would like to rely on the Turkish vote in order to pass the five percent threshold, below which it cannot win seats in the *Bundestag*, while the SPD is careful to support the large Turkish organisations out of a fear that their members will transfer their support to other parties (Sen 1994).

These developments highlight the link, or the absence of a link, between citizens and nationals that some would like to create, or develop. The desire to separate the elector from the basis of nationality – single or double – demonstrates the difficulty faced by public opinion and the political class in accepting 'foreigners' as constituent parts of the German nation.

Instead of limiting identification with an ethnic community to civil society, such an approach – given its foundation on dual citizenship – creates a permanent duality between minority in the national political community and citizen. In addition, such an approach, crystallised around the debate over dual citizenship, continues to perpetuate the idea of an 'Other' introduced into the political community. It reinforces the idea of a national minority with a separate identity, retaining the status of foreigner despite its accession to legal citizenship. The result is a distinction between real and false citizens. Although dual citizenship can be viewed as provisional and a pragmatic means to promoting inclusion in national citizenship, making it the touchstone of debates over a change in the law – despite the equality of rights ensured by the law – results in a separation of nationalities and renders both permanent and structural the status of foreigner. It serves to prevent the assimilation of dual nationals.

Conclusion

Dual citizenship relates importantly to two broader themes addressed by this volume: European integration and transnationalism. It is normatively and practically encouraged by the expansion of transnational 'solidarity networks' based on an identity – national, religious, linguistic or regional – and on common interests that transcend national frontiers. The networks develop in response to new communication technology, the emergence of large regional collectivities (particularly the EU and its institutions) and the expansion of migratory movements. They evince financial, cultural, social, political and even ideological transfer, but they emphasise also the multiplication, from a national basis, of transnational strategies. Drawing on an immigration experience linking two national spaces, transnationalism responds to a new identity space, tying together cultural references from the country of origin and the country of residence.

In this perspective, the very concept of dual citizenship is bound up with the concept of transnationalism insofar as both rely on multiple national references and national belonging, as well as on at least two arenas of political participation. Transnationalism also presents a paradox. Even if the extranational networks seek to circumvent national politics and thus constitute a challenge to nation-states, they increasingly appear as indispensable structures for demands that remain national and, as such, maintain the nation-state as a legal source of identity. Paradoxically, the transnational logic reinforces demands within the nation-state for equal rights and treatment for the immigration population, as well as for a struggle against racism. Transnational frameworks, in reality, act on states from the outside, as it is in the context of national citizenship that the limits of the recognition of difference and, as a result, the expression of identity permitted, are negotiated (Kastoryano, 1998).

However, dual citizenship does not necessarily imply a simultaneous participation in two political arenas. Citizens are only citizens of the state in which they fully exercise their rights and obligations. Naturalisation, the process through which an individual joins a political community, assures their inclusion, subject to certain conditions. These conditions, however, only concern the link between individuals and *their new political community*, in the framework of their territorially limited state. Naturally, neither a forgetting nor a cultural amnesia of the previous citizenship or nationality should accompany this process, but these can be reserved for private life. Their legal validity flows merely from agreements between states.[14] As a result, the argument developed around the 'democratic influence' of dual citizenship (Spiro: this volume) – the application in the countries of origin of western democratic values – has only limited applicability.

The meaningful question is thus not dual citizenship but simply citizenship itself. Dual citizenship can only constitute one stage in the negotiation of citizenship. This negotiation rests on the elaboration of new codes of coexistence in redefining certain cultural values or reinforcing others. The goal is to reconcile the unitary nation state with the 'fact' of modern pluralistic societies, to ensure a historical continuity and to recognise the particularities that crop up in the public sphere, in short to reestablish the link between the state and civil society in order to arrive at a recombination of the social and political contract. It is a question of a balance between civil society and the state, or of a link between cultural diversity and a citizenship that undermines neither civic principles nor the final identity of the entire collectivity.

In Germany, the right of children born in the country to citizenship, proposed by the new law, is evidence of an important step towards the acceptance of the 'Other'. Yet, changes in attitudes, reflected in discourse and political rhetoric, are as important as laws and institutional practices. It is here that the reconciliation of citizenship and identity gains importance. As Charles Taylor rightly emphasised, it is difficult to conceive of a democratic state actually stripped of all dimensions of identity (Taylor: 1992, 135–153). Germany, perhaps more than other nations, is, because of a past whose scars have not entirely healed, subject to intellectual and political scrutiny. Nationality laws must not go against the democratic route followed since the end of the War. Thus, the real challenge for the country is to encourage an identification of its 'new citizens' with Germany's institutions and its fundamental constitutional principles, to help them in developing a sense of responsibility towards the political life of their new 'community of destiny' and, finally, to affirm itself as a nation-state in Europe.

References

K.J. Bade ed., *Bevölkerung, Arbeitsmarket und Wanderung in Deutschland seit der Mitte des 19 juts*, (tome 1), Ostfilden, 1984.

K.J. Bade, *Deutsche im Ausland – Fremde in Deutschland – Migration in Geschichte und Gegenwart*, Munich, 1994, 442–455.

S. Berman, 'Civil Society and Political Institutionalisation', *American Behavioral Scientist*, vol. 40, no.5, March–April 1997, 562–574.

R. Brubaker, *Citizenship and Nationhood in France and Germany*, Cambridge, Mass., 1992.

J.H. Carens, 'Why Naturalisation Should be Easy', in *Immigration and Citizenship in the 21st Century*, N. M. J. Pickus ed., Littlefield, 1998.

L. Dumont, *L'idéologie allemande. France-Allemagne et retour*, Paris, 1991.

Dieter Gosewinkel, 'Citizenship and Nationhood: The Historical Development of the German Case', in *European Citizenship, Multiculturalism and the State*, U.L.Preuss and F. Requejo, eds, Baden Baden, 1998, 125–137.

J. Habermas, 'Immigration et chauvinisme du bien-être', in *Revue Nouvelle*, 10, 1992.

R. Kastoryano, *La France, l'Allemagne et leurs immigrés. Négocier l'identité*, Paris, 1997.

R. Kastoryano, 'Participation transnationale et citoyenneté. Les immigrés dans l'Union européenne'; *Culture et Conflit*, no. 28, 1998.

P.J. Katzenstein, *Policy and Politics in West Germany. The Growth of a Semi Sovereign State*, Temple University Press, 1987.

J. Leca, 'Individualisme et citoyenneté', in Pierre Birnbaum and Jean Leca eds., *Sur l'individualisme*, Paris, 1986, 159–213.

J.Leca, 'Nationalité et citoyenneté dans l'Europe des immigrations, in *Logiques d'Etat et immigration en Europe*, J.Costa-Lascoux and P.Weil, eds, Paris, 1992.

La lettre de la citoyenneté, no. 31, January-February 1998.

T.H. Marshall, *Class, Citzenship and Social Development*; Chicago, 1964.

Migration New Sheet, Brussels, December 1991, cited in *The Economic and Political Impact of Turkish Migration in Germany*, Zentrum für Türkeistuden, March 1993.

N.M.J. Pickus, *Immigration and Citizenship in the 21st Century*, Rowma, Littlefield, 1998.

P.H. Schuck, 'Plural Citizenship', in *Immigration and Citizenship in the 21st Century*, ed. N. M. J. Pickus, Littlefield, 1998.

F. Sen, *L'intégration des Turcs en RFA et ses limites*, *Migrations-Société*, May-August, 1990.

F. Sen, Yasemin Karakasoglu, *F.Almanya'da yasayan Türklerin ve diger yabancilarin seçme ve seçilme hakki, partiler ve çifte vatandaslik üzerine görüsleri*, Essen, September 1994.

C. Taylor, 'Les institutions dans la vie nationale,' in *Rapprocher les solitudes. Ecrits sur le fédéralisme et le nationalisme au Canada* (textes réunis par Guy Laforest), Sainte-Foy, Quebec, 1992, 135–153.

M. Walzer, The Civil Society Argument, in *Radical Democracy*, ed. C. Mouffe, London, 1994.

Notes

1. Translated by Randall Hansen.
2. In this paper, citizenship and nationality are synonymous in the context of the nation-state; French/German nationality/citizenship are identical. In the

context of dual citizenship I define citizenship as a right in the country of residence and nationality as a right to an identity stemming from the belonging to
a nation.

 4. The public debates are published in, *Etre Français aujourd'hui et demain*, Paris,
    coll 10/18 1988
 5. Joseph Carens distinguishes between three basic conditions that can be legiti-
    mately expected of those taking nationality: conformity to the law, an adjust-
    ment of attitudes in line with fundamental social norms and citizenship and an
    affirmation of the society's essential goals. Following Carens, the last is the
    most important criterion for naturalisation (Carens 1998).
 6. The contrast is even sharper in French: *le droit du sol* versus *le droit du sang*. A
    law adopted in 1999, granting individuals a conditional citizenship when they
    are born of individuals legally resident in Germany, will likely alter German
    citizenship considerably. As it is too soon to know the character of these
    changes, however, this chapter limits itself to the pre-1999 situation.
 7. Also see 'Trends and Issues of Historical Migration Research in the Federal
    Republic of Germany, in *Migration*, 6, no. 89, 7–28: 'Politik in der Einwan-
    derungssituation: Migration - Integration – Minderheiten', in Bade (1994).
 8. The association is superficially modelled on the *judische Gemeinde zu Berlin*,
    both in its discourse and its actions, as if the members wanted to advertise their
    good relations with both Turkey and Israel. More importantly, however, the
    appellative similarity reflects an effort to demonstrate their openness towards
    other communities and minorities. Even more than openness, it is as the
    organisation wanted to prove to German public opinion, as well as to its own
    supporters, its role in the formation of a 'minority' inspired by a 'model minor-
    ity', and to sensitise them to a fight against racism, of the sort that a support for
    Jewish organisations could only strengthen.
 9. It is this that led Peter Katzenstein to refer to the German state as a 'semi-
    sovereign state' (Katzenstein: 1987, 168–192). Also see Berman (1997).
10. Marshall (1964). In the same lecture, Marshall reexamined citizenship in terms
    of social class, blurring the legal and political content of the concept with the
    social.
11. For an examination of citizenship as a sense of belonging and as political
    involvement, see Leca (1986).
12. Statistics from the Union of Turkish entrepreneurs Berlin. See also Zentrum für
    Türkeistuden; *Konsumgewohnheiten und wirtschaftliche situation der türkischen
    Bevölkerung in der Bundesrepublik Deutschland*, Essen, September 1992.
13. The author emphasises the fact that the democratic constitution of Weimer
    (1919) placed the accent on a conception of civil society granting equal rights
    for men and women, coinciding with the legal status of citizenship defined as
    affiliation to the state. The 1935 Nuremberg laws overturned this law.
14. Schuck (1998) develops this argument.
15. Dual citizenship was integrated into the Turkish constitution, which permits
    the attribution of Turkish identity to a child born in Turkey but no longer pos-
    sessing Turkish citizenship, or to a child born in Germany of parents born in
    Turkey.

III

OTHER EUROPEAN TRADITIONS

CHAPTER 8

THE DOG THAT DIDN'T BARK: DUAL NATIONALITY IN THE UNITED KINGDOM

Randall Hansen

In the U.S., Germany and elsewhere in Europe,[1] dual citizenship is viewed with suspicion and hostility. Once tantamount to treason, American administrations and the U.S. Congress viewed dual nationality with intense distaste during the Cold War, and the very act of voting in a foreign election led directly to expatriation (Spiro: 1997, 1444). Despite a more open (at least informal) policy since the 1960s, a 1998 decision by Mexico allowing its citizens to acquire a second citizenship without relinquishing their Mexican one has inflamed Cold War fears of foreign influence and shadowy fifth columns infiltrating domestic U.S. politics. In Germany, the generally liberal constitutional court (BVG) claimed in a famous 1974 ruling that dual nationality was an 'evil' (*Übel*) that the state had every interest in avoiding (Hailbronner: this volume). More recently, the SPD/Green coalition's attempt to reform German nationality law in a manner accepting dual nationality met the intense opposition of the CDU/CSU, and the loss of the traditional Hessen stronghold in the *Landtag* elections forced the government to modify its proposal (Hailbronner: this volume).

By contrast, the striking feature of the U.K. is the country's liberal, even cavalier, view of dual nationality. The Home Office, Britain's Ministry of the Interior, views dual and even plural nationality as a matter of indifference. No effort is made to encourage applicants for naturalisation to make even token efforts to relinquish previous citizenship(s). This official indifference is mirrored in the public. In a country in which colonial immigration was one of the major issues of the early post-war decades, and in which opposition to non-white immigration reached hysterical levels in the late 1960s and early 1970s, not once has dual nationality served as the focus of anti-immigration campaigners or of public opposition.[2]

This chapter examines the U.K.'s current policy on dual nationality. It attempts to explain the current operation of dual nationality in practice and to offer an explanation of its liberality relative to the U.K.'s American and (some of its) European partners. The argument proceeds in three steps. It begins with a description of the United Kingdom's current policy towards dual nationality, briefly outlines past practice and, finally, offers an account of current liberality. To summarise briefly, dual nationality is accepted in the U.K. because it creates no discernable problems; this, in turn, reflects a particularly British approach to policy in which policies are developed on the basis not of abstract legal or philosophical principles but of the success or failure of previous policy efforts.[3] More positively, dual nationality is viewed as an instrument for promoting the integration of migrants into British society. This liberal attitude and expansive policy reflects, in turn, two factors: first, British identity/belonging was founded until 1948 not on *Staatsangehörigkeit* but on allegiance; and, second, when citizenship was introduced in 1948 it was, by definition, plural citizenship.

Current U.K. policy on dual nationality

The U.K.'s policy on dual nationality can be briefly described: there are almost no limits to it. Britons naturalising abroad are free to acquire a second or third nationality without informing the Home Office. Likewise, individuals acquiring British citizenship are not required to renounce their previous nationality, and the government uses no other means to encourage renunciation.[4] There is, for example, no equivalent to the American oath of allegiance containing a pledge to abjure other nationalities. The Home Office keeps no statistics on dual nationality.[5]

Diplomatic protection

The main implication of dual nationality for the British concerns the issue of diplomatic protection. In this case, the U.K. government is willing to provide diplomatic protection to all its nationals, except when they are in the country of their other nationality; in such cases, they are under the protection and, at times, at the mercy of the state of which they are a national. Thus, a Pakistani/British dual national can receive no formal assistance from the British embassy while in Pakistan. Informally, however, the embassy can provide assistance in the form of giving unofficial advice, contacting relatives in the U.K., and so forth.

Military service & security

The U.K. ended military service in the late 1950s. Before this time, dual nationals were subject to the military service obligation in the U.K., whether or not they were also subject to it in another country. Dual nationals would be called up sometime after the age of 17, but they could defer it until 21. At that time, if they had not formally renounced British citizenship, they were forced to complete their military service.[6]

In issues of security, it is important to distinguish between dual nationals by birth and descent and dual nationals by naturalisation. Dual nationals by birth and descent cannot under any circumstances be deprived of their nationality, even for High Treason. They can only be charged with treasonous activities. By contrast, a dual national by naturalisation (that is, a foreigner who acquires U.K. nationality and keeps his/her former nationality) may be deprived of his/her British nationality. As in all such cases, the decision is taken by an *ad hoc* committee on the deprivation of citizenship, which is appointed by the government and consists of 'the Great and the Good' (eminent politicians, judges, intellectuals, etc.). The essential factor here, however, is not dual nationality, rather, it is being British by naturalisation. Individuals who acquire British citizenship and renounce their former citizenship(s) remain, in principle, subject to citizenship deprivation, although British law prevents the deprivation of citizenship if this will lead to statelessness. Certain elements of the Home Office are unhappy with this provision, viewing it as an unjustified distinction between naturalised citizens and others, one that rests uneasily with Britain's obligations under international law, including the European Council's 1997 Convention on nationality.

Paths to dual citizenship

As elsewhere, dual nationality may be acquired through four processes, and U.K. policy differs slightly in each of these:

1. When a child is born in the U.K. of a dual national or of a foreigner permanently resident in the U.K., the child is British by birth and may hold another nationality by descent; as far as the U.K. is concerned, the child's British nationality is unquestionable.
2. In instances where dual nationality is acquired by birth abroad to a British citizen born in the U.K. (for example, a British citizen himself/herself born in the U.K. gives birth to a child in the U.S.) the child is unquestionably British; under the U.S. constitution, the child is also unquestionably American.[7]
3. In cases in which a foreigner naturalises in the U.K., the Home Office asks no questions about the applicant's intentions with respect to his or

her previous nationality, and it does not inform other states of their nationals' decisions to naturalise.

4. In cases where British citizens naturalise abroad, they retain their U.K. nationality unless they specifically apply for the renunciation of U.K. citizenship, which is only granted if the other citizenship is already acquired or is guaranteed. The U.K. thus does not recognise naturalisation abroad as 'implying' renunciation even if it so implies under foreign law, and it would not recognise a verbal renunciation as valid. Thus, a formula to the effect of 'In acquiring nationality X, I hereby renounce all other citizenships and shall henceforth consider myself solely a national of X' would be meaningless under U.K. law.

The U.K. does little to assist other states in preventing dual nationality. It does not inform other governments when their citizens acquire British nationality. The U.K. receives many requests for confirmation or denial of the claim that a particular citizen holding another nationality has acquired U.K. citizenship. The U.K. only provides this information with the consent of the naturalised citizen, whose right to prevent the information's disclosure is seen by the Home Office as protected under British data protection legislation. Germany recently asked the U.K. to provide it with lists of Germans acquiring British nationality; the U.K. sat on the matter until it was no longer relevant.

Dual nationality in previous centuries

The U.K.'s current tolerant or, depending on one's view, cavalier attitude is not new. The U.K.'s pre-1949 policy towards dual nationality developed in two broad phases: pre-1870 and 1870–1948. In the first period, judicial opinion was divided over the common law's implications for dual nationality, but policy towards it was nonetheless expansive; in the second, the government officially opposed dual nationality in certain instances, but the civil service (and above all the Foreign Office) facilitated it in practice. Since 1949, British nationality law has officially embraced dual nationality.

Policy pre-1870: Dual nationality in the common law & allegiance tradition

Before the late nineteenth century, the U.K. did not have a specific policy on dual nationality; rather, it was addressed, generally only by implication, through a combination of parliamentary acts and judicial decisions. Britons naturalising abroad retained their connection to the British Crown, although they may have faced penalties for doing so, such as losing inheritance rights (Parry: 1957, 125). Dual nationality, or, more accurately, dual allegiance, flowed inevitably from the basis of British 'belonging'. From the early seventeenth century until the 1940s, British citizenship (in the sense of *Staatsangehörigkeit*) did not exist; rather individuals were tied to the United Kingdom, derivatively, through their allegiance to the Crown. Simply put, the rights and duties that would be associated today with British citizenship flowed from an individual's allegiance to the King or Queen. The doctrine originated in a famous 1608 judicial ruling known as 'Calvin's Case'. English courts heard a case brought on behalf of a Scottish child, Robert Calvin, over the Scottish possession of English lands. At the time, Scots were aliens in England, even though King James VI of Scotland had become King James I of Great Britain in 1604. The courts ruled that Calvin was not an alien; all Scots born within King James' rule were English subjects, while those born before were not. This simple decision had two fundamental consequences. First, it introduced *jus soli*, or nationality by birth, into British law, where it rested until 1981. The most common means to becoming a British subject was birth within the monarch's realm. Second, the decision eventually meant that allegiance was not linked with birth or residence in England, Britain or the United Kingdom: all individuals born anywhere within what became the British Empire were, legally speaking, British subjects with equal rights. At the empire's peak early this century, some six hundred million individuals had a technical right to enter the U.K. and to avail themselves of all the rights now associated with British citizenship (Hansen: 1999). In terms of dual nationality, the allegiance tradition meant that it was inevitable. Individuals born within the U.K./Empire were British subjects irrespective of other citizenships they might acquire by descent, and British subjecthood, once acquired, could not be renounced. Allegiance was perpetual.[8]

In addition to furthering dual nationality, perpetual allegiance engendered major foreign policy dilemmas following the American Revolution. As there was no provision in British law for expatriation, individuals born in the American colonies before the revolution remained subject to Crown duties following it (Parry: 1957, 125). Thus, after 1807, British captains regularly stopped American ships and seized both deserters from the British navy and genuine American citizens (Dummett and Nicol: 1990, 87). The practice was one of the causes of the War of 1812 (Spiro: this volume). Later, the U.K. applied a similar policy to Irish British subjects by birth who naturalised in the U.S. When they protested against British policy in Ireland at the Canadian border, they were arrested and convicted in Canada of treason and sedition (Parry: 1957, 126).

Although dual nationality, or dual allegiance, seemed to create serious international problems in the nineteenth century, these were, in fact, problems of expatriation. They arose from the U.K.'s insistence on taking its nationality legislation to the logical extreme in order to place pressure on its erstwhile American colonies. They were finally regulated in 1870, when British legislation made provision for the renunciation of British nationality.

1870–1948: Dual nationality limited in law, encouraged in practice

The 1870 Naturalisation Act concerned both naturalisation and expatriation. In the former, it extended measures, adopted in 1844, that empowered the Home Secretary to naturalise aliens resident in the U.K. for at least five years; in 1870, as in 1844, the renunciation of one's existing nationality was not a precondition (Parry: 1957, 126). There was thus never a period in which individuals naturalising as British nationals were required to give up their other citizenship(s). The Act also implemented the Bancroft Convention with the U.S., which provided for the mutual recognition of naturalisation (Parry: 1957, 126). Individuals naturalising abroad could, for the first time, divest themselves of their status as British subjects.

Expatriation was not, however, automatic. Although scholars have held that Section 6 of the legislation led to the automatic loss of British subject-hood and a transferral to the status of alien (Dummett and Nicol: 1990, 87), the law was applied with considerable liberality. The British national archives contain a large number of documents concerning British nationals naturalising abroad; in all cases, the Foreign Office sought to ensure that they retained their British nationality. When, for instance, another country's laws dictated that acquiring its citizenship implied a renunciation of other nationalities, and when it informed the applicant of this, the British did not view this as tantamount to expatriation. Expatriation only occurred from the U.K. point of view when British nationality was explicitly renounced.[9]

A number of documents suggest that the U.K. was even keen to encourage dual nationality. In 1946, a dual American/British citizen had left the U.S. on her British passport (not yet holding an American one) and wished to return to the U.S. from Algeria. The American consulate refused to give her a visa, and informed her that she would have to apply for an American passport. To do so required surrendering her British passport. She took the matter to the British Foreign office, and the Acting British Consulate General wrote to London. He explained the situation and suggested he take her British passport and give her a certificate of British nationality, which would allow her to apply for a British visa on her American passport.[10] The Foreign Office replied that this was unnecessary, and that it had no difficulty with her holding two passports. It was suggested she surrender the U.K. passport to the Foreign Office, and that it would return it to her once she was in the United States.[11] In Holland, some forty years later, a similar policy on Italy's part towards Dutch/Italian dual nationals was important in encouraging the Netherlands to soften their opposition towards dual nationality (Groenendijk and Heis: 2001).

The archives also confirm the U.K.'s liberal policy towards those naturalising as British citizens and those foreign nationals entitled to a British passport. In all cases, the only issue in granting them the passport was whether they had a right to it; the other nationality was an irrelevance. In one instance, a dual Argentinean/British national gave up his British citizenship to avoid conscription and lived on his Argentinean passport during the war. Following the war, he applied to reacquire it. One Foreign Office official very much wanted to deny his application, and the legal rules were unclear. It was, however, ruled that if he had a legal claim to the passport, neither his failure to serve in the army nor his second passport could serve as an impediment.[12]

In 1948, the U.K. government adopted the first formal definition of citizenship through the British Nationality Act, 1948. Section 19 formalised this practice, stating that individuals acquiring another citizenship would only lose their British citizenship if they formally renounced it to the Home Secretary, and if the Home Secretary approved the renunciation. The policy still operates today.

With this background, the essay now turns to the issue of why the U.K.'s policy on dual nationality is so liberal.

Dual nationality's origins and goals

The single most important reason for the U.K.'s policy is that dual nationality creates no meaningful problems for the U.K. Policy in the U.K. is not guided by abstract legal principles, still less by philosophical aims. Even in the emotive area of immigration and 'race', policies are maintained or rejected on the basis of whether or not they 'work'; positively, this means achieving their goals, negatively, this means not giving rise to troublesome side-effects (Favell: 1998). Dual nationality seemed to create few problems in the era of military service, and it creates, for the Home Office, none now.

More positively, dual nationality is also seen by the U.K. as a tool for integration. Acquiring citizenship encourages migrants' identification with the U.K. and their integration into British society. This, in turn, improves 'race relations'. British policymakers speak incessantly about 'race relations', by which they mean harmony between different ethnic groups and an absence of threats to public order by any one group or groups. Dual nationality is an instrument in this policy. As a 1980 White Paper that formed the basis for the U.K.'s most recent nationality law reform put it,

> [T]his country has absorbed large numbers of immigrants in recent years from both foreign and Commonwealth countries, and it is to be expected that many of them will retain strong links with their countries of birth; and that

they would hope, where the law of that country allows, to retain their original citizenship and perhaps pass it on to their children born here. *If the retention of that citizenship on becoming a British citizen will assist them in the process of settling down in this country then the Government would see this as a good reason for our not requiring them to renounce it* (emphasis added) (Cmnd. 7987: 1980, par 89).

The role of dual citizenship in promoting integration is, however, secondary to that played by Britain's three acts against racial discrimination: the Race Relations Acts of 1965, 1968 and 1975, outlawing discrimination in employment and housing, and allowing the active recruitment of ethnic minorities.

Dual nationality often serves less progressive ends, allowing the national community to maintain ethnic and/or cultural links with the national community abroad. The U.K. once saw dual nationality as a means to maintaining ties to emigrés and encouraging the dissemination of British values. Another anecdote illustrates this aim. Just after World War II, a Brazilian/British dual national left Brazil on his Brazilian passport, and presented both his passports to the British authorities. The immigration officer stamped only the British; the individual asked to have the other stamped, as it would be hard to reenter Brazil with an unstamped passport. Following standard practice, the immigration officer stamped it and added the words 'entered the United Kingdom on his British passport'. As Brazil was opposed to dual nationality, this rendered the passport almost useless. Under Foreign Office pressure, the Home Office agreed to alter its policy.[13] The Foreign Office justified its demand as follows: 'the fact that in [Brazil] they are regarded as local, and not as British, nationals, is often of very considerable assistance to us. It would be a pity if, by administrative action at this end such action as that described [i.e., the landing on a U.K. stamp], their position were made more difficult than it already is, and our interests indirectly made to suffer'.[14] As a country that financially sponsored migration with the aim of maintaining British culture and values abroad, the U.K. saw a great advantage in large numbers of British citizens living abroad and acquiring other citizenships while still maintaining ties to Britain. Such an aim, however, no longer actuates British policy. The country has largely turned away from the Commonwealth as the foundation of its foreign policy and takes relatively little official interest in British communities abroad. It is doubtful that this quasi-imperialist sentiment plays much of a role any longer.

Citizenship vs. subjecthood

One of the many consequences of the tradition and history of allegiance (described above) was a British indifference to citizenship. When a formal definition of British citizenship was forced upon Britain by the Commonwealth in 1948, politicians derided the notion of citizenship as 'republican', 'alien' to British traditions (Hansard: 21 June 1948, cols 992–1083). The Government that passed the legislation, the British Nationality Act of 1948, seemed embarrassed by the concept, eager to stress its essential instrumentality to subjecthood (Hansard: 19 July 1948, cols 48–51). For most of the postwar period, British élites were uncomfortable with the language of citizenship, and even today senior politicians will refer to 'Her Majesty's subjects' (Hogg: 1990). This is not to claim that there is no tradition of British citizenship in the sense of an identifiable set of ideas or traditions about the rights and obligations of members of society; on the contrary. These values are, however, not seen to be importantly linked with a passport as such and, conversely, the possession of other passports does not preclude one from subscribing to those values. When individuals appear to violate those values, the issue is not seen to be one of dual nationality. At the height of the Rushdie Affair, when (a minority of) British Muslims were baying for Rushdie's blood and promised to carry out the Fatwa, some saw it as a failure of integration, multiculturalism and/or immigration. No one saw it as a problem of dual nationality.

It is also worth considering that Britain's first citizenship was essentially plural in character. The British Nationality Act, 1948 supplanted British subjecthood with a citizenship made up of 'citizenship of the United Kingdom and colonies' + 'citizenship of an independent Commonwealth country'. The former was an imperial category including Britons and all 'colonial subjects' (some six hundred million) under a single citizenship; the latter extended a form of British citizenship to Canadians, Australians, New Zealanders and South Africans. Thus, essentially four 'nationalities' were linked together: 'colonial subjects', (though it had no legal standing, British subjects in, for instance, Jamaica or Kenya likely had a sense of being Jamaicans and Kenyans), British citizens (as now defined), Dominions' citizens (Canadians, Australians, etc.) and citizens of independent Commonwealth countries. Even today, after Britain finally introduced an exclusively British citizenship, there are still four nationalities: British citizenship (for Britons), British national (overseas) citizenship (Chinese citizens of Hong Kong), British Dependent Territories citizenship (for the remaining 'colonies')[15] and British overseas citizenship (stateless individuals in what was the British empire). At the same time, the contested status of Northern Ireland leads to dual nationality. Irish nationality law claims Ulster as part of the Republic, and individuals born in Ulster automatically acquire, or can elect to acquire, Irish nationality; [16] as Ulster is of course part of the U.K., most also acquire British nationality. In light of the extraordinary complexity of British nationality legislation, and the immense anomalies it has given rise to, it is no surprise that migrants' deciding to retain their passports is viewed as an anodyne affair.

In summary, the U.K. has a liberal, even expansive, policy on dual nationality. Dual nationality is allowed because there are no problems associated with it, and because it furthers the integration of aliens resident in the U.K.

Conclusion: Britain and Europe

Nationality law and practice reflects particular, nationally bounded under-standings of belonging, the content of citizenship and the duties associated with it. It develops in response to particular national aims and impera-tives, and lessons should only be drawn with care. Nonetheless, the com-mon British and continental European experience of large-scale, non-European immigration in the post war period, and their common need to reconcile the cultural specificity of Islam with Western values, sug-gests that Europe – and perhaps the U.S. – can view Britain as something of a 'test-case' of dual nationality. For those uneasy about dual national-ity's consequences, the British experience should be reassuring. There is no evidence that the U.K.'s tolerance of dual nationality has resulted in any of the scenarios constructed by its opponents: it has not been a source of immigration, a threat to security, or an impediment to integration. In the first, the U.K. combines a liberal policy on dual nationality with an extremely strict policy on family reunification; all applicants must satisfy requirements on income, housing and spousal intent,[17] and success is by no means assured. Disloyalty and threats to security have not been issues for the simple reason that neither are caused by dual citizenship. Legal permanent residents and single nationals, by birth or through naturalisa-tion, may have no loyalty to the state, and they may engage in espionage. Indeed, anyone interested in the latter would be advised not to become a dual national, as this might draw the authorities' attention.[18] In the U.K., during the darkest hours of World War II, when it appeared inevitable that the country would fall to a Nazi invasion, the British government did not feel compelled to abandon its acceptance of dual nationality, and British/German dual nationals were not interned for being such.[19]

To be sure, the U.K. is not free of difficulties linked with integration. Although the British extreme-right is a spent force, there are a large num-ber of racially motivated attacks each year – broadly similar to those in Germany (Hansen: 1999, Human Rights Watch: 1997); British racist atti-tudes remain within the European median and cannot be held up as a model (Eurobarometer: 1997); in the 1980s, there were several inner-city riots started by disenchanted ethnic minorities; the Rushdie Affair created concerns over allegiance in a country with a large Muslim population; finally, a senior Conservative politician suggested as late as 1990 that West Indians take a 'cricket test' as proof of their loyalty ('which side do they cheer for? England or Jamaica?'). Again, these difficulties are not, however, occasioned by dual nationality; they all exist entirely independently of it.

Dual nationality has created few problems in Britain; indeed, in a country with arguably the fullest sense in Europe of its status as a multi-cultural society, it has served it well.

References

Cmnd. 7987, British Nationality Law: Outline of Proposed Legislation, London: HMSO, 1980, Quoted in Fransman, Laurie Fransman's, *British Nationality Law*, London: Butterworths, 1998.

A. Dummett and A. Nicol, *Subjects, Citizens, Aliens and Others*, London, 1990.

Eurobarometer: *Public Opinion in the European Union.* (Brussels: European Commission, DG X), 48: Autumn 1997), released March 1998.

A. Favell, *Philosophies of Integration: Immigration and the Idea of Citizenship in France and Britain*, Houndsmills, 1998.

K. Groenendijk and Eric Heijs, 'Immigration, Immigrants and Nationality Law in the Netherlands 1945–1980,' *Towards a European Nationality: Citizenship, Immigration and Nationality Law in the EU*, R. Hansen and P. Weil, eds, Houndmills, 2001.

Hansard Parliamentary Debates (Lords) (156), cols. 992–1083, 21 June 1948.

Hansard Parliamentary Debates (Commons) (454), cols. 48–51, 19 July 1948.

R. Hansen, 'The Politics of Citizenship in 1940s Britain: The British Nationality Act,' 20th Century British History, 10, no. 1, 1999, 67–95.

R. Hansen, 'Migration, Citizenship and Race in the EU: between incorporation and exclusion,' *European Journal of Political Research*, 35, no. 4, June 1999, 415–444.

R. Hansen, 'From Subjects to Citizens,' in *Towards a European Nationality: Citizenship, Immigration and Nationality Law in the EU*, eds R. Hansen and P. Weil, Houndmills, 2001.

Q. Hogg, *A Sparrow's Flight: Memoirs* (London: Collins, 1990). Human Rights Watch, Racist Violence in the United Kingdom, New York, 1997.

C. Parry, *Nationality and Citizenship Laws of The Commonwealth and of The Republic of Ireland*, London, 1957.

Clive R. Symmons, 'Irish Nationality Law,' in *Towards a European Nationality: Citizenship, Immigration and Nationality Law in the EU*, eds R. Hansen and P. Weil, Houndmills, 2001.

Peter J. Spiro, 'Dual Nationality and the Meaning of Citizenship,' *Emory Law Journal*, 46, no. 4, 1997, 1411–1485.

Notes

1. Notably Austria, Denmark, Luxembourg and Switzerland.
2. During the debates over the British Nationality Act, 1981, a few Conservatives, generally on the right of the party, expressed opposition on principle to dual nationality, but it came to nothing. Enoch Powell, who led a demonic campaign against immigration in the 1960s and 1970s, argued in 1981 that '[o]ne matter has not yet been mentioned at all, curiously enough, in the debate – dual citizenship. There is an immense quantity of dual citizenship in the United Kingdom at present, an immense range of possession of dual citizenship, dor-

mant or otherwise. Is dual citizenship really compatible with nationality? Is it really compatible with the inherent obligations and implications of allegiance that lie at the foundation of national status and nationhood?' (Hansard (Commons), Vol. 997, col. 967, 28 January 1981). The government, and implicitly the country, have answered yes.

3. One exception to this is economic policy; unlike on the continent, on which economic policy has largely been made by lawyers and/or professional politicians, macro-economic policy in the U.K. has been heavily influenced by economists, with debatable results.

4. The one very minor exception to this concerns a residual category – British subjects without citizenship. Under the British Nationality Act, 1981 (Section 35), such individuals lose this status if they acquire another citizenship. The 'citizenship', however, does not provide the right of entry to the United Kingdom, or any other right generally linked with citizenship. It is a legal status, originally created by Sections 13 and 16 of the British Nationality Act, 1948 (BNA, 1948), granted to those who (a) held or still hold that status because of the 1948 legislation; (b) were Irish citizens who applied for British subject status under Section 2 of BNA, 1948; (c) were entitled to that status through marriage or (d) were otherwise deemed, through Secretary of State registration for instance, a British subject without citizenship. See British Nationality Act, 1981, Sections 30–34.

5. Although it does keep statistics on the nationality of those acquiring British citizenship, these do not provide information on individuals who automatically lose their previous nationality, decide to renounce it, or keep it.

6. PRO, FO 372/4712, Letter from the Foreign Office to the Danish Minister, 14 March 1946.

7. The matter is more complicated for children born of British citizens by descent. See Section 3 of the British Nationality Act, 1981.

8. In nineteenth century Europe, perpetual allegiance was a common basis for nationality. See Spiro (1997)

9. PRO, FO 372/4754, Letter from E. W. Light, Foreign Office, to Under-Secretary of State, Home Office, 21 June 1946.

10. PRO, FO 372/4705 Letter from John Martin to His Majesty's Principal Secretary of State for Foreign Affairs, 23 August 1946.

11. PRO, FO 372/4705, Letter from the Foreign Office to John Martin, 5 October 1946.

12. PRO, FO 372/4752, Letter from Principal Secretary of State for Foreign Affairs, 20 September 1946.

13. For the file containing the full story, see PRO, FO 372/4683.

14. PRO, FO 372/4683, Letter to Perks, 5 July 1946.

15. The British Government has recently announced that it will grant all such individuals British citizenship.

16. The matter has recently been complicated by the 1998 Belfast Agreement – part of the Northern Ireland peace process. For the details, see Symmons (2000).

17. See R. Hansen, 'From Subjects to Citizens: Immigration and Nationality Law in the United Kingdom', in *Citizenship, Immigration and Nationality: Nationality Law in the European Union*, eds R. Hansen and P. Weil, Houndmills, 2001.

18. Spiro, Embracing Dual Nationality, p. 9.

19. Though they might be interned if it was decided that, according to other criteria, they constituted a threat to security.

CHAPTER 9

DUAL NATIONALITY AND THE FRENCH CITIZENSHIP TRADITION[1]

Géraud de la Pradelle

The concepts and reasoning that bind together legal principles are moulded by political ideology. This interrelationship has consequences for their practical application and, indeed, for their internal coherence. It is nonetheless plausible to believe that the law generally triumphs over ideology through its utility: the fact that its subjects share with jurists the same experiences facilitates the acceptance of those governmental norms validated by law.

This suggestion is readily verified in the area of nationality. In this domain, legal principles, or legal constructions, are formed through interpretations of reality, and above all of historical facts, which are as tendentious as they are impressive. This alchemy continually reinforces collective, and especially national, myths that the law holds (*revêt*) a surplus of legitimacy. At the same time, the law in turn legitimises governmental rules aiming at orienting the passions that develop through these myths. It thus allows the capture of their power so that it may serve the state's political ends. These are, in the main, remarkably realistic, to the point of contradicting in practice, where necessary, the ideology supposed to underlie legal principles.

This is, at any rate, the manner in which French law treats the fact of dual citizenship and reconciles powerful emotions, founding myths, and political calculations and contingencies. The coherence of this mish-mash's result often leaves something to be desired. This may not be true of its practical application, although it often serves inopportune ends. This seems to be a constant thread in history more or less everywhere.

In any case, the recent evolution of law governing dual citizenship has followed the same course in almost all countries. It is characterised by two stages.[2] The dawn of the nineteenth century opened the first phase. It was characterised by the dominance, in legal discourse, of ideology that was nationalist, imperialist and, above all, radically hostile to dual nationality. It justified, as a result, practices aimed at outlawing it. At the same time, however, this legal discourse nourished the seeds of a legitimisation of differing practices that itself engendered, however discretely, plural citizenship.

Despite the diversity of cultural traditions and national interests, hostility to dual nationality developed everywhere, and its strands were sufficiently convergent to influence the development of the law of nations. The preamble to the Hague Convention of 12 April 1930 stated that it 'is in the general interest of the international community to have all its members acknowledge that every individual should possess one nationality and only one'. Although the Convention was not universally ratified, this recommendation became part of customary law, of which it remains a part today.

Certain aspects of the reasoning that presumes to justify the recommendation in law have also passed into legal custom. It is organised around a universally accepted legal theory, forming, in the last instance, the thrust of the recommendation formulated by the Hague convention. This common theory has as its ideological pedestal an ideology of political independence, one expressed through the notion of sovereignty. It holds – following in particular French jurists – that the sovereign state is more than the sum of a territory, a governmental apparatus and a people subjected to the latter (Dinh, Daillet and Pellet: 1999, 265). The ideology of political independence additionally requires that there is an ultimate authority; the mastery over these elements must begin with the population, which includes the sum of individuals possessing its nationality.

Accordingly, the very notion of a sovereign state – as it was constructed by the jurists – provides strong and universally applicable reasons for prohibiting dual citizenship. In effect, since the population appropriated by the sovereign state through the attribution of its nationality forms the substance of the state itself, it cannot be held in common between several states without diminishing their sovereign independence. How, this theory continues, can the principle of sovereignty accommodate the fact that a state is constituted by the 'substance' of another state? What is more, the consequences of dual citizenship – above all dual allegiance – frustrate the exclusive fidelity that normally flows from the obedience of a population to the state constituted by it. In practice, this results in considerable loss, if not forfeiture, of nationality through the acquisition of a foreign citizenship and in the subordination of naturalisation to the repudiation of all other allegiance(s).

The intellectual edifice constructed by jurists is nevertheless not without flaws. If one element of judicial logic, built upon the concept of the state, leads to a condemnation of dual citizenship, another points – on the foundation of the same concept – to the necessary means for justifying its existence in cases of need. In effect, the judicial state is only sovereign in that it can attribute its nationality, in a unilateral and discretionary manner, to its constitutive population. International law entrenches this prerequisite in that it grants to each state 'exclusive competence' – in other words, sovereignty – in defining its nationals.[3] Paradoxically, the rigorous respect for this competence leads ineluctably to dual nationality, as its development is largely beyond the nation-state's control. As competence is 'exclusive', each state is only able to attribute a single nationality – its own. As a result, no state can either directly create a dual national or directly prevent his/her existence. Exclusive competence, moreover, gives more than a fortuitous origin to dual citizenship; it provides a possible justification. In effect, the exercise of legal competence under the law of nations is, fundamentally, legitimate; its inevitable consequences cannot be, *a priori*, subject to condemnation.

In practice, states have never rigorously applied the apparently accurate reasoning that prohibits dual citizenship. Without overtly repudiating this reasoning, many states have, throughout history, discretely but deliberately encouraged the multiplication of dual nationals. It was for them a matter of pursuing particular ends: at times 'defensive', through the maintenance of their citizenship for their nationals abroad, at times 'offensive', through the establishment of ties of allegiance to foreign populations (Darras: 1986). Such policies, always justified by local legal theory,[4] which was further – and opportunely – fortified by the universal principle of exclusive competence.

The existence of these selective precedents in favour of dual citizenship, which date from the first phase of its evolution, unquestionably facilitated the transformation characteristic of the next phase. For half a century, in effect, there were noticeable changes in the understanding of the fact of dual nationality, in the policies and practices of states confronting it and, in consequence, in the content of their laws (such as in international instruments). The emergence of new migratory fluxes explains in large measure these new developments.

At the same time, the ancient demand in a number of countries for an exclusive allegiance gave way to an increasing scholarly approval of relative tolerance towards dual belonging. In practice, this shift manifested itself in the conditions under which nationality was attributed and withdrawn: its acquisition by a foreigner depended less often on the repudiation of previous citizenship, and the acquisition of a foreign citizenship resulted less often in the automatic loss of existing citizenship. Indeed, the attribution of nationality is at times even facilitated by the possession of a particular foreign citizenship.

Finally, it is increasingly admitted today that it is not always in a state's interest to prohibit dual citizenship; on the contrary, in certain circumstances the opposite obtains. States have also recognised that multiple belonging is not necessarily contrary to the international community's general interest. It is moreover recognised – or at least, the idea has gained in credibility – that requiring dual citizens to renounce one of their nationalities, and/or systematically refusing to recognise multiple belonging, could violate a fundamental human right.

Despite these expansive developments, the heritage of an earlier epoch weighs heavily. Legal doctrines dating from that period, which condemn dual citizenship, are not spent; a number of practices serving as their point of reference remain in effect. One can thus observe, more or less everywhere and in both discourse and praxis, curious contradictions. Manifestations of a new course in matters of dual nationality continue to multiply, yet, they coexist with vestiges of a past that can only be considered outdated. The French example serves as a testimony to these opposing trends.

Dual citizenship in France

France's evolution has followed the general course, and its attitudes are, like those of other nations, contradictory. Nevertheless, the ideology that largely inspires France – which can be characterised for convenience as 'republican' – maintains a pretence of particularity. This particularity has not, however, isolated France from general developments. There are two reasons explaining this. First, the roots of republican ideology are more European than French, and they predate the establishment of a specifically republican regime (Kriegel: 1999). It could thus easily be accommodated within a legal theory of the state and nationality that has become part of customary law. Second, republican ideology is sufficiently flexible to serve, in France itself, as a common creed for highly diverse strains of thought (Kriegel: 1999, introduction). It legitimises a variety of measures that, in other states, have contrasting justifications.

One of these distinctive traits of French republicanism seems to have played a fundamental role in France's treatment of dual citizenship. It involves a particular conception of the state's constitutive population: rather than 'subjects', it is made up of 'citizens' characterised by the fact that they are *free*, *equal* amongst themselves, and able to participate fully in both *civil* and *political* life (Kriegel: 1999: from 183, Fougeyrollas: 1987, Schnapper: 1994). This special significance is granted by France's constitutional tradition to the terms French 'nation' and 'people'. Through it, sovereignty belongs in law to 'the nation', to 'the people' and thus to 'the universality of French citizens (Constitution of 4 November 1848)'. As a result, sovereignty belongs to the state's constitutive population rather than to its governmental apparatus.

In such conditions, the quality of being French – translated into the law through a *de facto* belonging to the nation[5] – is inseparable from citizenship itself; the two merge together. As a consequence, all French should be citizens according to the principles inscribed in the constitution since 1791.[6]

This principle, however, has long been of more value in its proclamation than its implementation, which was remarkably incremental. It suffices to recall that the *Code Noir* of March 1685,[7] establishing slavery in overseas France, remained in place until the decree of 28 April 1848, despite Article 1 of the 1789 Declaration of the Rights of Man;[8] that the voting system created, for some time, 'passive citizens' stripped of the right to vote; that French women were without political citizenship until 1945; and that, at least when they were married, they had only limited civil citizenship, the last traces of which lasted until 1985. Nonetheless, this aspect of the republican creed, despite its long-lasting bombastic dimension, reinforced a latent aversion towards dual belonging. Generally a metamorphosis of xenophobia, this aversion has corresponded in France to a universal norm, but one whose justification is three-coloured. The French citizen's belonging to civil and political society is conceived of as a complete and freely chosen integration, which by definition can only be exclusive. French jurists condemned dual nationality on the principle of republican nationality. Their hostility, inscribed in law derived from the 1804 civil code, accords well today with the customary recommendation figuring in the Hague Convention.

Despite this, the felicitous flexibility of 'republican' ideology has allowed the public authority to reconcile its prohibition of dual citizenship with the abandonment, when necessary, of that prohibition in the name of national cohesion. In France, national cohesion – so often presented as a given – would hardly exist but for state action. The French nation is much less homogeneous than 'republican' ideology would have us believe. It was always necessary to cement together, through robust efforts, its diverse (*épars*) elements: a population made up of multiple nationalities, a diversity stemming from indigenous cultures, and – compounding both – a profound social fracture (Yves Lequin: 1988, Schnapper: 1991). In addition, the 'preservation' of the nation requires, in reality, never ceasing to construct it. This necessity is reflected, in a particularly striking manner, in the legal principle through which the state appropriates its constitutive population: the French state literally created the population it appropriated. This particularity notably explains the French authority's relative indifference towards the foreign nationalities possessed by certain of its citizens.

At the very least, it is in the formulation of rules governing the attribution of 'Frenchness' that the manifestation of this indifference has ceaselessly, and ultimately openly, multiplied. It has resulted in ever-growing instances of dual citizenship.

It is important to attend to the meaning of this indifference. It is clear that the attribution of French nationality – in other words, the determination of the state's constitutive population – directly affects state sovereignty. It is naturally left to more elevated political organs to direct the action of the state in this domain. Conforming to tradition, and to Article

34 of the current constitution, this organ is Parliament, acting through legislative channels. It is thus at the legislative level that the fear of augmenting dual citizenship is no longer considered sufficient to justify preoccupation with the customary principle formulated in the Hague Convention.

Now, perspectives change entirely when examining the way in which individual instances of dual citizenship are treated. In these cases, it is a matter of ruling on concrete litigious situations that pose banal questions, often originating in private law as much as public law, that are complicated by dual citizenship. High politics is either no longer in question, or only certain of its distant consequences must be confronted. The organs of state government are no longer directly concerned. Instead, ordinary courts, referred to by individuals, public prosecutors or other representatives of the administration proffer rulings through a particular path: judgments. It is at this level that the division between indifference towards dual citizenship and its full acceptance could be breached. It would be sufficient if judges took account of the rights and obligations attaching to all nationalities held by an individual. Subject to being selective, such a process would be as practicable as opportune. Until the present, French justice has only made this leap in exceptional circumstances. Its extreme prudence amounts to a refusal to accept the fact of dual citizenship. This refusal finds a facile justification in the traditional conception of 'republican' citizenship and, more precisely, in the principle of equality among citizens. According to it, liberty must be equal: one French citizen must have – like all his or her co-citizens – all the rights and obligations flowing from French nationality, but he/she should have no other rights and obligations flowing from the possession of another nationality.

A definite contradiction thus affects the way in which France has followed the general shift towards a growing tolerance of the fact of dual citizenship. It is hardly logical to adopt, through the legislature, rules of attribution that increasingly expand multiple belonging, while simultaneously refusing, through the courts, to sanction the majority of concrete manifestations of these belongings. In truth, however, this incoherence is hardly exceptional in an international context.

The attribution of French nationality: indifference towards dual citizenship

The 'exclusive competence' granted by international law to states expresses itself principally in the general rules governing the attribution of nationality.[9] These rules, in all instances fundamental, are the ordinary means through which the sovereign state defines its constitutive population. Thus, it is natural that these rules express in every state both the traditional aversion towards dual citizenship and, when necessary, the indifference and/or tolerance of which it is also the object.

The general dispositions adopted in this domain by the French legislature in the last two hundred years have only been exceptional in one respect: from 1804, the civil code consecrated, with relative indifference, a number of derogations from its principled aversion. The manifestation of this indifference has never ceased to multiply.

The rules of the civil code

Hostility towards dual citizenship shows through in the most important and most visible nationality rules of the 1804 civil code. However, other, more discrete rules already so testify to a large dose of indifference.

Hostility in principle

From 1804, one finds abundant justifications in 'republican' ideology for hostility towards dual nationality, as the ideology links together French nationality and French citizenship. In accordance with ideology, citizenship implies the capacity to participate fully in both civil and public life. From this, the *Français*, because he is necessarily a citizen, is by definition perfectly integrated in society; he is in complete solidarity with the nation's destiny. At the very least, he is reputed to be such. At the same time, the citizen is a free individual. He is thus supposed to have adhered voluntarily to the nation's identity and, even to renew this commitment constantly.[10] A putative willingness (*volonté*) would thus explain, in the last analysis, the exclusive character of his fundamental choice in favour of France: it would be incompatible with foreign allegiance.

This discourse finds an echo in two sorts of civil code provisions. The first attributes the quality of being French in restrictive conditions rendering dual belonging improbable; the second kind forces the loss of it in the case of allegiance to a foreign power.

The attribution of 'Frenchness'

The 1804 civil code is characterised by exclusive recourse to *jus sanguinis* in the attribution of French nationality from birth (*nationalité d'origine*), which is the means by which the vast majority of the French population acquires nationality (Article 10). The break (*rupture*) with monarchical jurisprudence, putatively entrenched in *jus soli*,[11] was more spectacular than effective, as the majority of French citizens *jure sanguinis* at the time would have also been citizens *jure soli*. However, the authors of the code intended to reserve French nationality '*d'origine*' for individuals whose French stock (*souche*) would guarantee a profound belonging to the nation.

In pursing this goal, they did not entirely bow down before the altar of ethno-culturalism, which would have been grotesque in the light of the diversity of peoples (*peuplades*) in the nation. They rather hoped, thanks to education and the example provided by the family, for conditions favourable to the theoretically voluntary adhesion of nationals/citizens to the nation's collective destiny. They also hoped effectively to obviate the risk of dual belonging, at least among the French citizens who did not leave French territory (the majority of them). As this obviating measure might prove itself insufficient, the authors put into place, through the institution of 'the loss of French nationality', a precise remedy for this (perceived) ill.

The loss of Frenchness

The code provided for the loss of French nationality for those who, as it were, misused their putative liberty in fulfilling an act of allegiance to a foreign state. This loss was above all incurred when the 'allegiance' took some sort of indisputable legal form – in cases of 'naturalisation undertaken in a foreign country (Article 17(1))'. There were also, however, a number of other instances that had the same expatriating result: the acceptance of official functions without the authorisation of the French state (Article 17 (2)); expatriation without 'an intention to return (Article 17 (3))', and, for women only, marrying a foreigner (Article 19).

The hostility towards multiple attachments institutionalised in the 'republican' tradition, however, was never excessive. It did not inspire measures going beyond what appeared necessary to secure respect for this tradition, particularly the putative free will ascribed to citizens. In addition, from 1804 a number of civil code provisions on attributing French nationality expressed a measured, but significant, indifference towards certain instances of dual citizenship.

Calculated indifference

The civil code did not link automatic loss of French citizenship with the simple possession of a foreign passport. In reality, its provisions on loss sanctioned a perverse usage of a citizen's liberty: factual allegiance to a foreign state, whether or not it was accompanied by a corresponding nationality.[12] In the absence of an explicit voluntary act in favour of foreign nationality, the possession of a foreign citizenship did not supersede the French citizen's attachment to France. It was thus without consequence.

This is an early manifestation of indifference towards dual citizenship.

Discretely but certainly, it testifies to a large degree of confidence in the 'national cohesion' that would otherwise be guaranteed by *jus sanguinis*. At the same time, a politically more calculating indifference is found in the texts on the acquisition of French nationality by foreigners. In effect, neither the 1804 civil code, nor the subsequent regulations linked with it, make the acquisition of French nationality conditional upon the loss or renunciation of another citizenship. From 1804, the descendants of foreigners born in France and residing there at the age of majority (Article 9, civil code), the foreign wife of a French husband (Article 12) and a former French citizen reacquiring nationality (Articles 18, 19 (2), Articles 10 (2)) could, like the naturalising foreigner, become again French without regard to their foreign citizenship(s). They could be thus retained with impunity. This practice accorded with the requirements of a realistic nationality policy, the basic thrust of which was reinforced through similar provisions that multiplied in the nineteenth and twentieth centuries.

The subsequent evolution of the civil code

Certain elements of republican discourse could easily give the impression that the existence of the French nation and its permanence are the fruit of a quasi-miraculous determinism. At the same time, French authorities have always governed as if the nation were in the last instance nothing but the product of their efforts. This attitude explains the content of their particular policies on the attribution of nationality, in reaction to both a large growth in immigration and the development of French emigration.

The authority's overall attitude

The voluntarism displayed by the authorities, already noticeable at the time of the civil code, later increased through reforms to French nationality law. It was also, however, part of a global strategy extending beyond the legal sphere. It was as if governments have known for the last two centuries that national belonging can never be entirely spontaneous; rather, the willing commitment of individuals would always have to be encouraged by the state and would always result from a direct action on its part.

Without doubt, these rules attribute French nationality on the basis of meaningful ties with France (Lagarde: 1997, 73 and 110). However, they do not limit their action to the legal recognition of a pre-existing attachment. They rather aim at strengthening previously established links and thus at (partially) creating a practical belonging that is supposed to sustain this attachment. The modalities of their action differ appreciably according to the origin – whether French or foreign – of the individuals concerned. This creative role, however, explains the growing indifference towards the possible foreign nationality(ies) of both 'new' French citizens and those who are French by descent.

Policies towards naturalised and other new French nationals

It is well-known that France benefited after the 1850s from an increasing wave of immigration. French authorities, facing a labour shortage and haunted by fears of depopulation, were not content to control population flows and to encourage the development of a growing number of permanently resident aliens. They also implemented a policy of assimilating immigrants to the native French population, without attending closely to the resulting increase in dual citizenship. They judged, rightly or wrongly, that in granting French nationality, and all civil and political rights and obligations linked with it, they would effectively counter the weight of any original attachments. By contrast, to delay the grant of nationality, to maintain fundamental discrimination in law and rights, would only further solidify those attachments. The traditional conception of citizenship could be invoked to justify this calculation. On this view, all nationals were citizens, and all citizens participated fully in civil and political life; they thus enjoyed all rights and obligations implied by it.

It was also the case that, for immigrants, the attribution of French nationality served to further their attachment – which was in theory voluntary – to the nation. Naturally, this instrument did not act in a vacuum, but in harmony with the influence of meaningful links with France: birth, prolonged residence, marriage to a citizen and so on. The grant of citizenship was meant to lock-in this process.

This consolidation of individual attachment required a constant modification of the rules governing the attribution of nationality. A number of necessary reforms greatly extended, through an almost uninterrupted process, *jus soli*'s application. Two were particularly noteworthy. First, the laws of 22 and 29 January 1851 instituted double *jus soli* – a child born in France of foreign parents also born there is French at birth (now Article 19 (3) of the civil code). Second, the law of 26 June 1889 granted citizenship automatically to foreign children born in France and resident there until the age of 18 (now Article 21 (7) of the civil code).

It is also worth emphasising that the effect of marriage on French nationality has been radically transformed in two instances. First, from the law of 10 August 1927, a French woman marrying a foreigner – in most cases, an immigrant – no longer lost her French citizenship. Second, the law of 9 January 1973 granted foreign spouses of either gender the right to acquire their spouse's French citizenship (now Article 21 (1)-21 (6) of the civil code).

None of these laws took the least account of foreign nationalities retained by those individuals acquiring French citizenship as a result of immigration; French legislators never required their abandonment. The indifference towards dual citizenship detected in 1804 texts on nationality acquisition was thus maintained. The inevitable result was a multiplication of dual and plural nationality. One can observe a similar development in the case of French citizens by descent.

Policy towards French nationals by descent

For the products of *jus sanguinis*, the fullness of their links to the nation rendered the role of nationality attribution rules in manufacturing belonging almost invisible. Some of them appear to have no other role than recording a pre-existing sociological fact whose origin easily appears 'natural'. Certain demagoguery in France has recently developed the theme that 'only French citizens by descent are truly French', suggesting that the 'nature' at work here is biological.

Nevertheless, the 'factual belonging' (*l'appartenance de fait*) predating the attribution of French nationality through *jus sanguinis* is due, for the most part, to state action in a number of fields. The state largely constructed the social and cultural environment through which French descendants are constructed and through which they become 'naturally' French. It is French nationality attributed for generations on the basis of *jus sanguinis* that, in determining the rights and obligations reserved for citizens, fixes the conditions essential to this environment: raised as French nationals, by French parents, the children of French nationals also owe the core of their identity to the rules governing the attribution of French citizenship. The creative function of these rules is thus no less certain for being undetectable.

Nationality continues to play this creative role after attribution: the maintenance of French nationality, the status reserved for citizens, certainly contributes to the preservation and ultimate transmission of this identity, this attachment to the nation. The loss of the former could only weaken and/or compromise the latter, as witnessed in those French nationals – traditionally a very small number – who reside permanently abroad.

The example of these expatriates illustrates the recent evolution of French indifference towards the fact of dual citizenship. In this instance, it is explained by exactly this creative role. The 1804 code had already retained the right of French expatriates to pass French citizenship on to their descendants indefinitely. It was only lost when they demonstrated allegiance to foreign states, either through naturalisation (Article 17; also see Articles 12 and 21) or through the loss of the 'intention to return' (*l'esprit de retour*).[13] Outside of these two instances, the acquisition (other than through voluntary means) of a further citizenship – that is, multiple belonging – had no effect on an expatriate's legal attachment to France.

In the twentieth century, France took into account its interest in a number of its nationals who were well established abroad without severing their ties with the republic. As permanent residence under acceptable conditions normally presumes naturalisation, French nationality law was progressively reformed to permit it. In the first instance, the 19 October 1945 ordinance, creating the French nationality code, rescinded the automatic loss of citizenship for French nationals comporting themselves as nationals of and in foreign countries. From then, it has been necessary for the government to take a formal citizenship denaturalising them, namely a (rarely taken) decision by the *Conseil d'État*.

The decisive step was, however, taken through the law of 9 January 1973, holding that French citizens voluntarily acquiring another nationality retained French citizenship, unless the country of their new citizenship is a signatory to the 6 May 1963 Strasbourg Convention. They can thus only lose French citizenship under highly restrictive conditions: if they reside permanently abroad, are free of (now defunct) military obligations towards France and, most importantly, have made a formal declaration of their desire to renounce French nationality in the year following their acquisition of a foreign citizenship.

Finally, regarding the evolution of 'nationality practice' over two decades, policymakers have accepted that not merely naturalised French nationals, but also French citizens by descent, may possess two or more nationalities simultaneously. Its motivations for doing so are rooted in high politics, as it is a matter of determining the state's constitutive population which is, in the eyes of 'republican' ideology, the '*nation-citoyenne*'. 'Republican' ideology has adapted itself remarkably well to this relative tolerance, perhaps because it accords well with republicanism's emphasis on the free adhesion of each citizen.

At the same time, this ideology is ill-equipped to tolerate what are the concrete consequences of dual citizenship. In this matter, the obstacle it erects appears effective. It is not a matter of high politics; the national constitution is not at issue, and it is, in practice, the judge much more than the legislator, who, in ruling on individual situations, must confront the difficulty.

Intolerance towards the concrete implications of dual nationality

In law, an individual's nationality must be considered in terms of two inseparable issues: it is both a legal quality of the individual holding it and the basis of the large number of rules applied to the same individual. As a quality possessed by the individual, nationality is of substantial interest, both for the state conferring nationality and for the individuals themselves. For the state, nationality is an expression of its sovereignty, marking it off from all other states. For individuals, it is a fundamental part of their identity. Under these conditions, it is possible to elevate the 'quality of being a national' to the status of an autonomous legal question of great importance in itself. It is possible, but not inevitable. It is nonetheless the path that the French tradition has, no doubt to an excess, followed, resulting in the application of a specific legal regime.[14]

The reasons for what is ultimately a hypertrophy of nationality has not resulted merely from a single legal technique. Political ideology plays a large role, as testified by the fact that the particular legal regime is, more or less, that which governs the civil status of natural persons, particularly as the provisions governing nationality have, through a 22 July 1997 bill, been reintegrated into the French civil code. These provisions now appear in its first book. As a result, questions of nationality are governed as if, in the ideology underpinning the French legal construction, the image of citizenship had, as a constituent part of the state, engendered this other image: citizenship as a way of being for the individual. It is as if the identity of all its nationals reflects that of France itself, that of its popular image.

In practice, however, the interest of nationality, for the state and for the individual, relates to the importance and value of its consequences: it conditions the application of specific rules that in turn engender rights, obligations, liberties and powers in the most diverse of areas.[15] In international affairs, nationality is the foundation of diplomatic protection, and it affects the application of a number of treaties. In domestic politics – in addition to affecting these same treaties – it is the basis of almost all rights and obligations, civil as much as political, that are the very substance of citizenship. The most basic of these is the right to remain indefinitely on French territory. Nationality also exercises an influence over questions of jurisdiction.[16] Finally, it facilitates both the identification of the law relevant to the questions of personal status before the French courts and, indirectly, the efficacy in France of foreign judgments given on such questions. It is thus essential, as a condition for the practical application of innumerable rules of law, that nationality is used by practitioners of the law with an eye to the consequences brought about by its rules.

The problems linked with dual citizenship are not problems of dual citizenship as such; rather, these are problems linked with the consequences of one of the nationalities, problems that are in practice raised by individuals. More precisely, it is only as conditions governing the application of rules generating rights and obligations that these nationalities manufacture specific problems. Flowing from often irreconcilable imperatives engendered by the two citizenships, they arise in specific (and banal) instances whose solution depends on the particular individual's nationality(ies). In most cases, they are litigious problems dealt with by the courts. Although the state may set out the rules for treating them, judges play the essential role. Their task involves a choice: they must, in the case of a Franco-Polish citizen for instance, choose between French and Polish law.

204 | Géraud de la Pradelle

In other instances, they must rule on the treaty governing the right of a Tunisian/American to a commercial lease. In still others, they must decide on the fate of a young man called on to fulfil military service, perhaps in the event of a military conflict between the two powers the nationalities of which he holds.

In most cases, there is nothing tragic about the difficulties arising from dual nationality. The only exception is that of war, which is ever more rare among Western democracies. Otherwise, issues for which an arbiter must be located, namely a relevant law or jurisdiction, are no different than those that the courts face daily. Nonetheless, the way the choice is made, made necessary by the solutions themselves, remains in most cases surprisingly brutal.

In effect, the French courts ordinarily address the choice between nationalities in a manner resulting in a refusal to accept what is in fact a reality – the unique situation created by dual citizenship. At the same time, there are instances in which the courts depart from this negative stance, giving – admittedly only in exceptional circumstances and in a restrained manner – rulings that imply something of a recognition of dual citizenship. Legislators often chart the path to such exceptions. Finally, in even more rare instances these divergences highlight an alternative method for dealing with dual citizenship.

The standard rejection

The courts resolve the divergent consequences arising from an individual holding two nationalities in terms of a 'conflict of nationalities'. The judge overcomes such a 'conflict' by choosing one nationality. It would not imply any particular intolerance if it were simply a matter of opting for one decision (relating, for instance, to a question of personal status) while recognising that the matter could be looked at from a different angle (as, for instance, a matter of recognising civil rights). In practice, however, it rarely works like this. The judge transcending the conflict of nationalities treats the matter as if the individual's nationality were the fundamental issue. In fact, it is only a means to resolving an entirely different question, for example, as a factor linked with the law governing the dual citizen's personal status.[17] The French tradition explains in large measure this pattern of reasoning, as it regards the quality of 'national' itself as an autonomous and weighty legal matter governed by its own legal regime. One of the traits of this regime is that, in cases of serious difficulty, the *Tribunal de Grande Instance* (TGI) has exclusive competence over it (Article 29, civil code). Interlocutory in all other jurisdictions, even if it is incidental to the matter, the question of nationality benefits – for this reason – from an autonomy that remains unquestionable.

The most important consequence of privileging nationality in jurisprudence is that choice in favour of one of the nationalities 'in conflict' is made *une fois pour toute* in all respects. It is as if the judge is not only (for instance) ruling on a divorce or the renewal of a lease, but rather attributing to the individual his *one* nationality, in conformity with the Hague Convention's requirement that individuals 'should possess . . . only one nationality'. The result is that, in 'transcending' the nationality conflict over a banal affair of divorce or the end of a lease, the dual national finds himself perpetually defined in law as the national of a single state. He is literally stripped, at least in the eyes of the French authorities, of one of his nationalities.

Such reasoning cannot be considered the logical result of the simple indifference exhibited by French legislators in defining the content of French nationality; we are in fact far from the minimal tolerance implied by this indifference. It is rather a simple refusal, made possible by the particular French method for addressing nationality conflicts, to accept dual citizenship as a situation that must be taken into consideration.

The case of French nationals

When facing a case involving a French citizen who is simultaneously a citizen of a foreign state, French judges almost always choose to declare the individual French. The systematic pre-eminence of the nationality of the forum is effectively permitted by customary law.[18] It is practised by most states in internal affairs, and it blocks the official exercise of diplomatic protection in external affairs. In France, the practice is justified by the idea 'that, if French law declares an individual French, no legal authority or French administration can refuse to recognise this status without placing itself in conflict with the legal order from which it derives its powers (Largarde: 1997, no. 21)'. For this reason, the French dual national can neither assert his foreign nationality nor make claims on the basis of it. The *Cour de Cassation* – to say nothing of lower courts – staked out this position in diverse areas – for example, by determining the law governing divorce[19] and guardianship,[20] in refusing to confirm a foreign legal decision invoked in France, or even in ruling on the enjoyment of civil rights.

It is essential to understand that, in all these examples, the choice of French nationality was *definitive*. In other words, whatever the nature of the question leading to the choice, it can not later be modified. It imposes itself on all legal questions arising in the future, whatever they may be. This definitive character flows in the first instance from the reasoning that justifies the pre-eminence of French nationality law with reference to the judge's obedience to the law. The demand for this obedience weighs exactly the same each time the question is addressed. This translates, in terms of legal procedure, into the 'absolute' authority of judgements by *juge de droit commun* (i.e., the *tribunal de grande instance*) in matters of French nationality (Article 29 (5), civil code).

The refusal to treat French dual citizens as such, whatever the question before the judge, accords – entirely – with two ideological presuppositions. In the first instance, it is a question of a predisposition towards seeing nationality as an expression of the individual, and as an aspect of his or her personality that could only be divided at the risk of schizophrenia. This predisposition contributes, incidentally, towards the hypertrophy of questions of nationality. In the second instance, it is a matter of a 'republican' precept – the fundamental equality of citizens/nationals prohibits the recognition of another nationality for the purpose of attributing to them any statute except that which flows from their French nationality.

The case of foreigners

There is no explicit recognition in French jurisprudence of a particular treatment for dual citizens. Instead, all indications suggest that, in the eyes of the judge, it is natural for foreigners – like the French – to be definitively and perpetually trapped in the nationality recognised for them through some (relatively trivial) question of divorce or access to a restricted profession. This is despite the fact that 'republican' ideology is hardly relevant to the question and, more importantly, resolving nationality conflicts over foreign citizenship raises three particular issues in law that should prevent a judge from ever 'definitively' determining a dual national's citizenship.

Above all, questions surrounding a foreign citizenship – in contrast with those surrounding French citizenship, can never be presented before French courts as 'principal' or 'primary' (Largarde: 1997, no. 360, 263). They are always 'incidental' or 'secondary' to another issue, such as a divorce. A process with the sole objective of 'definitively' determining a foreigner's citizenship is thus impossible. Second, the authority brought by judgements on foreign nationalities can only be relative. Therefore, the courts' choice of one nationality is not binding in another case concerning the same individual: an identical court might choose the individual's other nationality. Third, all foreign nationalities are undifferentiated before French courts. This quality leads the French courts to overcome the nationality conflict through their respective *'effectivité'*.[21] This criterion – debatable, to be sure (Lagarde: 1988, 29, 37–38) – is at least less constraining than that requiring strict obedience to the law imposing French nationality. The *'effective'* nationality is, by definition, variable and relative. It would, therefore, be entirely natural to conclude that, for instance, nationality X is more relevant than nationality Y for divorce, because the individual retained strong familial attachments to country X, but that, by contrast, nationality

Y is clearly more relevant to his professional life, as the individual lives and works in country Y (Lagarde: 1988). In other words, the courts choose the nationality with which a dual national is *de facto* most closely connected. Yet, the courts have hesitated before the path of relativism in resolving conflicts among foreign nationalities. But they have not done so for purely legal reasons. Rather, they have ingrained habits in ruling on questions of French nationality, and consider it self-evident that any nationality is part of an individual's personal identity and so must be uniform.

This attitude is objectionable, but the courts at times agree to make exceptions to their practice in the case of both foreigners and French nationals. They thus agree, in practice if not in word (and all too rarely), to recognise the dual citizenship of both.

The exceptional recognition of dual citizenship

The acceptance – indeed, the official recognition – of dual citizenship is evinced in rare actions taken by governments and in equally rare decisions made by the courts without reference to any text.

Recognition by governments

Under certain conditions, the very act of respecting international convention governing diplomatic protection involves, for the French authorities, recognising dual citizenship. The practice – sanctioned by international law – of refusing official intervention in favour of French nationals wronged by another state of which they are also a national entails recognising both the foreign citizenship and the individual's status as a dual citizen. This recognition, however, takes the form of an adjustment, through general rules, of particular consequences of a French citizen's dual citizenship. These rules figure at some times in customary law, and at others in legislation.

Thus, military obligations have long been the object of bilateral[22] and, more recently, multilateral (6 May 1963 Strasbourg Convention), accords specifying the conditions under which French citizens can be freed of their obligations towards France on the basis of obligations towards another country. In the absence of these accords, the law – entitled, 'The Code of National Service' could unilaterally resolve the matter (Articles L 3 to L 38, Strasbourg Convention). It is worth noting that these agreements concern an ideologically sensitive area, because military service is one of the key obligations linked, in 'republican' ideology, with French citizenship. Finally, France is party to several treaties relating to issues of private law, such as judicial cooperation, names, guardianship and matrimonial property (Lagarde: 1997, from no. 40). These treaties take into account, albeit in a restrictive manner, the particular condition of dual nationals.

Recognition by the Judge

The rare judicial decisions, delivered in matters that are not touched upon by the above texts, recognise – albeit in a marginal and discretionary manner – the fact of dual belonging. The oldest of these concerned foreigners, and was taken during a state of war. Ruling on the sequestering of enemy nationals' property, judges were led to recognise the regularity of sequestering the goods of individuals holding citizenship of both an enemy state and a neutral country. They appear to have systematically chosen, for reasons of security, to give credence to these measures by recognising the enemy nationality as relevant, though without entirely discarding the neutral citizenship. It amounted to a certain, largely implicit, way of recognising the dual citizenship of those whose property was called into question (Darras: 1986, from 907).

The most significant French decisions gave effect to foreign judgements given in matters of divorce, and of the custody of infants following a divorce involving French dual nationals. The *Cour de cassation* twice accepted – in 1969 and 1987 – the fact that Swiss and Polish courts used, respectively, the Swiss and Polish nationality of French dual citizens in determining the law governing litigation among them. In the second case, the court stated that this tolerance of dual citizenship was essential to applying the Franco-Polish Convention of 5 April 1967.[23]

The court also agreed to recognise dual citizenship through the use of a method radically different from that usually employed.

The alternative method for recognising dual citizenship

Paul Lagarde has exhaustively analysed the method employed in the 1969 and 1987 decisions and characterised it as 'functional' (Lagarde: 1988, from 29). The alternative method consists of putting forward not questions of nationality as such, but rather the issues that led to legal disputes over it. The method recommends itself in that, in contrast to the usual refusal to accept dual citizenship, it allows judges to recognise the indisputably particular case of dual nationals. It is better adapted to procedural logic, and, moreover, manifestly reflects a different political ideology.

Under the usual method, French courts address nationality as if it were the fundamental issue (*la question principale*) in a pending case (Largarde: 1988, 32). This is appropriate when the courts are to decide if an individual is French under Article 29(3) of the civil code; in other words, when French nationality itself is the issue at stake. As a method for overcoming nationality conflicts, it is entirely inappropriate. In these instances, the question of nationality is 'incidental' to and 'dependent' upon a 'determined principal question' (Lagarde: 1988, 31) of an entirely different nature from that concerning an individual's (single) nationality. Under the alternate method, nationality is not treated in itself, but rather as a tool with which a judge can resolve a question of divorce or renewal of a lease.

It is worth noting that the incidental appearance, in a position of dependence, of nationality questions allows a judge to decide in a manner that would be forbidden if nationality were the principal question – namely, to determine whether the individual has a given foreign nationality.

From the point of view of legal technique alone, the same 'incidental' appearance allows the judge to make his choice under the usual conditions, namely not treating the nationalities as if they were 'in conflict' – whether they are both foreign or one is French – as issues in their own right. In fact, the process itself does not turn on nationality as such, but on some other element of a political or civil status deriving from it. It is thus not a question of nationality, but of divorce, a sequester, enjoying the right to vote or to remain on the territory, and so forth.

The necessary choice, therefore, between nationalities should be taken according to the function of the conditions governing the rules' application, in harmony with the principles governing the principal question (Lagarde: 1988, 31) and not as a matter of definitively attributing one nationality to the individual in question. This choice should be motivated by the particularities of the divorce, sequester, or lease at issue in the litigation. It is this that leads Lagarde to characterise the method as 'functional'.

In contrast with the common result, it is clear that the choice made this way leaves open the possibility of alternate choices later. This is perfectly logical, as nationality was not itself the issue, and was not indefinitely 'overcome.' Following the decision, we could conclude that the individual whose goods have been sequestered as an enemy subject is nonetheless not, despite this, deprived of his 'neutral' nationality; the wife viewed as Italian in order to spare her Islamic renunciation is not, for all that, stripped of her Tunisian citizenship.[24] It is clear that the legal technique alone both allows and encourages this form of legal reasoning seen in the *Cour de cassation's* miserly use of it, in 1961 and 1987.

If the 'functional approach' remains infrequently invoked, it is so for reasons that are not purely technical; they reflect political ideology, namely the traditional conception of equality among citizens in matters of French nationality. But it is also a question of the no-less traditional fusion of nationality and individual identity, a fusion that induces the legal hypertrophy of nationality questions, foreign and French. If French law is to follow the general evolution towards increased tolerance of dual citizenship, if it is to resolve the fundamental contradiction in which it creates dual citizenship that its courts refuse to recognise, then it is insufficient to look

to this legal technique. It is above all necessary to recast the political presuppositions of the legal constructions built up around French nationality.

References

L. Darras, *La double nationalité*, Paris III (doctoral thesis), 1986.
P. Fougeyrollas, *La Nation*, Paris, 1987.
V. Blandine Kriegel, *Philosophie de la Républicaine*, Paris, 1999.
P. Lagarde, 'Vers une approche fonctionelle du conflit positif de nationalités', *Revue critique de droit international privé* (1988), p. 29.
P. Lagarde, *La nationalité française*, Third edition, Paris, 1997.
J. Roman, *E Renan, Qu'est-ce qu'une nation? et autres essais politiques*, Paris, 1992.
L. Sala-Molens, *Le Code noir*, Paris, 1987.
D. Schnapper, *La France de l'intégration*, Paris, 1991.
D. Schnapper, *La communauté des citoyens*, Paris, 1994.
V. Yves Lequin, ed., *La mosaïque France*, Paris, 1988.

Notes

1. Translated by Randall Hansen, with the assistance of Patrick Weil and Géraud de la Pradelle.
2. It naturally has to be noted that not all countries are at the same stage. In addition, in all countries, each stage coexists with different levels of content-ment, as the process is far from complete.
3. 'Under international law, these questions in principle . . . fall within the domain reserved for States.' *Cour Permanente de Justice Internationale* (CPJI), advisory opinion no. 4 of 7 February 1923, série B, p. 24; also see opinion no. 7, série B, No. 7 p. 16. 'International law reserves for each state the discretion to determine the manner in which its own nationality is attributed'. *Cour Internationale de Justice* (CIJ), judgement of 6 April 1955, *Aff. Notteböhm*, Rec. p. 4.
4. The doctrine of exclusive competence (over nationality) justifies 'local legal theory' even when the latter appears to account for the growing incidences of dual nationality.
5. 'Nationality is generally defined as legal belonging to the state's constitutive population, (Lagarde: 1997, 3).
6. See Articles 2 and 3, title II of the constitution of 3–14 September 1791 and, despite the ambiguity of drafting (see, for instance, Articles 2 and 13 of the constitution of 22 August 1795), all constitutions until that, still in operation, of 4 October 1958, Article 3.
7. See the text and the commentary of Sala-Molens (1987); one can, however, doubt that slaves enjoyed French nationality.
8 'Men are born and remain free and equal before the law'.
9. Nationality legislation involves other rules, notably the legal regime governing it. Such rules are particularly developed in France. See, in particular, Articles 29 to 31–3 of the civil code.
10. Such is the elective conception of the nation, developed (not without

equivocation) by Ernest Renan (Qu'est-ce qu'une nation? conférence donnée à la Sorbonne en 1882) and rediscovered by the 1988 report of the Nationality Commission (*Être français aujourd'hui et demain*, 10–18 and Tome II, éd. 10–18). It has traditionally been contrasted (not without caricature) with Fichte's 'organic' conception of the nation. On this, see Roman (1992).

11. According to Pothier, *Traité des personnes*, Title II, Section 1, 'the true and natural French nationals (*Français*) are those born within the area 'of French domination' (that is, within the realm) as well as those born in our colonies, or even in foreign countries, such as Turkey or in Africa, where we have establishments assisting French commerce'. 'Children born in foreign countries, of a French father who has neither established domicile in this country nor lost the intention to return are also French; above all, those who would have been born of French parents are French . . . For the others, those born within the countries of the French dominion, who are only reputed to be French, are not considered to have been born either of French or foreign parent, irrespective of whether they were domiciled in the French dominion or were simply voyagers. Only birth within the dominion provides the right of naturalisation, independently of the origin of the Father and Mother, and of their residence.' Pothier, *Traité des Persinnes et des biens*, 1777, Title II, First Section.

12. In some circumstances, this created the risk of statelessness, such as when French nationality was lost through a *de facto* allegiance to a foreign state without an actual naturalisation.

13. Since 1945 (under Article 95 of the *Code de la nationalité française*), the loss of nationality is to be decided by the courts on the basis of a loss of *de facto* belonging to France (*perte d'état de français*) for more than fifty years and two generations (see, now, Article 23.6 of the civil code).

14. This regime's principal traits are: competence reserved for Parliament by Article 34 of the constitution; jurisdictional competence reserved for the *Tribunal de Grande Instance*, and the derogation of question of proof, procedure and authority to the common law. See Articles 29 to 31 (3) of the civil code.

15. Corresponding to the duality – civil and political – of citizenship traditionally defined.

16. On this, see the regrettable Articles 14 and 15 of the civil code concerning the attribution of jurisdiction to French courts in civil and commercial matters where competence is based on one litigant's French nationality.

17. In France, an individual's personal status is constituted by rules governing the status and capacity of persons, marriage, divorce and relations between parents and children. In other countries, it also governs matrimonial property, inheritance and gifts.

18. Article 44 of the 1930 Hague Convention attests to this.

19. Civ., 1, 17 June 1968, *Aff. Kasapyan* was a matter of the divorce of Turkish spouses, one of whom – the wife – also enjoyed French citizenship: 'The court rules that the Kasapyan (the woman) remained French . . . this nationality alone could be taken into legal consideration . . . it is with good reason (*à bon droit*) that the Court of Appeal in order to apply French law governing the conflict decided that the spouses were of a different nationality.'

20. Civ. 1, 27 January 1987, *Aff. Alamir*: '. . . Article of the civil code decrees a rule of exclusive competence founded on the defendant's French nationality . . . in

instances in which he possesses another nationality, only the French nationality can be taken into legal consideration.

21. Civ. 1, 15 May 1974, Martinelli, *Rev. cr. dr. int. pr.*, 1975, 260, n. Nisard; Cluete
    (1976), p. 298. N. .D *Alexandre* was a matter of an Italian/Tunisian '. . . having
    . . . sovereignly concluded that the '*effective*' nationality of the wife of Ben Khal-
    ifa was the Italian . . . the Court of Appeal rightly applied Italian law'.
22. See the list off accords published in the Ministry of Justice compendium, *La
    Nationalité Française, Textes and Documents*, Paris, La Documentation Française,
    1996, 307 and following and Lagarde (1997), 31 and following.
23. Civ. 1, 22 July 197, *Aff. Dujaque, Rev. cr. dr. int. pr.* 1988, 85 and *Chronique Lagarde*
    (1988), from p. 29: 'the judges applied with good reason the Franco-Polish Con-
    vention of 5 April 1967, although according to French law all the concerned
    parties were French . . . In effect, the spirit of this convention being such that
    the international legal relations are treated in terms of the rights of individuals
    and the family, it behooves us to conclude from this that the litigation concerns
    individuals holding Polish nationality, although they also have French nation-
    ality'. Also see Civ. 1, 10 March 1969, *Aff. Butez, Rev. cr. dr. int. pr.* 1970, 114, n.
    Batiffol.
24. As in the *Martinelli* case, cited above.

IV

SOCIAL RIGHTS, DUAL CITIZENSHIP AND NATIONALITY IN AN AMERICAN CONTEXT

CHAPTER 10

THE ATTACK ON SOCIAL RIGHTS: U.S. CITIZENSHIP DEVALUED

Susan Martin

Introduction

In the United States, 1996 proved to be a watershed year in defining the rights of legal permanent residents (LPRs) as distinct from two other groups: illegal aliens and U.S. citizens. For most of U.S. history, legal immigrants and citizens differed with regard to political rights but not, in fundamental ways, civil and social rights.[1] Citizenship conveyed the right to vote in all elections, serve on juries and obtain certain government jobs, but both citizens and legal immigrants were otherwise treated remarkably the same in law. Illegal aliens, on the other hand, had few social rights and still fewer political rights.

George Washington gave early voice to this conception of immigration: 'The bosom of America is open to receive not only the Opulent and respectable Stranger, but the oppressed and persecuted of all Nations and Religions; whom we shall welcome to a participation of all our rights and privileges, if by decency and propriety of conduct they appear to merit the enjoyment' (Fuchs: 1990).

While some may debate the truth of this assertion, few question the strength of this founding myth. In effect, immigrants were conceived as presumptive citizens who would quickly become Americans and, hence, should enjoy the same rights and privileges of other Americans. This is not to say that the U.S. welcomed all newcomers equally. Certainly, distinctions as to who could enter continued to be made on the basis of race. And, from the 1880s onward, applicants for admission could be denied entry if immigration officials determined they were likely to become public charges – that is, require income support from public authorities.[2] A recurrent complaint about nineteenth century immigrants was their apparent excessive use of public services. In 1856, a New York Superintendent of the Poor complained that 'whole towns and counties in Europe find it more economical to pay for the transportation of paupers to our shores than support them at home, and hence deposit them in shiploads in our cities.' An almshouse official wrote in 1846, 'they wander through the streets, in a state of utter desolation until some benevolent hand . . . guides them to the almshouse board (Joselit 1981)'. Although these two complaints led to requests for federal reimbursement of costs and, later, similar statements were used to justify restrictions on immigration, concern about costs did not generate proposals to restrict eligibility for services. Legislation adopted in 1996, however, seriously eroded what Lyndon Johnson referred to as the 'covenant' that had long existed between immigrant and society in the United States.[3] The Personal Responsibility and Work Opportunity Reconciliation Act (Welfare Reform Act) and the Illegal Immigration and Immigrant Responsibility Act (IIRIRA) reduced substantially the social rights of legal immigrants relative to citizens. Although parts of these laws have since been changed, the reversals halted retroactive application of the new standards to immigrants in the United States at the time of passage. The significant derogation of the social rights of legal immigrants entering now and in the future has not changed.

This paper explores one component of the changed concept of the social rights of aliens versus citizens: eligibility for benefit programs funded by the federal government.[4] It is only since the 1930s, and hence only with regard to the latest wave of immigration, that eligibility for federal assistance programs has become key to defining membership and rights in U.S. society. During earlier periods, there were few public programs funded or implemented by the federal government that served as safety nets for residents of the United States. Rather, the principal responsibility for helping individuals in need rested with private charities and local public programs, as indicated by the almshouse officials cited above. With the New Deal and, subsequently, the War on Poverty, a growing federal responsibility emerged. And, with this growth in federal activity have come questions about who falls within the safety net of federal responsibility.

The next section provides background on pre-1996 eligibility standards, followed by a description of the debate on the welfare reform changes. The new standards adopted by Congress are then described. The last section analyses the effects of these changes on naturalisation patterns and concepts of citizenship.

Pre-1996 eligibility for public benefit programs

Until 1996, no federal benefit program denied eligibility solely on the basis of alienage to permanent resident aliens. During the course of the 1970s and 1980s, however, the courts held that Congress (but not the states) could make distinctions among different immigration statuses and between aliens and citizens, paving the way for the 1996 changes.

The Supreme Court in the 1971 case *Graham v. Richardson* held State restrictions on the eligibility of legal immigrants for benefit programs to be unconstitutional because they violated the Equal Protection Clause of the 14th Amendment and encroached upon the exclusive federal power to regulate immigration. At the time, however, the Supreme Court did not determine whether the federal government could itself restrict eligibility on the basis of alienage. A later court ruling, *Mathews v. Diaz*, did address that issue, determining that a congressionally imposed five year residency requirement for LPR participation in the Medicare Supplementary Insurance program was constitutional. The Court held that 'it is obvious that Congress has no constitutional duty to provide *all aliens* with the welfare benefits provided to citizens.' As long as the distinctions between citizens and aliens are not wholly irrational, then Congress may draw such distinctions. Through legislative and regulatory actions, distinctions were then made between aliens residing permanently and legally in this country and undocumented aliens. Aliens in the U.S. with legal status were generally determined eligible for federal assistance while the unauthorised were generally barred from these programs.

During the 1970s, most restrictions on alien eligibility pertained to illegal aliens and temporary visitors to the United States. Then, in the early 1980s, in part because of concern about costs, legislation was passed to restrict access by legal immigrants, though not deny eligibility. In determining eligibility for three programs, Aid to Families with Dependent Children (AFDC), Supplementary Security Income (SSI) for aged and disabled persons, and Food Stamps, the income of sponsors was to be deemed during the first three to five years after entry. Under 'deeming' provisions, the income and resources of an alien's 'sponsor' are considered to be available to the sponsored alien when he or she applies for the applicable public benefits. A sponsor is someone who completes an affidavit of support to assist the alien in obtaining legal immigrant status. If the sponsor or the sponsor's spouse's income and assets relative to family or household size (depending on the program) would render them ineligible, the income and assets also render the immigrant ineligible for aid. Deeming held several advantages: it reinforced the responsibility of sponsors for family members that they brought into the country; it allowed access to public programs if the financial circumstances of the sponsor changed after the individual entered; and because the deeming requirement was for a limited period of time, it did not construct a permanent second class of resident who paid taxes but would not realise any benefits.

Two groups not subject to the deeming rules were resettled refugees and asylees (after receiving their grant of asylum). Refugees and asylees were not subject to the public charge provisions in the immigration act.

Under the Refugee Act of 1980, a special program of cash and medical assistance was established to help even refugees who were not categorically eligible for regular federal or state aid. The special rules permitted single persons and childless couples to obtain support equivalent to the aid provided to families with children under AFDC. The legislation provided for up to 36 months of coverage, but the period in actual use was significantly shorter (eight to twelve months depending on budget availability). Refugees eligible for AFDC, SSI and Medicaid were assisted under these mainstream programs and retained coverage as long as they met the program rules.

A further complication in the law pertained to individuals who were Permanently Residing Under Color of Law (PRUCOL). These individuals were neither illegal aliens nor legal immigrants on a citizenship track. They were known to the government and often had formal permission to remain in the United States indefinitely. Many in this category had entered under the parole authority of the Attorney General, who is able to admit individuals outside of the regular immigration provisions. The parole authority was used to admit large numbers of Cubans, Haitians, Southeast Asians, eastern Europeans and Soviets who did not qualify for refugee status but were otherwise of humanitarian or foreign policy interest to the United States. Other PRUCOLs include persons whom the government chooses not to deport but who do not qualify for legal immigration status. The courts had found these individuals to be eligible for assistance unless the federal program explicitly barred them.

By the time debate began on welfare reform, there were significant variations by legal status and program in alien eligibility for public benefits, with illegal aliens having least access, legal immigrants restricted access and refugees, quite generous eligibility. Table I summarises the rules in effect prior to 1996 for the four major federal programs: AFDC, SSI, Medicaid and Food Stamps.

The debate on welfare reform and immigration

Beginning in 1994, Congress began to explore more basic changes restricting eligibility of immigrants as it began consideration of fundamental welfare reform. The impetus for the restrictions in eligibility for public assistance programs stemmed from a number of different concerns as did the opposition to them. The following discussion of positions taken by supporters and opponents of reform is drawn from the *Congressional Record* of debates on the welfare and immigration bills, testimony presented to the congressional committees considering legislation, and an expert consultation on welfare reform held by the U.S. Commission on Immigration Reform, a federal body that advised Congress and the Executive Branch on immigration policy.

Support for restriction in eligibility

Budget pressures may have been the most important in stimulating discussion of restrictions in eligibility. In an era where funding for any new programs at both the federal and state levels must come from cuts in existing ones, restricting coverage of immigrants was seen as a possible source of revenues. The Clinton Administration led the way in this regard, although it expressed dismay at how far Congress eventually took the idea. In 1993, the Administration proposed increasing the deeming period for SSI from three years to five years in order to save funds to pay for an extension of unemployment benefits to workers affected by the economic recession. The next year, when Congress began consideration of welfare reform, further restrictions on eligibility of legal immigrants appeared to be a politically cost-free way (at least in the short-term) to find cost-savings. Unlike most other groups whose eligibility might have been restricted, immigrants could not vote. When the Congressional Budget

Table 1 Alien Eligibility for Selected Federal Programs: Pre-1996

	AFDC	SSI	Medicaid	Food Stamps
Legal Immigrants	Yes, but sponsored aliens are restricted for 3 years by deeming rules	Yes, but sponsored aliens are restricted for 5 years by deeming rules	Yes	Yes, but sponsored aliens are restricted for 3 years by deeming rules
Refugees and Asylees	Yes, with special eligibility for Refugee Cash Assistance during time limited period	Yes	Yes, with special eligibility for Refugee Medical Assistance during time-limited period	Yes
Permanently Residing Under Color of Law (PRUCOL)	Yes	Yes	Yes	No
Asylum Applicants	No	No	Emergency services only	No
Temporary Admissions	No	No	Emergency services only	No
Unauthorised Aliens	No	No	Emergency services only	No

Table 2 Alien Eligibility for Selected Federal Programs: Post Welfare Reform

	TANF	SSI	Medicaid	Food Stamps
Pre-Reform Population				
Legal Immigrants (Now called Qualified Aliens)	States are authorised to determine eligibility, except those who worked 40 quarters, veterans and aliens on active duty qualify regardless of state action. Deeming applies unless the immigrant has worked 40 quarters	Yes (includes those already on SSI and those who become eligible due to age or disability). Deeming applies unless the immigrant has worked 40 quarters	States are authorised to determine eligibility, except those who worked 40 quarters, veterans and aliens on active duty qualify regardless of state action. Deeming applies unless the immigrant has worked 40 quarters	No, except for elderly and children. Deeming applies unless the immigrant has worked 40 quarters
Refugees and Asylees	States are authorised to determine eligibility, except refugees in the country five years or less qualify. Special eligibility for Refugee Cash Assistance during time-limited period	Yes	States are authorised to determine eligibility, except refugees in the country five years or less qualify. Special eligibility for Refugee Medical Assistance during time-limited period	No, except those who have been in the U.S. for fewer than seven years and Hmong refugees who assisted U.S. military forces
Post-Reform Arrivals				
Legal Immigrants:	No during the first five years after entry; thereafter States are authorised to determine eligibility, except those	No, except those who worked 40 quarters, veterans and aliens on active duty qualify	No during the first five years after entry; thereafter States are authorised to determine eligibility, except those	No, except those who worked 40 quarters, veterans and aliens on active duty qualify

Table 2 continued

	TANF	SSI	Medicaid	Food Stamps
	who worked 40 quarters, veterans and aliens on active duty qualify regardless of state action. Deeming applies unless the immigrant has worked 40 quarters		who worked 40 quarters, veterans and aliens on active duty qualify regardless of state action. Deeming applies unless the immigrant has worked 40 quarters	
Refugees and Asylees	Yes during the first five years after entry; thereafter as above except deeming does not apply.	No, except those in the country for less than seven years after entry, who worked 40 quarters, veterans and aliens on active duty qualify	Yes during the first five years after entry; thereafter as above except deeming does not apply.	No, except those in the country for less than seven years after entry, who worked 40 quarters, veterans and aliens on active duty qualify
Unqualified Aliens (PRUCOL, asylum applicants, temporary admissions, unauthorised aliens, etc.)	No	No	Emergency services only	No

Office reported that elimination of eligibility for SSI, Food Stamps and other major programs would net a cost savings of about $25 billion, the move towards this option became almost irreversible. The foreign-born component of some federal public assistance caseloads had risen dramatically during the 1980s (Borjas: 1996). Of particular concern was the SSI program. A large proportion of the immigrants who applied for the program did so soon after their sponsor's income was no longer deemed in determining if they met the income eligibility requirements. This practice was not illegal but appeared to members of Congress to be a violation of the spirit of the immigration law.

The growing size and nature of immigration into the United States also contributed to support for restrictions. Some observers argued that the U.S. was admitting record numbers of immigrants, many of whom were lower-skilled immigrants who, they further argued, tended to utilise federal benefit programs at a higher rate than the general population or previous generations of immigrants. Pointing out that likelihood to become a public charge had long been a basis for denying admission, they argued that restrictions on eligibility were the only way to enforce this provision. (As discussed below, the statistics on welfare utilisation are far more complicated than this picture presents.)

Interestingly, though, proponents of welfare restrictions included many supporters of high levels of immigration. Senator Spencer Abraham, who successfully fought restrictions on the number of immigrants to be admitted, was a staunch supporter of the welfare changes, stating 'Immigration Yes, Welfare No'. Rick Santorum, one of the Senators responsible for managing the debate on the Senate floor, countered proposals to retain eligibility for immigrants already in the country with the following words: I am pro-immigration. I am the son of an immigrant. I am not one of those people who says, 'I'm in. OK. Close the door'. I believe immigration is important to the future of this country. . . . If we clean up [the abuse of welfare programs] I think we improve the image of immigration and there is less pressure on lowering those caps and doing other things that I think could be harmful with respect to the area of immigration and, I think, save the taxpayers a whole bundle of money in the process (Congressional Record: 1996).

Finally, there was a concern that public aid impedes adjustment to the United States, a sentiment that echoed criticism of the broader welfare policies. This line of argument picked up on views often expressed within the refugee resettlement program where AFDC and its refugee cash assistance counterpart were the principal means of providing transitional financial aid to refugees. Continued high levels of welfare utilisation in some states, particularly California, raised questions about the effect of public assistance on the attainment of economic self-sufficiency by refugees. Most of the refugee-concerned groups who made this point, however, wanted to pull the refugee program out of the welfare system not deny eligibility to all immigrants.

Opposition to restriction

Those who argued against restrictions on immigrant eligibility for public assistance programs generally pointed to the U.S. heritage as a country of immigration that seeks to quickly absorb its new arrivals. They further pointed out that legal immigrants paid taxes that supported these programs. Outright bars on eligibility would be discriminatory against one part of the taxpaying public, they claimed. Critics of restrictions on eligibility also pointed out that most immigrants did not overly utilise public benefits. The Congressional Research Service had concluded after a review of 1994 data that 'the vast majority of non-citizens receive no assistance from Federal and State welfare programs (O'Grady: 1995)'. In fact, given the large proportion of the immigrant population living under the poverty level (about twenty-three percent of the foreign born compared to fifteen percent of the native born), as well as the high proportion without health insurance (forty percent of non citizens compared with fifteen percent of citizens), the surprising finding was the low proportion utilising certain programs.

Only two groups of aliens appeared to utilise these programs disproportionately: the elderly and refugees (Fix and Passel: 1994). As discussed above, refugees had special eligibility based on their status as refugees. To the extent there was a problem, it was the refugee resettlement program's reliance on public assistance as a mechanism for providing transitional support to refugees. Once enrolled in AFDC, refugees in certain states, such as California, were likely to remain on the program because it is hard for them to find jobs with wages that exceed the benefit level of the public program.

The welfare utilisation patterns of the elderly were more complicated. Immigrants seemed to fall into two groups: those who grew old in the United States and those who came as elderly. The former group tended to apply for SSI many years after their arrival. They were generally eligible for SSI because they did not have enough work experience to qualify for Social Security, the social insurance program that covers most American elderly, or because their earnings were so low that they would otherwise live in poverty. The second group generally applied as soon as the deeming period was over. Most had been admitted as the parents of naturalised U.S. citizens who had guaranteed that their parents would not become public charges.

Many experts argued that the first group should not be penalised because of their low earnings, while the solution to the second group was to enforce the responsibility of their sponsors for longer periods. Others argued that elderly immigrants' use of public assistance reflected basic problems in the safety net. They pointed out that applications for SSI did not necessarily reflect an abdication of responsibility of children sponsors for their parents. SSI provides Medicaid coverage as well as income support. Even if sponsors were able to indefinitely provide financial support to their parents, they often found it difficult to fund medical care for elderly parents.

Some argued that the focus on eligibility for public assistance benefits was misplaced (Commission on Immigration Reform, 1995). If there was a problem related to immigrants and public funding, it was the lack of programs to help immigrants integrate fully into U.S. life. Arguing that immigrants need help in addressing language and other adjustment problems, and that communities require federal resources to help them absorb the impact of immigration, these experts believed there should be a greater investment in immigrant-related services.

Opponents also pointed out that restrictions on eligibility would increase poverty among immigrants. As discussed above, almost one-quarter of the foreign born were already living under the poverty level. Food Stamps, in particular, contributed to the household income of both the working and non-working poor. The effects on children and the elderly, two vulnerable populations, would be greatest. Even if they retained eligibility (as the newly passed legislation permits), families would still need to make hard choices about the purchase of food because adult members of the household would not be covered. Hence, fewer resources would be available overall to the family to meet its nutritional needs. For children, this could translate into lower school achievement and a continuation of the cycle of poverty.

A number of State and local officials also indicated their concern that restrictions on eligibility for federal programs may save money for the federal government but shift it to State and local governments. A member of the Virginia state legislature wrote: 'State legislators are deeply troubled by proposals to finance federal welfare reform by eliminating benefits for legal immigrants. The federal government's abdication of its responsibility to those it admits to the country does not eliminate immigrants' needs, and state and local budgets and taxpayers will bear the burden (Darner: 1996)'.

The final argument against the proposed welfare changes pertained to their effects on notions of citizenship. Some critics argued forcibly that linking eligibility, particularly for safety net services, to citizenship would debase citizenship. As early as August 1994, Barbara Jordan, Chair of the U.S. Commission on Immigration Reform, raised this issue before the Ways and Means Committee of the U.S. House of Representatives:

> I believe firmly that citizenship in this country is something to be cherished and protected. I want all immigrants to become citizens. I want them to seek citizenship because it is the key to full participation in our political community – to know first hand and understand the American form of democracy. I want unnecessary barriers to naturalisation – and there are many of them – to be removed. *However, I do not want immigrants to seek citizenship because it is the only route to our safety nets. To me, that would be a debasement of our notions of citizenship* (emphasis added) (Jordan 1994).

Post-reform eligibility rules

For the most part, Congress ignored the arguments made against categorical denials of eligibility for public benefits for legal immigrants. The 1996 reforms in the welfare system reduced significantly the eligibility of immigrants for public benefits, thereby restricting social rights purely on the basis of citizenship. As stated above, in 1997 and 1998, some of the most egregious provisions, specifically retroactive application of the new rules to persons already receiving assistance, were reversed. Additional proposals for reform were pending in 1999. The improved budget climate enabled consideration of these changes. Advocacy efforts by state and local governments and certain industries (e.g., the nursing home industry) concerned about cost shifts also contributed to a favourable atmosphere. The increased political clout of Latino and Asian voters, who in some highly publicised campaigns defeated Republican candidates who had supported the welfare reform provisions, added additional impetus to the reversals. It should be pointed out, however, that no changes have been made to the *prospective* application of the new restrictive rules on eligibility. The basic conceptual change, that immigrants can and should have fewer social rights than citizens, continues to hold.

More specifically, the principal provisions, as amended by IIRIRA and subsequent legislation, include: Legal immigrants are ineligible for Supplementary Security Income (SSI) and Food Stamps until citizenship or the immigrant has worked 40 qualifying quarters without receiving any Federal means-tested program during any such quarter. Exceptions are made for refugees, asylees and individuals granted cancellation of removal during their first five years (now seven for some programs) in the country and veterans and active duty service personnel and their immediate family. As amended in 1997, the bar on SSI eligibility applies only to legal immigrants admitted after enactment of the 1996 law. Legislation just passed by Congress would restore eligibility for Food Stamps for about 250 thousand of the more than 950 thousand legal immigrants who lost eligibility as a result of the welfare reform legislation. Aid would be restored to the elderly, children and certain refugees.

States received the authority to determine if they will permit legal immigrants (except those specified above) to receive temporary assistance for needy families (the amended Aid to Families with Dependent Children), social services under Title XX, and Medicaid. Immigrants living in states that determine legal immigrants ineligible would continue to receive assistance until 1 January 1997.

Legal immigrants (except those specified above) are ineligible for other federal, means-tested benefits during their first five years after entry. Exceptions in means-tested programs are emergency Medicaid not related to an organ transplant, emergency disaster relief, public health assistance for immunisations, public health assistance for testing and treatment of symptoms of communicable diseases, soup kitchens and similar such local programs, certain housing benefits if receiving them on the date of enactment, programs of student assistance under titles IV, V, IX, and X of the Higher Education Act of 1965, foster care and adoption assistance, assistance and benefits under the Child Nutrition Act and national School

Lunch Act, means-tested programs under the Elementary and Secondary Education Act of 1965, Head Start, and benefits under the Job Training Partnership Act (JTPA).

Legal immigrants are subject to deeming rules in determining eligibility for federal programs (with the exceptions listed above to the five year bar on eligibility) until citizenship or the immigrant has worked forty qualifying quarters and did not receive any Federal means-tested program during any such quarter. The deeming provisions apply to current recipients when they go through the normal eligibility review process. No affidavit of support may be accepted to establish that a legal immigrant will not be a public charge unless it is executed as a contract which is legally enforceable against the sponsor by the sponsored immigrant, the federal government and state and local governments that provide means-tested public benefits. The sponsor must agree to support the alien and submit to the jurisdiction of any federal or state court for reimbursement of government expenses. Sponsors will not be liable for reimbursement of the expenses incurred in providing assistance for the programs exempted from deeming (e.g., school lunches, Pell grants, JTPA, Head Start, etc.). The affidavit is to remain in force until the immigrant becomes a citizen. A sponsor must be a citizen or permanent resident, eighteen years of age or older, domiciled in the U.S., and the person who petitioned for the admission of the alien. Under IIRIRA, all immigrants sponsored under family-based categories must be sponsored by a relative who signs the affidavit of support and who can demonstrate an ability to support the immigrant and members of his or her immediate family at 125 percent of poverty level.

Illegal aliens are ineligible for federal public benefit programs, grants, contracts, loans, professional licenses or commercial licenses, with the exception of emergency Medicaid not related to an organ transplant, emergency disaster relief, public health assistance for immunisations, public health assistance for testing and treatment of symptoms of communicable diseases, soup kitchens and similar such local programs, and certain housing benefits if receiving them on the date of enactment.

States have wide discretion in limiting eligibility of migrants for their own programs. It makes illegal aliens ineligible for state or local public benefit programs, grants, contracts, loans, professional licenses or commercial licenses unless a state enacts a state law which affirmatively provides for such eligibility. States are given the authority to limit eligibility of legal immigrants (with the exceptions listed above) and nonimmigrants or deem sponsor income and assets for their own programs, with similar exceptions.

Prior to the 1997 and 1998 changes in federal law, most states with significant immigrant populations took steps to reduce the impact of these changes on those already residing under their jurisdiction. Many of the larger states, as well as many with smaller populations, continued benefits jointly funded by the federal and state governments. New York, California and other states also initiated new state-only-funded programs to give at least some immigrants (e.g., the elderly and children) Food Stamps and other assistance that had been covered by the federal government. Budget surpluses stemming from the thriving U.S. economy permitted these decisions to be made. It is not clear if states will provide Food Stamps to the immigrants who are not covered under the pending legislation to restore aid. Questions remain, moreover, about the capacity of states to continue benefits not covered by the federal government in the event of economic recession. Also, most states opted to restrict the eligibility of future immigrants.

Naturalisation trends and impact

The erosion of social rights for immigrants clearly has affected naturalisation patterns, although the precise relationship is not a simple one. Increases in applications for naturalisation began prior to passage of the welfare reform legislation, but debate about the rights of immigrants contributed to the greatly expanded interest in citizenship.

To provide some historical perspective, throughout most of the twentieth century, applications for naturalisation averaged fewer than 200 thousand per year. The peak came in 1944, during World War II, when about 400 thousand persons naturalised. During the late 1970s and into the 1980s, as levels of immigration increased, naturalisation numbers also went up but still did not exceed 300 thousand per year. Then, in 1992 almost 350 thousand applications were filed, followed by more than 500 thousand in 1993 and 1994. The big jump occurred in 1995 when almost one million applications for naturalisation were filed. Since then, the numbers have continued to grow. In 1996 alone, more than one million persons were granted citizenship.

The increase in applications was somewhat but not totally predictable. Several factors contributed. First, a large cohort of immigrants became eligible to naturalise in the 1990s. In 1986, Congress had granted legal status to about three million illegal aliens, all of whom obtained immigrant status within a relatively short time. In 1994, the legalised aliens began to become eligible for citizenship. Unlike many other immigrants, they had resided for a long time within the United States prior to becoming legal immigrants. Since naturalisation rates tend to increase with residence in the U.S., many were ready to apply as soon as they became time eligible. Further, to obtain legal status, they had to pass an English and civics test or take an approved course. Hence, many had already gone through a process similar to the naturalisation test.

The second contributor was a program to replace with counterfeit-resistant documents the 'green cards' that long-term permanent residents had been issued as proof of their legal status. Since applications for the new cards cost almost as much as naturalisation applications, many immigrants chose to forego the replacement and apply for citizenship instead.

Third, the new Commissioner of the Immigration and Naturalisation Service announced in 1993 that she intended to emphasise the 'N' in her agency's name. Commissioner Meissner encouraged outreach activities to immigrant communities to promote naturalisation. When the applications grew, partly in response to the new outreach, and processing time lagged, INS put in place an ambitious processing program, Citizenship USA, to reduce backlogs.[5] The new effort and publicity about INS' activities then stimulated even more applications.

A fourth factor was outside of U.S. control. The Mexican government reversed its long-standing opposition to Mexican nationals becoming citizens of other countries. For a variety of reasons, Mexican naturalisation rates had been very low. For example, in 1991, thirteen years after admission, only fifteen percent of Mexicans in the 1977 entry cohort had naturalised., (INS: 1991) In part, the low rates were attributable to proximity (Canadian rates were even lower), but loss of Mexican nationality and, hence, rights to own land and exercise other rates, contributed to the reluctance to naturalise. In the 1990s, the Mexican consulates in the United States began an information campaign that recognised that Mexicans might have a legitimate interest in naturalising and explained that it would not be difficult to re-obtain Mexican citizenship should a naturalised U.S. citizen wish to return to Mexico. Quickly, the Mexican political debate moved beyond this point to discussion of dual nationality. Legislation now in force permits dual nationality but not dual citizenship. In other words, Mexicans who become U.S. citizens retain certain rights, most notably land ownership ones, but they cannot vote in Mexican elections while living in the United States.

Clearly, a final factor is welfare reform itself. A portion of the immigrants who applied for citizenship did so to retain their own eligibility for public benefit programs (Migration News: 1997). Some of these applicants turned out to be the most egregious victims of welfare reform. Their experiences in the naturalisation process helped provide the impetus for restoration of eligibility. For example, public support for the changes made in SSI eligibility grew with the proliferation of newspaper reports about elderly immigrants and refugees struggling to learn English and U.S. history so they could pass their naturalisation examinations, retain eligibility for federal aid, and remain in their nursing homes. The very circumstance that made them need help made them so vulnerable to the new rules.

Other applicants, probably the majority, appear to have been only indirectly affected by the welfare reforms. They were motivated to apply not because they feared loss of eligibility for a specific program but, rather, because of concern about continuing encroachments on their rights as immigrants. This process had been unfolding for a number of years. The political debate about illegal migration in the 1994 California election precipitated fears about the growth of broader anti-immigrant sentiments. Many immigrants came to believe that they needed to become citizens in order to protect themselves against what they perceived to be public animosity. Others recognised that only through the ballot box could they hope to influence the political process. The emerging debate in 1995 and 1996 on welfare reform and national immigration legislation reinforced these views. The national election to be held at the end of 1996 served as a further stimulus, permitting newly naturalised citizens to give immediate voice to their concerns.

The interest in naturalisation did not wane after 1996. Applications in 1997 exceeded 1.6 million. Even though many immigrants saw a restoration of some of their own eligibility for benefits, most of the other factors discussed above were still in play. A study of naturalisation tendencies in California, based on Census data, indicates that the naturalisation rate among Latino immigrants in California increased more significantly between 1996 and 1997 than that of other immigrants living in other states. Immigrants with higher educational levels also demonstrated a greater increase in naturalisation rates (Johnson: 1999). In fact, the heightened interest in naturalisation, and the related political activity within Latino and Asian communities, have been important factors in Congressional decisions to restore limited social rights to immigrants already in the country.

Conclusion

In recent years, the United States has impressed on millions of immigrants the value of citizenship by taking away their social rights. I would argue that, in this respect, the U.S. is no model for other nations. Let me rephrase Barbara Jordan's statement quoted above: Making citizenship the only route to social rights does not exalt citizenship; it debases it. Democracy is hardly strengthened when immigrants choose citizenship to preserve basic social safety nets or to guard against rising anti-immigrant sentiment.

If democratic nations truly wish to encourage a robust sense of citizenship, there are far better and more humane ways. Let me offer four ideas in closing:

Civic education for citizens and immigrants alike. Civic education provides both immigrants and natives with a better understanding of the rights and responsibilities of citizenship. An understanding of the country's history and the principles and practices of its government are essential for all citizens, regardless of their place of birth. Civic education provides a common core of civic culture that can unite people from many different backgrounds and experiences. On a more practical level, civic education can help immigrants prepare for and appreciate the purposes of naturalisation.

Language training. Governments should make a commitment to help all immigrant children become fluent in the language of their new home country. Language training programs should also be available to adult immigrants who need and want it. Sharing the language of the native population enables immigrants to communicate more effectively and participate more fully in the civic life of their new country. This is not to say that immigrants should be forced to give up their native languages, but to emphasise the difficulty of full social, economic and political integration when immigrants are not given the opportunity to learn the new language.

Equality of the law and equality of opportunity. Making equality of the law and equality of opportunity real for all of our residents is a key element in how we define our own nations. Failure to provide full and meaningful equality to racial and ethnic minorities is likely to impede their interest and willingness to embrace membership in our polities.

Eliminating institutional and legal barriers to naturalisation that turn away those who would become our citizens. Some countries have such difficult criteria that few immigrants believe they can qualify. Others have legal requirements that are readily met but impose administrative or bureaucratic obstacles on those seeking to naturalise. Removing obstacles that have little or no relationship to the meaning of citizenship would not only help those who wish to apply but would also send a message to immigrants who believe that the host country does not want them to become full members.

To relate this in closing to a broader question informing this volume: has the possession of social rights rendered naturalisation largely redundant? My answer is an unqualified no. The U.S. experience of the 1990s demonstrates that a complex set of factors influences the decision to naturalise. In my view, full participation in the political process is, and I would hope, continues to be the prime motivator for naturalisation.

Glossary

Aid to Families with Dependent Children
In existence until 1996, AFDC was a joint federal/state program that provided cash welfare payments to needy children and certain other household members who had been deprived of parental support or care because their father or mother is absent from the home continuously, incapacitated, deceased, or unemployed.

Temporary Assistance to Needy Families
The successor program to AFDC, TANF provides assistance to the same population but gives states substantially greater discretion in setting rules and implementing programs. No one may receive TANF payments for

more than a cumulative total of 5 years. States may limit any one stay even further.

Medicaid
Medicaid is a joint federal/state program that provides health coverage for recipients of TANF and SSI. Other medically needy populations may qualify if they meet income standards.

Supplementary Security Income
SSI is a means-tested, federally administrated income assistance program that provides monthly cash payments to needy aged, blind and disabled persons. Aged are defined as persons 65 years old and older; blind are individuals with 20/200 vision or less with correcting lenses or those with tunnel vision of 20 degrees or less; disabled are those unable to engage in any substantial gainful activity by reason of a medically determined physical or mental impairment.

Food Stamps
Administered by the Department of Agriculture, the Food Stamp program grants low-income households monthly benefits to enable them to purchase food items. Households receiving AFDC/TANF or SSI are determined to meet the income requirements for eligibility for Food Stamps.

References

G. Borjas, 'Immigration and Welfare: Some New Evidence,' testimony before the U.S. Senate Subcommittee on Immigration, Washington, DC, 6 February 1996.

Congressional Record, Washington, D.C., 18 July 1996.

K. Darner, *Immigrant Policy News: Inside the Beltway*, 3, no. 2, March 1996.

M. Fix and J.S. Passel, *Immigration and Immigrants: Setting the Record Straight*, Washington, D.C., 1994.

M. Fix, J.S. Passel and W. Zimmermann, 'The Use of SSI and Other Welfare Programs by Immigrants,' testimony before the U.S. House of Representatives Ways and Means Committee,Washington, D.C., 23 May 1996.

L.H. Fuchs, *The American Kaleidoscope: Race, Ethnicity, and the Civic Culture*, Hanover, N.H., 1990.

Immigrant Policy Project of the State and Local Coalition on Immigration, Newsletter, Washington, D.C.,'Immigrants Retain SSI,' *Migration News*, 4, no. 8, August, 1997.

H.P. Johnson, B.I. Reyes, L. Mameesh, and E. Barbour, *Taking the Oath: An Analysis of Naturalisation in California and the United States*, San Francisco, Ca., 1999.

B. Jordan, testimony before the U.S. House of Representatives Ways and Means Committee, Washington, D.C., 1994.

J. Joselit, 'The perception and realities of immigrant health conditions, 1840–1920', Supplement to the staff report of the Select Commission on Immigration and Refugee Policy, Appendix A, Washington, D.C., 1981.

T.H. Marshall, *Class, Citizenship, and Social Development*, New York, 1964.

M.J. O'Grady, *Native And Naturalised Citizens And Non-Citizens: An Analysis Of Poverty Status, Welfare Benefits, And Other Factors*, Washington, D.C., 1995.

U.S. Commission on Immigration Reform, *Legal Immigration: Setting Priorities*, Washington, D.C., 1995.

U.S. Immigration and Naturalisation Service, *Statistical Yearbook*, Washington, D.C., 1991.

Notes

1. T.H. Marshall differentiated these rights as follows: 'The civil element is composed of the rights necessary for individual freedom – liberty of the person, freedom of speech, thought and faith, the right to own property and to conclude valid contracts, and the right to justice. . . . By the political element I mean the right to participate in the exercise of political power, as a member of a body invested with political authority or as an elector of the members of such a body. . . . By the social element I mean the whole range from the right to a modicum of economic welfare and security to the right to share to the full in the social heritage and to live the life of a civilised being according to the standards prevailing in the society' (Marshall: 1964, 71–72).

2. The public charge exclusion concept was even older. In 1645, Massachusetts enacted legislation prohibiting the entry of paupers and, in 1700, excluding the infirm unless security was given that they would become public charges.

3. Speaking in the context of efforts to reform immigration policy to eliminate the most discriminatory effects of U.S. immigration laws, Johnson described the covenant as 'conceived in justice, written in liberty, bound in union, it was meant one day to inspire the hopes of all mankind'.

4. IIRIRA, in conjunction with the Antiterrorism and Effective Death Penalty Act (AEDPA) of 1996, also included significant derogation of due process rights for legal immigrants as well as eased rules for their deportation if convicted of certain crimes.

5. Citizenship USA has been criticised for having led to the naturalisation of about 200,000 applicants prior to the completion of a criminal background check. Although the vast majority of these applicants had no criminal background, some immigrants who had committed serious crimes did obtain citizenship wrongly. Afterwards, new control mechanisms were put in place that have slowed down processing time once again. At present, the time between application and naturalisation can exceed two years in some heavily affected districts.

CHAPTER 11

SEEKING SHELTER: IMMIGRANTS AND THE DIVERGENCE OF SOCIAL RIGHTS AND CITIZENSHIP IN THE UNITED STATES

Michael Jones Correa

The goal of this chapter is to explore the intersection between social rights and citizenship, and in particular what has happened in the United States since social rights and citizenship have once again begun to diverge. What effects has the reversal of certain social welfare services, once taken for granted, had on the choices people make with regard to citizenship and political participation? What implication does this have for the way we think theoretically about social rights and political rights?

Apart from their theoretical relevance these questions are particularly pertinent today with ongoing immigration to industrialised democracies. There are larger population movements in the world today than at any other time in history. The United Nations reported in 1993 that there were one hundred million people living in countries other than their country of origin, double the number only four years earlier. At least two percent of the world's population resides in a country other than that of their birth, and this can only be expected to increase (United Nations Population Fund, 1993: 7). The numbers of people immigrating, migrating or simply dislocated from one country to another raises questions about their insertion and participation in the social and political life of their host countries, and their protection under the umbrella of social, economic and political rights.

Questions about social rights and citizenship have drawn the attention of an increasing number of scholars and policy makers, leading to lively debates on the issue of migrants' rights, the definition of citizenship, the place of participation and the role of the state. An increasingly influential strand of these debates has drawn on arguments that global international-isation and transnationalism have made the notion of national citizenship increasingly archaic and obsolete, and turns to a notion of 'postnational' citizenship instead. In this perspective, postnational citizenship should supplement, and better yet, supplant, citizenship in the nation-state.

The pages which follow sketch out some of the problems with the argu-ment for postnational citizenship, drawbacks which have been amply illustrated by recent events in the United States. The U.S. retreat from its commitment to guaranteeing a full complement of social rights to perma-nent resident non-citizens has served to highlight the vulnerability of social rights in the absence of full citizenship. Immigrants are fully aware of this vulnerability, and as the data indicate, they have been shifting *en masse* to full formal membership in the polity as their informal member-ship has come under fire. However, it is useful to keep in mind that full citizenship requires not only formal membership, but participatory inclu-sion as well. While vulnerable immigrant minorities like Hispanic-Americans have responded to their sense of being besieged with a turn toward naturalisation, there has not been a parallel increase in partici-pation in electoral politics.

Social rights and postnational citizenship

The idea of postnational citizenship draws its inspiration from the growing literature on globalisation and transnationalism (Rouse: 1995; Bamyeh: 1993; Sutton: 1992; Appadurai: 1990). Theorists of trans-nationalism have focused on 'the manner in which migrants, through their life ways and daily practices, reconfigure space so that their lives are lived simultaneously within two or more nation-states' (Basch et al.: 1994, 28).[1]

> Over time and with extensive movement back and forth, communities of origin and destination increasingly comprise transnational circuits – social and geographic spaces that arise through the circulation of people, money, goods and information . . . Over time, migrant communities become cultur-ally 'transnationalised', incorporating ideologies, practices, expectations, and political claims from both societies to create a 'culture of migration' that is distinct from the culture of both the sending and receiving nation. (Massey and Durand: 1992, 8).

The culture of migration which immigrants form, these authors write, encompasses a political space of its own.

This political space is not simply the politics of a 'deterritorialised state', in which the migrants' home state extends its claims across the boundaries of other states to include its citizens who may live physically dispersed, but who 'remain socially, politically, culturally, and often economically part of the nation-state of their ancestors' (Basch et al.: 1994, 8).[2] Instead, proponents of the transnational perspective stress that there is the emergence of a new formulation for citizenship: a *postnational* citizenship, with its basis in an international human rights regime (Jacobson: 1996, Soysal: 1994, 1, 165–166). With individual rights disassociated from the state the importance of national citizenship, these critics argue, fades away. Territorial boundaries are increasingly less relevant as an organising principle of social interaction (Basch et al.: 1994, 52; Duany: 1994, 2–3; Sutton: 1992, 237). Individuals' identities are increasingly characterised by fluid, multiple attachments that stretch across frontiers in a 'single field of social relations' (Basch et al.: 1994, 5). Postnational theorists are implicitly (or explicitly) critical of the nation-state for claiming full authority and demanding sole allegiance.

The implication is that traditional notions of citizenship are less relevant for permanent non-citizen residents, that their social and political lives transcend national borders, and that their rights are adequately safeguarded by a rights regime that also transcends borders. There is no question that many first generation immigrants (and some in subsequent generations) live lives spanning across countries, but this view assumes that transnational citizenship provides adequate protection from the vulnerability and marginality often associated with non-citizen status.

Postnational citizenship theorists think of citizenship as a set of rights that are extended like an umbrella over permanent residents (whomever they may be) in the polity. However, there are at least two major problems with this view. The first is that for rights to be protected there have to be institutional mechanisms to enforce these rights. One cannot simply proclaim that these rights exist in principle, as the international community has done on more than one occasion, and expect that these rights will be allowed in practice. The practice of rights depends on their enforcement in specific localities. The European Union, for instance, has an elaborate set of statutes setting out rights for citizens and non-citizens, but while these rights theoretically apply equally across the member states of the Union, their existence in practice varies substantially across states and even within states. Without adequate institutional guarantors, do rights really exist?

One response might be that the enforcement mechanisms to protect these rights must simply be developed. Even so, when these rights are enforced, they are enforced by states, not by international institutions. At best international institutions act *through* states. It is possible that one day international institutions will develop the capacity to enforce rights; this may be theoretically and even normatively desirable, but for the foreseeable future rights will be enforced by states.[3] The problem with relying simply on a rights regime to protect non-citizen residents is that these rights are extended at the whim of the state – as the state gives, so the state can take away. Rights for non-citizen residents are rarely part of a nation-state's core laws, its constitution. Because of this, I would argue, they do not deserve to be called *citizenship* rights.

'Postnational citizenship' is partial, insubstantial, and insecure. By itself, it is only a simulacrum of full citizenship. Even if the gap between the rights held by residents aliens and those held by citizens has been shrinking to the point of meaninglessness, as some authors have charged (Schuck: 1989; Schuck and Smith: 1985), these rights are still less secure and more easily modified than the rights of citizens (Carens: 1989, 36). Full citizenship is basic – constitutional – to a democratic polity. It cannot exist at the whim, or discretion, of the state. Recent events in the United States – most notably the curtailing of social services to both undocumented aliens and permanent resident – serve as a pointed reminder of the vulnerability of immigrants, even those with claims to social rights, in the absence of political rights.

There is no realistic substitute in the current world system for formal citizenship in the nation-state. This is true at another level as well. Postnational theories think of rights as an umbrella, extended from above. Rights are top down. Apart from making these rights vulnerable to changes of heart, as I mentioned above, the rights regime inherent in the concept of postnational citizenship is also non-participatory. Non-citizen residents themselves are not involved in the crafting of the rights which protect them, nor, if issues and debates come up later in which they would like to take part, is there provision for their doing so. If states would like to make provisions for local representation or workers' councils and the like, they can do so, but again, these participatory mechanisms exist at the whim of the state. They can be withdrawn at will. The American case, again, is a good example.[4]

Citizenship is more than a formal status of basic equality in a community, entitling one to a set of rights – it is also an expression of one's membership in a *political* community (Kymlicka and Norman 1995: 301). Citizenship presupposes that members can take part in the polity's deliberation and decision-making. Theorists of postnational citizenship see citizens as holding a set of rights, but not as participating in a deliberative project. The description of institutional mechanisms for participation by authors pursuing this line of thought tend to be thin, or more likely, non-existent.[5] In a sense, the problem with transnational citizenship boils down to the fact that it does not take politics seriously. The contention for a postnational citizenship is, perhaps, the logical extension of T.H. Marshall's influential argument including social and economic rights in addition to political rights under the conception of citizenship (Marshall 1950), but it turns Marshall's argument around and focuses on civil and social rights at the *expense* of political rights. The fact is, it is hard to think of having functioning democratic institutions without, in some form, the presence of the state.

In the following sections we turn to the practical implications of having social rights without corresponding political rights. The vulnerability of these social rights in the absence of full citizenship is amply demonstrated by events in the United States. What happens when these social rights are withdrawn? It is to a discussion of these events, and their consequences, that we turn next.

Immigration to the US

The debate over citizenship and social rights has its origin with the wave of immigration arriving in Europe and the United States in the postwar period. The effects of this immigration are inescapable. It is impossible, for instance, walking through almost any American city today, to ignore the signs of transformative change. These can be seen in the lettering of signs over the storefronts, which are not just in English but in a panoply of other languages as well; in the faces of store owners, street vendors, waiters, pedestrians, passengers on the bus lines, and in the remarkable mix of children of different national origins in the public schools.

Over the last thirty years the United States has absorbed the largest wave of immigration since the turn of the century. In 1994, the Census Bureau announced that the 8.7 percent of the U.S. population was made up of first-generation immigrants, the highest proportion since the 1940s, and nearly double the percentage in 1970 (4.8 percent). This means that 22.6 million people – nearly one in eleven U.S. residents – were foreign born. Four and a half million immigrants arrived from 1990–1994. 8.3 million immigrants arrived in the 1980s, and 9.8 million before 1980.[6]

Nearly half of these new immigrants are from Latin America. A common refrain is that by the year 2010 Latinos will be the largest minority in the United States, surpassing African-Americans.[7] Latinos, now over ten percent of the U.S. population, grew in number from 22 million in 1990 to 26 million in 1995, and surpassed 32 million in 2000. But if Hispanics are a 'minority' population, they are also increasingly an immigrant one. Just under half of all Latinos in the United States are first-generation immigrants, about two-thirds are first or second generation immigrants, and these proportions are likely to increase (Schmidley and Gibson: 1999). Because many of the new immigrants are from Latin America, and because the U.S. Census Bureau has kept political participation data on Hispanics but only inconsistently on other emerging immigrant/pan-ethnic minorities like Asian Americans, the empirical data which follows will focus on immigrants overall when possible, but on Latinos specifically when necessary.

Raising the costs for non-citizens

As immigration to the United States increased steadily through the 1980s, there was an increasingly vociferous debate not only about the desirable levels of immigration, but about the rights accorded to immigrants once they arrived. The revamping of immigration laws in 1965 coincided with the expansion and consolidation of the (admittedly attenuated version of the) American welfare state. As a result of a series of administrative and judicial decisions the general policy became, almost by default, that non-resident aliens received basically the same package of social services as citizens. By the late 1980s, however, there was a perception that immigrants were particularly likely to take advantage of the welfare system, and that the sheer number of immigrants had raised taxpayer expenditures on income transfer programs.[8]

The first manifestations of the backlash against immigrant recipients of social welfare benefits were felt at the state[9] level. The approval of Proposition 187 in November 1994 by a majority of California voters indicated that there was a considerable ground swell of support for restricting taxpayer-supported benefits to undocumented immigrants, who were not perceived to be full members of the polity.[10] Proposition 187 would have made illegal aliens ineligible for public social services, public health care services (unless emergency under federal law), and public school education at elementary, secondary, and post-secondary levels. It would also have required various state and local agencies to report persons who are suspected undocumented immigrants to the California Attorney General and the United States Immigration and Naturalisation Service.

Almost immediately after its passage, federal courts blocked California from enforcing most provisions of Proposition 187. In a final 1997 ruling, a federal judge barred the state from denying non-emergency health care, welfare and most public education to undocumented residents. The ruling also blocked another controversial Proposition 187 requirement – that police, health workers and teachers report anyone they suspected of being illegal to immigration authorities. The judge said that parts of the measure could pressure immigrants into leaving the country when they have a right to remain. That would constitute a 'scheme to regulate immigration' – something only the federal government is allowed to do (McDonnell: 1997; Lesher: 1997).

However, by August 1996, Congress had picked up on the anti-immigrant mood and passed legislation limiting eligibility for welfare and other public benefit programs. Following the lead of Proposition 187, the legislation barred undocumented immigrants from access to all federal public benefit programs. The welfare reform bill went beyond Proposition 187 in barring most legal permanent residents from participation in Social Security and Food Stamp programs, and in banning all new resident non-citizens from federal means-tested programs like AFDC (Aid for Dependent Children).[11] Social services, the reasoning went, were not intended for non-citizens, even if these individuals resided permanently in the United States. Immigrants were meant to contribute to the well-being of the nation, and not be a burden on the taxpayer. In addition, cutting immigrants from federal social programs would supposedly save the U.S. government tens of billions of dollars a year, a not insignificant amount in an era of budgetary constraints.[12]

The current of American politics, rather than moving toward lowering costs for non-citizens to enter the polity, seems to be flowing in the opposite direction. American politicians are intent on *raising* the costs for immigrants who are not citizens. In response to the perceived crisis of illegal immigration, local, state and federal governments began pursuing since the late 1980s a number of strategies for raising the costs of non-citizenship. It is now more difficult for non-citizens to receive social welfare benefits, to receive an education,[13] or to speak a language other than English.[14] These laws may be intended primarily as symbolic gestures or cost-cutting measures, but their general effect is to reduce the access of both legal and undocumented immigrants to government services, and to government more generally.

The move to naturalise

The most obvious consequence of these restrictive policies was the dramatic increase in the number of people applying for naturalisation in the United States. While there were 384,000 new citizens in 1992, more than one million people a year became American citizens in 1994, and again in 1995.[15] *Raising* the costs of non-citizenship may have turned out to be a much more effective spur to naturalisation than *lowering* the costs to becoming a citizen.

Table 11.1 Immigration to the United States

1941–1950	1,035,039
1951–1960	2,515,479
1961–1970	3,321,677
1971–1980	4,493,314
1981–1990	7,338,062
1990–2001	8,600,000

Source: figures for 1941–1990 are from Pachón and DeSipio (1994), 5 Table 1. Figures for 1991–2000 are from the U.S. Census, and are rounded to the nearest ten thousand.

However, it is hard to disentangle what actually caused the increase in naturalisation rates, as there were several different possible causes. One possibility is that the dramatic increase in naturalisation figures in the mid-1990s might have been a one-time occurrence, reflecting the bulge of undocumented aliens who became permanent residents under the 1986 Immigration Reform and Control Act (IRCA): slightly more than three million people became legal residents of the United States under the amnesty offered by the 1986 Immigration legislation. These new legal residents became eligible for citizenship beginning in 1991, so that one would expect a short-term rise in citizenship applications, as this group joins the normal numbers of immigrants seeking naturalisation.

Yet while the number of immigrant naturalisations slipped from the peak reached in 1996, it remains significantly higher than it had been previously. It seems that we may in fact be seeing a reversal in some (particularly Latin American) immigrants' long-standing reluctance to become citizens. Another possibility, then, is that these naturalisation rates are a response to the general anti-immigrant context of the mid-1990s. If this were the case, then we would expect to see naturalisation rates increase more rapidly in states where anti-immigrant sentiment has been much more overt than in states where anti-immigrant sentiment has been defused or downplayed. California, for instance, should have higher naturalisation rates than New York or Texas.

Finally, naturalisation rates may be a reaction to federal legislation targeted at immigrants, like the 1996 welfare reform. Permanent residents, some of them having lived in the United States for decades, are likely to have reacted to the cutbacks in federally-funded social services by reconsidering U.S. citizenship. In Los Angeles County, for instance, a survey of recipients receiving Supplemental Security Income (SSI), a federal program that provides monthly cash benefits to elderly, blind and disabled individuals found, that of the thirty-five percent of immigrant recipients who did not fall under one of the exempt categories of the Personal Responsibility and Work Opportunity Reconciliation Act (PRWORA), eighty-nine percent had lived in the United States for at least five years and presumably were most likely eligible for citizenship. Of those denied benefits and eligible for U.S. citizenship, ninety-one percent had applied for naturalisation.[16] Welfare reform should be reflected in an increase in naturalisation rates after 1996, and should be felt evenly across the states.

Of course, these three possibilities are not incompatible, and in fact the naturalisation figures collected by the Immigration and Naturalisation Service (INS) from 1988 to 1996 seem to indicate that all three factors may be going on simultaneously (thus, the explanation for rising naturalisation rates in the United States may be overdetermined). First of all, figure 11.1[17] – which shows naturalisation rates in the United States for major immigrant groups across this time period – indicates that there is, in fact, a turn upwards in naturalisation rates after 1991, at about the time that many of those amnestied under the 1986 IRCA would have begun to be eligible for naturalisation, followed by a steady increase in naturalisations over the next several years. That naturalisation rates slow down from 1993 until 1996 may say less about immigrants' desire to acquire citizenship than about the administrative capacity to handle the rise in naturalisation applications. It was only from late 1995 (and lasting only part-way through 1996) that the Immigration and Naturalisation Service (INS) allocated additional funds to a citizenship program, 'Citizenship USA,' to ease the backlog in naturalisation applications which had begun accumulating since 1993. The 1996 spike, therefore, may be somewhat artificial, granting citizenship in 1996 to people whose naturalisation applications may have dated back a year or two before.

Second, the data indicate that different nationalities behave very differently when it comes to citizenship. Immigrants from Asian countries exhibit much steadier naturalisation rates, consistent with their historical pattern. For example, immigrants (and refugees) from Taiwan, Vietnam, the Philippines and Korea show the same gentle turn upwards in 1991, followed by a period of fairly steady naturalisation, with a slight upwards trend, over the next four years. The naturalisation of Mexican immigrants is much more striking. Following several decades in which they ranked at the bottom, or close to the bottom, among immigrant groups acquiring citizenship, Mexican naturalisation began accelerating in 1992, and shows no sign of stopping. Why Mexican immigration in particular? Again, there is more than one possible explanation. The rise in anti-immigrant sentiment in California, which was particularly directed at undocumented Mexican immigrants, may have had a negative effect on all Mexicans living in the United States.[18] The severe recession in Mexico may have persuaded migrants to stay in the U.S. economy, and the passage in Mexico of dual nationality for Mexican nationals abroad in 1996 may have lowered the costs of acquiring U.S. citizenship. None of these explanations is fully satisfactory. The Mexican recession and dual nationality date from later than the beginning of the rise in naturalisations, and if naturalisations were being driven by a reaction to anti-immigrant sentiment then California should have had higher naturalisation rates than other states. The state-level data, discussed below, do not seem to indicate this is the case.

Third, the data also show that the biggest jump in naturalisation rates took place only in 1996. Mexican naturalisation rates, which had been increasing disproportionately through the mid-1990s, go off the chart in 1996. These figures give some indication of the huge pool of potential citizens among Mexican permanent residents in the United States. However, every other immigrant group also experienced a significant jump in naturalisation rates in that year, including immigrants from Asian sending-countries. The figures partly reflect the effects of the 'Citizenship USA' program, the all too brief opening-up of the naturalisation process which reduced the backlog of citizenship applications, but there is little doubt that the spike in naturalisations in 1996 was also a response to the passage of welfare reform in Congress. Either way, the data suggest that many immigrants who had been hesitant about making the commitment to naturalise were seeking shelter from the prevailing anti-immigrant winds in the refuge of citizenship.

State-level data refine these findings further. Comparing state-level naturalisation data from 1988–1996 for the six states receiving the largest number of immigrants (California, New York, Florida, Texas, Illinois and New Jersey, which account for about three-quarters of all foreign born residents in the United States) we see, as we did at the national level, that the effect of the 1986 IRCA was not immediately felt in most of these states, but that naturalisation rates did begin increasing after 1992. The data also show that all six states had dramatic increases in naturalisation rates in 1996 (see figures 11.2–11.7). This state level information confirms what was already evident at the national level: IRCA did have an effect on naturalisation rates, but this was overshadowed by the response to the INS citizenship program and the 1996 welfare reform bill.

A first glance at state level data does not support the hypothesis that the naturalisation experience differed by state, and that states with more virulent anti-immigrant campaigns had higher naturalisation rates than others. In particular, California's pattern of naturalisation does not seem all that dissimilar from those of the other major immigrant-receiving states.[19] This seems to suggest that anti-immigrant sentiment has been overplayed as a cause for naturalisation. However, the state data, like the national data, *does* point to significant differences among national groups. Latin American immigrants – Mexicans, Dominicans and Cubans – each of whom are dominant in their own regions, seem to have exhibited similar naturalisation patterns in the mid to late 1990s. Across all the major receiving states, these groups significantly increased their naturalisation rates after 1992, and their naturalisation rates took an even more dramatic jump in 1996 (some groups of Asian immigrants, as noted above, also exhibited some of the same patterns, particularly Chinese immigrants in New York, and Filipinos in California and New Jersey).

So why were some groups of immigrants, particularly Latin American immigrants, disproportionately naturalising in the 1990s? One possibility is that these groups were those most targeted by the anti-immigrant backlash. Perhaps this explains why Mexicans, who were singled out the most in the immigration debate, responded in the greatest numbers by seeking naturalisation. But why Filipinos in California? Or Cubans in Florida? A more plausible explanation for the commonality among national-origin groups naturalising is that these groups were those that had historically lagged behind in acquiring citizenship, had the largest proportion of non-citizen residents, and were most affected by the cut in benefits to permanent legal residents. When their members are finally confronted by the erosion of public benefits coupled with what looks to be, at least for the

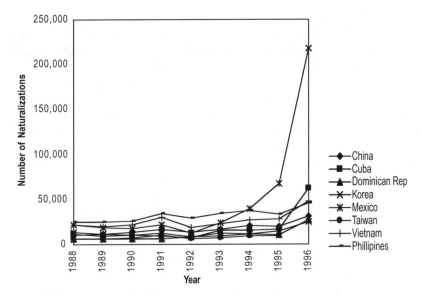

Figure 11.1 Naturalisation by Country of Origin, United States 1988–1996

foreseeable future, an anti-immigrant environment, they made the decision to naturalise *en masse*, which is what happened in 1996. Latinos had much higher naturalisation rates in the late 1990s because they had a much larger pool of non-citizen permanent legal residents eligible for citizenship. Historically Asian immigrants to the United States naturalise soon after they are eligible, regardless of public attitudes toward immigration (Barkan 1983), so when the 1996 welfare reform bill passed there was a smaller pool of permanent legal resident aliens to naturalise.

What about electoral participation?

Rising naturalisation rates by permanent resident aliens in the United States underscore the fragility of social rights in the absence of full citizenship. Immigrants are fully aware of the vulnerability of their position as permanent residents, and as soon as it becomes untenable, they seek the more secure status of citizenship. Some have gone so far as to argue that Proposition 187 in California, the cut-backs of benefits for legal and illegal immigrants by Congress, and the push for making English the 'official language' of the United States are all 'good things,' in the long run, because they encourage people to become citizens (Glazer: 1996). Even if it is the case that people became citizens as a result of the anti-immigrant backlash, do we really want people to choose citizenship under duress? Is revoking or removing benefits really the way we want to go about encouraging residents to become citizens? Having chosen naturalisation purely instrumentally, what kind of citizens will they be? What will citizenship mean to them, except a choice of status as a safe haven?

It may be that what motivated many permanent residents to acquire U.S. citizenship in the 1990s was the desire to be included under the same umbrella of rights, and to be protected by the same institutional mechanisms, as citizens. However, if we accept the principle that citizenship is solely an umbrella of rights, then we come back to the second flaw underlying the notion of postnational citizenship: citizenship becomes divorced from participation, and the umbrella of rights is simply held up from above. Naturalisation by intimidation may simply create a passive citizenry. This passivity may pass with the first generation, but it very well may not. If political behaviour is learned, particularly from one's parents, what does this say about the prospects for political participation in the second generation? If their parents are outside the polity, what opportunity will these new Americans have for civic education and participation in political life? Participation creates democratic citizens by fostering political learning, a sense of investment in the political system, and tolerance for the views of others. People learn to become citizens not by watching and waiting, but by *doing*.

The United States may have intimidated its non-citizens to naturalise, but it has not figured out how to encourage them to register and vote. The pool of potential participants is staggering. For instance, by the late 1990s there were more than a million legal immigrants in New York City – 1 in 6 adults in the city. The number of immigrants applying for citizenship in the New York metropolitan area alone more than doubled from 1992 to 1995 before rising even faster in 1996 (Dugger: 1996a). In California at this time there were almost ten million legal immigrants. INS statistics show that a record 879,000 immigrant adults were naturalised in California from 1994 to 1997. Another 623,000 had applications pending. The numbers of newly naturalised citizens have the potential to tilt the balance of electoral politics, particularly in those states in which they are concentrated. However, for this to happen, immigrants must not only naturalise, but also register and vote.

We might expect that naturalisation would lead smoothly to active engagement in the formal political system, and for this participation to be greater where immigrants feel a more palpable threat. Indeed, this is precisely the argument that many observers have made, arguing that there has not only been an increase in immigrant political participation, but that 1994 in particular – the year that California passed Proposition 187 – was a watershed for the mobilisation of new ethnic groups. While preparing for the 1996 elections, for instance, Alfredo Cruz, spokesman for the Los Angeles-based Southwest Voter Registration Education Project noted that '[e]verything we've experienced in the last year or so,

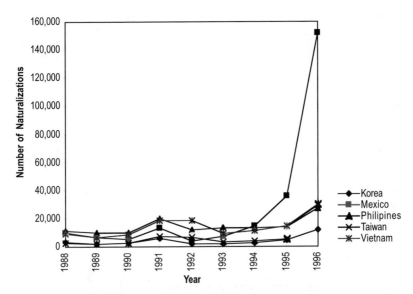

Figure 11.2 Naturalisation by Country of Origin, California 1988–1996

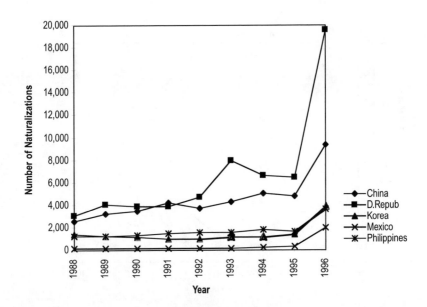

Figure 11.3 Naturalisation by Country of Origin, New York 1988–1996

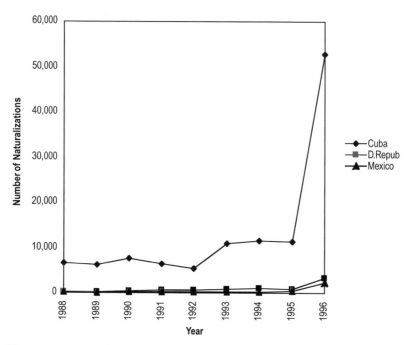

Figure 11.4 Naturalisation by Country of Origin, Florida 1988–1996

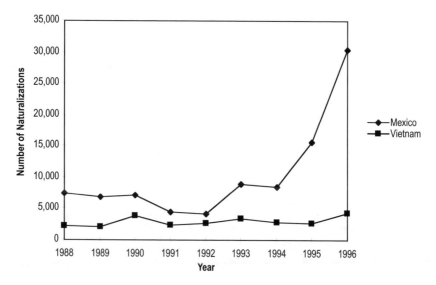

Figure 11.5 Naturalisation by Country of Origin, Texas 1988–1996

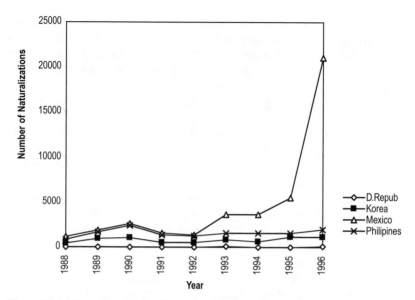

Figure 11.6 Naturalisation by Country of Origin, Illinois 1988–1996

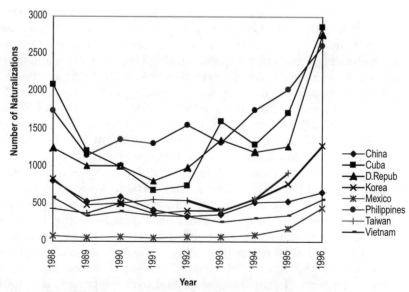

Figure 11.7 Naturalisation by Country of Origin, New Jersey 1988–1996

from Initiative 187 to the redrawing of voting districts, and [attacks on] affirmative action – that's stimulating people to participate more.' Proposition 187, he said, 'represents for the first time in history an imminent threat' to immigrant Latinos in California.[20] Observers have argued there has been a steady increase in immigrant, particularly Hispanic, electoral participation. However, these claims are only partly borne out by the evidence.

Because national level registration and voting data are available for Hispanics (but not for Asian-Americans), it makes sense to focus on Latino political participation. Hispanics have historically registered and voted at lower rates than the general U.S. population. In the 1996 presidential elections Latinos made up about 10.3 percent of the U.S. population of nearly two hundred and sixty million (about 9.3 percent of adults), but only 4.6 percent of registered voters in the November 1996 elections. About fifty-nine percent of eligible Hispanic citizens were registered to vote in 1994, compared to 71 percent of all U.S. citizens over eighteen.[21] Much, if not most, of this non-participation can be accounted for by non-citizens (Pachón and DeSipio: 1994, 6; Uhlaner, Cain, and Kiewiet: 1989). Breaking the Census numbers down, it is evident that more than a third of Hispanics of voting age are in fact first-generation immigrants who have not become citizens. So the question is, as these non-citizens naturalise, are they now entering into electoral politics?

There are only imperfect measures of immigrant participation. Because approximately forty percent of the Latino population in the United States in the 1990s were first-generation immigrants, and an additional thirty percent were second-generation, in this chapter we take the increase in Latino participation to reflect, in part, an increase in Latino *immigrant* participation. In the 1996 elections, Latino voter registration rose an impressive twenty-eight percent over 1992, making Hispanics easily the fastest growing segment of the American electorate – much of this increase was due to newly naturalised immigrants. According to the U.S. Census, the numbers of Latinos registered in the United States went up from 4,573,000 in 1988 to 6,573,000 in 1996, a forty-four percent increase. The numbers of Hispanics actually voting increased from 3,713,000 in 1988 to 4,920,000 voters in 1996, a thirty-three percent increase (see figure 11.8).[22]

However, the total Latino voting age population in the United States increased from 12,893,000 in 1988 to 18,426,000 in 1996, an increase of forty-three percent. So actually the number of Latinos registered just barely kept up with the increase in the Latino voting age population. If we look at Latinos of voting age registered (as a percent of the total Hispanic voting age population) we see that the figure basically stays constant over the period, at 35.5 percent in 1988 and 35.7 percent in 1996 (see figure 11.9). Latino voter turnout actually loses ground over the period. Turnout in 1988 was 28.8 percent of the Hispanic voting age population and only 26.7 percent in 1996.

This is all to say that the numbers of Hispanics registered and voting are not keeping up with the increase in the number of Latinos in the voting age population. So while the percentage of Latino voters does increase slightly relative to the total pool of voters, making up 4.7 percent of total voters in 1996 versus 3.6 percent in 1988, this is simply reflecting the greater size of the Latino population, and not any relative gains in participation rates (see figure 11.10). Naturalisation is not leading to a surge in electoral participation.

It might be the case that while Latino registration and voting rates lost ground relative to the growth of the Latino population nationally, this might not have been true of California. Because of California's history in the 1990s – most notably the passage of propositions 187, 209, and 227 – immigrants, particularly Latino immigrants, in California might be more inclined not only to naturalise but also to register and to vote. The voting data from 1988 to 1996 allow us to trace the effects of the highly contentious debates on immigration, affirmative action, and language on the state's voter registration and turnout.

In the interval between the Congressional elections of 1990 and 1994 the Latino voting-age population in California increased by twenty-one percent, while Hispanic voter registration increased by sixteen percent. What is interesting is that voter turnout across these two mid-term elections increased by thirty-nine percent (see figures 11.11 and 11.12). The year 1994, if we recall, was seen as a critical election for many Latinos, so perhaps it shouldn't be surprising that voting rates would increase. The implication of the Hispanic voting rate increasing relative to the population while registration lost ground relatively is that the voters voting in the 1994 election were more likely to be previously registered voters rather than new citizens. However, since the census does not ask whether a respondent is a first time voter, or newly naturalised voter, the limitations of the data do not allow us to do any more than speculate.

From the Latino perspective, even the higher turnout in the 1994 California election was still somewhat disappointing. Almost as many registered Hispanic voters stayed home as cast ballots. While almost eighty percent of registered non-Hispanic whites voted on November 8, only fifty-five percent of eligible Hispanics cast ballots. In 1994, Latinos made up 25.3 percent of California's voting-aged population, fifteen percent of registered voters, and eight percent of Proposition 187 voters.[23] Whites, in contrast, made up fifty-seven percent of California's population, but eighty-one percent of voters in the 1994 election. African Americans made up 7.5 percent of the population, and voted more or less in proportion to their numbers, while Asians (9.5 percent of the population), like Latinos, voted at significantly lower rates. The 1994 elections, which might have been expected to radically galvanise new Latino voters, did not seem to do so.[24]

The 1996 elections saw some significant changes in Latino political

participation, and the first real indications of involvement by newly naturalised citizens. One indication is that Latino voting registration increased
18.6 percent between 1992 and 1994, and Latino turnout increased 18.7
percent in this time period, while the Latino adult population increased
only 5.1 percent. Unlike the 1988–1994 period, between 1992 and 1994
Latino registration and turnout outstripped population increases (see
figures 11.11 and 11.12). In 1996, Latinos made up twenty-five percent of
adults in California, 12.8 percent of registered voters, and 11.7 percent of
those actually turning out to vote.

These changes were reflected as well in other, less comprehensive, interview and polling data. One 1997 poll indicated that recently naturalised
immigrants constituted up to one-third of Hispanic voters in the 1996 elections in California.[25] This finding was echoed by Political Data Inc., a non-
partisan vendor of voter histories in California, which released a study of
1996 registration data which suggested that up to forty percent of California's entire Latino electorate of two million had registered after President Clinton's first election in 1992 and before his reelection in 1996.[26] The
firm found that one-sixth of the Latino electorate in 1996 were new voters,
and over two-thirds of these went to the polls, surpassing the level of participation of all registered voters (Rohrlich: 1997). By 1998 *Los Angeles
Times* exit polls indicated that Latinos made up twelve percent of the
state's voters, about the same percentage as they had in 1996 and up from
nine percent in 1990.[27]

According to Political Data Inc. the upwards trend in Latino voting was
also visible at the county level. The Latino share of the Los Angeles County
vote rose from an estimated eleven percent to eighteen percent and the
share of the Orange County vote rose from six percent to nine percent in

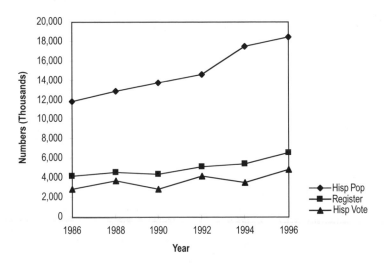

Figure 11.8 Hispanic population, registration, and voting 1988–1996

the 1990s.[28] The increase in Latino participation was particularly evident in central Orange County in 1996. In the 46th Congressional District, where Rep. Loretta Sanchez (D-Garden Grove) ousted Robert K. Dornan from Congress by 984 votes, the number of Latinos who registered went from about thirty thousand in 1992 to nearly forty thousand in 1996 (Rohrlich 1997). In the City of Los Angeles a *Los Angeles Times* exit poll found that Latinos accounted for fifteen percent of voters in the 1997 mayoral election, nearly doubling their turnout from four years before and surpassing the turnout rate of African-Americans for the first time. A *La Opinion* and KVEA-TV poll found that forty-eight percent of Latinos who voted in the April 1997 Los Angeles City elections had voted for the first time in the November 1996 Presidential elections,[29] which suggests that many were newly naturalised (or at least newly mobilised) citizens.

In 1994 the data seem to indicate that registration and voting turnout of Latinos in California were outpaced, as they were nationwide, by the growth in the Hispanic population. In addition, at least in California, rising registration rates were overshadowed by increases in turnout. The reason for the disjuncture between registration and voting rates is that Proposition 187 did not succeed in encouraging the registration or mobilisation of great numbers of *new* voters, but it *did* succeed in mobilising voters already registered. So while Hispanic registration rates did not keep up with population growth, Latino voter turnout rates, as we have seen, increased rapidly through the 1990s. What Proposition 187 did was to mobilise Latino activists.[30] This is reflected in turnout for the primaries, which determine the main parties' candidates in the general election. Latinos made up six percent of the primary vote in 1994, eight percent in 1996 and twelve percent in 1998 (Pyle, Mcdonnell and Tobar: 1998). Latinos

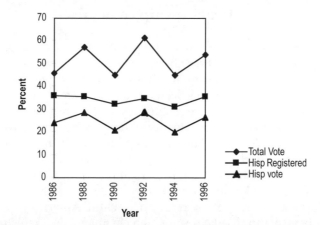

Figure 11.9 Hispanic registration and voting as percent of Hispanic voting age population, 1988–1996

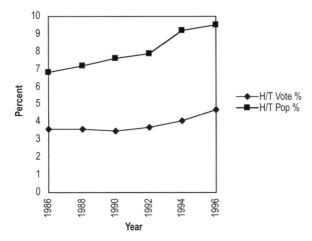

Figure 11.10 Hispanics as percent of total VAP and vote turnout

doubled their relative weight in the primaries between 1994 and 1998. This picture changed somewhat by the 1996 elections. Here, Latino registration rates and voting rates both increased significantly, indicating the mobilisation of both old and new voters. And for the first time, registration and voting rates outstripped population growth. This squares with the wealth of anecdotal evidence suggesting that there has been a dramatic increase in the mobilisation of Latinos in California, particularly following the passage of Proposition 187.[31]

Is citizenship enough?

The data indicate that although immigrants in the United States have been naturalising at record numbers, it is clear that citizenship does not automatically translate into participation in electoral politics. In the United States, at least, this has been a common pattern. Although immigrants, once naturalised, have historically had high registration rates,[32] these do not necessarily translate into actual participation in formal politics. The NALEO National Latino Immigrant Survey, for example, indicates that naturalised Latin American immigrants tend to have very high rates of voter registration, but significantly lower rates of turnout.[33] Among Asian immigrants to the United States, who, as a whole, have much higher naturalisation rates than Latin American immigrants (Barkan 1983), naturalised citizens still have much lower registration and participation rates in electoral politics than whites do, even accounting for socio-economic differences (Lien: 1995; Lien: 1994). It appears there are

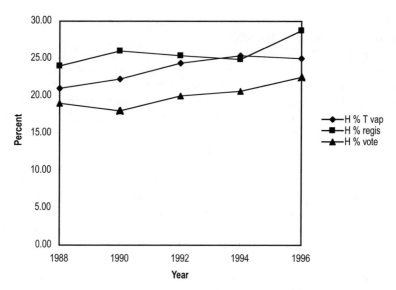

Figure 11.11 Percent Hispanic VAP, registration and voting

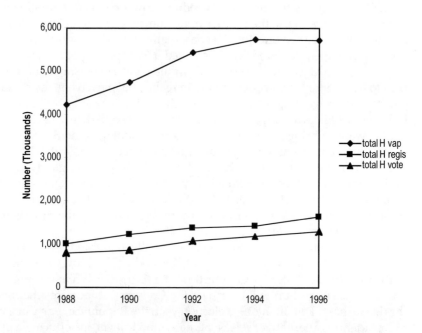

Figure 11.12 Hispanic population, registration and voting in California 1988–1996

other obstacles – low voter registration, low rates of turnout – to full participation (DeSipio: 1996; Schmidt: 1992).

Why should we be concerned about participation? If citizenship guarantees immigrant and minority rights, is that not enough? Why should participation make a difference? Again, recent events in the United States give some indication why immigrant advocates should not stop simply at guaranteeing rights. Rights, even citizenship rights, are never a done deal. They are part of the process of political contestation. In a participatory democracy rights and responsibilities are constantly being renegotiated among members of the polity. In the absence of participation, the interests of inactive members of the polity can be kept at the margins.

For instance, following the massive increases in naturalisation in 1995 and 1996, and fearing that many of these new citizens would be sympathetic to their Democratic rivals, Republican Congressmen accused the Immigration and Naturalisation Service (INS) of having encouraged fraudulent acquisition of citizenship. The INS's 'Citizenship USA' drive in the fall and spring of 1996, which had allocated more resources to naturalisation as well as allowing some naturalisation procedures to be contracted out, had apparently allowed at least six thousand and possibly as many as thirty thousand people to be improperly naturalised between August 1995 and September 1996 (Wilgoren: 1996). Funding for the program was promptly withdrawn, allowing huge naturalisation backlogs to develop once again, and causing delays in the process which persist today.

Facilitating the naturalisation procedure, critics charged, had allowed some immigrants to use the process opportunistically. Glenn Spencer, for instance, the executive director of a conservative lobbying group, Voices of Citizens Together, deplored what he called a 'cheapening of the [citizenship] process' (McDonnell: 1996, A-1). In his view, citizenship should be kept to those who truly appreciated it. In reality, people have many different reasons for wanting to become U.S. citizens. Some fear a cutoff of public benefits. Others are eager to vote, a privilege accorded only to citizens. Others want to bring family members to this country, something that is much easier for citizens. Others hope to get better jobs. Almost all who naturalise say it will be better for their children. Many speak longingly of the desire to travel back home with a U.S. passport. Most voice some combination of reasons (McDonnell: 1996, A1). If we require that citizens have the 'right' reasons to become citizens, the implication is that the citizenship process should be made more, not less, difficult.

To this end, one proposal on the table, initially suggested by Governor Wilson of California, is to do away with, or modify, the 14th Amendment to the Constitution guaranteeing birthright citizenship. While it is highly unlikely the suggestion will ever pass the Congress, it indicates the tone the debate has taken. In the 1996 election year, the Republican party began to consider this alternative, at least at the symbolic level, introducing a bill in the House and writing support for a constitutional amendment denying citizenship to children born to illegal immigrants into their party platform (Lewis: 1995, A 26; Rosenbaum: 1996, A12).[34]

There are also a number of proposals to tighten restrictions on voting. Following his 1996 defeat for the 46th Congressional seat in Orange County, California, former Republican Representative Bob Dornan asked for an investigation into what he called 'massive voter fraud' in the district. Dornan alleged that voting by non-citizens caused his narrow loss to Loretta Sanchez, a Democrat (Warren: 1998a).[35] The Republican-controlled House set up a task force to look into the charges of fraud, but more than a year later found that despite finding substantial voter fraud, it 'could not prove' there were enough illegal votes to overturn the election.[36]

Following the investigation, there were proposals both in Congress and at the state level to tighten access to the ballot by verifying the citizenship of voters (Knutson: 1998; Warren: 1998b). Sen. Spencer Abraham (R-Mich.) and Rep. Lamar S. Smith (R-Texas) called for a crackdown in light of an INS report that admitted that thousands of immigrants were improperly naturalised two years earlier. Their bills sought to codify many of the reforms that the INS has adopted in response to the controversy, such as requiring criminal background checks and having a standard citizenship test.[37] Similar proposals were considered in California and Massachusetts (Weintraub: 1998a and 1998b).

Rights, in and of themselves, are worth nothing without their practice. The protection of rights is carried out through an essentially agonistic, or conflictual, political process. By remaining outside that process, citizens, particularly those who are recent entrants, or who for one reason or another find themselves on society's margins, remain vulnerable to the machinations of other, more powerful, political actors. Formal citizenship may be a crucial first step to securing the protection of rights, but it is not a panacea.

Conclusion

The American retreat from its commitment to provide a full set of social rights to citizens and non-citizens equally serves as a useful object lesson for those engaged in debates on immigration, rights and citizenship elsewhere. The U.S. case is a valuable reminder that social rights that are not grounded in citizenship are inherently vulnerable to the whims of the state. Thus, the retraction of social rights in the United States serves to illustrate the weaknesses of the arguments for a 'postnational' citizenship, at least in the absence of any constitutional guarantees for the existence of rights, and any institutional framework for their enforcement. Immigrants fully realise the distinction, and this accounts for the massive increase in naturalisation rates over the last five years in the United States. For the present, there is no substitute for citizenship in the nation-state.

However, thinking of citizenship simply as protection under an umbrella of rights reproduces some of the flaws present in the conceptualisation of postnational citizenship. If citizenship is seen as largely passive and non-participatory, then many new citizens–whether because of differences in language, income, civic skills or other resources–will be left at the margins of the polity. Citizenship without participation leaves naturalised immigrants open to other kinds of abuses. This is the reason why the rise in naturalisation rates without a corresponding increase in registration and voting rates is so troubling. Simply acquiring the status of citizen is not enough; the American case also underscores the importance of the participatory aspect to citizenship.

References

A. Appadurai, 'Disjuncture and Difference in the Global Cultural Economy', *Public Culture,* 2, no. 2, 1990, 1–24.

M.A. Bamyeh, 'Transnationalism', *Current Sociology* 41, no. 3, Winter, 1991, 1–95.

E. Barkan, 'Whom Shall We Integrate?: A Comparative Analysis of the Immigration and Naturalisation Trends of Asians Before and After the 1965 Immigration Act (1951–1978)', *Journal of American Ethnic History,* Fall, 1983, 29–57.

L.N. Basch, N. Glick Schiller and C. Szanton-Blanc, *Nations Unbound: Transnational Projects, Postcolonial Predicaments, and Deterritorialised Nation-States,* Basel, 1994.

R. Bauböck, *Transnational Citizenship: Membership and Rights in International Migration,* Brookfield, Vt., 1994.

F.D. Blau, 'The Use of Transfer Payments by Immigrants', *Industrial and Labor Relations Review,* no. 27, January, 1984, 222–239.

G. Borjas and L. Hilton, 'Immigration and the Welfare State: Immigrant Participation in Means-Tested Entitlement Programs', *Quarterly Journal of Economics,* 111, no. 2, May 1996, 575–604.

G. Borjas and S. J. Trejo, 'Immigrant Participation in the Welfare System,' *Industrial and Labor Relations Review* 44, no. 2, January 1991, 195–211.

W. Connolly, 'Democracy and Territoriality', in *Rhetorical Republic: Governing Representations in American Politics,* eds F. M. Dolan and T. L. Dunn, Amherst, Mass., 1993, 249–274.

J. del Pinal and C. de Naves, *The Hispanic Population of the United States, March 1989: Current Population Report,* Washington, D.C., 1993.

L. DeSipio, 'Making Citizens or Good Citizens? Naturalisation as a Predictor of Organisational and Electoral Behavior Among Latino Immigrants', *Hispanic Journal of Behavioral Sciences,* 18, no. 2, May, 1996, 194–213.

J. Duany, *Quisqueya on the Hudson: The Transnational Identity of Dominicans in Washington Heights,* New York, 1994.

C. Dugger, 'Immigrant Voters Reshape Politics', *New York Times,* 10 March 1996.

C. Dugger, 'Immigrant Voters Target Public Issues that Affect Them Most', *New York Times,* 1996b.

N. Glick-Schiller, N.L. Basch, and C. Blanc-Szanton eds, 'Towards a Transnational Perspective on Migration: Race, Class, Ethnicity and Nationalism Reconsidered', *Annals of the New York Academy of Sciences*, v. 645, 1992.

L. Jensen, 'Patterns of Immigration and Public Assistance Utilisation, 1970–1980', *International Migration Review*, 22, Spring, 1988, 51–83.

M. Jones-Correa, *Between Two Nations: The Political Predicament of Latinos in New York City*, Ithaca, NY, 1998.

L.L. Knutson, 'Groups Criticize Citizenship Bill', Associated Press, 10 February 1998.

D. Lesher, 'Deadlock on Prop. 187 Has Backers, Governor Fuming', *Los Angeles Times*, Saturday 8 November 1997.

N. Lewis, 'Bill Seeks to End Automatic Citizenship for All Born in the United States', *New York Times*, 14 December 1995.

P. Lien, 'Contextual Change, Ethnic Identity, and Political Participation: The Case of Asian Americans in Southern California', paper presented at the American Political Science Association meeting, Chicago, 31 August–3 September 1995.

——, 'From Immigrants to Citizens and Beyond? The Political Participation of Asian Americans in Southern California', paper presented at the American Political Science Association meeting, New York, 1–4 September 1994.

P. McDonnell, 'Learning the Language of Citizenship: National Debate Spurs a Rush to Gain English', *Los Angeles Times*, 3 August 1996, A-1.

P. McDonnell, 'Prop. 187 Found Unconstitutional by Federal Judge', *Los Angeles Times*, Saturday 15 November 1997.

G. Marín and B. VanOss Marín, *Research With Hispanic Populations*, Newbury Park, Ca., 1991.

D. Massey, 'The Social Organisation of Mexican Migration to the United States', *Annals of the American Academy of Political and Social Science*, v. 487, September, 1986, 102–113.

D. Massey and J. Durand, 'Continuities in Transnational Migration: An Analysis of Thirteen National Communities', paper presented at a conference on 'New Perspectives on Mexico–U.S. Immigration', University of Chicago, Mexican Studies Program, 23–24 October 1992.

D. Massey and K. Schnabel, 'Recent Trends in Hispanic Immigration to the U.S.', *International Migration Review*, 17, no. 2, 1983, 212–244.

H. Pachón and L. DeSipio, *New Americans by Choice: Political Perspectives of Latino Immigrants*, Boulder, Co., 1994.

A. Portes and R. Grosfoguel, 'Caribbean Diasporas: Migration and Ethnic Communities', *Annals of the American Academy of Political and Social Science*, v. 536, 1994, 48–69.

A. Portes and R. Schauffler, 'Language and the Second Generation: Bilingualism Yesterday and Today', *International Migration Review*, 28, no. 4, Winter, 1994, 640–661.

A. Portes and R. Rumbaut, *Immigrant America: A Portrait*, Berkeley, 1990.

A. Pyle, P.J. McDonnell and H. Tobar, 'Latino Voter Participation Doubled Since '94 Primary', *Los Angeles Times*, 1998.

J.B. Raskin, 'Legal Aliens, Local Citizens: The Historical, Constitutional and Theoretical Meanings of Alien Suffrage', *University of Pennsylvania Law Review*, v. 141, 1993, 1391–1470.

T. Rohrlich, 'Latino Voting in State Surged in 1996 Election', *Los Angeles Times*, 31 December 1997.

G.M. Rosberg, 'Aliens and Equal Protection: Why Not The Right To Vote?', *Michigan Law Review* v. 75, April–May, 1977, 1092–1136.

D. Rosenbaum, 'Platform Unit Acts on Illegal Immigrants' Children', *New York Times*, 6 August 1996.

R. Rouse, 'Thinking Through Transnationalism: Notes on the Cultural Politics of Class Relations in the Contemporary United States', *Public Culture*, 7, no. 2 Winter, 1995, 353–402.

——, 'Making Sense of Settlement: Class Transformation, Cultural Struggle, and Transnationalism among Mexican Migrants in the United States', in *Towards a Transnational Perspective on Migration*, eds N. Glick–Schiller, L. Basch, and C. Blanc–Szanton, New York, 1992, 25–52.

——, 'Mexican Migration and the Social Space of Postmodernism', *Diaspora*, v. 1, 1991, 8–23.

P. Schuck, 'The Re–Evaluation of American Citizenship', *Georgetown Immigration Law Journal*, 12, no. 1, 1997, 1–34.

P. Schuck and R. Smith, *Citizenship Without Consent: Illegal Aliens in the American Polity*, New Haven and London, 1985.

A.D. Schmidley and C. Gibson, *Profile of the Foreign Born Population in the United States, 1997*, U.S. Census Bureau Current Population Reports, Series P23–195, 1999.

R.J. Schmidt, 'The Political Incorporation of Immigrants in California: An Institutional Assessment', paper presented at the American Political Science Association meeting, Chicago, 3–6 September 1992

C. Schmitt, 'A Law to Learn 'Em A Thing Or Two About The English Language', *New York Times*, 28 July 1996.

E. Schmitt, 'Immigration Overhaul Moves Toward Vote', *New York Times*, 2 August 1996.

R. Smith, ' "Los Ausentes Siempre Presentes": The Imagining, Making, and Politics of a Transnational Community Between New York City and Ticuani, Puebla', unpublished Ph.D. dissertation, Columbia University, 1993.

Y.N. Soysal, *Limits of Citizenship: Migrants and Postnational Membership in Europe*, Chicago, 1994.

C. Sutton, 'Transnational Identities and Cultures: Caribbean Immigrants in the United States', in *Immigration and Ethnicity: American Society – 'Melting Pot' or 'Salad Bowl'?*, eds M. D'Innocenzo and J. Sirefman, Westport, Ct., 1992, 231–241.

——, (1987) 'The Caribbeanisation of New York and the Emergence of a Transnational Sociocultural System', in *Caribbean Life in New York City: Sociocultural Dimensions*, eds C. R. Sutton and E. Chaney, New York, 1987, 15–30.

B. Turner, *Citizenship and Capitalism: The Debate Over Reformism*, Boston, 1986.

C.B. Cain Uhlaner and D.R. Kiewiet, 'Political Participation of Ethnic Minorities in the 1980s', *Political Behavior*, 11, no. 3, 1989, 195–231.

United Nations Population Fund, *The Individual and the World: Population, Migration and Development in the 1990s*, New York, 1993.

R. Waldinger, 'Immigration and Urban Change' *Annual Review of Sociology*, v. 15, 1989, 211–32.

P.M. Warren, 'Orange County Registrar Refuses State Request on Voters', *Los Angeles Times*, 10 March 1998a.

P.M. Warren, 'GOP Leaders Present Plan to Tighten Voter Scrutiny', *Los Angeles Times*, 18 January 1988b.

P.M. Warren and J. Wilgoren, 'House Plans to Drop Dornan's Vote Challenge', *Los Angeles Times*, 4 February.

D.M. Weintraub, 'Voter ID Bill Stymied in Assembly Panel', *The Orange County Register*, 21 May 1998a.

D.M. Weintraub, 'New Voters Would Have to Prove Citizenship', Associated Press, 6 May 1998b.

K. Weiss, 'Fewer Blacks and Latinos Admitted to Three UC Schools', *Los Angeles Times*, 17 March 1998.

J. Wilgoren, 'Democrats, GOP Seek to Speed, Restrict Immigration', *Los Angeles Times*, 6 March 1998.

Notes

1. The literature on transnationalism is large and growing by leaps and bounds. See for instance Duany (1994); Portes and Grosfoguel (1994); Smith (1993); Schiller et al. (1992); Rouse (1992); Sutton (1992); Rouse (1991); Sutton (1987); Massey (1986).

2. Many nations – Korea, Mexico, Turkey, Algeria among them – maintain a claim on their nationals abroad. One example of this was the 'tenth Department' popularised by President Aristide of Haiti when he was in exile in the United States in the early 1990s: in addition to the nine administrative divisions on the island, he included Haitians living in the United States (Basch et al.: 1994, 146–147). However, this claim is rarely more than rhetorical, stopping far short of equal political and civic rights. In spite of the language of the 'citizens abroad', for instance, the Haitian legislature turned down any inclusion of Haitians as dual citizens (Basch et al.: 1994, 212). Participatory citizenship is not encouraged.

3. It may very well be true that national, territorial notions of citizenship are inadequate, as some have argued (Connolly: 1993), so that we need a new theory of universalistic citizenship to fit an increasingly global economy (Soysal: 1994; Bauböck: 1994; Turner: 1986), but until an institutional framework is in place to guarantee democratic practices at the international level, it would not do to ignore the importance of political citizenship in the nation-state.

4. Non-citizen suffrage was allowed in the United States from 1789 to 1924. Immigrants had the right to vote in local, and sometimes national elections by signing 'first papers' – a declaration of the intent to become a citizen (Raskin: 1993; Rosberg: 1977). A total of eighteen states, mostly in the Midwest and western United States, experimented with non-citizen suffrage, before increasing hostility to immigrants led to a backlash and repeal of those voting rights. For a

fuller discussion of political rights for non-citizens, and their inherent vulnerability, see Jones-Correa (1998), 197–199.

5. Soysal might disagree with this characterisation of her argument; she does call for a 'postnational citizenship confer[ring] upon every person the right and duty of participation in the authority structures and public life of a polity, regardless of their historical or cultural ties to that community' (Soysal: 1994, 1). Nonetheless, this strand of her thought remains underdeveloped and rather vague.

6. For overviews of the new immigration see: Portes and Rumbaut (1990); Waldinger (1989); Massey and Schnabel (1983).

7. A note on terminology. 'Hispanic' is used by the Census Bureau and most mainstream sources to describe the population of Mexican, Puerto Rican, Cuban, Central or South American, or some other Spanish origin (de Pinal and de Naves: 1990). This paper uses the term 'Latino' – the term currently in vogue – and 'Hispanic' interchangeably. See Chapter 2 in Marín and VanOss Marín 1991 for a further discussion. 'First generation immigrant' here is used to describe permanent residents in the United States born in another country; the 'second generation' are their children.

8. The social science literature through the 1980s tended to find that immigrants used fewer social services than the native-born (Blau: 1984; Tienda and Jensen 1986). However, by looking at cohort and national origin effects Borjas has been instrumental in shaping the view that immigrants were increasingly availing themselves of benefits (Borjas and Hilton: 1996; Borjas and Trejo: 1991)

9. I should note here that 'state' from here on out in the paper refers to the regional units of the American federal system, not the national government.

10. Fifty-nine percent of voters approved of 187, including majorities of whites, Asians, and blacks. One-third of Latinos approved of 187.

11. Though there are numerous exceptions including emergency Medicaid, disaster relief, child nutrition, and some training and education (Shuck: 1997, 27). The legislation also allows states to deny state and local benefits to some categories of immigrants if they so wish.

12. Borjas and Hilton claim that 'immigrant households accounted for 16.6 percent of the costs of the AFDC program, 18.4 percent of the cost of SSI, 11.5 percent of the costs of Food Stamps, 14.1 percent of the costs of Medicaid, and 19.0 percent of the cost of subsidised school breakfasts and lunches. In sum, the 8.8 percent of persons residing in immigrant households accounted for 13.8 percent of the costs of the programs, almost sixty percent more than their representation in the population' (1996: 584). Regardless of the accuracy of these figures, arguments like these helped sway legislators in their decision to cut social programs for both legal and undocumented immigrants.

13. Proposition 209, which passed in California in the fall of 1996, banned affirmative action in the state of California, reinforcing the decision by the University of California Board of Regents, which had already voted to end affirmative action in the UC system. Both decisions have the effect of making it more difficult for immigrants, particularly Latinos, to enter into the upper tier of higher education in California (see Weiss: 1998). In addition, in the aftermath of Proposition 187, Congress seriously considered proposals to allow states to deny education benefits to the children of undocumented immigrants (see Schmitt: 1996).

14. Proposition 227, which passed June 2 1998 in California eliminates bilingual education from public schools in the state. This measure follows up on Proposition 63, passed in 1986, which declared English the official state language. Since 1986 at least twenty-three states, forty-one counties and fifteen cities have passed measures making English the official language of that jurisdiction (see 'Suffolk Vote Backs Making English Official Language', *New York Times*, 14 August 1996, B5). In 1996 a similar measure was approved by the U.S. House of Representatives making it likely that the matter will continue to be addressed at the federal level as well (see 'House Votes English Official Language', *Reuters*, 1 August 1996; see also Schmitt: 1996). This in spite of the fact that research on language acquisition has generally indicated that contemporary immigrants are learning English as fast, or faster, than earlier generations of arrivals. See Portes and Schauffler (1994).

15. Naturalisation rates for New York City almost doubled from 1994 to 1995, to 141,235. The number of new citizens in the city in 1992 was only 43,447 (see Dugger: 1996b).

16. 'Preliminary Results of Survey of Non-Citizen Recipients of SSI/IHSS, Los Angeles County' Tomás Rivera Policy Institute, 18 June 1997. Results are drawn from a non-random survey of 1,112 individuals (873 of whom were non-citizens) receiving both Supplemental Security Income and In-Home Supportive Services.

17. See appendix for figures.

18. Even if it only had an effect on Latinos in California this would be significant in itself; one third of all Latinos living in the U.S. live in California.

19. One possibility is that the pattern of naturalisation looks the same but that California might still account for a disproportionate number of the naturalisations taking place. However, this is not the case. About thirty-four percent of all foreign-born U.S. residents live in California. The percentage of permanent residents seeking naturalisation is greater than the percentage residing in the state in only two years, 1991 (when California accounts for forty-one percent of all naturalisations nation-wide) and 1996 (thirty-six percent). California's averages twenty-seven percent from 1986 to 1996 (including 1991 and 1996).

20. 'Hispanics Registering To Vote,' Associated Press, September 10, 1995.

21. In 1994, Latinos made up only 4.4 percent of registered voters in the November 1994 elections. About fifty-three percent of eligible Hispanic citizens were registered to vote in 1994, compared to sixty-seven percent of all U.S. citizens over eighteen.

22. There was only a twenty-three percent increase in the Latino turnout for off-year elections from 1986 to 1994.

23. The figures from exit polls are significantly different from those of the census. Exit polls show Latinos made up eight percent of voters in 1994, eight percent in 1990, and nine percent of the vote in 1992. The census data indicates that Latinos made up 7.7 percent in 1988, 9.4 percent in 1990, 9.2 percent in 1992, and 11.3 percent of voters in 1994. The census figures are substantially higher than those for the exit polls. Why this is, is uncertain. One interpretation is that the census figures rely on self-reporting after the fact, so there might be some inflation of the figures in retrospect.

24. 'Hispanics Showing Vote Apathy' Associated Press, November 24, 1994. How one interprets the 1994 turnout results may be a matter of the glass being half-empty or half-full. On the half-full side, one observer noted: 'Despite the fact that voter participation tends to decrease in non-presidential election years, in 1994 the Latino turnout in California equaled that in 1992'. As noted earlier, it was significantly higher than the previous mid-term election in 1990.

25. 'Latino Electorate Continues to Speak out on Issues: Tomás Rivera Policy Institute, La Opinion and KVEA-TV Reveal Results of New Poll' Tomás Rivera Policy Institute news release, 6 February 1997.

26. A statewide poll of Latino voters conducted just before the 1996 election by the Tomás Rivera Policy Institute found that twenty-seven percent of the Latino electorate had registered since 1992 (Rohrlich: 1997).

27. In 1998 Latino voters in California made up twelve percent of the vote in 1998 (compared with sixty-nine percent white, fourteen percent black, and three percent Asian). 'Profile of the Electorate' *Los Angeles Times*, 4 June 1998.

28. This data is far from definitive. The estimates are based on a Spanish-sur-name analysis of voter rolls statewide (which means they capture a good number of Filipinos, the largest Asian-American group in the state). They only analyse whether a name appears for the first time in an electoral district, so someone moving from elsewhere in the state is counted as a new voter along with true new voters: those turning eighteen, new citizens, etc. Voter rolls are also notoriously out-of-date, with a margin of error of as high as twenty percent. Different surveys also have different results. *Los Angeles Times* and Field Institute polls show a less pronounced trend, while the Willie Velasquez Institute, an affiliate of the Southwest voter Registration and Education Project, indicate that Latino voters have had a greater impact (Rohrlich: 1997).

29. 'L.A. City Elections Initiate Influx of New Latino Voters', Tomás Rivera Policy Institute, La Opinion, and KVEA-TV Conduct L.A. Exit Poll, 8 April 1997. The poll was conducted April 8, 1997 with 444 Latino voters who participated in the Los Angeles City election. Surveys were conducted in both Spanish and English. The poll had a margin of error of plus or minus five percent.

30. Although only sixteen percent of the Latinos surveyed in a Tomás Rivera Policy Institute (TRPI) poll of the five-country Los Angeles area indicated that they voted Democratic primarily to punish the Republican Party and Governor Pete Wilson for their anti-immigrant proposals ('Latino Electorate' TRPI). The Latino Voter Poll was conducted in January 1997 with 500 Latino voters who participated in the November 1996 elections and voted in the counties of Los Angeles, Orange, San Bernadino, Riverside and Ventura. The margin of error for the sample is plus or minus four percent.

31. One story on the new Hispanic activism noted, for instance, that:

> Southern California Hispanics, through hundreds of grass-roots fund-raisers the past four months, have contributed about $1 million of the total $3 million for anti-Proposition 227 commercials scheduled to run across the state.
>
> In Santa Ana, voter registration groups such as the Latin American Voters of America are seeing almost double the number of volunteers this year compared with the last two election cycles of 1996 and 1994. The organisation has jumped from 150 to 250 members this year.

The Orange County Democratic Party doubled its number of volunteers in 1998 from 1994, up from 25 to 50 workers, many of whom are Hispanics. The Republican Lincoln Club of Orange County drew about 350 people at its first Hispanic outreach breakfast last month. (Amber Arellano, 'Hispanics' Bloc Party' *Orange County Register*, 13 May 1998).

32. More than two-thirds of new citizens in New York City register immediately after the naturalisation ceremony, according to the New York Immigrant Coalition (see Dugger: 1996a). The NALEO National Immigrant Survey found registration rates of eighty percent or more for most groups of naturalised Latin American immigrants; Mexicans are the exception, with registration rates of 'only' seventy percent (Pachón and DeSipio: 1994, 87).

33. In Pachón and DeSipio's sample voter turnout for Dominicans, South Americans and Central Americans in the 1984 Presidential elections was around fifty percent; Mexican participation was the lowest at thirty-eight percent, and Cuban participation the highest at seventy-one percent (Pachón and DeSipio 1994: 88).

34. For a cautionary discussion see: 'Birthright Citizenship Amendment: A Threat to Equality,' *Harvard Law Review*, 107, 1994, 1026–1043.

35. During the investigation, Dornan tried to subpoena records from labor unions, voting rights groups, Sanchez and others in an effort to prove that he had actually won a 10th term in Congress. Few of the subpoenas were answered.

36. The task force found that about 750 non-citizens voted in the election (far fewer than the 2,500 illegal votes that Republican sources had initially said they had uncovered). During Dornan's investigation, the Orange County registrar of voters found about 125 illegally cast absentee ballots in the race (Warren and Wilgoren: 1998).

37. The bills also extend to five years the window for the INS to revoke the citizenship of newly naturalised immigrants. [Smith's bill was HR 2837; Abraham's was S 1382] (Warren: 1998b).

CHAPTER 12

VARIATIONS IN TRANSNATIONAL BELONGING: LESSONS FROM BRAZIL AND THE DOMINICAN REPUBLIC

Peggy Levitt

Many Americans expect migrants to loosen their ties to their countries of origin as they assimilate into the United States.* They assume that residence will eventually equal membership as migrants transfer their allegiance from the countries they come from to those where they settle. Increasing numbers of migrants, however, continue to keep feet in two worlds. Rather than cutting off their social and economic attachments, and trading one political membership for another, some individuals remain strongly connected to their homelands even as they become integrated into their new homes.

The proliferation of these long-term transnational ties challenges conventional wisdom about how migrants are incorporated into host countries and about migration's impact on sending-country life. Researchers have already identified a wide variety of transnational practices.[1] But what explains the variation in the ways in which ordinary people actually stay connected to two nations? What kinds of transnational communities emerge and how do we account for differences between them? How do different community forms affect host-country incorporation and continuing involvements in sending communities?

In this chapter, I present findings from an on-going comparative, historical study of transnational migration among six immigrant communities that begin to answer some of these questions. The larger study examines migration from Lebanon, Ireland, India, Israel, the Dominican Republic, and Brazil to the Greater Boston Metropolitan area, though in this chapter, I focus only on the last two groups. Each group was chosen because it sends large numbers of migrants from a particular sending-country locale who have settled near one another in the Boston metropolitan area. Since one of the goals of this project is to identify and explain differences in cross-border social groups, we felt that if some form of collective transnational activities were to emerge, they would be more likely to do so under these conditions. While this strategy allows us to compare variations in transnational community across groups, it does not shed light on how widespread these practices are.This study is being conducted by a team of graduate and undergraduate researchers and colleagues in each sending community. In the United States, we interview sixty first and second-generation men and women from each group. We carry out interviews with home and host-country political, civic, and religious leaders working with each community in the United States at the local, regional, and national levels. We also attend meetings and special events and review newspapers, promotional materials, and organisational documents. After each interview, we ask for the names of family members and leaders still living in the sending-country. We then conduct a parallel set of interviews with nonmigrant family members and organisational leaders working at the local, regional, and national levels in the country of origin.[2]

Theoretical assumptions

In many cases, the magnitude, duration, and impact of migration is so strong that migrant social networks mature into transnational social fields or public spheres spanning the sending and receiving country (Mahler: 1998, Fraser: 1991). These extend beyond the chains of social relations and kin that are specific to each person located within them (Glick Schiller: 2000). Though many migrants within these fields gradually weaken their ties to their sending communities, more and more ordinary and elite migrants continue to engage in a range of transnational practices or economic, political, and sociocultural occupations and activities that require regular long-term contacts across borders for their success (Portes et al.: 1999). Individual actors cannot be viewed in isolation from the transnational social fields in which they are embedded. Their activities are powerfully shaped by the social fields in which they are carried out. Those who live within transnational social fields are exposed to a set of social expectations, cultural values, and patterns of human interaction that are shaped by more than one social, economic, and political system.

The transnational social fields engendered by migration encompass all aspects of social life. Though migrants' economic activities are frequently their initial catalyst, social, religious, and political connections eventually emerge which constitute and are constituted by these arenas. The more diverse and thick a transnational social field is, the greater the number of ways it offers migrants to remain active in their homelands. The more institutionalised these relationships become, the more likely it is that transnational membership will persist.

Some researchers describe transnational social fields encompassing all migrants from a particular sending country residing in a key site of reception. Glick Schiller and Fouron (1998), for example, argue that Haitian young adults who have never migrated still live their lives within a social field connecting the United States and Haiti because so many aspects of their lives are permeated by Haitian immigrant influences. Transnational social fields, however, often form from connections between multiple localities. Although there may be large overarching fields between the United States and Mexico, the Dominican Republic or El Salvador, for example, these are constituted by smaller, bounded fields between particular sending villages and cities and specific urban or rural receiving points. Brazilian migration to the United States has created transnational social fields between the city of Governador Valadares and migrants in New York City; Pampano Beach, Florida; Danbury, Connecticut; and the greater Boston Metropolitan area (Margolis: 1994). Transnational social fields also unite Dominicans in Venezuela and Spain to those who stay behind.

Transnational arenas function at multiple levels. A political party can link migrants and nonmigrants to one another through personal ties between members in local sending and receiving-country chapters. These local, personalised ties often form part of coordinated efforts between the party's national level sending- and receiving-country operations as well. Similarly, relations between local parishes broaden and thicken existing ties between national and regional sending and receiving-country churches.

Studying transnational actors and the social fields which they inhabit helps clarify several things. First, the ways in which individuals distribute their resources and loyalty between the sending and receiving country is, in part, determined by the kinds of institutional opportunities available to them. If transnational social fields are institutionally complete, and create and are created by numerous political, religious, and social institutions that enable migrants to remain active in multiple ways, then more transnational practices are likely to occur. If the social field offers fewer institutional choices, then the volume of transnational activities is likely to be lower.

Second, focusing on social fields calls attention to nonmigrants and those who move only periodically but who also enact aspects of their lives within these arenas. Movement is not a prerequisite for transnational participation. There are those who travel regularly to carry out their routine affairs, whom some researchers have called transmigrants (England: 1999, Glick Schiller: 1995, Guarnizo: 1997). There are also individuals whose lives are rooted primarily in a single-sending or receiving-country setting, who move infrequently, but whose lives integrally involve resources, contacts, and people who are far away. Finally, there are those who do not move but who live their lives within a context that has become transnationalised.

The scope and intensity of the transnational practices that *frequent travellers, periodic movers,* and *those who stay in one place* engage in varies considerably. Guarnizo (2000) defines core transnationalism as those activities that (a) form an integral part of the individual's habitual life, (b) are undertaken on a regular basis, and (c) are patterned and therefore somewhat predictable. Expanded transnationalism, in contrast, includes migrants who engage in occasional transnational practices, such as responses to political crises or natural disasters. Itzigsohn et al. (1999) characterise broad transnational practices as those that are not well institutionalised, involve only occasional participation, and require only sporadic movement. He and his colleagues contrast these with narrow transnational practices that are highly institutionalised, constant, and involve regular travel.

These terms help to operationalise variations in the intensity and frequency of transnational practices. But cross-border engagements also vary along other dimensions such as scope. Even those engaged in core transnational practices may confine their activities to one arena of social action. Or the same person may engage in core transnational activities with respect to one sphere of social life and only expanded transnational activities with respect to another. There are those, for example, whose livelihoods depend upon the frequent, patterned harnessing of resources across borders while their political and religious lives focus on host-country concerns. In contrast, there are those who engage in regular religious and political transnational practices but only occasionally send money back to family members or invest in homeland projects. Some individuals whose transnational practices involve many arenas of social life engage in comprehensive transnational practices while others engage in transnational practices that are more selective in scope. Table One provides concrete examples of variations on these different dimensions of transnational activism.

The concepts of core and expanded transnationalism must also be extended to include the transnational practices of those who stay behind. Nonmigrants who engage in core transnational practices are those whose social and economic lives depend upon and are shaped on a regular basis by resources, people, and ideas in the receiving-country context. These may also be comprehensive or selective in scope. The nonmigrant grandparent who, along with her migrant children, is jointly responsible for income generation and raising children across borders participates in comprehensive, core transnational practices, although she may only travel once a year. Similarly, the nonmigrant who travels during a campaign to mobilize support for a sending-country candidate is enacting selective, expanded transnational practices.

In some cases, numerous individuals embedded within transnational social fields engage in high levels of transnational practices but few communal activities emerge. Colombian migrants in New York have created a complex web of multi-directional relationships but their mistrust and fragmentation impede community organisation (Guarnizo et al.: 1999). Often, however, certain sites within transnational social fields become sufficiently organised and institutionalised that some kind of transnational community is established. In such cases, it is not merely that numerous individuals live their lives within a social formation that crosses borders. It is that a significant number from a given place of origin and settlement share this experience collectively with one another, transforming the way they think of themselves as a group. Since transnational communities emerge from the social networks that first encourage migration, at least initially, members often know one another personally or have family members or acquaintances in common. They acknowledge that they belong to a collectivity constituted across space and express some level of self-consciousness about this membership by forming groups such as hometown organisations that attest to their transnational character.

Transnational communities lie between what M.P. Smith and Guarnizo (1998) call 'transnationalism from above,' or global governance and economic activities, and 'transnationalism from below,' or the everyday, grounded practices of individuals. Communities are one of several mechanisms mediating between 'high' and 'low' levels of transnationalism. When individual actors identify and organise themselves as transnational communities, a response from 'above,' by the state or by an international religious group, is more likely. Likewise, when national

Table 1 Variations in the Dimensions of Transnational Practices

	Comprehensive	Selective
Core	Transnational business owner who is also active home-country political party member, member of church with sister congregations in home and host country, and hometown association leader.	The political party official whose job it is to coordinate party activities between the sending and receiving country but who does not participate in any other kind of transnational group and maintains few cross-border social and familial ties.
Expanded	Periodically contributes to sending community projects, makes contributions to political campaigns, and provides occasional economic remittances to family members.	Periodically engages in only one of these activities.

political and economic actors reach out to local communities, they encourage individual members to maintain loyalties across borders.

By using the term community, I do not mean that all members feel a sense of affinity or solidarity toward one another. Long-standing patterns of privilege and access do not disappear merely because they are constituted across borders. In fact, transnational migration often exacerbates class differences because elite community members are better positioned to use cross-border strategies than their poorer counterparts. Migration also increases the layers in the stratification hierarchy because more community members are in a position to achieve a more diverse range of socioeconomic goals.

The kinds of transnational connections I describe are not new. Earlier groups, such as the Irish, Polish, and Italians, also remained involved in the affairs of their sending countries (Foner: 2000; Morawska: 2001). Several factors, however, heighten the intensity and durability of transnational ties among contemporary migrants and alter the nature of their connections to nonmigrants in significant ways. First, it is easier and cheaper for migrants and nonmigrants to stay in touch with one another than ever before. Relations enacted through telephone calls, video exchanges, and yearly visits differ qualitatively from those pursued through monthly letters and a single visit home. Second, increasing numbers of states are institutionalising ways for migrants to assert long-term, long-distance membership. In Latin America and the Caribbean alone, over 20 states have granted dual nationality to those living outside their borders (Jones-Correa: 2001). Countries such as Brazil and Columbia have also granted migrants the right to the expatriate vote. Third, economic restructuring makes it more difficult for some migrants to achieve levels of economic mobility that are comparable to their predecessors. Contemporary migrants often face discrimination and blocked opportunities because they are more likely to be people of colour.[3] Finally, heightened economic and political globalisation and greater tolerance for multiculturalism in the United States is also more conducive to the maintenance of enduring home-country ties.

In the following section, I compare two types of transnational communities suggested by my ongoing research on Dominican and Brazilian immigrants in Boston. I describe the characteristics of each community and the distinct ways in which their members manage their home and host-country attachments before turning to a discussion of selective factors which explain these variations.

Variations in transnational community form

Migration between Boston and Miraflores created a rural to urban transnational village. Miraflores, a village of approximately three thousand, and the neighbouring city of Baní, are located about 65 kilometers from the Dominican capital of Santo Domingo. Before migration began in the late 1960s, most villagers supported themselves by farming, though few families owned land of their own. Though Miraflores is only two kilometres away from Baní, a trip to town was a big event. Many Mirafloreños could count on their hands the number of times they had visited Santo Domingo.

Migration began in full force in the late 1960s when the commercialisation of agriculture and restricted access to land made it increasingly difficult to earn a living in agriculture. By 1994, over 65% of the 545 households in Miraflores had relatives in the greater Boston metropolitan area. Migration gradually distributed the functions of production and reproduction across borders. Numerous migrants left their children behind to be raised by nonmigrant family members. At the same time, nonmigrants' dependence on remittances increased. In 1994, almost sixty percent of the households in Miraflores said they received at least some of their monthly income from those in the United States. For nearly 40 percent of these households, remittances constituted between 75–100 percent of their income. Only 31% of the households earned their money entirely in the Dominican Republic (Levitt: 2001a).

Not surprisingly, migration has completely transformed village life. Any number of houses have been renovated with U.S. dollars. They are jam packed with the clothes, appliances, toys, and food that migrants bring back. Almost everyone in Miraflores can talk about 'La Mozart' or 'La Centre,' or Mozart Street Park and Centre Street, two focal points of the community in Boston. When someone is ill, cheating on their spouse, or finally granted a visa, the news spreads as quickly on the streets of Miraflores as it does on the streets of Boston.

Many Mirafloreños found apartments near one another, particularly during the first years of settlement. They met each other when they went out shopping. A number worked together in the same factories or for the same office cleaning companies. Someone could always carry money, packages, or messages between Boston and the island. During their visits, phone conversations, and through the videotapes they sent home, migrants introduced those who remained behind to the ideas and practices they observed in the United States. Nonmigrants gradually began to adopt these behaviors. Migrants' frequent contact with one another and their high levels of continued contact with those who remained behind gradually extended the life of the community across borders. This steady infusion of social remittances, combined with migrant and nonmigrants' growing dependence on one another, further encouraged transnational village formation (Levitt: 2000).[4]

Several new organisations also reinforced the community's sense of itself as extending across boundaries. Over the past thirty years, the Miraflores Development Committee (MDC), with chapters in Boston and Miraflores, built an aqueduct, funeral home, park, and baseball stadium and funded renovations to the school, health clinic, and community centre. Religious and political life has become transnational as well. Relations forged by Catholic parishioners circulating between local churches in Boston and Miraflores are reinforced by ties between priests, seminary students, and diocesan officials at the regional and national levels.[5] They are also reinforced by an institutional ideology that positions Catholicism as a universal church.

Furthermore, at least two of the three principal Dominican political parties have created U.S.-based organisations encouraging migrants' continued participation in Dominican politics. Constitutional reforms, approved in 1996, allow those who became naturalised citizens of other countries to retain their Dominican citizenship and grant citizenship to those born outside the country to Dominican parents, thus ensuring the formal inclusion of the second generation and beyond (Torres-Saillant and Hernández: 1998). In 1997, Dominican legislators also passed a bill allowing Dominican migrants to vote from abroad rather than return to the island, though the Central Election Board or the *Junta Central de Elecciones* has not yet agreed on how to implement this project.

The demands of work and family life, then, necessarily keep Mirafloreños with feet in two worlds. Religious, political, and social organisations also promote this by providing multiple opportunities for dual membership. But acting transnationally does not necessarily produce transnational results. To date, most Mirafloreños continue to devote most of their energies toward island concerns and remain on the margins of U.S. political and social life. In 1994, for example, while seventy-three percent of Mirafloreños in Boston were legal resident aliens, only one percent had become U.S. citizens (Levitt: 2001a). Only nineteen percent of all Dominicans in Massachusetts were naturalised. The Boston community displayed little political activism. Dominican political groups had few contacts with the Democratic or Republican parties. Only a few individuals had worked on campaigns or had relationships with individual politicians.

Political groups did better organising around Dominican causes. Candidates for Senator of Peravia[6] or Mayor of Baní campaigned specifically in Boston because so many Banilejos lived there. Both the *Partido Revolucionario Dominicano* (PRD) and the *Partido de la Liberación Dominicana* (PLD) have well-developed party organisations in New England. In 1994, the PRD had over one thousand members spanning Providence to the North Shore of Boston who contributed over one hundred and fifty thousand dollars to the Dominican presidential election campaign. In 1999, the party raised an additional fifty thousand dollars in support of Presidential hopeful Hipolito Mejía (Rodriguez: 1999). While some migrants participated in community organisations, such as parish councils and the PTA, the Miraflores Development Committee felt that to turn its attentions to migrants' concerns in Boston and away from needs in Miraflores would be like 'robbing Peter to pay Paul.'

In contrast, migration between Boston and Governador Valdares created an urban to urban transnational village. Governador Valadares is a city of approximately two hundred and seventy thousand located in Minas Gerais, one of Brazil's largest states. Valadares has a long history of contact with the United States. North Americans came to the city during World War II to get minerals for their war efforts. The Rockefeller Foundation funded major public health initiatives in support. After the war, the U.S.-based Morrison Company built the city's railroad. Its employees socialised with the Valadares elite, introduced them to the washing machines and dishwashers they brought with them, and established organisations like the Rotary and Lion's Clubs. They also gave scholarships to promising Valadareneses who became the first to migrate to study in the United States. Migration to Boston began when mining company executives brought young Valadarenese women back with them to the United States to work as domestic servants.

Valadares has little industry. Its economy has been based on mining, wood, sugar and ranching at various stages throughout its history. In the 1970s, when it became too difficult to earn a decent living raising cattle, Valadareneses took advantage of the social networks already established by the young women who migrated earlier and began to move in earnest to the United States. Migration increased considerably in the 1980s, following a failed economic stabilisation program which hit hard at the middle and working classes. By 1994, an estimated 1.5 million Brazilians had migrated, including six hundred thousand to the United States. Of these, approximately thirty thousand were from Gov. Valadares (Sales: 1999). An estimated twenty thousand settled in the greater Boston Metropolitan area. Though many Valadarenses live in other parts of the region, such as Allston and Somerville, our focus is on the Valadarense community in Framingham, where an estimated five thousand Brazilians lived in 1998. Most work in restaurants, hotels, or cleaning homes, though a good number have started their own small stores and home or car cleaning businesses. The Valadares economy has grown so dependent on *Valadolares* (or Valadollars) or migrant remittances that when the Brazilian government devalued its currency in 1999, Valadares was the one place in Brazil it was said to have a positive impact.

A 1994 survey of migration from Valadares found that while thirty percent of the migrants interviewed classified themselves as having settled definitively in the United States, an additional forty-nine percent considered themselves to be temporary, circular, or return migrants (Soares: 1995). Many of the Valadarenses we spoke with in Boston also planned to return to Brazil. In Valadares, we interviewed several target earners who had saved enough money and had so far been successful at returning home and finding a job. A larger group, however, were unable to establish themselves when they returned. The farms or businesses they invested in eventually failed. The real estate they bought was unprofitable because the market was already saturated. Many were in the process of returning to the United States or they planned to do so in the future. Community leaders in Framingham have also noted this shift toward more permanent settlement. They highlight the increasing numbers who seek help getting their income taxes in order or who wanted to explore real estate opportunities in the United States. In 1990, fourteen percent of all Brazilians in the state had naturalised; seventy-five percent of these individuals had arrived after 1984 (U.S. Census: PUMS, 1992).

The urban to urban transnational village linking Boston and Valadares differs from its Dominican counterpart. Brazilians widely recognize the strong connection between Valadares and Boston. That 'there is not one house in Valadares without family in the United States' is a constantly repeated refrain. Walking through poor and upper-class neighborhoods in the city, it is easy to identify houses with migrant family members because so many have been renovated with remittances from the United States. Yet efforts to build on these connections and to institutionalize this transnational community have not received widespread support. In many of our interviews, though respondents articulated a sense of belonging to a community that spanned borders, they distrusted organised efforts to institutionalise it, as Deva, a thirty-five-year-old migrant described,

> Everyone knows about the strong links between Boston and Valadares, that there are so many people from Valadares living in Boston. If you ask me what is my social circle I would say it still very much includes friends and family here and in Brazil. My church in Valadares is still a very big part of my life. But I am not sure about these programs that try to get us to invest in the city (Valadares) or that want to make a sister-city between Framingham and there. You know the government in Brazil is so corrupt. We left Brazil to get away from that government. I will stay connected to Brazil and loyal to my country but without the government's help.

Although Deva, and a number of migrants like her, engaged in numerous social and economic transnational practices, they generally rejected invitations to participate in organised, collective transnational activism. Churches formed the primary organisational arenas that constituted this transnational social group.

Those trying to institutionalise this Valadares-Framingham transnational community are generally its elites. Most of the initiatives they propose try to capitalise on migrants' potential economic contributions. The mayor of Valadares, for example, visited Framingham and several other East Coast cities with large concentrations of Valadarenses in 1997. Just as he visits his constituents in the neighborhoods of Valadareses, he said, so should he visit Valadarenses in the United States. The publisher of a Valadares daily newspaper, *O Diario Rio Doce*, added a two page section with news and advertising from community members in Massachusetts. The *Banco do Brasil*, in conjunction with the Mayor's office, created a Minas Gerais – focused investment fund that pays higher interest rates to those who deposit their remittances. The earnings generated by this fund were earmarked for development projects in the region. *The Federacao das Indus-trias do Estado de Minas Gerais* (FIEMG or the Federation of Industries in Minas Gerais) mounted a technical assistance program to help return migrants set up businesses in Brazil. FIEMG also organised a trade fair at the Massachusetts Institute of Technology to attract recent graduates to return to work in Brazil.

These efforts have met with only limited success. In addition, though some leaders attempted to establish a 'sister-city' relationship between Valadares and Framingham, no specific association like the hometown associations so common among other immigrant groups, has emerged. The *Partido dos Trabalhadores* (Brazilian Workers' Party) is the only party that is active in the Boston Metropolitan area and it has attracted few sup-porters. The community organisations that have emerged generally focus on U.S.-based goals. Business owners, for example, created a Framingham branch of the Brazilian Business Network, an effort supported by the Con-sulate to promote small business development. Other community mem-bers have begun working with State Representative, John Stefani, who, in turn, has acted as an informal intermediary between the Brazilian com-munity and the Framingham town fathers.

Unlike Mirafloreños, then, who continue to place a high priority on remaining active in Dominican affairs, civically-engaged Valadarenses are directing more of their energies toward U.S. concerns and traversing a more traditional route toward incorporation. Despite the emergence of a diverse, complex transnational social field linking Framingham and Val-adares, the transnational community vision proposed by elites has not been embraced wholeheartedly by all potential members. Those who do express formal transnational membership, tend to do so within religious arenas. Though Valadarenses live their social and emotional lives across borders, few have adopted the notion that they should live their collective civic and political lives transnationally as well. Because this village is con-stituted by larger, more dispersed numbers who are less likely to know one another personally, the community cannot exert the same pressures on those members who do not subscribe to its proposed vision.

What explains these variations in transnational activism?

Several factors explain the different patterns of civic engagement exhibited by Mirafloreños and Valadarenses. I focus on four salient influences.

The Characteristics of Transnational Social Groups

One factor that explains the different participatory patterns Valadarenses and Mirafloreños exhibit are variations in the transnational communities themselves.

Rural transnational villages like Miraflores have a set of characteristics that make long-term sending-country involvements more likely. These groups arise when a large proportion of a relatively small community leaves a well-defined locale and settles within easy reach of each other in the host-country. High levels of social and economic interdependence link migrants and nonmigrants. Migrants and nonmigrants tend to know one another or each other's families personally. In the receiving country and at home, their social lives continue to be so entwined that those who do not send money to their families or do not 'do right' by the community feel the consequences of their actions. Values like enforceable trust and bounded solidarity still hold sway (Portes: 1995). The sending community is still the reference group against which most migrants gauge their status (Goldring: 1998, Berry: 1985). The many benches in the park in Miraflores that are inscribed with the names of benefactors in Boston serve to demonstrate migrants' enhanced status but they also attest to their continued membership in the community.

Urban-to-urban transnational villages share some of these character-istics. Valadarenses also expressed a sense of belonging to a transnational social group to which they were loyal and responsible. Ethnic entrepre-neurs, community leaders, and clergymen created institutional settings that encouraged transnational practices. But sheer numbers, wider spaces, and weaker connections make it more difficult for urban-to-urban trans-national groups to exert the same hold over their members. Urban village members exercise greater agency because their communities are more loosely constituted and less interdependent than their rural counterparts.

While rural-to-urban transnational village members often know one another personally, members of urban-to-urban transnational groups are linked by increasingly attenuated ties to individuals who are much more dispersed. These characteristics render members less capable of pressur-ing each other to adhere to the same set of values. They make it harder to create strong boundaries that keep social capital from leaking out and new ideas from permeating in. While Mirafloreños ostracised those men who stopped providing for their families, Valadarenses could not exert the same kind of pressure on men who acted in a similar manner. Because urban transnational villages are larger and more differentiated, using membership as a means to display enhanced status is less satisfying. There are multiple stages that divert the attention of the desired audience, thus creating fewer incentives to remain a loyal community member.

The disjuncture between sending and receiving-country life is also greater in the case of urban-to-urban transnational villages. Mirafloreños recreated a Miraflores in Boston that was very similar to its counterpart on the island. Life in Boston and in the Dominican Republic remained in sync to a large degree. Social remittance transmission, which also reinforces community ties, functions especially efficiently within these kinds of tightly-bounded groups. Because urban collective life is more complex and multi-faceted, social life does not span borders as seamlessly. Valadarene-ses have more freedom with which to reorient themselves to the United

States. Since migration only intensifies the social differentiation that is more acute in urban communities from the outset, successful collective action is more difficult to bring about.

Finally, a higher proportion of Mirafloreños depend on migrant remittances while Valadarenses are more likely to receive remittances periodically or when a particular need arises. Because Mirafloreños need remittances to continue, they need to maintain strong ties to migrants and to do what it takes to remain in their good graces.

Migrants' socioeconomic characteristics

Differences in Mirafloreños' and Valadareneses' socioeconomic characteristics also explain variations in transnational participation.

First, active transnational participation is much easier when migrants have legal status. Though actual movement is not a prerequisite for transnational activism, unrestricted mobility clearly facilitates continued home and host-country ties. While most Mirafloreños entered the United States illegally, seventy-three percent had obtained legal permanent residence by 1994 (Levitt: 2001a). In contrast, community leaders estimated that sixty percent of the Valadareneses living in Framingham in 1998 were in the United States illegally, making it much more difficult for them to travel.

Second, migrants' motivations for participating transnationally and their ability to do so vary by class. Migrants with less education and fewer occupational and language skills face greater barriers to economic advancement. They may feel forced into long-term participation in sending-country activities to compensate for their blocked host-country mobility.

Most Mirafloreños in this study had less schooling and fewer English-language capabilities than Valadareneses. In 1990, 58% of the Dominicans in Massachusetts had no formal education or had only completed primary school. Fifty percent claimed to have poor language skills (U.S. Census, 1992). Most Mirafloreños worked in low-level factory and office-cleaning jobs involving little contact with native-born workers or U.S. institutions. They learned little English and despite their extended length of stay, continued to live, work, and socialise within a pan-Latino, if not Dominican, world. These experiences compelled some Mirafloreños to pursue transnational strategies because they could not gain a secure foothold in the United States.

In contrast, Valadarenses came to the United States with higher levels of education and language skills which facilitated their integration into the host society. In 1990, only twenty-two percent of Brazilians said they had no schooling or had only completed primary school. Thirty percent had some college education. Forty-five percent reported poor English language skills. Though like Mirafloreños, large numbers of Valadarenses also worked in the service sector, they were more likely to find jobs in restaurants and hotels or to start small cleaning businesses of their own. These positions involved more contact with the general public and required migrants to master a new set of skills. Because Valadarenses made greater economic gains, they had more choices about whether to pursue transnational strategies. [7]

The role of the state and political groups

Thus far, I have focused on how the characteristics of individual migrants and the local-level transnational social fields in which they are embedded shape migrants' transnational involvements. Other factors, operating at broader levels of the transnational social field, also influence cross-border activism. Political and civic institutions create participatory opportunities that channel migrants' energies and loyalties. The more institutionally complete the field is, the more arenas there are competing for migrants' attention, and the more dispersed their commitments may become. The political cultures surrounding these institutions also shape transnational politics.

Dominican political parties and migrants were the primary supporters of the legislation allowing dual nationality and the expatriate vote that was approved in the mid-1990s. The proportion of Dominicans in the United States grew so large that the biggest voting block outside of Santo Domingo lived in New York. According to Carlos Dóre, an advisor to former President Leonel Fernandez (1996–2000), economic remittances are 'sine qua non for Dominican macro-economic stability, including monetary exchange rates, the balance of trade, international monetary reserves, and the national balance of payment'(Guarnizo: 1997). Actors of all political persuasions realised they needed to ensure the continuation of remittance flows and that to do so, they would have to respond to migrants' demands for greater voice.

At the same time, some political groups began articulating a dual agenda that encouraged migrants to stay active in Dominican politics while they also become politically active in the United States. This strategy would enable migrants to improve their access to government programs and be in a better position to influence policies in favor of Dominican interests. The *Partido Revolucionario Dominicano* and the *Partido de la Liberacíon Dominicana* both created organisations in the United States that are integrally connected to their activities on the island. The emergence of a rhetorical climate favouring dual involvements and the creation of organisational structures to act upon them facilitated enduring home and host-country participation for those wishing to pursue such a path.

Despite generally low levels of U.S.-oriented political activity in Boston, increasing numbers of Dominicans in New York appear to be exercising their rights as members of both polities.[8] They continue to exert a significant influence over Dominican election outcomes (Sontag: 1997). At the same time, they have established a wide range of community organisations and have achieved greater representation in the formal political arenas. In response to concerted pressure by community groups, the New York City Districting Commission created District #10 in northern Manhattan, where there is a large percentage of Dominican residents. Guillermo Linares, the first Dominican to serve on the New York City School Board, has represented the district since 1991. Dominicans also gained politically from New York State Assembly redistricting in 1992 (Pessar and Graham: 2002). Adriano Espaillat became the Assembly's first Dominican-born member in 1996. Candidates for Mayor of New York regularly travel to the island to campaign, attesting to the Dominican community's increasing clout. Former Mayor David Dinkins, for example, received the endorsement of Rafael Corporan de los Santos, the Mayor of Santo Domingo, when he campaigned in the capital in 1992 (Moreno: 1992).[9]

The experience of Dominicans in New York, however, clearly differs from that in Massachusetts. It is not just smaller numbers or relative youth that differentiates the New York and Boston experiences. In New York, Dominicans encountered a critical mass of minority allies with whom to join forces while in Boston, powerful minority coalitions have been absent from the political landscape. Furthermore, when Dominicans first came to New York, there were activists who willingly socialised them into U.S. politics while in Boston, there were few individuals able or ready to do so (Levitt: 2001a). This combination of institutional opportunities and partners engendered greater transnational participation among Dominicans in New York while in Boston, the institutional landscape encouraged greater home-country involvement.

In contrast, the relatively underdeveloped nature of Brazilian transnational politics means that Valadareneses have more limited opportunities to participate in homeland politics. Brazilians earned the right to vote for President from abroad in the late 1970s, though democratic elections were not held until 1989.[10] Since the estimated 1.5 million emigrant Brazilians represent less than one percent of the Brazilian population, their impact on elections is negligible. According to Licenciado Lucio Pires De Amorim, the Former Director General for Legal and Assistance-Related Consular Affairs for Brazilians Living Abroad, only fifty thousand Brazilian migrants registered to vote in the 1998 election, and of these only twenty-five thousand actually cast their ballots.

Brazilians were granted the right to dual citizenship through a constitutional amendment approved in 1993. These reforms did not arise in response to widespread popular demand nor did they form part of a strategic plan on the part of the government to encourage migrants' enduring transnational ties. Instead, according to Licenciado Pires de Amorim, they emerged from Brazil's process of coming to terms with itself as a country of emigration as well as immigration. Media coverage of migrants' alleged mistreatment abroad and numerous letters from concerned family members prompted legislators to take steps to demonstrate their continuing concern for those living outside the country. By approving dual citizenship, Foreign Ministry officials hoped migrants would improve their access to host-country services. Legislators also recognised that, in a global economy, membership in two polities did not raise the same kinds of conflicts as it had in the past.[11]

Political culture also plays a role in explaining why so many Valadareneses reject their government's offer of long-term membership without residence. Their experience contrasts with the Dominican Republic, where following the demise of the thirty-one year old Trujillo dictatorship (1930–1961), the Dominican government actively promoted the creation of civic organisations. The Miraflores Development Committee, the community's sport committee, and its farmers' association are the contemporary fruits of these earlier organising efforts. Political party loyalty also runs deep. Mirafloreños often spoke about having a particular political party 'in their genes' because their family backed that group for generations. Politics figures so large in the everyday lives of some Dominicans that the next presidential election campaign is said 'to start the day after the last election is held.' The weekly car caravans and block parties held to support candidates are big events in small towns like Miraflores as Nicolás, a 40 year old migrant, describes,

> Let me tell you that Santo Domingo is one of the countries where they talk the most about politics. It is a country that is so politicised that you can't get any work done. The problem is that this has never been serious. There is no substance to it. The people enjoy politics. They like motorcades. They like flags. It is something that was restricted for many years. For many years, they did not have the right to fall in love so now, they fall in love with whoever comes along.

Valadarenses bring no comparable tradition of long-term party loyalty with them. In fact, most of the Valadarenses we interviewed adamantly distrusted the Brazilian government's efforts to reach out to them. Why would the state care about us now, they asked, when it has done so little to help us in the past? Furthermore, some researchers argue that Brazilians are disinclined to form community organisations. According to Margolis (1994: 195), 'the lack of community ethos and community associations was one of the most striking, and for a time, most puzzling features of the Brazilian immigrant scene' that she studied in New York. While we found that Brazilians in Framingham did organise community groups, there were clear ebbs and flows in activism (although these did not seem more pronounced than in the Dominican case). Since 1997, at least four organisations have been created to promote community development, primarily in the business sphere. All focused almost entirely on immigrant community concerns. Each of these efforts subsequently failed only to be resuscitated again by a new group. Because these groups were so unstable, they gained little momentum and the community had to begin again after each new round.

In sum, the Dominican government's clear outreach projects, high levels of transnational institutional development, and Mirafloreños' strong culture of participation encourage continued home-country political activism. In contrast, more limited institutional opportunities, a weaker tradition of party loyalty, and a strong distrust of government projects contributed to Valadarenses' lesser likelihood to be involved in homeland affairs.

Though my focus in this section has been on how sending-state policies influence transnational participation, receiving states strongly affect these activities as well. Immigration and naturalisation policies and policies regulating immigrants' access to social services also channel transnational involvements. First, undocumented migrants are less likely to take part in any kind of social or political activities, be they home or host-country focused. These individuals tend to be more recent arrivals who are dealing with issues of basic survival. They are also less likely to participate in organised activities because they fear contact with the law.

Second, both documented and undocumented migrants are more likely to engage in transnational practices when their relatives remain in their sending communities. Many Gujarati Indian families, for example, reported that their transnational practices declined when the majority of their relatives came to the United States. When receiving-state policies restrict family reunification, they may indirectly encourage transnational practices.

In addition, when receiving states restrict immigrants' access to social services, migrants may turn to sending states to get what they need. At one time, the Brazilian government offered a group health insurance plan to Brazilian workers living in New York because it realised that insurance costs were so high. *CONASIDA* (a Mexican health care agency) opened offices in the Los Angeles Consulate to help fight AIDS in the Mexican community. The Mexican *Instituto Nacional de Educacíon para Adultos* (INEA) signed an agreement with the One Stop Immigration and Education center (OSIEC) to distribute materials and provide technical support to help migrants learn to read in Spanish before they attempted literacy in English (González Gutierrez 1993). The fact that U.S. government policies made it more difficult for migrants to access health and educational services encouraged migrants to turn to their sending states for help. In exchange, migrants may be more willing to remain advocates for sending-states concerns.

The role of religion

The political arena is only one of several ways in which migrants express dual membership. In the Valadares case, religious participation supercedes politics as a means to dual belonging among the minority who choose to participate in collective transnational practices. Valadares is known as the evangelical capital of Brazil. In contrast to much of the country, where Catholicism still predominates, Protestantism has always figured large in Valadares' seventy-year history. While in the Miraflores case, Catholic Church ties form the primary religious links between migrants and non-migrants, Valadarenses in Massachusetts and Brazil are connected to one another through a diverse, overlapping set of relations between Catholic and Protestant congregations.

An estimated seventy percent of Valadarenses are said to belong to Protestant churches. These range from traditional mainline denominations such as Presbyterians, Baptists, and Methodists to evangelical churches such as the Assemblies of God or the *Igreja Universal*. Since most of these churches have at least some members who are either return migrants themselves or who have family members currently residing in the United States, strong ties connect individual church goers on both sides of the border. Relations between individuals are reinforced by institutional linkages between churches. Some churches, like the Assemblies of God, actually plant new churches by sending members to the United States to create new congregations. Though most become self-financed and governed within a short time, they generally remain in contact with their 'mother' church. In other cases, Brazilian pastors in the United States maintain their membership in their Brazilian denominations while they also forge a variety of connections to their denominational counterparts in the United States. Pastors from the Baptist National Convention (BNC) in Brazil, for example, formed their own Brazilian Pastors Alliance in the United States. In addition, some pastors have become affiliated with the American Baptist Convention at the same time that they maintain their membership in the BNC in Brazil.

The collective religious ties linking Boston and Valadares are more numerous and complex than their political equivalents. They are likely to thicken and diversify even further for several reasons. First, while more Valadarenses say they are settling permanently in the United States, the majority report that there are still significant numbers who travel back and forth between Boston and Brazil on a regular basis. Each time these individuals rejoin or visit the churches they leave behind, they solidify these religious connections. Second, a number of the Valadarenses we interviewed reported that they had changed churches at least once in the last five years. Both Catholic and Protestant clergy agreed that this was quite common. People often look to other denominations, they said, when the churches they attend fail to meet their spiritual needs, particularly during times of heightened social and economic crises. According to Pastor Waldo, 'the extraordinary that once delighted soon becomes ordinary', prompting a continuous cycle of seeking further miracles in other Evangelical groups once the new becomes routine. The hardships of migrant life also prompt many non-believers to seek religion. As more people join churches, and exit one church to enter another, the web of transnational religious ties between Boston and Valadares thickens and expands, allowing those wishing to do so to participate equally on both sides of the border.

Transnational religious belonging influences home and host-country civic engagement in ways I am still trying to disentangle. Because there is such a wide variety of Protestant experiences, and my analyses are still preliminary, I will offer just one example. The experiences of a group of Renewed Brazilian Baptist Churches highlights the ways in which churches can play the primary role in host-country integration. In this case, it is not merely that the immigrant experience makes religious beliefs more salient. It is that religious institutions replace political and civic ones as the arena through which migrants are socialised into the host-country public sphere. Pastor Eliana, for example, describes how she felt invisible in her encounters with political and educational institutions and the Census. She says she began making a place for herself in the United States when her church entered into the American Baptist Convention. It is her identity as a Baptist that roots her in the United States rather than her emerging identity as a Brazilian-American.

> What I see the Brazilian population searching for here in Massachusetts is that we would like to have a sense of belonging. When we go back to Brazil we are no longer Brazilian Brazilians and being here we are not considered EuroAmericans. So we are a people without identity, without a connection, and we are very family oriented. But when we leave our country, our family, our neighbors and we come here after time goes by, we search for a way to belong to this culture. We want to belong to something that we could call family because we are struggling to identify who we are. We have become bicultural, we have changed. But so far, who are we?

> Q: Why wouldn't one be a Baptist? Could you imagine a world where the salient identity would be a Baptist rather than Brazilian or American?

> I think that this identity already exists. I mean being a Brazilian person and being a Baptist is synonymous with being smart. It is synonymous with wisdom because among us we know that Baptists are capable of thinking or being in a relationship with one another, of having disagreements but at the same time finding solutions and agreement among ourselves. Calling ourselves Baptists is something that we as a community are proud of. When the denomination showed that it was open to establish this relationship with us, giving recognition to us, it was something that we celebrated because it is giving to us the recognition that we are no longer invisible. So far, we have been an invisible culture without any connection with the new system that we are in. But now, this kind of feeling is so strong because we really feel that we are becoming family in a very constructive way. We are no longer invisible. Even through the census, if I go to fill out an application in any school

or any place, I can identify myself as Hispanic or other. And usually I go other. This is what I call invisible culture. I mean we are here but nobody knows yet.

Because Eliana knows her members feel alienated and unacknowledged, she believes she should use her role as a religious leader to help them negotiate a political space.

Q: Do you see the church as substituting for the political citizenship route?

This is my personal expectation taking into consideration that we are a population that does not have well prepared people to be advocating for us. My hope is that someday that the pastors after becoming bicultural and after understanding more and knowing about the EuroAmerican laws and society in general, hopefully they will making this effort to be advocating for the population.

She tells of accompanying the parents of a child with special needs in her church to demand that they got the services they were entitled to. She also tells,

We do a lot of advocating and clarification of how our culture works. We have a different sense of privacy. Privacy is more kind of feelings and emotional than space. We can sleep together in the same bed, there is no sexual relationship going on. It is because we don't have two beds and we always sleep in one bed. And then sometimes we come to Massachusetts. And I have one teenager in my congregation. She used to sleep with her father in the same bed when her mother was away and for some reason she said that in her school. That she was sharing beds with her father. And then the whole system came to her home thinking that she was being sexually abused by her father. They were Christians, a very healthy family and suddenly they saw their whole family being approached by the system and once again we had to go and explain and testify to the people involved.

The integrative role played by Brazilian Baptists evolves as such because they form part of what I call a *negotiated transnational religious organisation* (Levitt: 2001b). Because there is no one leader or administrative hierarchy setting policy and dictating how things are done, issues like power sharing, accountability, financing, and organisation need to be worked out. These negotiations give rise to a diverse, loose set of partnerships that may be unstable and shift over time. The ways that negotiated transnational institutions function are akin to the network society described by Manuel Castells (2000). They are decentralised, flexible yet integrated networks providing customised services and goods to individuals and communities in ways that enable transnational belonging because they can be adapted fairly easily to each denominational scenario.

Dominican and Brazilian Catholics belong to an *extended transnational religious organisation* (Levitt: 2001b). Dominicans in Boston and on the island were already members of the universal Catholic Church. Migration simply broadened, deepened, and customised a global religious system that is already legitimate, powerful, and highly organised. Membership in extended transnational religious groups also enables migrants' simultaneous belonging in their sending and receiving communities. It also integrates them into resource-rich, well-connected institutional networks that are potential sites for expressing interests and making claims.

As migrants and nonmigrants circulated in and out of local parishes and personal relations developed between individual priests, a constant exchange of parishioners, clergy, and resources occurred between Boston and Santo Domingo. In contrast to Brazilian Baptists, who established new churches and negotiated relations with an American denominational sponsor, Mirafloreños became integrated into an existing church structure which affected their participation in sending-country civic life in very specific ways. First, religious integration required little self-mobilisation. Mirafloreños did not reap the benefit of the energy and skills that arise from creating new churches or congregations within congregations. Second, because the Church offered them a pan-Latino package of services it had already developed for earlier arrivals, migrants encountered something familiar and easy to adapt to but that channeled their participatory energies in specific ways. In most churches, Mirafloreños became incorporated into 'separate-but-equal' Latino parish structures. They organised their own Spanish-language masses, parish councils, and youth groups but had only minimal contact with Anglo parishioners. These organisational arrangements confined their focus to Latino religious life, mitigating against their complete integration and reinforcing their Latino, if not Dominican, focus.

Transnational communities and participation

In this paper, I have presented findings from a comparative, historical study of various immigrant communities to identify different types of transnational communities and to begin to suggest how these different forms affect migrants' integration into home and host-country life. Two types of communities emerged – a rural-to-urban transnational village whose members continued to remain oriented toward their sending community and were only minimally integrated into the civic life of the United States, and an urban-to-urban transnational village, whose members participated more actively in the U.S. civic arena.

Given that transnational connections are likely to persist, what are the implications of these findings for social and political life? Each transnational community creates different combinations of political, religious, and social membership options ranging from continued sending-country citizenship, and long-term partial membership in the host society to dual citizenship. The nature of the rural-to-urban transnational village suggests that many members will be slow to naturalise and will experience social and economic marginalisation in the United States while they continue to participate in local-level sending-country affairs. In contrast, the urban-to-urban transnational village experience suggests a more traditional path toward host-country incorporation with some periodic involvement in sending-country affairs, particularly through religious arenas.

These findings, and the context of increasing economic and political globalisation in which they take place, bring to light new participatory forms which decouple citizenship and membership. Migrants can opt for long-term partial membership in the places that they live and continue to be full, but partially-active members in the places they come from. We need to sort out the meanings and reasons behind different participatory choices. Naturalisation clearly does not signal a shift in allegiance and an end to sending-country involvements. Even migrants who become U.S. citizens may still remain active indefinitely in their home-country polities while they exercise their rights in the United States. Similarly, those who participate actively in sending-country political parties, though they are citizens or long-time residents of the United States, may do so to promote sending-country development rather than to influence political outcomes. The proliferation and maturation of the kinds of communities I describe will enable increasing numbers to balance dual involvements whose motivations may be different than they first seem.

What happens to those who choose not to become citizens but continue instead as long-term, long-distance participants in their home polities? What costs and benefits does this entail and for whom? This study makes clear that dual citizenship is just one way that individuals keep feet in two worlds. Many religious, social, and political organisations occupy transnational public spheres that migration gives rise to. The tradeoffs in protection and representation that migrants gain by participating in these different kinds of arenas must be better understood. Some sending states will always be better able to intervene on emigrants' behalf than others. Finally, we must explore the consequences for civil society when migrants' primary political socialisation and membership occurs within religious rather than political arenas.

References

L. Basch, N. Glick-Schiller, and C. Szanton Blanc eds, *Nations Unbound: Transnational Projects, Postcolonial Predicaments, and Deterritorialised Nation-States* Switzerland, 1994.

S. Berry, *Fathers Work for Their Sons*, Berkeley and Los Angeles, 1985.

M. Castells, *The Power of Identity*, Malden, MA: Blackwell Press, 1997.

S. England, 'Negotiating Race and Place in the Garifuna Diaspora: Identity Formation and Transnational Grassroots Politics in New York City and Honduras', *Identities*, 6, no. 1, 1999, 5–53.

T. Faist, 'Cumulative Causation in Transnational Social Spaces: The German-Turkish Example.' Paper presented at the International Sociological Association's meeting on 'Inclusion and Exclusion: International Migrants and Refugees in Europe and North America,' 5–7 June 1997, New School for Social Research, New York.

N. Foner, *From Ellis Island to JFK: New Immigrants in New York*. New Haven: Yale University Press.

N. Fraser, 'Rethinking the Public Sphere: A Contribution to the Critique of Actually Existing Democracy,' in *Habermas and the Public Sphere*, Craig Calhoun ed., Cambridge, Mass, 1991.

N. Glick-Schiller, 'From Immigrant to Transmigrant: Theorizing Transnational Migration', *Anthropological Quarterly*, 68, 1995, 48–63

N. Glick Schiller and G. Fouron, 'The Generation of Identity: Haitian Youth and the Transnational Nation State.' Paper presented at Transnationalism and the Second Generation Conference, Harvard University, April 1998.

S. Gold, 'Transnational Communities: Examining Migration in a Globally Integrated World', in *Rethinking Globalisation(s): From Corporate Transnationalism to Local Intervention*, Preet S. Aulakh and Michael G. Schechter eds, London, 2001.

L. Goldring, 'Diversity and Community in Transnational Migration: A Comparative Study of Two Mexico U.S. Migrant Communities', Ph.D. dissertation, Cornell University, 1992.

L. Goldring, 'The Power of Status in transnational social spaces,' in *Comparative Urban and Community Research* Vol. 6, Michael Peter Smith and Luis Eduardo Guarnizo eds, 1998, 615–196.

C. González Gutierrez, 'The Mexican Diaspora in California: The Limits and Possibilities for the Mexican Government', in *The California-Mexico Connection*, Abraham Lowenthal and Katrina Burgess, eds, Stanford, Ca., 1993, 221–235,.

L. Guarnizo, 'The Emergence of a Transnational Social Formation and the Mirage of Return among Dominican Transmigrants', *Identities*, 4, 1997, 281–322.

L. Guarnizo, 'The Rise of Transnational Social Formations: Mexican and Dominican State Responses to Transnational Migration', *Political Power and Social Theory*, 12, 1998, 45–94.

L. Guarnizo, A. I. Sanchez, and E. M. Roach, 'Mistrust, Fragmented Solidarity, and Transnational Migration: Colombians in New York City and Los Angeles', *Ethnic and Racial Studies*, 22, 1999, 367–395.

Hernández, Raymond, 'Guiliani, in Visit, Pledges Storm Help for Dominicans', *The New York Times*, 4 October 1998

J. Itzigsohn, C. Dore Cabral, E. Hernandez Medina, and O. Vaquez, 'Mapping Dominican Transnationalism: Narrow and Broad Transnational Practices', *Ethnic and Racial Studies*, 22, 1999, 2316–2340.

M. Jones-Correa, 'Under Two Flags: Dual Nationality in Latin America and Its Consequences for the United States', *International Migration Review*, forthcoming (2001)

R. Kastoryano, 'Mobilisations des migrants en Europe: du national au transnational', *Reveu Europeenne des Migrations Internationales*, 10, no. 1, 1994, 169–180.

P. Landholt et al., 'From Hermano Lejano to Hermano Mayor: the Dialectics of Salvadoriean Transnationalism', *Ethnic and Racial Studies*, 22 no. 2, 1999, 290–315.

P. Levitt, 'Migrants Participate Across Borders: Towards an Understanding of Its Forms and Consequences', in *Immigration Research for a New Century: Multidisciplinary Perspectives*, Nancy Foner, Rubén G. Rumbaut and Steven J. Gold, eds, New York, 2000.

P. Levitt, *The Transnational Villagers*, Berkeley and Los Angeles, 2001a.

P. Levitt, 'They Prayed in Boston and It Rained in Brazil'. Paper presented at Department of Religious Studies, University of California at Santa Barbara, March 2001b.

S. Mahler, 'Theoretical and Empirical Contributions Toward a Research Agenda for Transnationalism', in *Comparative Urban and Community Research* Vol. 6, eds Michael Peter Smith and Luis Eduardo Guarnizo, 1998, 64–103.

M. Margolis, *Little Brazil: An Ethnography of Brazilian Immigrants in New York City*, Princeton, 1994.

A.C. Martes, 'Respeito e Cidadania: O Ministério das Relacoes Exteriores e os Imigrantes Brasileiros em Boston'. Paper presented at the First Symposium on Brazilian Emigration, Lisbon, 1997.

E. Morawska, 'International Migration and Consolidation of Democracy in East Central Europe: A Problematic Relationship in a Historical Perspective', in *Immigrants, Civic Culture, and Modes of Political Integration*, Gary Gerstle and John Mollenkopf eds, New York, 2001.

S. Moreno, 'Dinkins Scores With Visit', *Newsday*, 22 May 1992.

A. Mountz and R. Wright, 'Daily Life in the Transnational Migrant Community of San Agustin, Oaxaca and Poughkeepsie, New York', *Diaspora*, 5, no.3, 1996, 403–428.

P. Pessar and P. Graham, 'Dominicans: Transnational Identities and Local Politics', in *New Immigrants in New York*, Nancy Foner ed., New York, 2002.

E. Popkin, 'Guatemalan Mayan Migration to Los Angeles: Constructing Transnational Linkages in the Context of the Settlement Process', *Ethnic and Racial Studies*, 22, no. 2, 1999, 267–289.

A. Portes, 'Transnational Communities: Their Emergence and Significance in the Contemporary World-System', in *Latin America in the World Economy*, R.P. Korzeniewicz and W.C. Smith, eds, 1996.

A. Portes, L. Guarnizo, and P. Landholt, 'Introduction: Pitfalls and Promise of an Emergent Research Field', *Ethnic and Racial Studies*, 22, no. 2, 1999, 217–237.

P.L. Rodriguez, 'Caem Remessas de Residentes no Exterior', *Net Estado*, 28 December 1997.

C. Rodriguez, 'From Island Politics to Local Politics: Dominicans Making Gains in City Offices', *The Boston Globe*, 14 November 1999.

R. Rouse, Mexican Migration to the United States: Family Relations in the Development of Transnational Circuits. Ph.D. diss., Stanford University, 1989.

T. Sales, 'Identidade etnica entre imigrantes brasileiros na regiao de Boston, EUA', in *Do Brazil Migrantes*, Rossana Rocha Reis and Teresa Sales, eds, San Paulo, 1999, 7–44.

M.P. Smith and L. Guarnizo, eds, *Transnationalism from Below Comparative Urban and Community Research*, 6, New Brunswick and London, 1998.

R. Smith, 'Transnational Localities: Community, Technology, and the Politics of Membership Within the Context of Mexico and U.S. Migration', in *Comparative Urban and Community Research* Vol. 6, Michael Peter Smith and Luis Eduardo Guarnizo, eds, 1998, 196–240.

W. Soares, 'Emigrantes E Investidores: Redefinindo A Dinamica Imobiliaria Na Economia Valadarense', PhD Dissertation Universidade Federal Do Rio de Janeiro, 1995.

Sontag, Deborah, 'Advocates for Immigrants Exploring Voting Rights for Non-citizens', *The New York Times*, 31 July 1997.

Torres-Saillant and Ramona Hernández, *The Dominican Americans*. Westport and London, 1998

United States Bureau of the Census, 'Census of the Population: General Social and Economic Characteristics, PC(1)-C23.1', Washington, D.C., 1992.

Notes

* I gratefully acknowledge research assistance from Rafael de la Dehesa, Waldo Cesar, and Erin Collins. Comments from Reed Ueda, Irene Bloomraed, and several anonymous reviewers helped improve this paper. This research is funded by the Ford Foundation, the Social Science Research Council, the Spencer Foundation, and the American Sociological Association Fund for the Advancement of the Discipline.

1. See, for example, Portes (1996), Smith (1998), Rouse (1989), Mountz and Wright (1997), Goldring (1992), Popkin (1999), Landholt et al. (1999), Faist (1997), Kastoryano (1998), Basch et al. (1994), and Mahler (1996).
2. The initial round of field work on the Dominican community is complete, though we continue to update our materials periodically. Sixty interviews have been conducted with migrants from Governador Valadares in Brazil. Over fifty interviews with organisational leaders have also been carried out. Field work in Brazil was carried out in Summer 1999; a second research trip is planned for 2002.
3. As Gold (2001) correctly points out, new migrants also enjoy certain economic opportunities earlier migrants lacked. Earlier in this century, even native-born minority men would not be hired for jobs in certain universities, industries, and the public sector. It is also true that migrants today benefit from anti-discrimination and affirmative action laws that are now in place.
4. Social remittances are the ideas, behavior, social capital, and identities that flow from receiving to sending country communities. They are the north-to-south equivalent of the social and cultural resources that migrants bring with them that ease the transition from immigrants to ethnics.
5. Though evangelical churches are becoming more prominent in the Dominican Republic, they were not an important presence in Miraflores when I conducted my field work.
6. The Province where Baní is located.

7. Margolis (1998) calls into question the validity of the category 'immigrant' for Brazilians. In her study of migrants from Rio de Janeiro living in New York and in subsequent interviews she conducted with return migrants in Rio she found that many of her informants were reluctant to identify themselves as immigrants. Martes (1997 as quoted in Margolis) also found that the Valadarenses she studied in Boston expressed comparable sentiments. We have not found this to be the case. In fact, more and more of the individuals in our study seem to be coming to grips with the idea that they are likely to remain permanently in the United States. One factor that might explain our different findings is that Martes conducted her field work earlier on in the life of the community. By the time we began our interviews, greater numbers may have been ready to make that psychological switch.

8. An important difference between Dominican migrants in Boston and New York is that the first to arrive in New York were political refugees. To quell political unrest following the U.S. invasion of the island in 1965, the U.S. government granted a higher number of visas to diminish political opposition to the government on the island. Though many of the first to arrive in New York were political refugees, subsequent flows can only be characterised as economic migrants.

9. Ruth Messinger also travelled to the Dominican Republic during her campaign against incumbent Mayor Rudolph Guiliani in 1997. Though Guiliani has not visited Santo Domingo to campaign, he did travel to the island to supervise relief efforts supported by New York City after Hurricane Mitch in 1998 (Hernández: 1998).

10. Brazil was under a dictatorship between 1964–1985.

11. While, in the past, the Brazilian Foreign ministry, *Itamaraty*, established consulates to promote trade, as migration increased, it shifted its focus toward providing services to Brazilians abroad and restructured its operations as a result. The office at the Foreign Ministry in charge of consular affairs was elevated to a General Directorate. This heightened the profile of consular services, decreased red tape, and increased access to high Ministry officials. Regional offices of *Itamaraty* were also opened in various Brazilian states. These structures, which are still quite new, are designed to give state governments a greater voice in foreign policy formulation. They may also serve as contact points for Brazilian consulates when arranging visits by foreign officials.

V

REINVENTING CITIZENSHIP: DUAL CITIZENSHIP, FEDERAL CITIZENSHIP AND EUROPEAN CITIZENSHIP

CHAPTER 13

EU CITIZENSHIP AT THE 1996 IGC

Carlos Closa

EU citizenship has emerged as the transnational embodiment of dual citizenship, constituted by both member state and European citizenship. Examining events and arguments at the 1996 Intergovernmental conference, this chapter reflects on the relationship between, on the one hand, European citizenship and, on the other, national citizenship and migrant integration. It begins by considering a number of methodological issues. These concern the contextual setting for the concept of citizenship and a possible analytical distinction between nationality and citizenship. The second part of the chapter focuses on the implicit understanding that emerges from the 1996 IGC.

European citizenship: methodological considerations

The huge increase in the literature on citizenship (and, specifically, on European citizenship) in recent decades reveals an important effort to substantiate a category around which the main current political and social problems can be examined. But puzzlement also arises from this flow of bibliography that is characterised by its diversity, heterogeneity, methodological pluralism, etc. Three factors account for this result.

There is, first, a disciplinary problem: citizenship is both a concept and a meeting point for law (public mainly), politics, sociology and even psychology. Thus, interdisciplinary perspectives add to our understanding of citizenship, but also reduce its conceptual precision. Applying the well-known rules about concept formation in social sciences (Sartori: 1984), the increase of denotation (i.e., the number of phenomena to which a concept may be applied) decreases its connotation (i.e., the substantial characteristics of this concept). In this context, for instance,

Ferrajoli has pointed out two very significant inconsistencies between juridical and sociological uses: first, the association of *all* rights with the status of citizenship and, secondly, the theoretical inconsistency *rationae constructione* of the sociological typologies of rights (Ferrajoli: 1994, 263–268).

A second difficulty arises from the ongoing conversation between normative and empirical analyses of citizenship, as much as between normative analyses themselves. Moreover, methodologists have warned of the danger of emptying a concept when it is used mainly for polemical purposes. EU citizenship has become an arena for this conflict between normative, empirical and polemical uses: for example, some authors conceive it as the centrepiece for EU fundamental rights while, at the same time, others criticise it as a potential source of discrimination.

The third type of difficulty is more specific and has to do with the emergence of a new 'paradigm' (in Kuhn's terminology). Citizenship has been tightly linked with the prevalent form of political control and domination in the last centuries, the nation-state and the so-called Westphalia system of sovereign states. This alone should suggest caution in simply transferring the model of national citizenship to the EU level.

These issues form the methodological framework of this chapter. There is, first, an obligation to clarify the interdisciplinary position from which research on the concept of European Union citizenship is carried out. Second, the alternative use of empirical and/or normative discourses and discussions must be explicitly framed. Finally, European citizenship must be examined in the context of the polity in which it is framed – the European Union, a new set of institutions. The first question considered is how can a concept developed within nation-states be applied to a supranational form of political power? In other words, how can this concept be disentangled from the nation-state? The thesis here is that this development is possible if the underlying differences between nationality and citizenship are taken on board.

The conceptual environment of citizenship: the nation-state

One of the assumptions of this chapter is that citizenship is a concept currently built on the experiences deriving from nation-states, although it is subjected to theoretical and normative reelaboration. Thus, the starting point in this inquiry is unveiling the connection between states and citizenship. In the classical theory of the state, state sovereignty implies the recognition by other states of the supremacy of a legal order, within a certain territory and over a certain population. Nothing can be deduced about the quality of the relationship between sovereignty and the people. In fact, in an approach from strict legal positivism, Kelsen stresses that the existence of a state depends on the existence of individuals subjected to its jurisdictional order (i.e., the personal scope of legal validity), but it does not depend on the existence of nationals (Kelsen: 1949, 286).

A second dimension of state sovereignty is participation. Theoretically (and practically), this connection was consolidated during the French revolution. Previously, the struggle for rights was against arbitrariness of either feudal or royal power, and it stressed legal equality. During the French revolution, the concept of citizenship was reconstructed around Rousseau's notion of self-determination or the idea of positive freedom; i.e., the freedom to participate in political life. The convergence of citizenship (as positive freedom) and the nation derives from the necessity of specifying the individuals entitled to participate in political life of the state. Republican doctrine had questioned royal sovereignty but it did not contain specific criteria to single out the individuals that composed the nation to the effect of exercising sovereignty through political rights. But there was a latent criterion, as Habermas suggests. The new political role of individuals demanded a high degree of compromise – to the point of personal sacrifice. In this context, nationalism served to increase the identification of bearer of right with this new role. In a word, nationalism and republicanism fused in the necessity to fight and perhaps to die for 'the country' instead of the king (Habermas: 1994, 23).

If the assumption that the concept of citizenship is linked with self-determination is accepted, then there is the option of drawing an analytical line between nationality and citizenship. Capturing this analytical distinction depends, of course, on the existence of two different words with a distinctive etymology. This perception depends also on concrete historical experiences that shape linguistic uses: if state-creation and people sovereignty is the same process, then differences are less evident.

Distinguishing nationality and citizenship

In the following paragraphs, three selected and interlinked criteria substantiate an analytical difference between nationality and citizenship.

Different bonds

The most direct definition of nationality is the 'juridical link between a person and a State', as recently reaffirmed by the *European Convention on Nationality* of the Council of Europe.[1] This Convention clarifies that nationality does not refer to the ethnic origin of a person. All major definitions follow this line: nationality as subjecthood of a determinate state (Jennings and Watts: 1992, 851); membership of the community which is the personal dimension of the state (Rezek: 1986: 351); or ascription of ultimate legal jurisdiction or diplomatic protection (O'Connell: 1967, 468).

These definitions distinguish those who are nationals, but they do not address the foundational issue, i.e., why is a particular group of people entitled to this specific juridical link? This is not explicitly addressed because formal, descriptive definitions contain, in fact, underlying criteria. Since states give political form to nations and, in parallel, nations have been traditionally considered the personal scope of state power, the transcendent link on which nations are constructed comes to be the substantial link between a person and the state. From this, the legal status of nationality came to mean both a connection to public power and to the human collectivity that has historically been the subject of that power.

A few decades ago, this transcendent understanding of nationality was a common feature, unambiguously stated. It appears in this form in the notion of effective nationality, which was established by the *Convention on certain problems relative to conflicts on nationality laws*.[2] Article 5 established that, in the case of a person with more than one nationality, a third party should exclusively recognise either the nationality of the country of principal and habitual residence or the nationality of the country with which the person is more *intimately* linked. It is worth noting that the connection is identified not in the public sphere, nor in the private one, but in the intimate. The notion of effective nationality was fully developed by the International Court of Justice which, in the *Nottebohm*[3] case, ruled that nationality is a legal link, which has as its basis a social fact of attachment, a genuine connection of existence, interests and feelings, as well as the existence of reciprocal rights and duties. Consequently, the Court argued that the individual to whom nationality is granted is *de facto* connected in a tighter form with the population of that state than with any other state. Accordingly, the International Court questioned if the nationality link between the individual (Nottenbohm) and his state (Liechtenstein) was primary to any other connection between him and any other state. A large part of juridical doctrine has evolved towards the opinion that the evaluation of the quality of the attachment was an erroneous basis on which to rule in that case.[4] Moreover, some legal experts have commented that the notion of effective nationality, which was implicit in this view, draws on a romanticised stage of international relations.[5] Regardless of this opinion, the belief that nationality conveys some form of communal identity (which is not necessarily expressed in a positive form) is still part of its implicit configuration.

Citizenship, constructed as the internal face of nationality, is a concept that inherits the exclusivist character of nationality. In this sense, Arendt describes citizenship as the right to have rights, i.e., the entitlement to rights. This statement can be interpreted in two different forms. The first is that only individuals with the nationality are entitled to have rights. This interpretation conflates a realist view on the validity of rights (only state power can guarantee them effectively) with the moral source of these rights (membership of a community). A second interpretation is based on the opposition of the status of *subject* (the person that does not have rights), which can be equally linked to nationality, with citizenship as a capability for actively shaping political decisions (for instance, on specific rights and duties). Understood in this sense, citizenship comes closer to reflecting the self-determination of individuals. If the assumption that citizenship implies personal self-determination is accepted, then, the link constructed between state and citizen is capable, in some form, of determining state will. This capability does not logically derive from the existence of a nationality link, but, rather, from a specific configuration of the state. In summary, nationality ascribes a person to a determined human collectivity, which is characterised by its 'stateness' (sovereignty). Citizenship, in turn, conveys the idea that the person is entitled to participate in the formation of sovereignty.

Right associated

Drawing inspiration from Kelsenian positivism, nationality forms the basis of a state juridical order for certain rights and duties: military service (which is simultaneously a right and a duty), fidelity (a general obligation to comply with the juridical order which also applies to foreigners), political rights (which exist only, of course, in democracies), the right not to be expelled from national territory (which can also be derogated in specific states) and the right to protection in foreign states (also a discretionary power in certain states). None of these rights, however, constitutes an essential right of nationality, in the sense of its presence being essential for the existence of the state.

In democratic states, nationality implies the entitlement to unrestrained freedom to stay, or move in and out of, the territory of the state, including the right to return to one's own state. In fact, control of this right of access and movement is the instrument securing the closure of national citizenship (Brubaker: 1992, 28) and some constitutional orders of EU Member States (i.e., Spain) *explicitly* guarantee this right to their own nationals only.

The most widespread form of characterising citizenship is by reference to a personal status of rights. The classical explanation of the modern process of creation of citizenship is that of Marshall's tripartite distinction (civil, political and, finally, social rights). In his writing, Marshall was highly influenced by the new social contracts, which marked the development of the welfare state after World War II. Although the growth of social rights was related to this context, this has not been the universal sequence of rights creation. Thus, Lorenz von Stein argued in favour of a paternalistic monarchy with a rich content of social rights, as was the German practice during the Prussian monarchy in the last half of the nineteenth century (while, simultaneously, political rights were marginalised). Nowadays, the tendency is towards the development of the so-called 'fourth generation rights', such as environmental rights, differential group rights, etc. around the statute of citizenship.

In any case, if citizenship is not merely a synonym for nationality, it implies the existence of a bunch of rights whose precise content and process of acquisition depends on specific historical trajectories.

The logic inspiring nationality and citizenship

The qualitative difference between nationality and citizenship is reflected in the logic that inspires each of them. A restrictive logic informs nationality as a legal status: states have reinforced the mechanisms excluding foreigners from the enjoyment of its most characteristic benefit, the freedom of access and movement within the national territory. Access becomes more difficult and this mechanism allows preservation of the rights of citizenship. In this respect, nationality (or the external dimension of citizenship) functions as a privilege (Ferrajoli: 1996, 154).

The logic of citizenship, constructed as successive acquisition of rights, has followed the opposite direction; there has been an historical enlargement of the categories of persons entitled to them. First, there was an expansion in rights enjoyed by nationals. Specifically, political rights were progressively released of qualifications such as income or gender. Secondly, rights were extended to legal residents. In practice, these (with the only exception being those political rights attached to the exercise of sovereignty) tend to be available for all persons legally resident on the territory of a state. This availability is based on the normative self-perception of the democratic state as an arena for effective solidarity. Exclusions within this arena are difficult to admit. In this context, the decisive marker of rights is the border. This limit, however, does not exactly coincide with nationals but it separates those who are 'within city walls' from those outside (Faist: 1994, 7). Particularly, the trend seems to direct towards the application of the principle of redistributive justice to any person legally established within the limits of the community.

Nationality and citizenship are concepts that belong to different contexts, but they are connected as the internal and external dimensions of perceptions of personal statutes (nationality implies a link to the state from the international law point of view and citizenship is the parallel internal expression attached to individuals' self-determination). Consequently, the logic governing each of them is also connected: citizenship (constructed as a sociological concept that reflects the relationship between a person and public power) acts as a correcting of nationality's exclusiveness through an expansive logic. Both the logical development of moral requirements for the statute of citizenship and discursive processes of democracy have extended almost the full catalogue of rights to all legal residents within the territory of the state. Modern constitutionalism advances in extending fundamental rights to almost all residents and only political rights are restricted to citizens.

EU citizenship embodies this decoupling of citizenship and nationality (as the exclusivist entitlement for rights). In parallel, the perception of EU citizenship as an expression of postnational citizenship has gained currency (Bauböck: 1997, 10, Shaw: 1997). What must be borne in mind, however, is that the process of rights construction leads directly towards a reinforcement of *personhood vis-à-vis* citizenship. The preeminence (and confusion) of citizenship probably derives from the lack of a parallel definitive change in the structure of political authority. What has not changed so dramatically in this new setting is that nation-state authorities (political and judicial) are still the ones in charge of guaranteeing this decoupling. States are still the basis for the granting of rights.

The following section illustrates how citizenship has become a banner for the legitimisation of rights and policies within the European Union, drawing on the evidence of the 1996 Intergovernmental Conference (IGC). While the IGC offered a chance to draw a clear statute around the rights for individuals' political self-determination *vis-à-vis* public power, the practice has been an open-ended and diffuse exercise that, nevertheless, has improved the general position of the person (understood as a rights-bearer) within the EU.

Reconstructing EU citizenship: the negotiation of the Treaty of Amsterdam

Scholars working on EU citizenship may opt between two analytical perspectives. In the context of the 1996 IGC and the Treaty of Amsterdam, Jo Shaw has labelled these the descriptive focus and the 'conceptual heritage' focus, preferring the latter (Shaw: 1997). Consistent with the methodological considerations discussed at the beginning of this paper, the approach adopted here is descriptive in order to avoid the context of the concept of citizenship – first and foremost, the state – permeating the analysis.

The drafting of EU citizenship provisions during the 1996 IGC relied on a body of positive provisions, some scarce (and not very encouraging) case law, a huge amount of academic writing and the political experience of the post-Maastricht actors. Despite this, little progress was made. Although some of these actors had called for an improved definition of the concept of EU citizenship, specific proposals were not forwarded. This likely reflected not only ignorance or bad faith, but also the sheer difficulty of conceptually recasting EU citizenship. Instead, efforts were directed towards a piece meal approach that sought to undermine or reinforce specific connotations of implicit concepts of citizenship. Specifically, two issues were implicitly at stake: the scope of EU citizenship, and its rights content.

These two issues were embedded in the two different attitudes that were prevalent during the 1996 IGC (Blázquez: 1998, 264). The first emphasised the subordinated role of EU citizenship to national ones. In parallel, certain actors sought an expansion of rights. Almost without exception, institutions and actors involved in the discussions of the 1996 IGC kept the hegemonic view of citizenship as the central category arbitrating on any aspect of the human condition. Consequently, heterogeneity marks proposals submitted under the heading 'citizenship', as any aspect of EU politics and policies has 'citizenship effects'. It should be noted, though, that many actors adopted both expansive and restrictive positions.

The reinforcement of citizenship's derivative character

The first attitude could be generally labelled restrictive. It echoed the concerns on the (supposed) threat to nationality reflected in the Edinburgh Declaration.[6] The guidelines of the European Council after the Florence summit pointed in the direction of respect for nationality and no replacement of national citizenships. There was near-unanimous support for Treaty articles stating that EU citizenship does not substitute national citizenship,[7] and is without prejudice to the rights and responsibilities of every individual *vis-à-vis* his country of origin.[8] Among these, it is worth recalling the strict Danish interpretation: the Edinburgh Decision regarding *inter alia* citizenship cannot be amended without Denmark's consent.[9] This paved the way for a new provision, article 17.1, (citizenship of the Union shall complement and shall not substitute national citizenship).

Concerns about the effects of EU citizenship on third country nationals justified appeals to both theoretical and political proposals on granting EU citizenship and/or the creation of a distinctive European nationality. In this context, Bauböck argues that the architecture (i.e., structural features) of EU citizenship has major negative impacts for the third country aliens remaining outside this framework. Most importantly, it missed the opportunity to improve their position throughout the Union, it increased inequality of their position between the different member states and it induced a relative deprivation of their status within member states (Bauböck: 1997, 12). Similarly, Lyons argues that EU citizenship is unexceptional in that it reflects the key foundations of citizenship: discrimination and deliberate exclusion. Moreover, if anything, EU citizenship has highlighted and increased the discrimination already inherent in the most tangible rights attached to citizenship (Lyons: 1996, 98).

These perceptions conflate two issues. On the one hand, citizenship – rather than personhood – is still perceived as the entitlement for rights. On the other hand, criticism of EU citizenship becomes a palatable alternative to criticism of nationality: discrimination associated with EU citizenship derives primarily from discrimination in national citizenship. EU citizenship could only be a discriminating instrument if it derived from an EU nationality, but as EU citizenship has not been equipped with autonomous criteria for determining its personal scope of validity, it still depends on nationality of a Member State and it is here that its discrimination – and other limitations – are located.

Improvement of current provisions

Apart from the former restrictive attitude, there was a general mood in favour of an improvement of citizens' entitlements. This involved three different lines: improvement of current provisions, creation of new rights and a simplified mechanism for future developments.

In relation to the improvement of current provisions, this proved more a rhetorical declaration than a summary of specific proposals. Regarding freedom of movement and residence, there were expectations that significant changes might occur. Legal and political doctrine has been predicated on the significance of this right as the cornerstone of the concept of Union citizenship, yet this provision had not been fortified by judicial scrutiny. The Court of Justice has held that the free movement right in article 8 is residual and not the starting point for the analysis of the constitutional nature of free movement.[10]

The European Parliament proposed a far-reaching change: granting direct effect to these provisions (Hall proposed the same; Hall: 1995), a move that could definitively consolidate the freedom of movement through judicial review. However, the general mood of other actors was restrictive. The Commission itself regarded this provision as merely declaratory,[11] although immediately after the conclusion of the Amsterdam Treaty it asked for a revision of free movement and residence provisions, in order to clarify the kind of rights of residence that exist under primary and secondary legislation.[12] In Jo Shaw's opinion, this reflects the contradictory tendencies within the Commission (Shaw: 1997).

For the European Council, freedom of movement and residence had a rhetorical value as a legitimisation of other agenda issues; specifically, control on the external frontiers of the Union.[13] The scarce number of governmental proposals (just two of them) shows the marginal interest for the improvement of these rights.[14] Against this background, the only effective change had an incremental character: the introduction of codecision with Council unanimity following a Commission proposal.[15]

Regarding the remaining provisions in the statute designed by the Maastricht Treaty, the EP asked for the elimination of current restrictions on voting rights introduced by current directives and the clarification of diplomatic protection.[16] Finally, there were also proposals for the adoption of a more flexible instrument for future enlargements via article 8(e). This 'flexibilisation' would consist in changing the requirement for unanimity to qualified majority and substituting national parliaments' ratification by an enhanced EP role, either through codecision or an assent procedure.[17] This 'communitarisation' of the procedure for enlarging the statute of EU citizenship was not accepted and article 8(e) remained unchanged.

Enlargement of citizens' rights: material contents and personal scope of rights

The most ambitious proposals aiming at improving citizens' status focused on the introduction of new rights, either as a general proposal[18] or through specific rights. To avoid ambiguity, the Italian presidency clarified the three criteria for the constitutional revision of citizenship at the conference's outset. First, new rights should not have a direct effect. Second, the financial and economical consequences of their implementation should be taken into account. Third, any right added should be relevant to the issue of citizenship.[19]

Among these three criteria, the third deserves a closer look, as it points directly to two significant theoretical and political issues raised by this 'inflationary tendency'. The first concerns the appeal of casting these issues in the language of rights. De Búrca has provided a convincing explanation for this tendency. In her opinion, the appeal to rights constructs a language with legitimising and integrative force. Specifically, the language of rights affords a means of introducing a range of different values other than predominant market values into the Community's legal and policy-making processes (de Búrca; 1996). Thus, during the 1996 IGC, there was an expansion of proposals on policy-related rights. Among these, the Treaty of Amsterdam has included a mention in the preamble to the promotion of a higher level of knowledge through access to education; [20] the right to receive an education that takes into account the cultural legacy, common values and cultural diversity of European civilisation, including the opportunity of learning a different language,[21] and a reference to public services of general economic interests.[22] These were not the only proposals; there were petitions to enlarge social rights *in abstracto*:[23] the right to a healthy environment,[24] the protection of health, the creation of a European voluntary service,[25] and the right to participate in the activities of a European humanitarian service of civil protection.

This overdevelopment derives from the very fact that the statute of EU citizenship is not a closed one in the double sense that new rights can be added and, significantly, that EU citizens can avail themselves of rights beyond those explicitly listed in article 8. Commentators commonly accept that rights attached to EU citizens can be found throughout the EU Treaty

(Lyons: 1996, 102). This inspired proposals for the simplification of citizen-ship provisions, such as the one from the EP which reclaimed its consoli-dation in a single chapter under the heading Declaration of basic rights and provisions governing the exercise of European citizens and resi-dents,[26] or the looser one of the Spanish government on the simplification of Treaty articles relating to citizenship.[27] Either of those were difficult options and the final reference contained in Article 17.2 follows the line suggested by doctrine: citizens of the Union are entitled to the rights and duties foreseen in the Treaty.

This large number of proposals reveals a blurring of the structural dif-ferentiation of rights between 'empowerment rights' (which recognise the capability of the person to act and to create juridical consequences with their actions) and 'anticipatory rights' (which basically mean an expecta-tion of behaviour from other persons or public powers). Most of the rights referred to above in the context of the 1996 IGC fell into the second cat-egory. Their efficacy depends not only on their construction as rights but also on the existence of positive public policies to implement them.

The second issue regards the previous clarification of the personal scope of validity of these rights, i.e., whether it includes all persons or only EU nationals. The salience of EU citizenship as the main reference for rights within the EU runs in parallel to governments' suspicion of alterna-tive provisions, specifically, those protecting human rights in general. Despite proposals for codification[28] and repeated calls to reinforce the protection of human rights and fundamental freedoms,[29] most delega-tions rejected a chapter of fundamental rights recognised to all persons in the EU. De Búrca writes that the concept of human and fundamental rights may be seen as capable of providing a moral grounding to a legal order which, at its face, was established principally to support the pursuit of economic goals, and also to forge an identity which could simul-taneously (1) have a cross-national appeal to individuals and to groups within the Community and (2) emphasise shared or common values already existing within member states (de Búrca: 1996, 43). However, this position was not unanimous; the British conservative government voiced its well-known view:

> the British government does not think that the European Union is appropri-ate for the maintenance of fundamental rights nor for the introduction of a general clause banning discrimination on grounds of sex, sexual orientation, race, religion, age or disability. In general terms, the British government also expresses concern at the possibility that the creation of new rights would result in the need to establish reciprocal rights, something which in its view cannot happen given that the European Union is not, properly speaking, a state.[30]

Implicitly, most actors (and commentators) accept the view that citizen-ship, rather than personhood, is the foundation for almost all rights. Thus, most contributions to the 1996 IGC linked EU citizenship with fundamental rights, but without specifying the content of those rights or their application to non-citizens. In general, two suggestions[31] addressed this issue: either developing a substantial enlargement of the catalogue of rights in the chapter of citizenship of the Union, or drawing up a charter of fundamental rights of *citizens* of the Union. Along these lines, the EP stated that European citizenship must imply that the EU guarantees the protection of all fundamental rights contained in the European Convention on Human Rights and Fundamental Freedoms.[32] In both cases, citizenship constitutes the referent statute for rights. This untidy mixture can even be perceived in more hesitant contributions. Thus, the Danish government declared in favour of some fundamental rights being dissociated from the concept of European citizenship, but, in parallel, the Danes argued that some parts of the Declaration of Human Rights (freedom of expression, right of property, right to a clean environment),[33] could be included in the section on EU citizenship.

In summary, it can be argued that the Italian Presidency's warning to include only rights relevant to the citizenship issue was probably grounded on an implicit definition of citizenship: rights applying to all individuals were fundamental rights, not rights of citizenship (Blázquez: 1998, 266). While this probably prevented an enlargement of EU citizenship provisions, it did not limit proposals for new rights. This development must be welcomed because it enhances personhood as an alternative to citizenship as the entitlement for rights and, assuming the words of Lyons, because an association between fundamental rights and citizenship would render the concept even more élitist in excluding fundamental rights protection for non-EU citizens in the field of EC law (Lyons: 1996, 106). This particular point can be illustrated by reference to non-discrimination clauses.

The non-discrimination clause

The introduction of a non-discrimination provision found widespread consensus among scholars and institutions. Its location and substantive contents depended on previous ideal-types of citizenship. For those commentators and institutions that implicitly identified citizenship and fundamental rights, the interest was placed within substantive contents. Thus, Jo Shaw pointed out that the idea of a general non-discrimination clause would significantly extend the 'civil' rights of EU citizens (Shaw: 1997, 424). In the same context, the Court of Justice indicated that it would wish to be involved in considering the implications for judicial review if there were to be a large-scale revision of the existing approach to the protection of fundamental rights.[34]

The path towards this provision was set very quickly. The Dublin paper proposed the introduction of a new Article 6A EC providing a specific legal basis for the adoption of non-discrimination law (not directly applicable). The clause draws out a specific and fairly lengthy list of criteria for non-discrimination: gender, racial, ethnic or social origin, religious belief, disability, age and sexual orientation.[35] The *Non-Papers* of the Dutch Presidency watered down the provisions, removing mentions to disability, age, social origin and sexual orientation. Instead, it was proposed to address them within specific policies.[36] In the Amsterdam Treaty, all of them appear with the exception of social origin. In the opinion of Shaw, this reinforces mainstream tendencies within the Union (Shaw: 1997, 430).

While entirely accepting the importance of this clause within the design of fundamental rights, its connection with EU citizenship should be logically based upon the differential characteristics between citizenship rights on the one hand, and fundamental and human rights on the other hand. In this sense, this provision makes sense within EU citizenship provisions as far as it is addressed to nationality; i.e., discrimination addressed to shelter communitarian understandings of rights attached to national citizenships *vis-à-vis* nationals from other Member States. Immediately, the Italian Presidency noticed that the inconvenience and risk of including the principle of non-discrimination within citizenship provisions derived from the possible limitation to its application to citizens only and not to juridical persons, goods and services.[37]

Political rights

The summary of arguments from the previous section provides the background for the discussion of political rights. To start with, it is obvious that EU citizens (as well as legal persons) benefit from rights other than the ones listed under the heading EU citizenship. It has been argued that most of the rights normally constructed as EU citizenship rights should be made available for any person, which implies a reinforcement of the statute of personhood as a meaningful alternative to citizenship. Conceived in this form, the material scope of EU citizenship becomes slim but not at all unimportant.

If the assumption set above that citizenship refers primarily to the possibility of self-determination for individuals is recovered, then political rights appear as the cornerstone and main element in the construction of EU citizenship. The EU, as an emergent form of political domination, faces two different dimensions in this respect: the new relation of EU citizens *vis-à-vis* the component units, i.e., states and, particularly, Member States different to their own, and the structure of the political relationship between citizens and polity, i.e., the EU.

With respect to the first dimension, the crunch of the issue lies in the legitimacy of invoking EU citizenship as a justification for overcoming the traditional arguments associated with the justification for the non-participation of non-nationals in political life. In a brief summary (Masso Garrote: 1998), the arguments are: only nationals experience and wish the common good for their country because only they feel attached to it. Next, foreigners are seen as a potential enemy of the State and they may have a partial or false view of state interest. Finally, foreigners lack an innate and intuitive knowledge of State issues. Only strong integration and rooting would allow participation in political rights. Constitutionally, this is expressed in the convention that a foreigner cannot participate in national sovereignty since he/she is not part of the nation. So far, the only possibility for loosening such a tight association has been the establishment of a difference between elections implicating national sovereignty and administrative elections (i.e., local). This was, of course, the line consolidated by the Maastricht Treaty, but even this limited option met opposition. Massimo LaTorre has described how the case-law of the German Constitutional Court which ruled out granting voting rights for aliens in district councils was inspired by a constitutional theorist, Josef Insensee, bearing a view of the people as an ethnically and culturally homogeneous entity (La Torre: 1998, 91–92). The same theorist influenced the restrictive view of the German constitutional court on European citizenship.[38]

During the 1996 IGC, a number of proposals drew on a richer political relationship between EU citizens and their Member State of residence. In general terms, the EP asked for measures that facilitate third country nationals' participation in the State of residence.[39] Specifically, a proposal was tabled establishing the right to participate in local referendums in Member States (since the practice is not widespread, it would amount to an asymmetric right).[40] Also, the extension of voting rights to intra-state levels (i.e., regional) was mentioned.[41] However, the perception of regional elections as some form of expression of sovereignty still prevails, with the result that so far they are excluded from the scope of EU citizenship.

A second dimension pertains to the political relationship between citizens and the Union. Related proposals are more solidly grounded. There is, firstly, the normative and legal claim that the existence of formal political rights is an essential element for EU legitimacy. Such proposals are also permeated by a certain communitarian understanding of political participation: the realisation of citizens comes through political participation. Actors forwarded proposals on the right to create EU level political parties (which would be promoted through a change in article 138.A of the Treaty),[42] the right to participate in associations and political groups.[43]

Also, the enhancement of specific legislative empowerment for citizens was sought through the proposal on the right of European citizens to address institutions directly in order to ask for the adoption of Community measures affecting them.[44]

Transparency and open government

Since the Maastricht Treaty, improving the 'transparency' of EU decision-making featured has been one of the key elements for the improvement of EU democratic credentials. The principle of transparency involves two different dimensions. First, it provides a principle of government for the EU: the democratic principle of publicity of decisions and deliberations. In this way, the concept is identified as capable of suggesting an effective transition from the conventional secrecy of diplomacy to a notion of 'public' democracy in every sense. It is generally accepted that, at present, the work of the Council is carried out in a culture of secrecy, tempered by leaks, official and unofficial, and ministers putting 'spin' on Council proceedings for consumption by domestic electorates.

The second dimension pertains to the construction of transparency as a political right of EU citizens. It was argued that the creation of a 'right to open government' would address the considerable *lacunae* existing with regard to the 'political' rights of EU citizens (Shaw: 1997, 24). In this second dimension, transparency means the right to public access of information.

Previous to the 1996 IGC, EU institutions had positioned themselves on the issue drawing on Member States' constitutional experiences. Thus, the Commission undertook a systematic analysis as the basis for its proposed code of conduct and the case-law of the ECJ recognised, in Netherlands v. Council, 'the domestic legislation of most member states now enshrines in a general manner the public's right to access documents held by public authorities as a constitutional or legislative principle'.[45] In this case, Advocate General Tesauro argued that 'an innate feature of any democratic system is the right to information, including information in the hands of public authorities'.

There was also a widespread consensus among IGC actors; thus, the Reflection Group expressed the opinion that citizens should be granted a specific right to information on Union matters and on how the Union functions:

> Citizens are entitled to be better informed about the Union and how it functions. Many of us propose that the right of access to information be recognised in the Treaty as a right of the citizens of the Union. Suggestions have been made on how to improve the public access to Union's documents.

Proposals were tabled by Sweden, Denmark, Finland and the Netherlands, as well as the Italian, Irish (as the right to information on EU affairs and functioning) and Dutch presidencies. The Swedish government believed that the most effective way of increasing the degree of openness and transparency in the European institutions is to give the citizens access to the documents forming the basis of the debates and decisions.[46] Along the same lines, the Spanish government considered that a specific right to information on the affairs and operations of the Union should be accorded to citizens.[47] This was far from being a unanimous position; the initial position of the U.K. government was that no change should be made to the present system, whereby documents may be requested but their relevance is subject to the confidentiality of the Council's proceedings (Öberg: 1998, 11).

The final configuration of this right is contained in Article 255, which recognises the right to access documents of EU institutions (EP, Commission and Council) (Article 255). The Council and the EP will establish the general principles and the limitations deriving from public or private interest through the codecision procedure. Several observations can be made.

The first pertains to the position of Article 235 within the Treaty. It was recorded that the Netherlands wanted the inclusion of the new rule in the EU citizenship provisions (Öberg: 1998, 12). This would again raise the previously discussed issues concerning the personal scope of validity of rights: is this a right that can be limited to nationals from Member States, or is it constructed as a fundamental right of any person? Perhaps everyone could avail himself or herself of this right.

Secondly, Jo Shaw noticed that the EU has not adopted a rights-based approach to the question of transparency (Shaw: 1997, 435). The new provision confirms the tendency towards the construction of an anticipatory-type right: rather than empowering individuals, it designs an obligation for institutions. The provision singles out the legislative institutions of the Union and, explicitly, it submits only these to the specific principle of transparency. Some authors argue that this limitation of the institutional scope derives from a misconception that the main purpose of such rules is to allow ordinary citizens to take part in the already complex decision-making process within the European Union (Öberg: 1998). While the practical effects will depend very much on whether citizens avail themselves of this right (and the judicial scrutiny that may follow), it is doubtful whether it effectively constructs a mechanism to become involved in real decision-making, i.e., whether this is an empowering political right.

At the same time, it is argued that a more modest purpose of such rules – to strengthen the democratic nature of institutions, the public's confidence in the administration and the principle of good administration in general – would have called for all Community institutions and other bodies to be submitted to a general public access provision in the Treaty. Ironically, the limitation to institutions does not seem to refer to the production of documents. Declaration 35 of the Treaty of Amsterdam states that Member States may request their previous agreement before communicating to third parties a document originating from that state. This declaration strengthens the view that access to documents applies, as a general rule, not only to documents drawn by a Community institution but also to all documents held by the institutions, irrespective of their author.

A new Treaty article, which included within citizenship a provision that establishes the right to write in one's own language to Community institutions and to receive an answer in the same language, completes the transparency provision.[48] While the provision sanctions the right to use official EU languages in communications with individuals when originating from outside of the institutions, the ends pursued by a Union citizen in availing herself/himself of this right are not too clear.

The proposal to abolish asylum rights for EU citizens

The proposal presented by the Spanish government to abolish asylum rights for EU citizens raises some critical issues in the design of EU citizenship (Closa: 1998b). The proposal derived from practical reasons linked to Spanish anti-terrorist policy, but it developed a full set of arguments on EU citizenship. It was grounded in the principle of equality. Equal did not mean uniform but, rather, non-discriminatory, treatment. The reasoning was this: a national of an EU Member State should not be treated unequally by his/her own country's legislation. Regarding the issue at stake, asylum, it is, of course, inconsistent and illogical that national authorities grant asylum to their own nationals. Consequently, if nationals of other EU Member States are to be treated equally, it is equally inconsistent to grant them the right of asylum.

The underlying argument of Spanish thinking suggests a federal conception of EU citizenship. If anything, EU citizenship comes closer to national models than to the idea of an individual personality with a set of basic rights drawn from a host of international rules. In this way, the proposal for ending the right of asylum would merely reflect, according to Spain, the advances in the integration process. Moreover, it develops the philosophy of the statute of EU citizenship, which is incompatible with asylum in EU Member States.The proposal faced sharp criticism from NGOs, governments and institutions; it was argued that European citizenship was, at the moment, insufficient as the legitimising basis for such a proposal precisely because of its lack of civic and social rights (Ugarte and Garrido: 1995). Thus, despite the initial Spanish intentions to create a treaty article within EU citizenship provisions, it became reduced to a Protocol annexed to the Treaty, which, substantially, confirms the existence of the right to asylum for EU citizens.

Conclusion

The Austrian paper for the 1996 IGC argued that European citizenship has not been successfully implanted in the collective consciousness. The process will likely take decades rather than years. In the meantime, several issues remain.

From the perspective of the development of positive statute (i.e., taking into account rights specifically included within EU citizenship provisions) the advance has been limited. However, parallel to this, citizenship has polarised, to a large extent, the proposals on EU reforms, driving the process towards a rights-justified approach (i.e., policy proposals are legitimised with reference to citizenship). Provisions regarding rights have been strengthened and new rights have been introduced. The prevailing will seems towards increasing the rights of citizens but not towards reinforcing the political concept of citizenship. This is mainly reflected by the underdevelopment of political rights.

In conclusion, the process is one of rights-construction, and citizenship can be an excellent auxiliary word for it. The main challenge, however, is to develop, from this rich rights-context the central dimension of citizenship: the political.

References

R. Bauböck, *Citizenship and national identities in the European Union*, Harvard Jean Monnet Working Papers, no. 4, 1997.

M.D. Blázquez Peinado, 'Los derechos de ciudadanía y otros derechos reconocidos a los ciudadanos de la Unión: De Maastricht a Ámsterdam', *Revista de Derecho Comunitario Europeo*, 3, no. 2, 1998, 261–280.

R. Brubaker, *Citizenship and nationhood in France and Germany*, Cambridge, Ma., 1992.

G. de Búrca, 'The language of rights and European integration', in *New legal dynamics of European Union*, J. Shaw and G. More eds, Oxford, 1996, 29–54.

C. Closa, 'Supranational citizenship and democracy: normative and empirical dimensions', in *European citizenship: an institutional challenge*, M. La Torre ed., The Hague, 1998, 415–433.

C. Closa, 'International limits to national claims in EU constitutional negotiations: The Spanish government and the asylum right for EU citizens', *International Negotiations*, 3, no. 3, 1998, 389–411.

T. Faist, *A medieval city: transnationalizing labour markets and social rights in Europe*, Zentrum für Sozialpolitik Universität Bremen ZeS Arbeitspapier no. 91, 1994.

L. Ferrajoli, 'Dai diritti del cittadino ai diritti della persona', in *La cittadinanza. Appartanenza, identitá, diritti*, D. Zolo ed., Bari, 1994, 263–292.

J. Habermas 'Citizenship and national identity', in *The condition of citizenship*, B. Van Steenbergen ed., London, 1994, 20–35.

S. Hall, *Nationality, migration rights and citizenship of the Union*, Dortrecht, 1995.

R.Y. Jennings and A. Watts, *Oppenheim´s International Law*, London, 1992.

H. Kelsen, *Teoría general del Estado y del derecho*, México, 1949.

M. La Torre, 'European identity and citizenship. Between law and philosophy', in *European citizenship, multiculturalism and the state*, U. Preuss and F. Requejo eds, Baden-Baden, 1998.

C. Lyons, 'Citizenship in the Constitution of the European Union: rhetoric or reality?', in *Constitutionalism, democracy and sovereignty*, R. Bellamy and D. Castiglione eds, Aldershot, 1996, 96–110.

M. F. Masso Garrote, 'Aspectos políticos y constitucionales sobre la participación electoral de los extranjeros en el Estado nacional', *Revista de Estudios Políticos*, 97, 1998, 159–194.

U. Öberg, 'Public access to documents after the entry into force of the Amsterdam Treaty: much ado about nothing?' *European Integration online Papers* (EIoP), 2, no. 8, 1998, http: /eiop.or.at/eiop/.

D.P. O'Connell, *State succession in municipal law and International Law*, vol.1, Cambridge, 1967.

J.F. Rezek, 'Le droit international de la nationalité', *Reueil des Cours de l'Academie de Droit International*, 1986-III.

J. Rodríguez Ugarte and D. López Garrido, 'La emergente Europa social y el asilo', *El País*, 25 April 1995.

G. Sartori, 'Guidelines for concept analysis', in *Social science concepts: a systematic analysis*, G. Sartori ed., Beverly Hills, 1984, 15–85.

J. Shaw, 'European Union Citizenship: the IGC and beyond' *European Public Law*, 3, no. 3, 1997, 413–439.

Notes

1. Art. 2 European Convention on Nationality and Explanatory Report [Dir/Jur (97) 6, 14 May 1997.
2. Adopted by the Conference of Codification. The Hague 1930.
3. Case Nottebohm, Liechtenstein v. Guatemala, Second Phase ICJ Reports 1955.
4. J. D'Oliveira Note on Case C-369/90, M.V. Micheletti y otros v. Delegación del Gobierno en Cantabria, 30 CML Rev., 623–637.
5. Opinion of G. A. Tesauro in the Micheletti case. In fact, the ECJ had adopted a similar formal and antiessentialist attitude in the *Poulsen* case. The fulfilment of formal requirements of nationality by a ship (such as register and flag) was considered by the Court as establishing the substantive link with a state. The *effective nationality* (which was obvious through previous flag and register and the nationality of owner and crew) was not taken into account. Case C-286/90, *Ankalgemgigheden v. Peter Michael Poulsen et Diva Navigation Corp.* (1992) ECR I-6019.
6. The 1992 Edinburgh Declaration simply stated: Provisions on citizenship of the Union do not take the place of national citizenship.
7. EP, Resolution of 13.03.1996 on the European Council in Turin; Commission Report on the operation of the TEU, point 18, European Council Report from the Presidency and conclusions of the European Council. Florence, 21–22 June 1996 Bull. EU 6–1996; Italian Government *Position of the Italian Government on the Intergovernmental Conference on the revision of the Treaties*; Portuguese Government *Portugal and the Intergovernmental Conference on the revision of the Union Treaty*; Austrian Government *Fundamental positions of Austria for the Intergovernmental Conference* and the joint *Contribution on Union citizenship* (art. 8.3) submitted by the Austrian and Italian delegations to the IGC. Slightly different

in wording, the Finnish proposal underlined that citizenship of a Member State is a precondition for Union citizenship *Memorandum concerning the Finnish points of view with regard to the 1996 IGC of the European Union.*

8. Wording of the Portuguese contribution *Portugal and the Intergovernmental Conference on revision of the Union Treaty.*

9. Danish Government *Agenda for Europe.*

10. Case 193/94, Skanavi and Chryssanthakopoulos (1996) ECR I-929.

11. Commission Report on the operation of the Treaty on European Union, SEC (95) 731 final, 10 May 1995.

12. Second Report of the European Commission on Citizenship of the Union COM (97) 230.

13. *A Union closer to the citizens.* Conclusions of the Turin European Council 29 March 1996 Bull.-EU 3–1996

14. In general terms, Spain called for achieving unrestricted freedom of movement and residence. *Elements of a Spanish position at the 1996 IGC.* In more specific terms, the Austrian-Italian proposal stated (art. 8b.1) 'Every citizen of the Union shall have the right to enter, move and reside freely within the territory of all Member States, including that of which he/she is a national, and shall enjoy the same rights as the nationals of the Member States where he/she resides, subject to the limitations and conditions laid down in this Treaty and by the measures adopted to give it effect'. Contribution on Union citizenship.

15. Commission Report of 3 July 1996 on the scope of the co-decision procedure.

16. OJEC no. L 314/73 28.12.1995.

17. Card on EU citizenship elaborated by the General Secretary of the Council. Italian Presidency SN 1802/1/96 8 March 1996.

18. For instance, *Report of the Finnish government to the national parliament of 27 Feb. 1996,* which asked for the introduction of new rights. Equally, the Italian government called for the inclusion of other civic and social rights. *Position of the Italian government on the Intergovernmental conference on the revision of the treaties.*

19. Introductory note of the Italian Presidency. CONF 3878/96 26 July 1996.

20. Approach suggested by the Irish Presidency on 8 October 1996.

21. Draft on the revision of the Treaties of the Irish Presidency CONF/2500/96 5 Dec. 1996.

22. The origins of this proposal can de traced in the conclusions of the Turin European Council of 29 March 1996; in the Proposal by the French delegation CONF/3911/96 17 September 1996 and in the Proposal by the Belgian Delegation CONF/3914/97.

23. Memorandum concerning Finnish points of view with regard to the 1996 IGC of the European Union; Greek document *'Towards a democratic European Union with a political and social content'* called for the addition to the Treaty of a catalogue of fundamental social rights as listed in the European Social Charter and the protocol on social policy.

24. Conclusions of the Turin European Council of 29 March 1996.

25. Approach suggested by the Irish Presidency on 8 October 1996. Report of the reflection group.

26. EP Resolution on the European Council in Turin PE Doc. A4–0068/96 13.3.1996.

27. Elements of a Spanish position at the 1996 Intergovernmental Conference 28 March 1996.
28. Joint declaration by the German and Italian Foreign Ministers.
29. See, for instance, the Greek document *Towards a democratic European Union.*
30. IGC 96 Task Force – European Commission *A Partnership of Nations.* The British Approach to the European Union Intergovernmental Conference 1996(Summary) 13 March, 1996. http://europa.eu.int/en/agenda/igc-home/ms-doc/state-uk/ukwhit.html.
31. These two options are identified in the Spanish document 'The 1996 Intergovernmental Conference: basis for a discussion'.
32. Opinion of the Committee on Legal Affairs and Citizens' Rights.
33. Danish government *Agenda for Europe.*
34. Report of the Court of Justice on certain aspects of the application of the Treaty on European Union, paragraphs 19–23.
35. *The European Union Today and Tomorrow. Adapting the European Union for the Benefit of its People and Preparing it for the Future. A General Outline for a Draft Revision of the Treaties,* Brussels, 5 December 1996, Conf. 2500/96. (It is worth noting the expression 'its People', conveying the implied meaning of a single people, in contrast with the Peoples of the Preamble.) The Irish government had positioned itself in favour of reinforcing anti-discriminatory provisions. White Paper External challenges and opportunity 26 March 1996.
36. Non-Paper No. 6 *Fundamental Rights and Non-Discrimination* Brussels, 26 February 1997, Conf/3827/97.
37. CONF 3878/96.
38. Theoretical arguments on the central question of the definition of the European demos can be founded in La Torre: 1998 and Closa: 1998.
39. Resolution of 17 May 1995 on the functioning of the Treaty on European Union with a view to the 1996 IGC.
40. Art.8d Contribution on Union citizenship submitted by the Austrian and Italian delegations to the Group of Representatives to the Intergovernmental Conference.
41. Approach suggested by the Irish Presidency on 8 October 1996.
42. Ibid.
43. The Austrian-Italian paper added trade Unions and other associations and groups, Art. 8g. Replacing 138.
44. Draft on the revision of the Treaties of the Irish Presidency CONF/2500/96 5 Dec. 1996. Art. 8e. Austrian Italian proposal.
45. Case C-58/94 Netherlands vs. the Council (1996) ECR I-2169; (1996) 2 CMLR 996 34–35.
46. Written statement to the parliament.
47. Elements of a Spanish position.
48. Its origin can be traced to a Belgian proposal on cultural diversity which mentioned a modification in this sense CONF/3993/96.

CHAPTER 14

THE QUESTION OF NATIONALITY WITHIN A FEDERATION: A NEGLECTED ISSUE IN NATIONALITY LAW

Olivier Beaud

In an otherwise highly interesting work, Rogers Brubaker undertook a comparative analysis of legislation regarding nationality, during the course of which the distinction between the French civic community (conceived of as a territorial collectivity) and the German civic community (conceived of as a collectivity founded upon lineage) emerges quite clearly (Brubaker: 1997). His intention was to 'explain this striking difference in the definitions of nationality and in models of civic incorporation, (Brubaker: 1997, 15). The work rests on the fact that nationality is invariably linked to the nation and the nation state. One may observe this presupposition in the foreword to the French edition, which defines the social function of legislation on nationality. This legislation is defined as 'a system of classification permitting all modern states to reconstitute themselves permanently as a collectivity of citizens which may be precisely defined, appropriating to itself certain individuals (most frequently, independently of their active effort or desire) and transforming all others into foreigners. This is a codified practise, which allows, via innumerable common diacritical procedures, to distinguish those who belong to a state . . . from those for whom such is not the case; it is obviously an essential practice for any modern state' (Brubaker: 1997, 8). One may perceive this state-centric dimension of the analysis in various passages on Germany and the right to nationality in Germany. German history is divided into two periods: before and after the nation-state; in other words, before and after 1870.

It is therefore striking that the author does not take into consideration the fact that the two countries in question have different politico-legal structures. France is a highly centralised polity, and Germany is, and was once before, a federation. This federal component continued to distinguish the country even as it came to resemble a state (beginning in 1870, and especially after 1919). Brubaker must raise the issue of the distinction between federal nationality and federated (sub-national) nationality, as it is a decisive one from the point of view of a constitutional theory of the Federation. Regarding the constitution of the German Empire, he writes the following: 'There was no unified German nationality: *Reichsange-hörigkeit* (nationality of the Empire) was derivative of *Landesangehörigkeit* (nationality of one of the constituent states) . . .' (Brubaker: 1997, 36). Clearly, the articulation between federal and federated nationality points to the need for a certain investigation into the specificity of the Federation.

This chapter analyses nationality in a federation, a neglected question in the legal analysis of nationality. From this standpoint, Rogers Brubaker merely endorses the state-centric, unitary vision of nationality promoted by jurists. In legal scholarship, nationality is based exclusively on the state. Nationality is defined as 'the legal belonging of a person to the population that constitutes a state' (Battifol and Lagarde, 1974, 66). Some jurists have questioned the terminology – one of them, in the 1920s, noted that 'pre-scriptive legislation acknowledges the idea of nationality as an intrinsi-cally complete notion, because it supposes that the Nation in question has attained that definitive state of its development which causes it to be identified as a state. Therefore, nationality is only a legal linkage uniting the individual to the state of which he is a subject. One should not fail to note, at this time, that the term nationality is, in and of itself, relatively poorly chosen, and the term 'stateality,' for example, would be more appropriate' (Louis-Lucas: 1927, 1).

In addition, there is another vantage point on nationality: that of domestic public legislation. Whereas contemporary legal doctrine com-monly associates legislation regarding nationality with the protection it offers its beneficiaries (the nationals), that is, whereas it has the tendency to treat legislation on nationality either as an institution of international law (public or private) or private law (a question of civil status), this chap-ter highlights the domestic dimension of public law. Nationality must pri-marily be considered as an institution of domestic public law, and furthermore as a 'constitutional' institution. The term was used by Marcel Prélot in the first edition of his manual. Here, he defines constitutional law as the laws determining 'policies bearing a relation to the structure of the state'.

Thus, amongst the different aspects of public constitutional law, he includes legislation on nationality, based on the logic that 'those who are governed themselves (of whom we have already noted that of their differ-entiation from others the state was born) belong to a constitutional nation-ality. The nationals physically constitute the nation. It is with nationality via birth or acquisition that 'not only the form, but the being and substance of a state is created. In order to understand public constitutional law, one must thus go back to the issue of nationality' (*Droit constitutionnel*: 1948, 12).

Dual nationality in a Federation, from the vantage point of constitutional theory

The comparison between the United States and Europe in nationality law highlights the specific issue of nationality within a federation, as the U.S. clearly forms (or formed) the model of federalism. Europe, in its new institutional form as a Union is confronted with the challenge of federalism, despite the semantic tricks used to mask this fact ('supranationality,' 'subsidiarity,' and so forth). Still, a primary intellectual obstacle confronts the analyst: the natural tendency, in the study of nationality within a federation, to draw decisive conclusions based on the schematic difference between a confederation and a federal state. This sort of deductive reasoning is not new – from 1824, the German jurist Robert von Mohl in his first work on American federal legislation argued that this distinction had decisive consequences for the status of nationality. He wrote:

> An institution demonstrating the unquestionable character of a distinction between Confederation (*Staatenbund*) and a Federal state (*Bundesstaat*), is a federal citizenship, or the immediate relationship of inhabitants to a Federation regarded as a state. Since the Federation (*Bund*) consists of a duality of states, the federal state and the member states (*Bundesgliedern*), the inhabitants benefit from a dual nationality (*Bürgerrecht*): that of the specific state in which one lives, followed by that of the general federal nationality (*Allgemeinen Bürgerrecht des Bundes*). Such an immediate liaison of the individual with the Federation is impossible in a Confederation because there is no state, in such a configuration, of which the citizens could be the aforementioned individuals (von Mohl: 1824).

For this author, a confederation implied a particular nationality: that of the member-state (the sole sovereign), while the existence of a federal state presupposed a status of dual nationality: sub-national and federal. This deductive analysis of legislation regarding nationality, based on the *summa divisio* between confederation and federal state, has remained until now. A very recent article by an economist, for example, reads that the subjects 'of a federation are individuals; the individuals of a confederation are the states of which it is composed' (Mueller: 1995, 789). From this duality stems a different status for nationalities: 'in a confederation, the definition of citizenship (in the sense of nationality) is basically residence in one of the member-states', while in a federation (a federal state) the definition should be 'defined in a unilateral manner' (von Mohl: 1824, 790).

In other words, the federal state would feature a unique and uniform nationality, defined by federal authority, while a confederation would feature a multitude of varying nationalities depending on each of the member states. Against this thesis, which does not admit of either prescribed law or constitutional history, this chapter maintains that a federation features only one true form of nationality: that of dual nationality. By dual nationality we mean not the classic state-based notion, according to which an individual would be at the same time a national of two different countries (the definition adopted in this volume), but the coexistence of two nationalities that do not necessarily depend on the existence of two separate countries.

Such an opinion is only conceivable if we accept the initial hypothesis: that there exists an intrinsic difference between the state and the federation that would allow a transgression of the classical distinction between a federal state and a confederation (Beaud: 1995, 1997, 1998). Among the numerous judicial consequences of a distinction between state and federation (status of the constitution, of power, of the distribution of responsibilities, etc.), one concerns nationality law, which has a different status in each of these two cases. In the case of the state, there is ordinarily only one nationality, following from the exclusive nature of the link between sovereignty and nationality (dual citizenship in the state-to-state sense of the term, being an exception). Citizenship in a federation is by definition *dual citizenship* – federal as well as sub-national – as the inhabitants of this Federation are simultaneously those of the member state to which they belong. Consequently, if dual citizenship is conceived of as an anomaly in the case of the state, it becomes, on the contrary, a prerequisite of the federation. One may express this idea otherwise: a state-based conception of nationality presupposes a marked and bipolar distinction between nationals and foreigners – those who are not nationals are foreigners, or to use Brubaker's language, those who are not 'admitted' are 'excluded.' Be contrast, nationality in a federation introduces a tertiary relationship, that of the federative nationality. The relationship ceases to be bipolar (nationals/foreigners) but becomes triangular: nationals of the member state, nationals of the federation, and foreigners to the federation. From the point of view of citizenship, the uniqueness of a federation is precisely due to the fact that its member-states, which were previously foreigners to one another, cease to be so once their states become part of a federation, without meanwhile becoming the same type of nationals (with respect to one another) as those of a state (country).

It is worth noting that the recognition of dual nationality within a Federation is not entirely original. It was hinted at in a French legal doctrine during a discussion of the 'community' of the '*pays d'outre-mer*', dictated by the Constitution of the 4th of October, 1958 on the nature of nationality and citizenship with respect to those regions (Gonidec: 1959, 748). The idea was above all affirmed in a collective reference work on the thematic topic of federalism in which the following is found:

The individuals in a federation have a dual relationship, as citizens of both the federation and the member state. Within their respective areas of competence, both the federation and the member states create rights and obligations for such individuals. Accordingly, in the fields of federal power the citizens of the member states, upon the creation of the federation, become directly subject to the central authority (Bowie: 1955, 655).

In contrast with the majority of authors (notably Bowie), this chapter does not associate 'dual citizenship' with the (federal) state, but rather to a federation alone. By placing the emphasis on the dual nationality that necessarily characterises all true federations, the chapter aims at a better comparison between the European experience and the United States, a federal country *par excellence*. In fact, before becoming a centralised state, with unified nationality and the exclusivity of obligation which this implies, the United States was for a long time a federation recognising dual nationality. In this respect, this country constitutes a laboratory of interest for the study of the Europe currently forming, since if there were ever an institution which was progressively approaching the status of federation, it is Europe. In fact, the notion of '*ressortissant communautaire*' (community member) is in the progress of erasing the distinction between foreigners and nationals which characterised the relations among members of the formerly independent European states.

If we turn now towards the constitutional theory of a federation, we find an illustration of dual nationality in the report made by Pellegrino Rossi, the Italian jurist exiled in Switzerland in the nineteenth century and naturalised Genevan (Dufour: 1998), on the revision of the federal Pact of Switzerland (1832). In this magisterial doctrinal presentation on the nature of a federation, he raised the question of the free movement between the cantons (making of this right one of the characteristic traits of federative nationality) for the members of the Helvetican Confederation. He argues that, 'if free circulation within Switzerland, free commerce, the right of succession, the abolition of all '*droit d'aubaine*' between the cantons, the equal treatment of the cantons, the equal treatment of creditors, whichever canton they belong to, were not recognised and guaranteed, we would not be worthy of the title of Confederation' (Rossi: 1997).

Federations, as such, are intrinsically inseparable from the notion of common status among inhabitants of the member states; nation states that cease to be foreign to one another, even if they do not necessarily enjoy the exact same political rights.[1] The treatment of the liberal establishment of federative rights proposed here attempts to realise a compromise in the relationship between the Federation and its member states (Rossi: 1997, 38–40). If a federative nationality and its corollary – the right to free movement from one member state to another – are decisive, however, then these two features translate into a common identity: the common belonging to a political entity that transcends, without abolishing, the belonging of its constituent parts. From this stage forth, this other patriotism (allegiance to the Federation) forbids the consideration of the inhabitants of different member states as foreigners to one another. Let us once more cite Rossi, describing the federal ideal towards which Switzerland must strive:

And next, we would revise the federal Pact, try to place the Confederation on more solid bases, make the effort to satisfy the demands of the times, the signs of the times and this sentiment of nationality which has developed and allied itself in our hearts as much as that of the sovereignty of the cantons, and the Swiss of differing cantons would not continue to view each other any less as foreigners, in such a way as the Swiss are not treated in foreign countries!

Let us proclaim without circumlocutions: if the Swiss still had insufficient civilisation and patriotism to make the cantonal barriers which restrain their fellow confederates fall, and to receive each other's presence otherwise than through a disdainful and precarious tolerance, it would be necessary to despair in the noble attempt at federal regeneration that the assembly has charged us with preparing. The Swiss refuse their fellow Swiss water and fire. The Swiss refusing to the Swiss: We are ousting you from our territory, or a least, you will not stay there under our pleasant disposition; we wish to exercise upon you an arbitrary power; you must be the puppet of our every whim! (Rossi: 1997, 38–40).

It is the sense of common patriotism, the sentiment of Swiss nationality (in the Helvetican, patriotic sense of the term) that, according to Rossi, forbids the expulsion of one Swiss citizen from an adopted canton to his canton of origin. Here again, it is useful to recall the following discourse:

Who, then are these men which you wish to expel? These men are the same ones who, in the event of danger, would go die at the borders of Switzerland, the same who would embrace you on the battlefield, your brothers-in-arms by the sacred fraternity of the national flag . . . These men belong perhaps to the same canton only in the event of exterior or interior danger when you would call defence to your territory; defence of your liberties and your government. And today, because the danger is not imminent, because you think you have no need for them, today you would say to them: there is no hospitality here for you: this land rejects you: you are foreigners; you would be our brothers once again, but only the day when we will have need for your arms (Rossi: 1997, 40–42).

Thus, Rossi accurately describes how the emergence of a federal state, of a common patriotism implicates the disappearance of the notion of foreigner within the category of inhabitants of a common federation. Solidarity between such inhabitants is no longer random and exceptional (in the event of war for example), but becomes permanent and institutionalised. The deepest meaning of the federal mission is to transform the entirety of the different regions into a political community (from which stems the theme of fraternity), all the while safeguarding the initial allegiance of the individual members with respect to the member-state (the cantonal sovereignty in question). Dual citizenship, essential to federations, is then nothing but the duplication of the fundamental law of duality of political entities constituting them. In contrast to the state, the Federation here is characterised by a 'political dualism' to the extent that 'the essence of the Federation resides in the dualism of the existing political scheme, combined as a federative association (*Verbindung bundesmassiges Zusammenseines*) and political units, on the one hand, and the persistence of a plurality (*Merhheit*) of distinct political units, on the other (Schmitt: 1928, French translation 1993, 518).

Dual citizenship within a federation from the standpoint of legal dogma

From the point of view of the Federation, nationality poses a problem to the extent that there exists a dual nationality: federal nationality and subnational citizenship. The most difficult question, then, concerns the distinction between the two nationalities. The difficulty is to know whether the federative nationality proceeds from the federal nationality, or vice versa. In general, in a federation (distinct from the Federal state), the federal nationality precedes the federated nationality. A classic formulation of this rule appears in article 42, (paragraph 1) in the Helvetican constitution of 1848 (which founded the Swiss Federal state): 'All citizens of a canton are Swiss citizens.' Inversely, once the federated nationality begins to depend on federal nationality, one is in a phase of 'nationalisation' (or centralisation) of nationality which gives evidence of an evolution which we might term '*etatisation*' of the Federation (its development into a federal state).

We may use the United States as an example. The difficulty in this case comes from the fact that the Constitution of 1787 is tacit on the delicate question of citizenship, because the citizenship it implies raises the question of sovereignty. Americans did not wish to assign sovereignty to either the Federation or the member states (Bowie: 1955, 426–427). The entire text contains only a few allusions. Article 4(2), notably, states that: 'citizens of each state will enjoy the same rights and privileges and immunities as the citizens of every other state'. An embryonic federal citizenship was created by the constitutional clauses making this nationality a perquisite for becoming President of the United States or a Member of Congress, as well as by those granting Congress the power to naturalise foreigners. Also, from 1787, it was clear that 'from this moment onwards, citizenship of the United States will be the result of birth within the territory, following in this respect the doctrine of *jus soli* consecrated by English common law' (Bowie: 1955, 426). A definite lesson drawn from the 1787 Constitution is the simultaneous recognition of an 'American citizenship,' or federal citizenship, and a federated citizenship.

Still, there is widespread agreement about the ambiguity of the constitutional text with respect to the articulation between the two citizenships. 'The relationship between these two citizenships, state and national, . . . the Constitution did not expressly determine' (Willoughby: 1910, vol. 1, 260). Neuman recently made the same point. 'The 1787 Constitution . . . did not specify the intended relationship between citizenship in a state and in the nation'. Still, the dominant opinion, until the *Dred Scott* decision (1856), was that state citizenship *ipso facto* implied citizenship of the United States; in other words the federal citizenship (Story: 1858, 260). It also admitted that the relationship was reciprocal, and that the simple case of a federal citizen residing in a member state accorded him/her the citizenship of this state, the federated citizenship. What remained seemingly disputable was which citizenship was predominant. We should not be surprised to note that there were jurists in favour of 'states' rights'. John Calhoun, as their leader, defended the pre-eminence of the antecedent of the citizenship of the states (federated citizenship). From this point of view, the politico-legal quarrel evidently espoused the idea of sovereignty.

The *Dred Scott* verdict (1856) put the question of citizenship at the forefront of legal debate. It raised the issue, notably, of whether a black slave from the state of Missouri (a state where slavery was legal) might be considered a 'national citizen,' and if so, whether he/she should be considered an American citizen, thus entitled to 'privileges and immunities'.[2] In order to argue that the person in question was not a 'citizen' of the United States in the sense of the American Constitution, and therefore that he could not initiate legal action in this specific circumstance, the Supreme Court (through the vehicle of Chief Justice Taney) excluded blacks (free or enslaved) from the category of American citizens and forcefully dissociated federal citizenship from state citizenship.[3] In dissent, one judge expressly underlined the need to maintain this liaison between the two nationalities,[4] and the right of the member states to designate as 'citizens, those people relevant to their jurisdiction'. According to the same dissident, the 'privileges and immunities' of the American citizen, mentioned in article IV(2) are attributed first and foremost to the citizens of the federated states.[5]

This famous verdict was reduced to nothing by the edict of the Thirteenth and Fourteenth Amendments (Equal Protection) and the federal law on Civil Rights, a determining event in the American history of citizenship.[6] The Thirteenth Amendment (1865) is directed against the famous *Dred Scott* verdict. From this point on, it is written in the American Constitution that 'all persons born in the United States and not subject to any foreign power, excluding Indians not taxed, are hereby declared to be citizens of the United States'. As to the 1866 law on Civil Rights, there is a §15 expressly entitled 'right of citizenship': Sect.1992: 'All persons born in the United States, and who are the subjects of no foreign state, excluding Indians not taxed, are hereby declared to be citizens of the United States'.

It is, however, the Fourteenth Amendment, proposed on June 16, 1868 and ratified on July 28, 1868, which is the fundamental text. If the pre-eminence of state citizenship had continued to be admitted, the Southern states would never have accorded citizenship to Black Americans, who could never have become American citizens with respect to citizenship of the state. This is why the creators of this Amendment wished to protect Black Americans by according citizenship directly, which was supposed to qualify the American (federal) citizenship as foremost with respect to the state (federated) nationality. The first section of this Article, 'All persons born or naturalised in the United States and subject to their jurisdiction, are citizens of the United States and the state in which they reside', contained two major ideas: 'the affirmation that national citizenship is first and superior to state citizenship, and the grant to Blacks of the dual citizenship, both national and state' (Willoughby: 1910, 270). Such an amendment forbids 'that the member states withdraw state citizenship from those who enjoy the national citizenship; the national citizens' (Neuman: 1996, 64). This superiority of federal citizenship over state citizenship is in some respects guaranteed by the second section of the Amendment, which says 'No state will enact or enforce a law which would restrain the rights or privileges of citizens of the United States, or would deprive a person of life, liberty, or the pursuit of happiness without due process of law, or would refuse to anybody enjoying its jurisdiction the equal protection of the laws'.

If we then examine the Fourteenth Amendment from the point of view of citizenship, we may conclude that 'it is not necessary that one be a state citizen to be a national citizen. The Amendment was voted essentially to affirm the supremacy of national citizenship and to guarantee that Blacks be considered as citizens if they were born in the United States' (Bowie: 1955, 427). More concretely, he by whom the federal citizenship has been acquired acquires automatically that of the state. 'The Fourteenth Amendment grounds a right to state citizenship in residence. The notions of the acquisition of the citizenship of state by birth or naturalisation do not exist: an American citizen who fixes his residence in a state, be it at the time of his birth or later, becomes automatically a citizen of that state. One may consequently change their citizenship by changing their state of residence; and, in fact, by going to live abroad . . . the person in question may lose all citizenship without compromising federal citizenship' (Bowie: 1955, vol 2, 430–431).

Two points flow from this. First, the Supreme Court in the Slaughter House Cases (1873) restrained considerably the interpretation of the clause 'privileges and immunities of citizens' of the Fourteenth Amendment. Even if it admitted the American citizenship of blacks, it rejects the thesis of the primacy of federal citizenship, and readopts the earlier thesis on the duality of citizenship.[7] Judge Miller, author of this decision, was attempting to defend federalism and to fight against the centralising imperialism of the partisans of the Fourteenth Amendment.

Second, the Supreme Court gave a very extensive interpretation of the Fourteenth Amendment, this time using the 'due process of law' and 'equal protection' clauses of the Fourteenth Amendment. Progressively, the judicial problem changed its meaning; the question arising was not that of citizenship but rather that of knowing whether the due process clause implicated the application of the Declaration of Rights to the states (the issue known as the incorporation of the Bill of Rights). This jurisprudence radically changed the entire theory of the relationship between the federation and the member states (Bickel: 1973, 379). In fact, through jurisprudence, the American Union, the federation, was henceforth perceived as the 'supreme protector of individual rights – of Blacks as ordinary citizens just like anybody else' (Toinet: 1987, 92). This legitimisation of the federation via the defence of rights had an unmistakably centralising effect, as Theodore Lowi commented, 'if the notion of citizenship has a meaning, and if the citizenship of a nation includes an inherent notion of rights, then a nationalised definition of citizenship should constitute a nationalisation of citizenship itself' (Lowi: 1990, 114).

The Fourteenth Amendment thus had an incontestable 'nationalising substance'[8] in that, whatever the Supreme Court's intention, the amendment consecrated the pre-eminence of national citizenship over its state counterpart. The duality of citizenship that had once rested on the equality of two citizenships and on an equality of bases (equality between the federation and its member states) made way for a progressive 'hierarchisation' of the legislation regarding citizenship, in favour of the federation. The federation progressively became a federal state.

Individual federative rights as effects of the federal nationality

The last section considers the issue of nationality from a legal standpoint. Today, jurists of international law continue to associate it with the protection it accords its beneficiaries (the citizens), while domestic jurists concentrate their study on the conditions of acquisition and loss of nationality. The latter thus evaluate the right of nationality as a function of the respective incorporation of the principles of *jus soli* and *jus sanguinis*. This approach is clearly driven by the current political climate and by the attempt, for example in France, of certain political parties to modify nationality law and *jus soli*. However, if we de-centre the study of nationality and examine, from this point onwards, the point of view of the constitutional theory of the federation, then the richest perspectives are much less the study of the conditions of acquisition of citizenship than that of its legal effects. Among these, it is appropriate to focus on the specific rights certain individuals enjoy as members of a federation. We may term these rights, stemming from the federative nationality, federative rights. We must not content ourselves to determine the rights implied by a federative nationality, but also examine which rights are excluded by this common belonging.

Among the most important effects of nationality in a federal regime, one must mention the rights that this regime confers on individuals with respect to the member-states of which they are not citizens, in the strictest sense of the term. In other words, the recognition of national citizenship has the effect of creating certain federal rights that some call 'interstate privileges'. These are rights that citizens of one member state in a federation may successfully claim against other member states. We have seen that certain rights were at the core of the Dred Scott verdict. Seen from this angle, the question posed by this affair was that of knowing whether a black could freely move to a neighbouring member state that opposed slavery (the right of free circulation and residence) and if he/she could initiate legal procedures. Incidentally, still from the legally technical angle, such rights are rights stemming from the very existence of a federation. More specifically, they flow from a fundamental principle: the inability of one member state to define another's residents as foreigners. Consequently, these federative rights have the particularity of being unwritten rights, stemming from the federative principle. One may illustrate this analysis of the effects of a federative nationality, on the one hand by the study of federal theory, and on the other hand, by the examination of certain constitutional measures.

To evoke federal theory, we will cite central examples of residence. Pellegrino Rossi, whose report concludes that 'the commission would have thought to abdicate its mandate if it had not proposed to recognise as a fundamental principle, the right to free settlement, and to surround it with the necessary guarantees to assure its exercise' (Rossi: 1997, 38). In the bill to revise that policy, which the commission of 1832 would propose (in vain), Article 36 states: 'freedom to reside is guaranteed to all the Swiss, in the entire domain of the confederation'. To this effect,

1. No Swiss citizen may be impeded from residing in any canton, as long as he is armed with an act of origin or an act stating that he belongs to a canton, an attestation of moral standing, and an attestation that he is the master of his rights.
2. The federal authority fixes a limit on fees.
3. In settling in a different canton, the Swiss citizen enters into the right of all the entitlements of the citizens of this canton, with the exception of political rights and the participation of common goods and of the corporations. In particular, the liberty of industry and the right to acquire and cede property are assured to him, in conformity with the laws and ordinances of the canton, to which in all respects must render the quality of the Swiss citizen, simply lodged, equal to the citizen of the canton.

4. The communes may not impose upon their residents belonging to other cantons stronger burdens than inhabitants belonging to other communes of their own canton.
5. The Swiss citizen living in a canton other than his own may be sent back to his own once he is condemned by legal sentence, or once he is convicted of transgressions of laws or ordinances, including those on good moral behaviour (Rossi: 1997, 222).

The fundamental principle of free inter-federal establishment of residence implies a series of federative rights attributed to an inhabitant of a member-state based solely on his belonging to a federation. These rights are usually private rights, and essentially economic and social ones. Rossi believes this judicial dimension of free establishment is closely linked to the economic development of the Swiss federation. The moving of the inhabitants from one canton to another is the source of industrial emulation and 'a source of national richness' (Rossi: 1997, 42). He pleads in favour of a common market on the global scale of the federation. If the principle of free establishment and free industry were guaranteed by cantonal laws this 'would make of Switzerland a vast workshop and of each city, a common market of all Helvetican productions, so that work, capital capacities, all would take on a natural and national level. There would be employment for all'[9].

The other advantage of this recognition of free intrastate establishment is to impede immigration outside of the Swiss federation. The richness of the population is preserved at the heart of the larger entity. Inversely, these federative laws inevitably entail obligations on the part of state or national authorities, such as equal treatment. The Swiss Federal Constitution of September 12, 1848, which institutes a federal state, recognised this right of residence, in terms largely taken from Rossi's report. According to article 41, 'the confederation guarantees to all the Swiss of one Christian denomination the right to establish themselves freely in all the extent of the Swiss territory in conformity with the dispositions' of this article.

Germany provides a second example suggesting remarkable continuity – reflected in legal and constitutional principles – of inspiration between different constitutional texts of the nineteenth century. Article 18 of the Federal Act (*Bundesakte*) provides an instructive enumeration of the rights pertaining to federal nationality, or belonging to the *Bund*:'the German princes and the free townships agree to assure to subjects (*Untertanen*) of German member states (*Bundesstaten*) the following rights:

The right to property outside of the state in which they live
The right: a) to leave a German member state for another which is ready to accept the person in question as an inhabitant and b) to enter in the civil and military public service, so long as military service in the state is not a violation of obligations towards the Fatherland.

The exemption from all immigration taxes (*jus detractus, gabella emigrationis*). The assembly will then handle upon its first session the drafting of common dispositions relating to freedom of press and the guarantee of the rights of authors and editors against pressures.[10]

Two lessons may be drawn from these provisions. First, the fact of belonging to the German federation (*Deutsche Bund*), being a subject (*Untertan*) in the strictest sense of the term, of a member-state of this federation implies the enjoyment of particular rights. Second, federative laws are of a very different nature. They are either private rights (the right to property), or political rights (for example the equal access to public employment), or a combination of both. How would one classify the right to circulation and residence?

Movement between the members of the German federation was not 'internal migration': 'it was rather migration between states.'[11] As Fahrmeir (1997, 731) argues, 'in practice as in theory, the nationality law must derive from the competence of the states of the Federation'. In other words, the nationality of the state implied federal nationality, and migration between states was migration from one state to another. From this point of view, Article 18 of the Federal Act of 1915 does not truly represent a break with previous legislation (Fahrmeir: 1997, 730–731). The federal pact does not recognise a liberty of circulation within Germany for all the inhabitants of the member states, as is proven by the notion of *Freizügigkeit* (which had only a fiscal meaning at the time, and did not signify the idea of free circulation), such that the German federal law of the time continued to treat Germans as foreigners. For an inhabitant of a given member-state of the German Confederation, travelling to another German state qualifies as emigration, and the inhabitant could be expelled from this same territory. In fact, in the middle of the nineteenth century, German nationality law was contained less in the federal constitution or federal law than in bilateral or multilateral treaties.

As a matter of historical fact, this disposition of Article 18 fell into disuse; it expressed mainly the ideal of 'federalisation' of the German nationality. But this historical reality does not invalidate the systematic link existing between these federative laws and the federative nationality.

A similar conclusion could be drawn regarding the article on 'fundamental rights of the German people' of the Constitution of the Parliament of Frankfurt of 1848. This article first fixes as a principle: 'All Germans possess the German nationality of the Reich. The rights deriving therefrom may be exercised by him in any of the German states.'[12] We find in this the same logical structure as in the Federal pact of 1815: the granting of federal nationality (that of the Reich) has the effect of attributing certain rights that may be exercised in all of Germany, at least in the sense indicated by the constitutional text stating 'all the German states'. In addition, individual (federal rights) stemming from German nationality are relatively close to those recognised by the Confederation of 1815. We find there, first of all, the freedom of establishment and the freedom of industry,[13] and then especially, the principle of non-discrimination between Germans of different member states in criminal and civil matters.[14] But the *status quo* remains on one major point: the federative nationality was only the consequence of the nationality of the member state (Fahrmeir: 1997, 746).

These constitutional elements have been interpreted as an 'intention to create a direct nationality of the Reich while removing the nationality of the different states. It is an idea that was only realised by the law of February 5th 1934' (Rudy: 1949, 24).' This interpretation is anachronistic. It is true that the German revolutionaries of 1848 wished to create a German nation and the unity of the Reich, but, from the standpoint of nationality, the interest resides in association between a principle (the unity of the status of the Germans) and the entirety of rights pertaining to the common, federal nationality.

The disappearance of the German Confederation after the Austrian-Prussian War did lead to the eclipse of federal nationality. Its permanence is illustrated in the important law on free circulation within Germany (1 November 1867),[15] which enumerates the principle rights (the right of temporary stay, establishment, acquisition of the right to property and free industry) recognised to all federal inhabitants (*Bundesangehörige*) within the federal territory (*Bundesgebiet*). This law figures largely in Article 3 of the constitution of the German Reich of April 16th, 1871 (the 'Bismarck constitution', as it is sometimes called) which contains an essentially functional definition of German federal nationality. The structure remains identical: the causal link between the federal nationality in enumerating the following list of federative rights:

> There exists throughout the territory of the Confederation a common homeland right (*Heimatsrecht*) in virtue of which all inhabitants (subject, citizen, etc.) of all the confederated states will be treated as a nationals (*Inländer*) in each other member state of the federation. Consequently, they may have a fixed residence, benefit from freedom of industry, have equal access to public employment, the acquisition of goods and enjoy all the other private rights on the same terms of the inhabitants of these other states, and must be treated equally in matters concerning judicial protection of these rights.[16]'

Article 3 discusses the Reich's obligations with respect to its inhabitants. 'All Germans have the equal right to receive the protection of the Reich against a foreign state'.[17] The disposition confirms the importance of the principle of legal equality between Germans, which forbids any type of discrimination between them on a political and civil basis. 'No German may be limited, in the exercise of his rights, by the authorities of his own country or by the authorities of another member state' (Article 3 al. 2).[18]

Once they have the obligation to respect these individual federal rights, these rights of other inhabitants of other states of the federation, the member states of the German federation are limited in their sovereignty. The sole fact of possessing a federative nationality automatically brings (*de jure*) a protection benefiting the inhabitant of a member-state with respect to other member states. From today's perspective, the striking aspect of these rights is that they have not changed greatly since the Federative Act of 1815.

References

B. Ackerman, *We, the People, II, Transformations*, Cambridge, 1997.

A. Auer, J.F. Flauss, ed., *Le référendum européen*, Bruxelles, Bruylant, 1997.

H. Battifol and P. Lagarde, *Droit international privé*, 6th ed., 1, no. 59, 1974.

O. Beaud, 'La fédération entre l'Etat et l'Empire', in *l'Etat, la finance, le social*, B. Théret ed., Paris, 1995.

O. Beaud, 'Fédéralisme et souveraineté. Notes pour une théorie constitutionnelle de la Féderation', in *Revue du droit public*, no. 1, 1998, 83–122.

O. Beaud, 'Propos sceptique sur la légitimité d'un référendum européen ou plaidoyer pour plus de réalisme constitutionnel', in *Le référendum européen*, A. Auer and J.F. Flauss eds, Brussels, 1997.

A. Bickel, 'Citizenship in the American Constitution,' *Arizona Law Review*,

R. Bowie and C. Friedrich, eds, *Études sur le fédéralisme* (French translation), Brussels, 1955.

R. Brubaker, *Citoyenneté et nationalité en France et en Allemagne* (French translation), Paris, 1997.

A. Dufour, 'Hommage Pellegrino Rossi (1787–1848)', in *Genevois et Suisse à vocation européenne*, Berne, 1998.

A. Fahrmeir, 'Nineteenth-Century German Citizenship: a Reconsideration', *Historical Journal*, 40, no. 3, 1997, 728.

P.F. Gonidec, 'Note sur la nationalité et les citoyennetés dans la Communauté', *Annuaire français de droit international*, 1959, 748.

T. Lowi, 'Le fédéralisme américain', in *Et la Constitution créa en Amérique*, ed. M. F. Toinet. Nancy.

P. Louis-Lucas, *La nationalité française*, Paris, 1927

D. Mueller, 'Fédéralisme et union européenne: une perspective constitutionnelle', *Revue d'économie politique*, 105 (1995), 789.

R. von Mohl, *Das Bundes-Staatsrecht der Vereinigten Staaten*, Berlin, 1824.

G. Neuman, *Strangers to the Constitution*, Princeton, 1996.

P. Rossi, *Per la patria commune* (ed. Lacché), Bari, Piero Lacaita, 1997.

M. Ruby, *L'évolution de la nationalité allemande*, Baden-Baden, 1949.

C. Schmitt, *Théorie de la Constitution* (French translation), Paris, 1993.

J. Story, *Commentaries on the Constitution of the U.S.* (3rd edition), Boston, 1858.

B. Théret, ed, *L'Etat, la finance, le social*, Paris, 1995.

M. F. Toinet, *Le système politique des Etats-Unis*, Paris, 1990.

P. Willoughby, *The Constitutional Law of the United States*, New York, 1910.

Notes

1. 'We do not demand, wrote Rossi, political rights for residents. They are not citizens of a canton, they are not members of this political unity . . . We respect cantonal sovereignty' (Rossi: 1997, 48).
2. Willoughby (1910), 262.
3. 'In discussing the question, we must not confound the rights of citizenship which a State may confer within its own limits, and the rights of citizenship as a member of the Union. It does not by any means follow, because he has all the rights and privileges of a citizen of a State, that he must be a citizen of the United States' (Judge Taney).
4. Judge Curtis: 'My opinion is that, under the Constitution of the United States, every free person born on the soil of a State, who is a citizen of that State by force of its Constitution or laws, is also a citizen of the United States'.
5. On this, see Willoughby (1910), 268.
6. See on this subject, the important book of Ackerman (1997).
7. 'It is quite clear that there is a citizenship of the United States and a citizenship of a State, which are distinct from each other and which depend upon different characteristics or circumstances in the individual.'
8. On this point, see Ackerman (1997), 199.
9. *Ibid.*, p. 46.
10. Die verbündeten Fürsten und freien Städte kommen überein, den Unterthanen des deutschen Bundesstaates folgende Rechte zuzusichern:
   a) Gemeindebürgerrecht außerhalb des Staates, den sie bewohnen, zu erwerben und zu besitzen, ohne deshalb in dem fremden Staate mehreren Abgaben und Lasten unterworfen zu sein, als dessen eigene Unterthanen.
   Die Befugniß
   1) des freien Wegziehens aus einem deutschen Bundesstaat in den andern, der erweislich sie zu Unterthane annehmen will, auch
   2) in Civil- und Militärdienste desselben zu treten, beides jedoch nur insoferne keine Verbindlichkeit zu Militärdienste gegen das bisherige Vaterland im Wege stehe; und damit wegen der dermalen vorwaltenden Verschiedenheit der gesetzlichen Vorschriften über Militärpflichtigkeit hierunter nicht ein gleichartiges für einzelne Bundesstaaten nachtheiligesVerhältnis entstehen möge, so wird bei der Bundesversammlung, die Einführung möglichst *gleichförmiger* Grundsätze über diesen Gegenstand in Berathung genommen werden.
   c) Die Freiheit von aller Nachsteuer (*jus detractus, gabella emigrationis*) insofern das Vermögen in einen andern deutschen Bundesstaat übergeht und mit diesem nicht besonder Verhältnisse durch Freizügigkeits-Verträge bestehen.
   d) Die Bundesversammlung wird sich bei ihrer ersten Zusammenkunft mit Abfassung gleichförmiger Verfügungen über die Preßfreiheit und die Sicherstellung der Schriftsteller und Verleger gegen den Nachdruck beschäftigen.
11. On this point, see Fahrmeir (1997), 728.
12. § 132 : 'Jeder Deutsche hat das deutsche Reichsbürgerrecht. Die in ihm kraft dessen zustehenden Rechte kann er in jedem deutschen Lande ausüben (. . .)'.

13. § 133 : 'Jeder Deutsche hat das Recht, an jedem Orte des Reichsgebietes seinen Aufenthalt und Wohnsitz zu nehmen, Liegenschaften jeder Art zu erwerben und daraber zu verfügen, jeden Nahrungszweig zu betreiben, das Gemeindebürgerrecht zu gewinnen'.

14. § 134 : 'Kein deutscher Staat darf zwischen seinnen Angehorigen und anderen Deutschen einen Unterschied im bürgerlichen, peinlichen und Prozeß-Rechte machen, welcher die letzeren als Ausländer zurücksetzt'.

15. *Gesetz über die Freizügigkeit*, BGB1, p. 55.

16. 'Für ganz Deutschland bestett ein gemeinsames Indigenat mit der Wirkung, daß der Angehörige (Untertan, Staatsbürger) eines jeden Bundesstaates in jedem anderen Bundesstaates als Inländer zu behandeln, und demgemäß zum festen Wohnsitz, zum Gewerbebetriebe, zu offentlichen Ämtern, zur Erwerbung von Grundstücken, zur Erlangung des Staatsbürgerrechtes umd zum Genusse aller sonstigen bürgerlichen Rechte unter denselben Voraussetzungen wie der Einheimische zuzulassen, auch im betreff der Rechtsverfolgung und der Rechtsschutzes demselben gleich zu behandeln ist'.

17. 'Dem Auslande gegenüber haben alle Deutschen gleichmäßig Anspruch auf den Schutz des Reichs'.

18. 'Kein Deutscher darf in der Ausübung dieser Befügnis durch die Obrigkeit seiner Heimat oder durch die Obrigkeit eines anderen sundesstaates beschränkt werden'.

INDEX